*The World of Opera*

# The Work of Opera

Genre, Nationhood, and Sexual Difference

RICHARD DELLAMORA AND DANIEL FISCHLIN, EDITORS

*Columbia University Press    New York*

Columbia University Press

*Publishers Since 1893*

New York    Chichester, West Sussex

Copyright © 1997 Columbia University Press. Chapter Fourteen copyright © 1997 by
Rebecca A. Pope and Susan J. Leonardi.

Chapter Five is adapted from material in "Structures of Identity and Difference in *Carmen*,"
which appeared in *Women: A Cultural Review*, 3, no. 1 (Summer 1992): 1–15, published by
Oxford University Press, © 1992 Oxford University Press. Reprinted by permission.

Chapter Seven is adapted from material in "Constructing the Oriental 'Other': Saint-Saën's
*Samson and Delilah*," which appeared in *Cambridge Opera Journal*, 3, no. 3 (November
1991): 261–302, published by Cambridge University Press, © 1991 Cambridge University
Press. Reprinted by permission.

Chapter Ten is adapted from material in "Otherhood Issues: Post-National Operatic
Narratives," which appeared in *Narrative*, 3 (January 1995): 1–17, published by the
Society for the Study of Narrative Literature, © 1995 Ohio State University Press.
Reprinted by permission.

Chapter Thirteen is adapted from material in "Review of *The Queen's Throat* by Wayne
Koestenbaum," which appeared in *19th-Century Music*, 17, no. 3 (Spring 1994): 274–285,
published by the University of California Press, © 1994 University of California Press.
Reprinted by permission.

Chapter Fourteen is adapted from material in Susan J. Leonardi and Rebecca A. Pope, *The
Diva's Mouth: Body, Voice, Prima Donna Politics*, copyright © 1996 by Susan J Leonardi
and Rebecca A. Pope. Reprinted by permission of Rutgers University Press.

Library of Congress Cataloging-in-Publication Data

The work of opera : genre, nationhood, and sexual difference / edited by Richard
   Dellamora and Daniel Fischlin.
    p.   cm.
   Includes bibliographical references and index.
   ISBN 0–231–10944–X (alk. paper). — ISBN 0–231–10945–8 (pbk : alk. paper)
   1. Opera—History and criticism.   2. Nationalism in music.   3. Sex in opera.
I. Dellamora, Richard.   II. Fischlin, Daniel.
ML1700.W67   1997
782.1'09—dc21                                                                                97–19867

⊗

Casebound editions of Columbia University Press books are printed on permanent and
durable acid-free paper.

Printed in the United States of America

*Designed by Linda Secondari*

c 10 9 8 7 6 5 4 3 2 1
p 10 9 8 7 6 5 4 3 2 1

*For Robin Carlson and Alan Orenstein*

## ACKNOWLEDGMENTS

---

When he was ill with AIDS, my close friend and colleague Alan Orenstein, the Canadian philosopher and dramaturge, gave me a personal copy of Peter Conrad's *A Song of Love and Death: The Meaning of Opera* (1987). *The Work of Opera* is a gift in return. I would like to think that this is the sort of book that Alan, had he been granted reprieve, might today be reading and debating with the same pleasure I took in Conrad's book.

The proximate occasion of this book was a special session on opera, national ideologies, and sexualities that took place at the annual meeting of the Modern Language Association in Toronto, Ontario, in December of 1993. I am grateful to the Planning Committee for supporting the important interdisciplinary work of that session. The MLA's meeting in Toronto, the first held there in many years, proved to be memorable for the February chill that descended upon the city on the day the convention opened and that continued for its duration. For the warmth they brought to our session I am grateful to Daniel Fischlin, Felicia Miller, and Linda and Michael Hutcheon. I am grateful as well to Susan McClary, who initially helped prompt the session.

This project has been unusual for the sustained enthusiasm of all those involved. To my co-editor, Daniel Fischlin, I owe thanks for hard work, intellectual challenge, and many delightful conversations, including a memorable evening in Toronto spent attending a performance of Philip Glass's *Beauty and the Beast*. Linda Hutcheon has been, throughout, an engaged and generous interlocutor. I owe her thanks for her advice and assistance through the long process of assembling this book. Two anonymous reviewers for Columbia University Press ensured that the book would be as good as we could make it. Ann Miller, our editor at Columbia, has been consistently supportive. The contributors proved to be ideal collaborators.

I owe thanks too for assistance from the Social Sciences and Humanities Research Council of Canada. Without the award of a time-release stipend in 1992–1993 I could not have launched the original panel. I am especially grateful for this most precious gift of time since, because of budgetary cutbacks, SSHRCC has subsequently canceled time-release support for Canadian faculty.

As editors we would also like to thank Mark Morris, Mina Filardo, and Rhombus Media for making available the cover image from the Rhombus Media production of Henry Purcell's *Dido and Aeneas*, directed by Barbara Willis Sweete.

A portion of the royalties for this book is dedicated to the Casey House AIDS hospice in Toronto.

*Richard Dellamora*
*Toronto, Ontario*

Years ago as a young boy visiting my grandparents at Emma Lake in central Saskatchewan I had my first contact with the voice I've always associated with opera, Lotte Lehmann. Passing by the half-open door of my uncle's room facing onto the lake, I heard the scratchy 78 playing the distinctive tones and immediately set to parodying them with my insouciant boy soprano. My uncle, Robin Carlson, who to this day has the same Eaton's Viking record player and the same collection of Lehmann recordings, chased me out into the forest ready, I'm still convinced, to thrash me within an inch of my life. I hid in the deep forest surrounding the lake all afternoon, terrified. In the distance Lehmann resumed singing and her voice taunted the forest quiet with its impalpable presence. When my mother returned I tearfully repented. But she was not overly sympathetic, perhaps because she had similar passions to those of her brother, having played as Jon Vickers' accompanist on live radio in the Canadian hinterlands when both were local talents starting to emerge on the national musical scene.

In my mind, even though we still laugh at this bit of family lore, Robin has yet to forgive me and I have yet to tell him what that afternoon taught me about music. Music as something to cultivate in the privacy and intimacy of a world apart, as a talisman to guard against the encroachments of a world with little tolerance for fantasy and difference. Today when I visit with Robin, who cares for my nonagerian grandparents, Stanley and Violet,

I can still listen to the recording that prompted my afternoon terror. This book is dedicated to Robin, who somehow conveyed the significance of the secret space that music hollows out of things. I also wish to thank my co-editor, Richard Dellamora, for helping me remember the story through his own patient listening, his own talismanic generosity.

*Daniel Fischlin*
*Guelph, Ontario*

Richard Dellamora and Daniel Fischlin

I

On September 15, 1996, the Lombard League, Italy's secessionist political party, declared the symbolic independence of Padania—a mythical realm constituting the basin of the Po River valley and a number of adjoining territories in Italy. When Umberto Bossi, head of the League, decided recently to attend a performance of an opera by Giuseppe Verdi in Verona, he encountered an unpleasant surprise. Hecklers in the audience, perhaps responding to the movement's "dark overtones of racism and intolerance" (Drohan, A14), greeted him with the cry: "Long live a united Italy" (Bohlen, A10). Unpleasant, but not surprising, because as readers of this book are probably aware, Italian grand opera, the name of Verdi, and Italian nationalism are virtually synonymous. The incident offers a reminder of how intimately and dramatically nationalism and nineteenth-century opera are conjoined. In the Verdi of such works as *I vespri siciliani* and *Simon Boccanegra*, nationhood is eroticized as love of country (Parker et al., 1). In the context of secessionist politics, the symbolic power of Verdi to constitute a national community reminds readers that the interpellation of national subjects is not only an imaginary but, at times, an imaginative and creative, even a necessary act.

Perhaps Bossi should have chosen Puccini instead. The propriety of father–daughter relations or those of a young man and woman en route to marriage are the most familiar but by no means the only ways in which the coming into being of nationhood occurs in opera. There are also the homosocially bonded male choruses of Verdi's operas and Gioacchino Rossini's *William Tell*. There is the perversion of domesticity in fornication, adultery, and illegitimacy; in the murder of children by parents and of parents by children—all available as synecdoches for the fate of the nation. At precise moments, opera also signifies same-sex desire beyond the limits of the conventionally domestic as well as ideas of nationhood resistant to the politics of the imperial nation-state of post-Napoleonic, Western Europe, as Patricia Juliana Smith observes in her essay in this collection. By contrast, as Todd Gilman describes, at an earlier date these moments exist in political struggles originating in the importation of Italian opera into northern Europe. In a much later context, addressed by the final group of essays in this collection, national tensions are articulated in a wide range of operatic productions at a time when the AIDS epidemic has been construed as a sexual plague.

Efforts to think of opera in these terms have been made possible not only in new productions of standard works and by composers and librettists of new work but also by artists such as Derek Jarman and Diamanda Galas, who cross opera with other genres. Critically, a steady stream of studies has opened conventional opera criticism to questions about national politics, the construction of gender, and the implications of sexual dissidence in the performance and reception of opera. Catherine Clément's *Opera, or the Undoing of Women* (1979), Anthony Arblaster's *Viva la Libertà: Politics in Opera* (1992), and Wayne Koestenbaum's *The Queen's Throat: Opera, Homosexuality, and the Mystery of Desire* (1993) are cases in point. After publication of Corinne Blackmer's and Patricia Juliana Smith's *En Travesti: Women, Gender Subversion, Opera* (1995), it is impossible to discuss opera without addressing the significance of lesbian representation and cultural production; and David J. Levin's collection, *Opera Through Other Eyes* (1994), invokes Theodor Adorno's classic essay "Bourgeois Opera," as it declares this most theatrical of genres a suitable topic of contemporary critical theory.

## II

Nations embody and refract desire; that is, like opera, they give shape to the pleasures and pains, the mystifications and material effects that are a product of desire. But desire, like opera, is mediated by the politics of community and the individuals who articulate the apparent collectivity of the desires that constitute nation. The potent seductions of nationhood entail a symbolic discourse by which an apparently natural will (of the people, of a leader)—deemed the national, formed of shared language, common geography, ethnicity, vision of the future, and so forth—produces the phantasm of collectivity that becomes nation. Thus nation is illusion materialized and requires a symbolic language by which the imagination of nation becomes thinkable and enters into the realm of representation. Opera figures in such a symbolic landscape in a number of ways. First, as Lawrence Kramer's essay in this collection demonstrates, opera functions in the realm of pleasure, *jouissance*, and therefore operates at a figural level that makes its illusions and realities potently attractive. But *jouissance* is only part of the story, because opera also gives shape to a symbolic landscape by producing and contributing to myths of national authenticity and legitimacy. Adorno has argued that "[s]ince the mid-nineteenth century a country's music has become a political ideology by stressing national characteristics, appearing as a representative of nation, and everywhere confirming the national principle" (1989:155). But this "national principle" is contingent on the material and performative dimensions of the symbolic practices—musical, literary, and other—that give meaning to nation. And the creation of those dimensions is, like the pleasures afforded by operatic representation, the work of opera. The politics of operatic production reinforce the capacity of illusion to shape reality, precisely the capacity required of individuals who participate in imagining nation.

Beyond the somewhat obvious truisms implicit in such observations lies the notion of nation as an enactment of voice. Desire is mediated by voice, from the *fort/da* of early childhood to the "I want" that drives the psychic capital of Western economies predicated on patterns of inexhaustible production and consumption. Voice mediates desire, speaks it, enacts it, makes its phantasms real, calls forth the Siren song against which no resistance, even the ploy of Odyssean bondage, is possible, for the narrative of desire spins out of the eternal return of its forbidden voicings. Opera frames its narratives in a collective imaginary that follows a particular logic dependent upon a vision of nation as the imagination of a collective will yoked to the common goal of production; or, as Anthony Arblaster argues, in discussing nineteenth-century operas, "The collective voice of the chorus takes us at once into the public realm" (4). James Parakilas suggests, along somewhat similar lines, that "[t]he divided chorus allows nineteenth-century opera to dramatize issues of irreducible difference among social groups that have to live with each other despite their differences. The differences may be of gender, race or nation, class or profession, religion, or even age" (199). Opera produces, in this sense, the public realm of nation, insofar as opera voices an archetypal model of what nation is: a chorus, not always harmonious, against whose backdrop a small oligarchy of soloists intone the desires that give nation its illusory meaning.

Michael Chanan gives salient examples of the significance of operatic voice in figuring nation when he observes that the "social space" of the castrato voice used in the seventeenth century, which "signifies the chronotype of myth and the world of ancient civilization favoured by absolutist rulers, peopled by gods and superhumans" (46) gives way to "a new image of the family belonging to nineteenth-century bourgeois ideology, an imaginary image with deep sexual undertones: the oedipal family, where the soprano struggles against the paternal bass in order to pair off with the tenor" (47). Both instances of operatic social space, as described by Chanan, use voice to translate ideology into performative presence, the castrato signaling a mythic divinity used to authorize absolutist political practice, the constellations of vocal relations figured in nineteenth-century operatic practice instating a crucial model of submission, revolt, and the latter's containment. Both versions of voice, trailing their filaments of gendered relations, also articulate significant dimensions of a cultural practice that has its place in the formation of national identity.

The play of gender in such a political aesthetic is inscribed at every level of production, as it is in the politics of nation. Imagined community, as Benedict Anderson calls it, is "*imagined* because the members of even the smallest nation will never know most of their fellow-members, meet them, or even hear of them, yet in the minds of each lives the image of their communion" (6). Imagined communities require the invention of relations—both enabling and disabling, both fictive and material—that produce sexual and gender orthodoxies. In turn, those orthodoxies refract the politics of both the local and the national. The figuring of sexual difference—femaleness and maleness, homosociality and heterosexuality, homophobia and heterosexism—that opera stages has as much to do with the genderedness of national identities as it has to do with the erotics of nation and the performative tropes by which gender operates as a form of agency for national order. Opera's agency in the creation of myths of national order and thus, necessarily, of gendered order, is a function of "how deeply opera as a consumer product," in Adorno's words, "is entangled in calculations regarding the public" (1994:32). Such calculations about the public occur, as Adorno argues, because "dramatic form implies the audience" (1994:32–33) and the audience is in relation to the product before it as the subject is to the state, the individual to the nation. The representation of operatic collectivities—soloists, chorus members, orchestral members, stage crew, design team, and so forth—is regulated by a carefully controlled hierarchy. The hierarchy reflects in microcosm a form of social order, an order, moreover, with its versions of tolerable disorder as manifested in opera's staged riots and drunken merry-making.

Opera in production consistently emplaces authoritarianism—that of the composer, the conductor, the director—reproducing the hierarchy of governance it reflects. The conditions of production are such that this hierarchy is staged publicly, emblematizing the spectacle of orthodoxies on which a certain version of the social depends. The fable of the Canadian soubrette singing her first mainstage role as Papagena who was asked by a well-known U.S. director to squawk her lines so as to seem more birdlike but who refused to do so on opening night, thus provoking the wrath of the operatic hierarchy, is instructive. "Taking direction" for the better interests of the production (read director's or conductor's concept of a certain aesthetic ordering) comes to have curious affiliations with the notion of ordered representation, itself one of the key building blocks of nation. In the tale of the resistant soprano the specificities of the local confront the expectations of opera as an international medium that nonetheless insistently inscribes national norms. But the story is incomplete where we left it. The soprano had been trained in the bel canto tradition by a small group of nuns at an Acadian music school on Canada's east coast. The aesthetics of that tradition, within the highly charged political and national context of Acadian culture in Canada, could only result in resistance to the American director's notion of Papagena's sound, derived from a postmodern fantasy about the hyperreal. The anecdote recounts a classic decolonizing gesture in relation to the collision of a number of cultures and the expected subsumption of the less powerful in the dominant.

The linguistic politics of opera in relation to its consumption as product also figure here: not only does opera entail the parroting of languages that are "other," frequently learned syllabically, with little need for the singer to speak the language, but opera also imposes a version of language as mediated by the powerful colonizing gestures implicit in the director's, singing coach's, chorus and orchestral conductors' versions of what language is and means. Further, the commonplace use of surtitling in North American opera houses, in which large screens above the proscenium flash translations of the singers' words, engages yet another dimension of linguistic politics. Surtitles attempt to efface the very linguistic differences that European operas stage for North American audiences. Surtitling is as much about fulfilling consumer demands for a predictable product as it is about the national imposition of one language upon another. Surtitles literally require a lifting of the eyes from the stage to attend to the sequencing of translation occurring above the audience, thus displacing the staging of linguistic "otherness" with the homogeneous "real" of the recognizable.

The politics of nation cannot be dissociated from such a strategy. Nor can the politics of gender. For the screen on which the surtitle appears effaces (symbolically) sexual difference, producing the word as ungendered, desexualized, unmediated by the very voice singing on the stage below. Thus, the queerness of operatic representation, a queerness produced out of the disjunction between the visual and vocal reality of say, a Cherubino, an Arsace, or a Romeo, all of whom embody a form of cross-dressing *and* cross-voicing, is effaced in the subjection of the audience's attention to the screen, a theatrical dynamic that reproduces the familiar passivity of the TV audience, whose subjectivity is mediated by the semiotics of the screen. The efficacies of such a dynamic in producing a compliant national, not to mention gendered and sexed, subject cannot be ignored. This is especially true in the context of the gradual movement in operatic performance practice away from an active audience in which opera houses "well into the nineteenth century, were the locus for conversation and other activities," only quieting down "to hear favourite musical bits," to the gradual "silencing of talk" (Leppert, 24–25) that is now customary. As Richard Leppert observes: "The etiquette of physical passivity, simultaneously imposed and self-imposed, reflects the achievement of social hegemony in part through cultural practice" (25).

In North America, the Disneyification of fantasy and spectacle has contributed to the generic movement of sung spectacle in a direction that demands opera Americanize its otherness. The concerted attempt to turn opera into a commodity that abides by the logic of late capitalism exemplifies this movement. A recent instance of this sort is the fund-raising efforts made by the Canadian Opera Company's Operathon '96, in which "24 consecutive hours of music theatre on video laserdiscs" (Sumi, C7) were played under the general thematic focus of "Murder and Mayhem" to attract donations. This form of technological displacement, yielding to commodity and market imperatives, instates an aesthetic at several removes from the performative, not to mention historical, contexts traditionally associated with opera. Fredric Jameson describes this form of displacement in postmodern terms: "You no longer offer a musical object for contemplation and gustation; you wire up the context and make space musical around the consumer" (299–300). The creation of this "wired" space in relation to opera explicitly confirms the symbolic place opera is taking in the "New World Order," a putatively postnational eradication of traditional national boundaries whose sign is the very mutability and reproducibility of the cultural, economic, social, and historical capital upon which it depends.

In the case of the soprano who refused to squawk, the logos as the law (of the director, of the state) is also a function of the melos as an embodiment of harmony, a musical ordering that resonates with the overtones of the social. Or, as Kaja Silverman puts it: "The voice is the site of perhaps the most radical of all subjective divisions—the division between meaning and materiality" (44). As a result of this radical division, the public shaping of voice that is the work of opera frames a version of the meaning of materiality. Opera mounts this relationship in a spectacular, or what Herbert Lindenberger has called an "extravagant," way: the excessiveness of the resources, wealth, and leisure called for to create opera signifies its importance as national cultural artefact. But because the meaning of materiality is fraught with the arbitrariness of hermeneutic systems, of the specificities of local time and place, of the conditions of performance, reception, and so forth, opera is also the site of important contestations about meaning.

The apparent autonomy of voice, embodied in the soloist upon whom opera is predicated, is subsumed in the architectonic of musical and literary figuration, the score that, consciously or not, exfoliates ideology as surely as does the union placard, the editorialist, the corporate logo, the TV commercial. The work of opera, in this last regard, is the work of ideology transumed by aesthetics into the phantasmagoria, the spectacle, of a false consciousness. Take, for instance, the catcalls, bomb threats, and disruptions that followed from the Frankfurt Opera's staging of *Aida* in January 1991, in which, when the curtain rose, the audience was confronted with "something like its mirror image: the original first-night audience of the opera's European premiere at La Scala in 1872" (Weber/Levin, 107). The disruptions were caused, in part, by the recognition that false consciousness was being exposed, laid bare by the self-reflexive, meta-narrative imposed by Hans Neuenfels's staging. The exposition of the work of opera as a secular ritual of bourgeois self-identification, at once parodied and reinstated by the Neuenfels production, poses a threat to what Benjamin calls "the unique value of the 'authentic' work of art," whose "basis in ritual [is] the location of its original use value" (1969:224). In Neuenfels's production the panoptical relation of audience to performers and vice versa was suddenly exposed, the logic of such a strategy being one step removed from the exposition of the stage mechanics, and from the audience's point of view, the exposition of its own constructedness in relation to the spectacle. The spectacle makes the audience as much as the audience makes the spectacle. And once the epistemological contingencies of such a relation are exposed, the possibility of sustaining the pleasurable false consciousness associated with high cultural spectacle becomes more difficult, more fraught with the possibilities that such a mirror is itself a falsehood, a device that exposes the very constructedness of production as an extension of the arbitrariness of ideology.

The ruses of operatic art depend upon a version of mimetic idealism operative within the predictable boundaries that shape an audience's suspension of disbelief. At the same time, however, that version of mimetic idealism is strained beyond credulity in the hyperbole and sheer egregiousness of the spectacle. Subjectivity in opera is therefore deformed and reshaped in a potent spectacle that is analogous, in microcosm, to the very operations of nation as it "produces" the political subject. The *vox populi* is given heroic proportion even as the spectacle of that proportion reenacts the political relations between ruler and ruled, conductor and performer, all conjoining to produce the work of nation and of opera. The recent example, cited by Eric Hobsbawm, of "a Puccini aria sung by Pavarotti" that came to be associated "with the World Football Cup in 1990" (509), the latter a classic instance of the staging of putative national identities, merely reinforces the degree to which even the marginal presence of opera in popular culture refracts a certain ideological content with both national and gendered implications. The heroic masculinity of the football player is aligned with the sentimentality of a Puccini aria, constructing national identity through the tenor voice that echoes the homosocial authority of patriarchal discourse.

Similarly, the spectacle of tenors Plácido Domingo and José Carreras making "an impassioned plea . . . in Hungary to end injustice" at the same time as they "asked for lenient treatment when they sing arias with lyrics in tongue-twisting Hungarian" (Reuters, April 5, 1996) associates operatic pronouncement with ending injustice at the same time as it appropriates and defaces (proleptically) the particularities of a specific national language. Here opera acts as unifying and appropriative moral discourse, reinforcing its status as a privileged narrative of liberal values. Domingo, somewhat naïvely, asserts in the same news report, "I just don't know how the governments, powers, rulers, any kind of government can wake up in the morning with a conscience knowing that they are just doing something wrong to the people" (ibid.). Yet Domingo would not have to look far within his own operatic discipline to find numerous examples of complicity with the kinds of "conscience" that allow for state injustice. The meta-narrative of grand opera is one that subsumes (and makes palatable) discourses suitable to nation-building. The aesthetic values of opera as the most extravagant form of high culture are necessarily interwoven with the forms of oppression and myth creation required by that culture for self-legitimation.

Genderedness and the public representation of sexual artifice, so crucial to the visual allure of opera, are also decisively tied to the creation of meaning through the materiality of voice. Hence operatic spectacle is intensely imbricated in questions of orthodoxy and subversion related to both gender and nation. The public voicing of *the meaning of meaning*—the oratorical and highly artificial representation of sung speech extending from early recitative and monody evident in Claudio Monteverdi through to Rossinian and Verdian vocal display to Alban Berg's and Kurt Weill's versions of *sprechstimme* through to Philip Glass's minimalist rendering of the same— determines in part the symbolic and aesthetic shape of nation. In Jenny Lind's "mid-nineteenth-century American tour," to cite but one instance of this sort of dynamic, "her audience looked to Lind to provide them with a quasi-religious experience that would, through the magical power of her desexualized body and voice, heal the social divisions of the nation" (Blackmer and Smith, 13). John Dizikes's account of Lind's American tour notes how "Someone said: The Age of Music had come to America" (127) while also observing that "Jenny Lind's success had the effect of stamping almost anything European in music with the label 'best'" (135). This effect, despite Felix Mendelssohn's remark that Lind "sings bad music the best" (cited in Dizikes, 134), was intensely associated with the "uncritical admiration of European art in American [nineteenth century] culture, rooted in the lack of self-confidence of the American middle class" (Dizikes, 135). Lind embodied in her operatic voice the illusion of national taste, the false consciousness of an emergent national identity seeking self-validation through an authoritative, European other. The associations of operatic stardom with delusions about national self-worth are frequent, as if the voice of the singer somehow represents some essential quality of unvitiated national demeanor. Glory is the destiny of great operatic voices, and it is a glory that carries with it the symbolic dimensions of national greatness, as it did for Elizabeth I, the "Gloriana" of Benjamin Britten's eponymous opera (1953).

Opera as genre stages the epic of imperial culture. The epic requirements of the materials of operatic production are correlative with its place in the symbolic landscape of nation. It is no accident that there is no such thing as Third World grand opera. As Hobsbawm notes, "The international operatic repertoire [has] remained essentially what it had been in the Age of Empire, with composers born in the early 1860s (Richard Strauss, Mascagni) or even earlier (Puccini, Leoncavallo, Janáček) at the outer limits of 'modernity,' as broadly speaking, it still remains" (181). Even in the so-called "first world," establishing operatic legitimacy is no easy task. The example of English opera and its putative failure to produce a first-order national school of opera worthy of international recognition, with the flawed exceptions of Henry Purcell and Benjamin Britten (and possibly Michael Tippett), is a case in point. Adorno argues, for instance, "that the British musical genius dried up from the early seventeenth century on," an atrophy Adorno associates with the "rise of Puritanism" (1989:159–60). Blackmer and Smith observe that "[c]ontemporary musicologists, approaching opera through a priori assumptions about the inherent superiority of nineteenth-century German music, have labeled [Henry Purcell's] *Dido* a queerly flawed anomaly because it 'failed,' perhaps like an impotent parent, to 'engender' an English national opera" (8). Of course, *Dido and Aeneas* (1689) is itself about a particular colonial relation, about a movement toward the foundation of empire (what Joseph Roach calls a "mythic reiteration of origins" [51]), and about the power relations between men and women whose erotic relations are played out against the backdrop of national desire. In the context of post–civil war England *Dido* projects a suggestive meta-narrative of the struggle to achieve a form of national identity. The struggle, interestingly enough, is focused "around the actions of women" (Blackmer and Smith, 8) and the opera was originally written for performance "at Mr. Josias Priest's Boarding School at Chelsey. By Young Gentlewomen" (cited in Abraham, 369), both indicators of the queerness that opera refracts through its dreams of nation. The joking reference to "Dildo and Anus," common among opera types, punningly foregrounds (while deforming) the queer erotics of Purcell's spectacle at the same time that it effaces the national dimensions at stake in its complex of representations. The contemporary performance practice of *Dido* has generally sought to neutralize the same-sex gender relations of its original performance, as if its queerness can be authoritatively rescripted as a performance orthodoxy that reflects the heterosexual norms traditionally associated with national identity. Rare productions such as Mark Morris's dance and film adaptation of the opera, done in concert with the Toronto baroque ensemble, Tafelmusik, reshape Purcellian queerness by queering Dido, danced by Morris himself, who also plays the Sorceress. The sensual appeal of Aeneas's first confrontation with Dido is particularly charged as a result of the gender-bending staged by Morris's casting and choreography, especially within the context of an identity politics that puts the heteronormative to the question. The result is a further revisioning of the politics of nation subsumed in Purcell's score and Nahum Tate's libretto.

Another notable example of the way in which nation and gender rub up against each other in operatic contexts occurs in Giuseppe Verdi's *Aida* (1871). Edward Said describes *Aida* as the embodiment of "the authority of Europe's version of Egypt at a moment in its nineteenth-century history, a history for which Cairo in the years 1869–1871 was an extraordinarily suitable site" (1993:125) and observes that "[a]s a visual, musical, and theatrical spectacle, *Aida* does a great many things for and in European culture, one of which is to confirm the Orient as an essentially exotic, distant, and antique place in which Europeans can mount certain shows of force" (1993:112). Verdi's Orientalism extends to his treatment of priests who, in the opera, are converted into "priestesses, following the conventional European practice of making Oriental women central to any exotic practice: the functional equivalents of his priestesses are the dancing girls, slaves, concubines, and bathing harem beauties prevalent in mid-nineteenth-century European art, and by the 1870s, entertainment" (1993:121). The transsexualized Orient embodies the dream of national empowerment, the capacity to refigure the exotic "other" as oneself. Orientalist revisionism encodes a national vision of self that becomes self-empowering, especially in the context of Verdi's remarks about Egypt as a land that "once possessed a grandeur and a civilization which I could never bring myself to admire" (cited in Arblaster, 142). *Aida* is but one of many operas that frame the conjunction between national empowerment and the capacity to figure gender *as spectacle*, a characteristic of nineteenth-century, romantic operas "in which soprano *prime donne* are the sacrificial victims at the crossroads of heterosexual romance and nationalistic rivalries" (Blackmer and Smith, 7).

So much for the inherent heterosexism of opera that locates it as a particularly public site of production for patriarchal values. But opera also encodes homosociality and homosexuality and thus articulates notions of sexual difference as a function of its theatrics. Homosocial bonding entails a form of communal relations fraught with the peril of overstepping the unclear line that separates the homosocial from the homosexual. But such a line also brings the homosocial and the homosexual into close proximity, thereby framing difference within the normative strictures that generic opera articulates. The pattern is similar to larger-scale patterns evident at the level of nation, where the homosociality particular to governing bodies (the senate, Congress, parliament, the Supreme Court, and so forth) is authorized in relation to ideals of state unity, legitimacy, and law. As George Mosse argues, "Masculinity provided the norm for society; its symbol had to send out clear and unambiguous signals. Therefore nationalism tried to exorcise homoeroticism from masculine beauty and to make it respectable. It also attempted to absorb all the latently erotic aspects of personal relationships among men, as the history of friendship will show us" (16). But such an absorption could not wholly reduce the truth of masculinity to a deeroticized respectability as operas such as Britten's *Billy Budd* (1951), with its all-male cast; *Peter Grimes* (1945); *The Turn of the Screw* (1954); and *Death in Venice* (1973) demonstrate, pulsing as they do, with "queer subtexts" (Gill, 17). Such operas play against the norm of a stereotypical masculinity, suggesting possibilities for a queerness that cannot be eradicated by national will, for a sensuality figured in the vocal intertwinings of same-sex duets, the vocal "tops" and "bottoms" whose harmonizations and dissonances echo other bodily and imaginative configurations.

Opera is bourgeois art—no matter how many beer tents are put up at summer festivals with abridged versions of the stock-in-trade repertory that has become operatic canon; no matter how many parks or stadia resound to the high notes of the season's hot new star. And in bourgeois art, "the phantasmagoria of 'cultural history,'" as Walter Benjamin notes, allows "the bourgeoisie [to savor] its false consciousness to the last" (1978:158). At least in part, *the work of opera* is to stage the pleasure of the false consciousness that is nation, to figure and voice the contradictions implicit in any production of imperial order, to display the allure of the heterogeneous, the differend that will not be eradicated, the queer.

The staging of the Jew by Wagner—"The gold-grabbing, invisible, anonymous, exploitative Alberich, the shoulder-shrugging, loquacious Mime, overflowing with self-praise and spite, the impotent intellectual critic Hanslick-Beckmesser," what Adorno calls "caricatures of Jews" (1991:23)— participates in a particularly insidious form of the national urge to manipulate the "other" in the service of state values. Wagnerian Jews are demonized in the service of a form of national unity based on hate and prohibition. As Adorno notes, Jewish caricatures in Wagner "stir up the oldest sources of the German hatred of the Jews" (ibid.), a form of anti-Semitism that Wagner "shared with other representatives of . . . the German Socialism of 1848" (ibid.), and later, of course, with elements of German National Socialism. Adorno concludes that Wagner's "hatred [of the Jews] is so extreme that, if we are to believe [Carl F.] Glasenapp, the news of the deaths of 400 Jews in the fire in the *Ringtheater* in Vienna inspired him to make jokes. He had even conceived the notion of the annihilation of the Jews. He differs from his ideological descendants only in that he equates annihilation with salvation" (Adorno, 1991:26).

The allure of Wagnerian opera rests not only on transcendental notions of redemption and salvation, but also on how those concepts are aligned with forms of German national identity. To this day the fascination with these notions persists. Hans Jürgen Syberberg's film version of Wagner's last opera, *Parsifal* (1882), for instance, "cannot be seen in isolation from [Syberberg's] *Hitler* trilogy," for what lies behind the films "is the fascination with the imbrication of high art, of German romanticism, in Nazism, high culture and Fascism" (Tambling, 194). The demonized "other" of the Jew, though, authorizes the myth of transcendental and purgative salvation by virtue of its presence *as otherness*. Transcendence of this sort is unattainable without the other, and the curious bind that Wagnerian opera finds itself in is the promulgation of a perverse national legitimacy that cannot be dissociated from the other it seeks to eradicate. Marc A. Weiner frames this national dynamic in relationship to "stereotypes of Jewish sexuality," Alberich representing the "lascivious, irrepressibly horny Jew" and Mime "his sexual opposite, an effeminate, childless wimp" (185). Weiner argues that "the Jew is both obviously different from the German and at the same time chameleonic, mimicking and thereby infiltrating German society.

The anxiety behind this tension is precisely that involved in the polarization of images of the male Jew as both effeminate and . . . a malevolent threat, the very tension at the heart of Wagner's differing anti-Semitic caricatures in the *Ring*" (185). The desired purity of race and nation is subverted by the eternal return of the Jewish differend in performance after performance after performance. This makes Bayreuth a place of nested and embittered ironies in its significance to German culture.

It is not accidental that the emergence of grand opera in the nineteenth century coincides with what Julia Kristeva calls the "Romantic enthusiasm for the national genius *(Volksgeist)*," a form of imaginary self-identification that called for a "cultural nationalism . . . [resting] upon the need to display one's *own* while modifying it through confrontation with the sacred or classical canon" (1991:178). According to Kristeva, "the secret notion of *Volksgeist*, one that is intimate and indeed mystical (in the sense of *Gemüt* and *Einfühlung*), appears to me as favoring hegemonic claims" (1993:33), which is to say, precisely those claims that assert one nation's desires relative to another's. Opera, in such a context, works to produce a form of cultural nationalism profoundly tied to dreams of hegemony, but equally tied to dreams of a *Volksgeist* that authorizes values associated with masculinist, national ideologies.

## III

The authors of the essays in this volume examine the tense, often contradictory relation between opera's musical signifiers and its verbal signifieds. They test too the gaps, overdeterminations, reversals, and resistances that attend the continual reworking of opera in production. There could, for example, scarcely be a better demonstration of Adorno's contention that opera becomes possible only when mythological belief—both Christian and classical—is in decline than Simon Callow's 1996 Glimmerglass Opera production of Francesco Cavalli's *La Calisto* (1651). In Callow's rendition the doctrine of Neoplatonic metamorphosis uttered in the Prologue licenses the riot of perverse play and misrecognition that succeeds it. This contrasting but mutually generative pairing further connotes the culture of intellectual dissidence in which opera finds its origin. As Adorno remarks, the genre was invented not by philosophers or by members of an aristocracy but by "literati . . . namely, a Florentine circle of connoisseurs, writers, and ascetic-reformist musicians toward the end of the sixteenth century. The genre first blossomed in the republic of Venice, that is, under the social conditions of an evolved bourgeoisie, and the first great opera composers, Monteverdi, Cavalli, Cesti, belong there" (1994:31). At the same time, much of the play in *La Calisto* is a ruse of Jove's power. In the essay that begins this book, Victor Anand Coelho supplements such recognitions by bringing to light a long-forgotten piece of musical theater, composed and performed in Rome a generation earlier, in 1622, as part of the canonization ceremonies for Saint Francis Xavier, the "Apostle of the Orient," and Ignatius Loyola, founder of the Jesuit order. Coelho shows how the incipient genre inscribes at its outset the relation of empire to colony in the gendered relationship of Portugal to India. He also shows that the same performance is overwritten by the authoritarian claims of the post-Tridentine Roman Catholic church even as a new male homosocial institution accrues prestige and privilege within it.

Todd Gilman, deploying concepts of gender and nation in a very different context, shows that continual attacks on Italian castrati in seventeenth- and eighteenth-century English pamphlet literature tend to rebound against the heteronormative masculinity to which they are contrasted. Castrati were accused of transgressing conventional norms, and Gilman contends that the projection of hypervirility upon the figure of the castrato inadvertently called into question not only the sufficiency of the manly stance of the satirist but also a construction of English citizenship that was based upon the conflation of the ideal, in classic republican discourse, of the virile citizen-soldier with the Tory ideal of the country gentleman. This effect was scarcely avoidable. Both Italian opera and its virtuosi were associated with what the Tories did not like: namely, the Whig aristocracy and politicians; the Hanoverian dynasty; the growing power of the City (and along with it, the enhanced presence of Jews in English life and the declining value of land); and the imperial expansion necessary to support the growth of commerce. Paradoxically, the most egregious examples of contemporary decadence—namely, aristocratic patronage of Italian opera and its castrati celebrities—were associated with the most conspicuously modernizing agencies of eighteenth-century English political and economic life. Hence an attack on opera could hardly fail to imply the inability of the Country party either to thrive in or to manage the modern state.

In an essay that resonates with similar divisions based on national identity, Felicia Miller reads *Farinelli, Il Castrato*, the recent European coproduction as a conventional bio-pic, at pains to soothe the egos of European Union (male) viewers by producing an (Italian) Farinelli who, in effect, proves that castrati too can generate offspring, and a (French-speaking) gentleman who wows the ladies while eschewing the self-promotion that was part of the careers of actual castrati. Miller links the celebrity of the eighteenth-century castrato Farinelli with the cross-dressed singing of the nineteenth-century contralto Pauline Viardot and the technological "morphing" of the voices of a coloratura soprano and a countertenor to simulate the effect of castrato vocalization in *Farinelli*. In contrast to Gilman, who associates Farinelli with the image of bisexual glamour on stage and a lifelong intimacy with the librettist Pietro Metastasio, Miller uses the figure of the double-gendered voice to associate him with representations of the hermaphrodite.

In *The Mechanical Song: Women, Voice, and the Artificial in Nineteenth-Century French Narrative* (1995), Miller follows Michel Poizat in pointing out that in early nineteenth-century France, *travesti* roles and castrato parts were transposed for the female bel canto voice. As a young man, Viardot's father and voice instructor, Manuel García, had visited Italy to study with teachers who had studied in turn with followers of the operatic composer and tutor of Farinelli, Nicolo Porpora. Her training as a contralto continued the tradition in which leading castrati had been formed. The shift to a more "natural" gendering of high tessituras sought to leave behind the assorted embarrassments of the excess of the castrato voice, perceived to be too Roman, too Italian, too effeminate, too sexy. Instead a contradictory set of associations with the contraltist voice—its transcendent and otherworldly connotations—is transferred onto the "angelic" voice of a woman. This voice becomes a trope of aesthetic disembodiment and sublimation at the obvious expense of feminine subjectivity. Miller argues that in the twentieth century this tendency has been further exacerbated by the identification of female vocalization with technological processes such as the phonograph and radio so as to move the soprano voice "beyond" gender altogether. In the "morphed" voice of Farinelli, this tendency reaches an extreme through the technological sublimation of male and female voices in a sound that is literally inhuman.

Eve Kosofsky Sedgwick has drawn attention to the persistent triangulation of desire between men, mediated by a woman, in Victorian fiction in *Between Men: English Literature and Male Homosocial Desire*. Adopting Sedgwick's model to the topic of desire *between women*, Terry Castle has shown that female same-sex attraction is likewise often mediated by the contest between two women over a single male figure (66–91). In "*O Patria Mia*" Patricia Juliana Smith considers two operas that turn upon such a triangle: Vincenzo Bellini's *Norma* (1831) and Giuseppe Verdi's *Aida* (1871). In the first opera an ardently avowed love between the two women rescues Norma from the threat of treason and restores her both to her *patria* and to the religion of her forefathers. At the conclusion of the duet "Mira, O Norma," in Act II, Scene 1, Adalgisa and Norma sing together:

> Yes, you will have me as your companion
> until your last hour;
> the world is large enough
> to be a shelter to both of us together.
> With you I shall set my face
> firmly against the shame which fate may bring,
> as long as I feel your heart
> beating on mine.

In 1831 Bellini was able to affirm both the fervent expression of romantic friendship between women and, in his sympathy with the Druids' cause, a form of national identity often at odds with the politics both of empire (represented in *Norma* by the Roman invaders) and the modern nation-state.

In the forty years that separate *Norma* from *Aida*, however, the meaning of nation had changed in Italy, where the modern nation-state came into fragile existence in 1861 and where religion and the state had been forced into enmity over the issue of the secular power of the papacy. In response, Pope

Pius IX threatened with excommunication all who participated in Italian politics. Verdi's unsympathetic portrayal of the Egyptian priests in *Aida* resonates with his anger at the church's interference in the politics of representative government. Smith notes a number of ideological effects pertaining to this situation. First, the affirmation of personal love is accentuated at the expense of its place in affirming either religious faith or collective identity. Smith understands this tendency as a further *heterosexualizing* of opera that continues in *verismo* opera and in Puccini. The process appears ultimately to deprive operatic composition in Italy of any public significance. Second, although anticlerical, the opera is Roman Catholic in its characterology. Ancient Ethiopian background notwithstanding, Aida is very much a Catholic type. In this situation too, love between women is transformed, so that when Amneris interrogates Aida, she adopts what Smith calls a pretense of "sorority and equality" in order to learn whether she, her slave, is a rival for Radamès's affections. Smith contextualizes Amneris as a "virago," one part power-hungry feminist, the other part, in her inversion of conventional gender attributes, degenerate and lesbian.

Whereas both *Norma* and *Aida* articulate, in Smith's readings, a not-so-sublimated discourse that links nation with sexual identity, Lawrence Kramer bluntly asks what is left to be said about Richard Wagner's music in terms of sexual identity and anti-Semitic nationalism. Using Nietzsche's *The Case of Wagner* as a point of departure, Kramer examines the dialectic between nationalism and eroticism. In the case of *Götterdämmerung*, Kramer affirms that the national hero, here Siegfried, can exist only as a result of the mystification of political consciousness that is paralleled by an erotic sensibility that cannot recognize its object. For Kramer this structure is keenly evident in the *Ring*. Heroic (read national) identity is not a function of what the hero actually is so much as what he is imagined to be by others. Here again the staging of this othering is crucial to the work of opera, which gives public voice to the collective imaginaries of gender and nation. At the same time, opera's erotic fusion of media in the Wagnerian *Gesamtkuntswerk* produces a form of aesthetic *jouissance* that works to contradict the powerful ideological forces that make of opera a microcosmic and imaginary national polity.

By the 1860s, French grand opera was twinned with the Empire. Jean-Louis-Charles Garnier's plans for the Paris Opera, for example, included a separate entrance for Napoleon III, who had been the target of an assassination attempt while attending the opera in Paris in 1858. By the time the building opened in 1875, however, France had been humiliated in a brief war with Prussia in 1870 and the emperor had been deposed. Once again France was a republic. Nonetheless, as Susan McClary shows in her essay on *Carmen*, even in the less select bourgeois precincts of the Opéra-Comique, where Bizet's opera premiered the same year, imperial ambition had scarcely dissipated. Indeed, the musical potpourri of *Carmen*, which combines ethnographic citations; conventionally "Oriental" motives; cabaret songs, including an African-Cuban popular song that became the "Habañera"; and the

Wagnerian yearning of Don José's music is scarcely imaginable apart from the metropolitan milieu of Walter Benjamin's "Paris, Capital of the Nineteenth Century." Within the terms of this musical representation, the "Spain" of the action, like the country of the same name that had been subject to French invasion under Napoleon Bonaparte, is scarcely a singular reality. McClary traces in the musical structure of the opera a continual struggle for mastery over the contradictory elements of otherness—Spanish, feminine, gypsy, Oriental, working-class, and popular—that the music both conjures and, with limited success, works to dispel.

These contradictions are amplified in Camille Saint-Saëns's *Samson et Dalila*, begun in 1868 and premiered in 1877 in German under the sponsorship of Franz Liszt at Weimar, after French producers balked at the operatic use of sacred material and the opera's debt to Wagner. Arguing that *Samson et Dalila* is not so much Oriental as Oriental*ist*, Ralph Locke contextualizes the opera in terms of Edward Said's by now familiar discussion of the discursive construction of "Orientalism" by European writers, mainly English and French, in the nineteenth century. Juxtaposing musical citations from Eastern material with fragments drawn from the tradition of European sacred music, Saint-Saëns's composition performs the work of textualizing the Orient for Western consumption in the form of a luxury commodity. This commodity, moreover, is sexualized, observing the same heterosexual modeling that Said adopts in characterizing "the relationship between Occident and Orient" as "a relationship of power, of domination, of varying degrees of a complex hegemony" (1979:5). Locke further contextualizes Orientalism in relation to the intense interest French colonizers took in North Africa and the Near East. In this light he observes that the opera characterizes in wholly negative terms the male Philistines, stand-ins for modern Arabs. Examining the music and words of Dalila's aria "Mon coeur s'ouvre à ta voix," however, Locke finds Dalila to be represented as something besides an exotic, sexualized, and gendered other, object of desire and fear. Dalila's opacities and ambivalence, her equivocal status as a subject of desire, make her a focal point of both anxiety and identification on the part of operagoers.

Ruth A. Solie's "Fictions of the Opera Box" directs the attention of readers to the status opera enjoyed as a commodity spectacle in the United States by the fin de siècle. The installation of a "golden horseshoe" of no fewer than 122 boxes, for which subscribers drew lots when the Metropolitan Opera opened in New York in 1883, offers probably the most familiar illustration of what Thorstein Veblen refers to as conspicuous consumption in *The Theory of the Leisure Class* (1899). Writing a chapter in American social history, Solie describes how opera boxes became a setting in which social warfare was waged between patrician members of New York's old Knickerbocker society, on the defensive, and the *nouveaux riches*—including the Vanderbilts, Rockefellers, Morgans, Astors, Goulds, and Whitneys. Considering scenes set in opera boxes in a wealth of American novels, serious and popular, of the

Gilded Age, Solie pursues the disturbing topic of the young women who surveilled and were surveilled in opera boxes. Because women, as Veblen and
Henry James pointed out, were the bearers of high culture in the United
States and because their nervous temperaments were judged to be especially
liable to musical stimulus, particularly by Wagner's "modern" music, the
opera box provided an ideal site for reading the truths of female passion.

In these essays, issues of gender and sexual difference do not simply displace earlier associations among opera, nationhood, and empire. Daniel
Fischlin reads Britten's last opera, *Death in Venice*, by way of the issues that
"come out" when gender and sexuality are overwritten upon notions of
national identity, political subjectivity, state formation and regulation, especially within the historical trajectory from pre- to postfascist aesthetics. Both
Thomas Mann's novella and its operatic rescripting explore homoerotic
desire and the regulations, internal and external, that lead to its repression.
Mann's novella subtly links that repression with the emergence of nationalist (and what was to become National Socialist) ideology, whereas Britten's
musical version of the novella effaces such connections by aestheticizing the
narrative's sublimated political discourses. Aschenbach's repression of his
love for Tadzio is transmuted into transcendence, the eerie pall cast by the
contagious plague that Aschenbach dies of as a result of his closeted pursuit
of the boy, having disconcerting resonances in the context of the contemporary AIDS crisis. The essay asks why Britten's version of the story aestheticizes and transcendentalizes the closet, literally staging repression in an
operatic tour de force, while sanitizing the complicated national (and bourgeois) contexts Mann addresses in his narrative. The politics of sexual
repression, in which state values are reinscribed and internalized by closeted
artists in a postfascist context, demand attention, especially if elements of
complicity with fascist aesthetics, which represses desire through appeals to
unconsummated, Platonic transcendence as a substitute for the closet, are to
be avoided and undermined. Fischlin's essay invites a radical revision of the
performance practice traditionally associated with the opera, one that will
queer its repressive political, erotic, and aesthetic fantasies while recognizing the historical conditions that produce those fantasies.

Writing self-consciously *after* the end of both grand opera and the nineteenth-century concept of the nation-state grounded in a single linguistic
culture and ethnic identity, Linda and Michael Hutcheon argue, paradoxically, that at the very moment when state patronage promoted the development of specifically Canadian opera during the nation's centennial in 1967,
Canadian composers were at pains to write operas, admittedly on national
subjects, that contest ethnic and linguistic chauvinism (both Anglophone
and Francophone). The Hutcheons follow the work of Canadian opera into
the 1990s with Harry Somers and Rod Anderson's 1992 opera *Mario the
Magician*, premiered by the Canadian Opera Company in Toronto. October
1992 is also the date of a national referendum in which a new constitutional
accord, designed to address the demands of Québécois nationalists, aborig-

inal leaders, and members of other constituencies, failed to win support of a majority of voters, either in Québec or in the western provinces. The resulting impasse has brought Canada closer to breakup than at any earlier point in its history. The opera offers an apt warning, remarkably prophetic in the Canadian context, of the dangers posed by populist nationalism. Somers and Anderson, however, make their case obliquely, turning to Thomas Mann's 1929 novella *Mario und der Zauberer*, which tells the story of a group of Germans vacationing in Mussolini's Italy. There they learn the dangers both of nationalist xenophobia and of the music that spurs it on ("Giovinezza, Giovinezza," the fascist anthem, is sung in the course of the performance). Commenting ironically on the work of nation formation performed by such nineteenth-century composers as Verdi, Anderson repeatedly introduces into the libretto the phrase "acoustic contagion" to refer to the rabble-rousing effects of musical sound. Sexually, both Mann and Anderson refer to the hypnotic power of the Magician/"Forzatore," or strong-man, to seduce the audience. In the opera this effect is allegorized in yet another spin on male homosocial triangulation. "Cipolla teases Mario about his love for—and suffering over—a young woman named Silvestra" (see chapter 10 of the present volume). But after Cipolla hypnotizes Mario in front of an audience, he unmans him by calling upon him to kiss him under the delusion that he is, in fact, Silvestra. Mario does so. After he realizes what has happened, he "runs away—but then turns and shoots his mocker dead" (ibid.). Subjection, operatic and political, is figured as a veiled homosexual seduction.

IV

Lecturing in Western Germany in the mid-1950s, Theodor Adorno described most operatic productions as paying nostalgic tribute to a traditional bourgeoisie whose actual prospects had been in decline since the end of World War I. At the same time, Adorno's "Bourgeois Opera" continues to be the single most prophetic utterance devoted to opera in the past half century. In the final sentence of the lecture, he says, "Only when the entire fullness of musical means in the face of a complaint worthy of humanity awakens something of that tension between the musical and the scenic mediums . . . only then could opera once more match the power of the historical image" (1994:43). The final essays in *The Work of Opera* locate such a complaint in the AIDS epidemic of the *fin de millenium*. They address the future of opera in terms of the ways in which—in new productions of standard operas, in refurbishments of familiar productions, in new operas, in work that combines opera with other media such as film and performance art—the work of opera continues. Why has AIDS been so important in operatic work? Part of the answer lies in demographics. The AIDS epidemic was first widely reported in places such as New York City, San Francisco, and London, which are major centers of opera production. Second, theatrical and musical communities have been disproportionately hard hit by AIDS. For example, Christopher

Keene, the former general director of the New York City Opera reported that by the early 1990s "dozens of the City Opera's members and two administrators had died" as a result of AIDS—a fate to which Keene himself succumbed on October 8, 1995 (Oestreich, A12). The presence of queer subjects behind the footlights—and behind the scenes—in opera houses has demanded that they communicate the catastrophe they continue to experience in daily life. In the most unsettling ways, the freshly experienced vulnerability of those involved in opera has provided a reminder of the queer affinities of this genre.

Today queer critics are also observing that, since the very origins of opera with Claudio Monteverdi's *La Favola d'Orfeo* (1607), the power of music has been associated with cross-gendered or otherwise specially marked voices (Koestenbaum, 178–80). In the premiere production of Monteverdi's opera, for example, the roles of the Prologue (La Musica) and of Eurydice were sung by castrati. Throughout the sixteenth century, Orfeo could be sung interchangeably by either a male or a female singer. In the eighteenth century Gluck wrote the lead part in his *Orfeo* for a castrato; and when Pauline Viardot sang the role in cross-dress in 1859, her appearance carried with it feminist and socialist connotations of the figure of the androgyne/hermaphrodite in French political radicalism. Later, when Natalie Barney temporarily lost her lover, Renée Vivien, to another woman, she enlisted the help of the diva Emma Calvé. Calvé visited Vivien and began to serenade her with Viardot's best-known aria from the opera, "J'ai perdu mon Euridice." In these instances heterosexual representation provides a highly permeable screen for connotations of sexual difference that contravene conventional assumptions about gender and sexuality.

Wolfgang Amadeus Mozart is usually represented as an international figure and his operas interpreted in terms of Enlightenment, even Revolutionary values. In "Mozart and the Politics of Intimacy" Dellamora turns to Peter Sellars's 1990 production of *The Marriage of Figaro* to argue that precisely by attending to issues of gender and sexuality that exist in both the Mozart–Da Ponte opera and the play by Pierre de Beaumarchais on which it is based, a director can find reasons to contextualize a new production in national terms. Doing so, however, requires the subversion of the domestic ideology that commentators usually impose on the opera and the restoration of arias sung by Marcellina and Basilio that address questions of misogyny and sexual abuse. The Sellars production of this opera is one of the few that foreground class and national issues in terms of gender and sexuality that are fully reversible; that is, although the abuse by the count of his wife and servants exemplifies the abuse of others by financial wheelers and dealers during the Reagan years, the representation of corruption at the Trump Tower similarly underwrites the complaints of feminists and members of other subordinated groups. Sellars places economic, gender, sexual, and national issues on a single plane. In contrast, Robin Phillips's 1993 production of the same opera for the Canadian Opera Company in Toronto effaces gay subjectivity—his own and that of Toronto's large and diverse communities of sexual dissidents—in favor of a heterosexual reinscription of the opera. Dellamora observes that doing so requires Phillips to suppress the questioning of conventional ideas of subjective interiority that occurs both in the text by Beaumarchais and in Figaro's fourth-act aria "Aprite un po'." Dellamora further contextualizes the production in terms of the position of sexual dissidents within Anglophone Canada's theatrical establishment. Although the careers of many gays and lesbians are virtually synonymous with the development of an "English" Canadian national theater over the past generation, the price of admission has been the explicit demand that people like Phillips emphasize "universal"—that is, hegemonic—values. This demand leaves the national organs of Anglophone culture in no position to address the actual heterogeneity of Canadian existence today.

In contrast, Jim Ellis shows how Thatcherite politics, in particular the passage of Section 28 of the Local Government Act in 1988 in a climate of AIDS hysteria, have prompted counterarguments from cultural practitioners such as Derek Jarman. Section 28 prohibits local authorities from "intentionally promoting homosexuality" as a "pretended family relationship" (Jeffery-Poulter, 5–6). Drawing on an alternative political tradition, Jarman contends that feminists and gay artists in England have long contested the conflation of nationalist belligerence with a narrow construction of "family values." Jarman's film adaptation of Benjamin Britten's *War Requiem* (1961) went into production in March 1988, simultaneously with passage of the Government's bill. In his version Jarman emphasizes the pacifist affirmation of the lives of young men in Britten's work. Likewise, Britten himself in this work refers to the homoerotic, antiwar poetry of Wilfred Owen, which Virginia Woolf likewise enlists in her critique of British patriotism in *Three Guineas* (1938). Ellis pursues these aspects of Britten's thinking into *Owen Wingrave*, the opera written for television that Britten began writing in 1968, at the height of anti–Vietnam War agitation in the United States and Britain. The work of interpreting opera today, according to Ellis, requires critics to be willing to rethink a composer's operatic oeuvre in light of adaptations such as Jarman's, which import specifically operatic techniques into other musical genres.

With the publication in 1993 of Koestenbaum's previously mentioned *The Queen's Throat*, opera in the United States came definitively out of the closet. Koestenbaum's book is an Orphic exercise whose object of ambivalent desire, glimpsed across the abysses of the politics of gay liberation and the AIDS epidemic, is not Eurydice but the 1950s-style opera queen. Turning to an elegy by Koestenbaum, written in memory of a friend who died as a result of AIDS, Kevin Kopelson argues that the loss attributed to homosexual identity, which inhabits as well generational shifts in gay culture, is today seconded by losses due to AIDS. In this respect Koestenbaum's outing of opera has been compelled by the impact of AIDS. Although this context makes *The Queen's Throat* very much a "New York" book, Kopelson argues that Koestenbaum's admitted amateur status as a fan of opera signals the gap that continues to exist between homosexual fantasies of escape from the American hinterlands and the dream of genuine citizenship in a metropolitan culture.

The book ends with Rebecca A. Pope and Susan J. Leonardi's study of Diamanda Galas's operatic *Plague Mass*. Like Koestenbaum, Galas turns to familiar aspects of operatic tradition to find materials for reversing the abject terms on which, as feminists such as Clément have argued, divas perform and women are represented in opera. First staged in 1991 and based on earlier work recorded in 1986 and 1988, the *Plague Mass* marks the high-water mark of direct action, centered in groups in New York City such as ACT UP, in protest against the indifference and/or hostility of politicians, the media, and public agencies in face of the growing epidemic. Hence the difference in tone between Koestenbaum and Galas, whose *Mass*, like Jarman's film *Edward II* (1992), represents and calls for militant response in the face of AIDS.

Galas is widely known as a performance artist. She herself, however, regards the term as relegating her work and that of other artists such as Laurie Anderson to a secondary role, that is, to a female ghetto. Preferring instead to refer to her work as that of an *auteur*, Galas sees her performances as forms of *Gesamtkunstwerk*, the term Wagner used for his version of opera theater. The diversity of musical means that Galas brings to her work makes it an ideal point at which to bring the present discussion to rest. Drawing on the electronic manipulations of avant-garde rock music and on classical voice training technique—including the three-and-one-half octave contralto range employed by Viardot and Calvé—Galas makes opera new by grafting it with other high cultural musical forms such as the Requiem Mass and with material from different traditions, including *moirologia*, dirges and lamentations for the dead, sometimes seeking vengeance, sung by women in Sicily and Greece. Crossing opera with materials and techniques from very different musical media and genres, Galas's work provides a powerful example of the transformations of style and content in contemporary versions of operatic practice, which make it far more pertinent today than it was when Adorno spoke a half century ago.

WORKS CONSULTED

Abraham, Gerald. *The Concise Oxford History of Music*. Oxford: Oxford University Press, 1986.

Adorno, Theodor. "Bourgeois Opera," trans. David J. Levin. In *Opera Through Other Eyes*, ed. David J. Levin. Stanford: Stanford University Press, 1994:25–43.

——. *Introduction to the Sociology of Music*, trans. E. B. Ashton. New York: Continuum, 1989.

——. *In Search of Wagner*, trans. Rodney Livingstone. London: Verso, 1991.

Anderson, Benedict. *Imagined Communities: Reflections on the Origin and Spread of Nationalism*. London: Verso, 1991.

Arblaster, Anthony. *Viva la Libertà: Politics in Opera*. London: Verso, 1992.

Attali, Jacques. *Noise: The Political Economy of Music*, trans. Brian Massumi. Minneapolis: University of Minnesota Press, 1989.

Benjamin, Walter. "Paris, Capital of the Nineteenth Century." In *Reflections: Essays, Aphorisms, Autobiographical Writings*, ed. Peter Demetz; trans. Edmund Jephcott. New York: Schocken Books, 1978:146–62.

——. "The Work of Art in the Age of Mechanical Reproduction." In *Illuminations*, ed. Hannah Arendt; trans. Harry Zohn. New York: Schocken Books, 1969:217–51.

Blackmer, Corinne E. and Patricia Juliana Smith, eds. *En Travesti: Women, Gender Subversion, Opera*. New York: Columbia University Press, 1995.

Bohlen, Celestine. "Plans for Mythical State Go Ahead." *The Globe and Mail* [Toronto], August 24, 1996, A10.

Brett, Philip, Gary C. Thomas, and Elizabeth Wood, eds. *Queering the Pitch: The New Gay and Lesbian Musicology*. New York: Routledge, 1994.

Castle, Terry. *The Apparitional Lesbian: Female Homosexuality and Modern Culture*. New York: Columbia University Press, 1993.

Chanan, Michael. *Musica Practica: The Social Practice of Western Music from Gregorian Chant to Postmodernism*. London: Verso, 1994.

Clément, Catherine. *Opera, or the Undoing of Women*, trans. Betsy Wing. Minneapolis: University of Minnesota Press, 1988.

Dizikes, John. *Opera in America: A Cultural History*. New Haven: Yale University Press, 1993.

Drohan, Madelaine. *The Globe and Mail* [Toronto], September 14, 1996, A14.

Frank, Felicia Miller. *The Mechanical Song: Women, Voice, and the Artificial in Nineteenth-Century French Narrative*. Stanford: Stanford University Press, 1995.

Fulcher, Jane F. *The Nation's Image: French Grand Opera as Politics and Politicized Art*. Cambridge: Cambridge University Press, 1987.

Gill, John. *Queer Noises: Male and Female Homosexuality in Twentieth-Century Music*. Minneapolis: University of Minnesota Press, 1995.

Gilman, Sander L. *Jewish Self-Hatred: Anti-Semitism and the Hidden Language of the Jews*. Baltimore: Johns Hopkins University Press, 1986.

Hobsbawm, Eric. *Age of Extremes: The Short Twentieth Century, 1914–1991*. London: Abacus, 1995.

Hutcheon, Linda and Michael Hutcheon. *Opera: Desire, Disease, Death*. Lincoln: University of Nebraska Press, 1995.

Jameson, Fredric. *Postmodernism, or, The Cultural Logic of Late Capitalism*. Durham: Duke University Press, 1992.

Jeffery-Poulter, Stephen. *Peers, Queers, and Commons: The Struggle for Gay Law Reform from 1950 to the Present*. London: Routledge, 1991.

Koestenbaum, Wayne. *The Queen's Throat: Opera, Homosexuality, and the Mystery of Desire*. New York: Poseidon Press, 1993.

Kristeva, Julia. *Nations Without Nationalism*, trans. Leon S. Roudiez. New York: Columbia University Press, 1993.

——. *Strangers to Ourselves*, trans. Leon S. Roudiez. New York: Columbia University Press, 1991.

Leppert, Richard. *The Sight of Sound: Music, Representation, and the History of the Body*. Berkeley: University of California Press, 1995.

Levin, David J., ed. *Opera Through Other Eyes*. Stanford: Stanford University Press, 1994.

Lindenberger, Herbert. *Opera: The Extravagant Art*. Ithaca, N.Y.: Cornell University Press, 1986.

McClary, Susan. *Feminine Endings: Music, Gender, and Sexuality*. Minnesota: University of Minnesota Press, 1991.

Mosse, George L. *Nationalism and Sexuality: Middle-Class Morality and Sexual Norms in Modern Europe*. Madison: University of Wisconsin Press, 1985.

Oestreich, James R. "Christopher Keene Is Dead: Head of City Opera Was 48." *New York Times*, Monday, October 9, 1995, A12.

Parakilas, James. "Political Representation and the Chorus in Nineteenth-Century Opera." *19th-Century Music* 16, no. 2 (Fall 1992): 181–202.

Parker, Andrew, Mary Russo, Doris Summer, and Patricia Yeager, joint eds. *Nationalisms and Sexualities*. New York: Routledge, 1992.

Purcell, Henry. *Dido and Aeneas: A Danced Opera*. Performed by Mark Morris, members of the Mark Morris Dance Company, and Tafelmusik Chamber Orchestra and Choir. Film directed by Barbara Willis Sweete. Toronto: Rhombus Media, 1995.

Roach, Joseph. "Culture and Performance in the Circum-Atlantic World." In *Performativity and Performance*, eds. Andrew Parker and Eve Kosofsky Sedgwick. New York: Routledge, 1995:45–63.

Said, Edward W. *Culture and Imperialism*. New York: Vintage, 1993.

——. *Orientalism*. New York: Vintage, 1979.

Sedgwick, Eve Kosofsky. *Between Men: English Literature and Male Homosocial Desire*. New York: Columbia University Press, 1985.

Silverman, Kaja. *The Acoustic Mirror: The Female Voice in Psychoanalysis and Cinema*. Bloomington: Indiana University Press, 1988.

Solie, Ruth A., ed. *Musicology and Difference: Gender and Sexuality in Music Scholarship*. Berkeley: University of California Press, 1993.

Sumi, Glenn. "Notes from an Operaholic's Notebook." *The Globe and Mail* [Toronto], Saturday, March 9, 1996, C7.

Tambling, Jeremy. *Opera, Ideology and Film*. New York: St. Martin's Press, 1987.

"Tenors Want to End Injustice." Reuters News Agency. *The Globe and Mail* [Toronto], Friday, April 5, 1996, C4.

Weber, Samuel. "Taking Place: Toward a Theater of Dislocation." In *Opera Through Other Eyes*, ed. David J. Levin. Stanford: Stanford University Press, 1994:107–46.

Weiner, Marc A. *Richard Wagner and the Anti-Semitic Imagination*. Lincoln: University of Nebraska Press, 1995.

## Part I

# Constituting Opera

St. Ignatius, the founder of the Jesuits, holding a host whose rays subdue the female figures representing the Jesuit conquests of the Americas, Africa (mistakenly shown in reverse in the engraving), and Europe. From Daniello Bartoli, S.J., *Historia della Compagnia di Gesú* . . . (Rome, 1650). (Courtesy of Brera Library, Milan.)

## CHAPTER ONE

# Kapsberger's Apotheosis . . . of Francis Xavier (1622) and the Conquering of India

Victor Anand Coelho

It was so that in a single month I baptized more than ten thousand men, women, and children. My method, upon arriving in a heathen village, was to assemble the men and the boys apart, and to begin by teaching them to make the sign of the cross three times as a confession of faith in Father, Son and Holy Spirit. . . . I then recited in a loud voice the General Confession, the *Credo*, the Commandments, the *Pater Noster*, the *Ave Maria*, and the *Salve Regina*. . . . The baptisms over, I told the new Christians to demolish the shrines of the idols, and saw to it that they crushed the images into dust. I could not express the consolation it gave me to watch the idols being destroyed by the hands of those who so recently used to worship them. I went thus from village to village making Christians. . . .
—*Francis Xavier*[1]

Fittingly, Francis Xavier's imperishable relics now lie in the Renaissance ghost town of Old Goa at the Minor Basilica of Bom Jesus, a Baroque church that was built, like most other churches in Portuguese India, where ancient Hindu temples once stood before they were demolished by the European "discoverers." Situated on the monsoon path some 500 kilometers south of Bombay, Goa was the undoubted emporium of the East and has been coveted throughout history for its spectacular terrain and strategic location. Following the landings of Vasco da Gama (1498) and Afonso de Albuquerque (1503–1504), the city was the capital of the Portuguese Asian empire and a magnet for both traders and evangelists. Goa was established as a diocese in 1533 and soon became the main theater for the Christian-ization of the "heathen" that constituted the aggressive missionary program of the Jesuits, the educated and obedient church soldiers who were recog-nized as an order by Pope Paul III in 1540, and arrived in Goa two years later in the person of Francis Xavier. His presence coincided with the founding of the Goan Jesuit College of St. Paul in 1542, which instructed newly con-verted boys from all races in the fields of theology, music, grammar, and

Latin toward the formation of a native clergy. A strict, cohesive education was central to Jesuit training, since much of their subsequent missionary work would depend on their ability to articulate a narrative of history and of destiny. Drama was especially effective as a pedagogical tool in the Jesuit colleges through its representation of martyrdom and other biblical stories on stage, enhanced by special effects and all-embracing metaphors.[2] For similar reasons, singing and instrumental music were permitted in the Jesuit college churches of Goa, Cochin, and Bassein as a means of evangelization.[3] These pedagogical methods strengthened the concept not only of a Society of Jesus but of a "nation" of Jesus in recognizing that the success of conversion is predicated on shared cultural and national values.

To demonstrate the political and nationalistic motives implicit in the Jesuit campaigns, an appropriate parallel might be drawn between the Jesuits of the late sixteenth and early seventeenth centuries, and a modern right-wing political party. For many years the right-wing party exists on the fringe, trapped by its own unreasonable ideology of nationalism and rhetoric of "Christian values" but thriving anyway as a result of the "mission" being crusaded by its constituents. The networks of the party are comprehensive and involve local representatives, bureaus, and media outlets. The indoctrination of youth is key. The group is tightly knit, fraternal ("My method . . . was to assemble the men and boys apart [from the women]"), gender and racially exclusive, and usually fundamentally racist and homophobic. (The new native clergy in Goa trained by the Jesuits were always referred to as dark-skinned and shown disrespect for this reason.[4]) Its members are highly critical of opposing parties. Eventually, a charismatic spokesman emerges, one who links the aspirations of the party with a newly constructed definition of nation, citizenry, and patriotism. They build infrastructure through vigorous campaigning and recruitment, advocate the use of force in cases of noncompliance, and develop a rhetorical language that employs officially sanctioned themes. They willfully carry out the most conservative policies, as seen in the Jesuits' strict following of the rules imposed by the Council of Trent: censorship of books, strengthening of the Inquisition, rigid control over the lives of clergy, and the instilling of high morals through conservative education. The party soon develops alliances with influential figures with capital (the Jesuits found their ally in Pope Urban VIII) and finally enter the mainstream.

In the decade following Xavier's arrival on the shores of Goa, his letters described in passionate detail the mass baptisms and conversions he administered in India and Japan. Before about 1545, Europe's knowledge about India came mainly through the Portuguese spice trade, but now Xavier's correspondence provided models for the Jesuit histories and newsletters that gave European intellectuals their image, however distorted, of Asia.[5] To counter reports that filtered back to Europe about the failure of missionary activity in India and about the tormented lives of martyrs, these documents set the foundations of an *imagined* history, in which the success of the missions, the efficacy of Jesuit teachings, and the urgency of Christianizing much older non-Western societies became stories for edification and inspiration. Part recruitment, part moral teaching, the Jesuit letters constructed a history that relied on the "irreproachable" Western techniques of claiming historical facticity and chronology. They succeeded in creating a concept of *nation* that was a complete abstraction in an India divided many times over by caste, language, ethnicity, and religion. At the same time it was altogether clear to the Jesuits that although there were pockets of success in conversion, India's deep, complex, and ancient culture would not give itself over easily to Christianity. Undaunted, the Jesuits continued their campaign of missionary recruitment through the persuasion of Xavier's correspondence, now rife with hyperbole in order to assuage fears back home. In the letter quoted earlier—which became the best-known item of his Asian envelope—he claims to have baptized 10,000 Mukkuvas on the fishery coast in a month; in another he estimated that 100,000 could be baptized in a single year. And in a famous passage reported widely in Europe, he alleged that 635,000 heathens had been converted in various parts of Portuguese Asia by 1545, an unreasonable figure that exceeded all previous estimates.[6] By the end of the sixteenth century, Xavier's letters circulated throughout Europe, and as printed editions of the letters were frequently appended to Xavier's biography, a hagiography was clearly in the making.

Xavier's martyrdom in 1552 on Sanchwan, an island off mainland China, inspired the central themes of most Jesuit theater and histories: "the highly emotional lives of the saints, sensual tortures of Jesuit martyrs in Japan and America, and allegories—all aimed polemically at pagan and licentious subjects fashionable among unbelieving, hypocritical, or simply nonconformist high society."[7] In 1619 the Brief of Beatification was issued by Pope Paul V, and in 1622, Xavier, the "Apostle of the Indies," along with Ignatius Loyola, the founder of the Jesuit Order, and three others were canonized at an ornately decorated St. Peter's by Pope Gregory XV in one of the largest and most lavish celebrations that Rome has ever seen.[8] The canonization marked a turning point for the Society of Jesus. It was an undisputed triumph, the end of a long road to acceptance; the Jesuits had entered the mainstream. In particular, the canonization was an investiture of the Society of Jesus as the greatest force in defending Counter-Reformation Catholicism and promoting it militantly to the "pagan" sectors of the world, such as India.

The Jesuits now had their first two saints, and this was celebrated by weeks of solemn processions and special services, as well as by three new Jesuit dramas. The most opulent of these was an important musical production entitled *The Apotheosis or Consecration of Saints Ignatius Loyola and Francis Xavier*, which was performed at the Roman College, the pod of Jesuit knowledge.[9] The music was composed by Giovanni Girolamo Kapsberger [Kapsperger] (1580–1651), a virtuoso lutenist, a prolific and successful composer of instrumental and vocal music, and a well-connected Roman musician who was appointed to the papal court in 1624, where he served under

Pope Urban VIII and his nephews for the next twenty years.[10] The Latin libretto was by Father Orazio Grassi, the chair of mathematics at the Roman College and the architect of the new church dedicated to St. Ignatius in Rome. We will see later how the libretto and Grassi's concept of St. Ignatius are connected in stating a unified cultural policy of the Jesuits. Grassi would gain more notoriety a year later as Galileo's most bitter adversary.[11] Grassi's Latin text recounts the missionary conquering by the two new saints and features personifications of countries—including India, China, Japan, and Palestine—in which Xavier was most active. The five-act work was a great success "as much for the excellence of the composition, as for the wealth of the actors and their sprightliness of delivery [*lor vivezza nel recitare*], the wealth and beauty of the machines, and finally for the abundance and organization of the decorations . . . ."[12] According to Verzellino, it "played three times in the Roman court, always to renewed applause."[13]

Because the work is in Latin, contains no real action (the characters sing to the audience), and the libretto neither creates tension nor seeks a resolution, it should not be included in the same genre as the earlier Florentine/Mantuan operas of Peri and Monteverdi, or the Roman operas performed at the Barberini Court after 1631, even though there are many similarities. On the one hand, the *Apotheosis* follows directly in the didactic tradition of the Jesuit dramas, whose stories entwined Christian literature with pagan mythologies around a core of moral teaching.[14] On the other hand, mainstream operatic traits in the *Apotheosis*—insofar as an operatic "mainstream" can be identified in early seventeenth-century Italy—involve recitative style, participation of a chorus, and the inclusion of instrumental dances. The *Apotheosis*, although indebted to both opera and theater, is a unique genre that is more political and didactic in nature. The libretto establishes a history—a summing up and prognosis—and a politics that constitute something between an apology and propaganda for the "spiritual conquests" of the Jesuits. These themes are rendered most powerfully not by the musical setting, as is the case in Monteverdi's brilliant *L'Orfeo* of 1607, but by the stunning visual component of the work, which promotes an "official" iconology that ensnares the subjects in the matrix of a highly subjective and political Jesuit program. The *Apotheosis* is closest to a large allegorical painting with music, employing the theatricality and sensuality that are so much a part of Baroque art in the early seventeenth century.

The scene takes place at the Field of Mars, located in the heart of Baroque Rome just to the north of the Roman College. The pre-Christian backdrop sets the stage for a Christian conquest of paganism. In the Prologue, Wisdom appears in a cloud and asks the youths of the Roman College to honor the saints Ignatius and Loyola by reenacting the pagan rites used by the ancient Romans to celebrate their (false) gods. In Act I Rome instructs the architect Metagenes to build a temple, which is done hastily. (The parallels to Grassi, the architect commissioned to build St. Ignatius, are clear.)

Spain and Portugal appear in their own chariots and offer Ignatius the weapons he used in battle and present to Xavier the vessel that took him to the shores of India. Portugal concludes the act by claiming that "Xavier proclaimed God to the Indian world as the dawn of a new day."[15] Act II opens with the appearance of India in her own chariot, and while seventeen Indian youths amass pearls at Xavier's feet, India praises "the mighty right hand by which Xavier conquered India." After a large globe is built, the Indian chorus proclaims "Francis' valor which, poorly confined within a narrow circle, is now challenging and hardly to be contained in one world." Later in the act India celebrates the "triumphs on the Eastern shores" achieved by the saints and praises Xavier, whose "authority subdues conquered India." Acts III and IV introduce other countries along the saints' missionary itinerary, each of which bears gifts: France offers its lifeline of the Seine; Japan, palms and laurel as a gesture of peace in view of the martyrdoms on its soil; China, silks; Italy, flowers and aromatic herbs. In the final act India, China, Palestine, and Japan are on stage, and statues of the saints are carved. A spectacular earthquake gives way to an opening in the heavens and all the countries prostrate themselves before the two new saints and a chorus of angels, while prayers of thanks and adoration are given to the saints, the church, and Pope Gregory XIV.

Grassi's text clearly requires scrutiny as an early example of colonial history and its representation of the other. In particular, the images in the libretto drawn from pagan and ethnic sources, insofar as they relate to Christian images used to validate a colonial narrative, need to be carefully examined. Further, the relations between Jesuit homosociality—that is, the web of strategies that define patriarchal relationships—and colonial narratives of subjugation are deeply and intentionally embedded in this work. Finally, gendered representations of European creativity and fecundity are also used as part of the appropriative function of the colonial imperative of the *Apotheosis*.

So how do we reconcile this work—easily the most elaborate musical production in Rome prior to Landi's *Sant' Alessio* of 1632—with our present reformulations of missionary and colonial activity during this time, and what is its relationship to, and influence on, opera? The characterization of a penitent (and colorfully plumed) India willfully subordinate to the Holy Church is one of the most troubling aspects of the work, and it betrays an official and already revisionist history constructed by the Jesuits themselves. Moreover, it anticipates by a century the binary Orientalism of Occident–male/Orient–female relationships in operatic librettos, whose origins Edward Said has located in the late eighteenth century.[16] With its gendered formulation of India's subordination to the Catholic Church and the themes of procreation as its *modus operandi*; its strangeness of genre, which lies somewhere between Jesuit drama and opera; and the constructed sense of nation to promote the paternity of the church, the *Apotheosis* is ideal for investigating the themes of gender, nation, and genre.

Using sixteenth- and seventeenth-century documents from Indian archives, as well as travelogues, Jesuit histories, dispatches from Italian and Portuguese missionaries, and candid European reactions to life in Baroque Goa, I shall attempt in this essay to (re)position the *Apotheosis* at the nexus of cultural confrontation and nationalist history, rather than at the altar of the Jesuit church in post-Tridentine Rome. By confronting the characterizations of India in the *Apotheosis* with the largely different picture of the denigration of Hindu and ancient Indian aesthetic values that emerges from other sources, this discussion of the *Apotheosis* will move us closer to identifying issues of cultural politics and ethnic representations that are embedded in operas written during the early modern period of global maritime exploration.

## Gendering India

Working just beneath the surface of the *Apotheosis* in the portrayal of India's submission to the church is a Magdalenesque program of converting sexuality to penitence, for sexuality is a traditional attribute of the "heathen," and in Western iconographic discourse, of the female. Said has remarked that sexualizing is a common manifestation of the anxiety of empire,[17] and although the trope of equating the colonized landscape and the female body has been overextended in postcolonial scholarship, it is an integral part of colonial rhetoric.[18] In the *Apotheosis*, India is feminized both in dress and through subordination, as is traditional in representations of Asia in Western discourse and in the visual arts. She is also implicitly linked to heathen or pagan sexual (deviant) practices and sensual images, of which India is cleansed in the *Apotheosis* through submission and conversion. In short, India, being both feminine and sexual, embodies attributes that are almost archetypes in the Western formulation of colonialism. For example, in psychoanalyst/musicologist Maynard Solomon's analysis of one of Beethoven's dreams, in which the composer remembers a "very long journey, as far even as Syria, as far as India, back again, as far as Arabia . . . ," he delineates the gendered codes that are behind the archetypal profile of the conquering nation: "The conquistador here fuses with Don Juan, for distant nations are the embodiment of the (taboo) female. Simultaneously, these lands represent the exotic bisexual religions of the East and Mediterranean . . . ."[19]

This feminization and exoticization of India were already well understood within the iconographic lexicon of the Renaissance. In Cesare Ripa's famous guide to symbols in art, the *Iconologia* (Rome, 1597/1603), the personification of Asia is a woman crowned by a garland of flowers and wearing clothes adorned with gold and pearls—symbols both of the Orient and of maritime abundance (see figure 1.1). In her right hand she holds leaves, cassia, pepper, and cloves, and in her left hand there is an incense burner emitting perfumed smoke. A camel reposes behind her.[20] All these attributes are promoted in the *Apotheosis:* India arrives wearing clothes of feathers, and China of beautiful silks; India's inhabitants present Xavier with gifts of pearls, while disheveled and weeping Palestine, depicted by Kapsberger with a more agitated rhythmic motion, appears as an old abandoned woman (for Palestine is no longer venerated) and offers to Loyola the gift of smoky incense.

The themes of procreation, church paternity (conqueror), and Oriental femininity (conquered) are introduced into the work at its outset. Loyola and Xavier are scored for bass voices, whereas the countries, including "mother" Rome, are soprano parts—an interesting example of gender inversion because these roles would have been sung by castratos. (Women were forbidden to sing in the Roman College, though cross-dressing—men playing female roles—was acceptable, as it always has been in boys-only clubs.) The prologue introduces us to Loyola, "Father of an indefatigable race," which promotes themes of progeny and nation, and Xavier, who "ennobles the offspring of an illustrious Father." In Act 1, Spain, the birthplace of Loyola, is positioned as a "foster mother of Kings" and "fertile parent of the stars"; similarly, Portugal, "the powerful matron of the Lysians," is the womb of Xavier, who is also the "foster child of the Virgin Mother." These themes suggest a complex relationship among power, gender, and colonialism, and can further inform about the characterization of India in Grassi's libretto.

Figure 1.1

*Asia*, from Cesare Ripa, *Iconologia* (Rome, 1603).

## Encountering the Lingam

Krishna's offerings of divine love to the maidens and his playful bantering with them; cults of suprasensual goddesses like Parvati; the fine line between sex and worship codified in some Tantric philosophy; the activities of cleansing, adorning, touching, releasing, and fulfilling found in Hindu texts; and the lingam of Shiva. . . . The missionary position (that is, the ideological position of missionaries) on these practices, whether they encountered them in philosophical or iconographic manifestations, was one of general contempt and ignorance. "Limited by their cultural and religious hostility to Hinduism," writes Lach, citing documentary evidence, "the Jesuits were naturally unable to penetrate beneath the surface of Hindu life."[21] They learned almost nothing of Hindu doctrine or their sacred representations, and lumped together most Indian idols in the category of monsters or devils, the latter inspiring the image of the famous Idol of Calicut that was promoted in the German edition of Varthema's influential *Itinerario* of 1515 (see figure 1.2).[22] Indian music and dance were also considered to be demonically inspired and sexually transgressive. A Jesuit dispatch of 1598 complains that Hindu and Moslem dancers in Goa "include many vile and indecent things and obscene songs, and other things that they can only perform through some diabolical art, and in their songs they include their temples and idolatry, which are all opposed to the common good of the Christian republic, and against good upbringing."[23]

The Jesuit reaction to Indian erotica must be seen within the context of the zero tolerance they had already demonstrated in their condemnation of

Figure 1.2

_____

L. de Varthema: *Die Ritterlich von Lobwirdig Rais\[* (Augsburg, 1515), p. 1: Idol of Calicut.

Jews, Moors, and the Portuguese for their practice of sodomy—the *pecado nefando* analogous to the "unspeakable" trope in English literature.[24] Sexuality for the Jesuits was by no means seen as culturally variable, and their punishment of sodomists reveals more of the Jesuits' evolving concept of nation, which I discuss in some detail later. As Parker et al. have remarked, "Typically represented as a passionate brotherhood, the nation finds itself compelled to distinguish its 'proper' homosociality from more explicitly sexualized male–male relations, a compulsion that requires the identification, isolation, and containment of male homosexuality."[25] Although this is not in itself a theme in the *Apotheosis*, it is crucial to the image of a Jesuit "nation," which is one of the most emphatically articulated themes in Grassi's libretto.

Not surprisingly, the Christian missionaries in India showed some respect for the Brahmin yogis, who practiced celibacy and devoted their lives to acquiring and contemplating knowledge. But many of the most holy Indian art forms frequently involve ceremonies in which the object of veneration is the phallus, such as the *Shiva-lingam*[26]; and their rituals, along with the equally gendered zoolatry in Indian worship,[27] were subjects of considerable concern to the Jesuits. Even the Italian traveler Pietro della Valle, whose tastes in music, as we know from his valuable *Discorso dell'età nostra* (1640),[28] leaned clearly toward the adventurous, exposed a characteristic hypocrisy by his incapability of equating the images he saw in an Indian temple with the sacred sensual images he admired in his own Baroque Rome. While visiting a temple in Honelli, he complained that "many of these figures represented dishonest actions. One was of a Woman. Another was of a Man and a Woman kissing, the Man holding his Hands on the Woman's Breasts, and sundry such representations fit indeed for a Temple."[29]

The point of this discussion is that the Jesuits in the end saw the sacred context of the lingam as proof that India was a society—with the exception of certain Brahmins and yogis—of unrepressed sexual motivation, ignorant of the fact that the lingam denotes the male creative energy of Shiva and is often placed in balance with the yoni, the female symbol of energy, both of which symbolize the cooperative forces of the sexes.[30] But the relegation of the lingam to a purely sexual object was a useful taboo for the Jesuits, because it brought India into line with the paganism of licentious pre-Christian and similarly polytheistic Egyptian and Greek cultures. These associations swirl behind the personifications of countries in the *Apotheosis* and its setting of Christian deeds playing out on a pagan field, evoking the Jesuit campaigns in India and elsewhere. India's conversion is predicated on the rejection of its own history and its "erotic" ritualistic practices, symbolized by Xavier's method of demolishing the shrines of the Indian idols. India must be reborn (or reformed) through baptism. The Prologue thus defines the Jesuit College (or the Church of the Gesù) as a "chaste Queen," which "influences good conduct." Stripped of its cultural and aesthetic roots, India submits to the church: "That bold spirit of Francis penetrated into the remotest kingdoms of India, conquering seas under his broad sway" (Act

II). These hegemonic and gendered distinctions between "pagan" and Christian cultures, as well as the Christian solution, are formed through the important role that nation plays in the *Apotheosis*.

### Nation: Locating India

*V. A. Coelho*

"Loyola endures as Father of an indefatigable race"—by positioning the Jesuits as a *race* in the very Prologue of the *Apotheosis*, Grassi introduces the theme of nation and defines the powerful role of nationalism. The claim to racial status evokes consanguinity and nationalism, which are powerful and troubling issues within the intricacy of the Indian caste system, about which the Jesuits were always perplexed. Five castes of Brahmin in Goa alone can be found, all of them descendant from either Aryan or Dravidic race, and thirty other castes and subcastes can be identified.[31] Caste and race are crucial issues when dealing with Indian culture and religion. They provide(ed) unwritten laws that govern(ed) marriage, diet, worship, professional standing, and social interaction, with severe penalties for any transgression of caste protocol. Caste also plays a role in the most terrifying by-products of a consanguine or strictly insular culture: highly restrictive marriage laws, legal privilege, obligatory head shaving of divorced Brahmin women, and the despicable practice of *Sati*, or widow burning, which Pietro della Valle describes as an eyewitness.[32] It is clear that a criticism of the *Apotheosis* from the "other side" could trigger highly sensitive concerns about the role and empowerment of nation, particularly when the employment of race in the work serves to ally the Jesuits with those same structures of caste authority in India. As if caught in the web of the Indian caste system itself, India the character in the *Apotheosis*, is voiceless to define herself as India the country, not only because of the authority of race and singularity of nation that were imposed in the Prologue, but also because such concepts of nation are alien to her.[33] In the *Apotheosis* India is devoid of both national identity and an autonomous voice. This homogenization exposes one of the more rapacious strategies through which "nation" is defined in the *Apotheosis:* we meet India only after her conversion; we are unaware of her prior history. The work offers no cultural sanctuary in which India can avoid the gaze of the Jesuits. Stripped of her own cultural past, India offers no resistance.

As we have mentioned earlier, the Jesuits employ the same homosocial strategies used in nationalistic movements: fraternity, exclusion of others, "union between men," their willingness to die in the line of duty, and the memorializing of such martyrs in the name of *patria*, all of which is made explicit at the beginning of the *Apotheosis*. Consequently, India remains voiceless except to support a Jesuit concept of nation that is destined to be a singular, male history. India is indeed "a nation subdued" (Act II) and the "mute but necessary allegorical ground for the transactions of nationalist history."[34] If the creation of nationalism is dependent on a "project of deracination"[35] as it is in many parts of the world today, the sublimation of India in the *Apotheosis* can be seen as part of that process, in which conversion is a metaphor for alienating her from an "unreasonable prehistory."[36]

## Genre: Repositioning the *Apotheosis*

Even recognizing the fluidity of genres that exists in music of the early *seicento*, this work is not opera in the traditional or evolutionary sense. We have already remarked upon the absence of dialogue between characters (they speak to the audience) and the relative dramatic stasis of the work. Unlike opera, too, Kapsberger does not attempt to carve out individual profiles through stylistic means. He sets Grassi's libretto in a fairly unbroken, syllabic, recitative style with many cadential and motivic clichés. There are no experiments with chromaticism, no unusual or surprising rhythmic gestures. The style is identical to Kapsberger's setting of Pope Urban VIII's poetry, the *Poemata et Carmina* of 1624, which was composed throughout with what we might call a "purity" of monody. In 1626 the neoclassic music theorist Giambattista Doni wrote to the French Jesuit Marin Mersenne that "you will never find [the *Poemata*] full of affectations, but rather a melody that is pure and simple *and of which you will be the better judge* [italics mine]," which suggests that the music conformed to a certain Jesuit aesthetic.[37] In her detailed study of seventeenth-century Roman opera, Margaret Murata describes the use of the recitative soliloquy in some of these works as demonstrating the "struggle for spiritual purity against incursions of secular institutions."[38] The musical and textual styles in the *Apotheosis* are thus united by their austerity and solemnity; the work proceeds reflectively, and the staid, obedient, predictable musical characterizations of the countries evoke various degrees of cohesion, loyalty, sublimation, penitence, and shame until the apotheosis in the final act, when the new saints appear amid elaborate effects from stage machinery.

Acknowledging the presence of dance sections sprinkled throughout the work, Ambros places the *Apotheosis* within the genre of a "grand ballet with song" (*Prachtballet mit Gesang*).[39] Forbes feels the work is a unique combination of Roman opera and Jesuit drama, in which the idea of spectacle is an "integral part of the *Apotheosis* and essential to the understanding of it."[40] Hammond distinguishes it from the Jesuit dramas and is content with the moniker *opera*.[41] Parallels can indeed be drawn between the *Apotheosis* and Roman opera as cultivated during the pontificates of Urban VIII (*reg.* 1623–44) and his nephews, and Alexander VII (*reg.* 1655–67). Urban and the most important librettist of this period, Giulio Rospigliosi (*reg.* Pope Clement IX, 1667–69), were educated at the Jesuit College, and their guiding principle of Roman opera, *Delectare et docere* ("instruction and delight"), is also one of the aims of the *Apotheosis*.[42] Other common themes include religious subjects and stories of saints (*Il Sant'Alessio*, 1631–1632), and the trepidation of Christian conversion (*Il Sant'Eustachio*, 1643; *La comica del cielo*, 1668) and/or martyrdom (*I Santi Didimo e Teodora*, 1635; *San Bonifazio*, 1638).[43]

Musical productions with dance on an operatic scale were certainly not unknown in the Jesuit institutions; similar works by Agazzari (1606), Mazzocchi (1628), and others were used in the service of Jesuit education. Although Catalani's work *David musicus* (1613), set to a text by the Jesuit Alessandro Donati, is in Latin, Murata refers to this work as an opera, perhaps because of the dramatic scenes, and possibly because of the strong prosodic elements of the text (which survives) that bring this work into line with the humanistic origins of the genre, neither of which, however, is characteristic of the *Apotheosis*.[44] She does not place the *Apotheosis* along her evolutionary line of Roman operas that begins with Cavalieri's *Rappresentazione di anima e di corpo* (1600) and continues through Landi's *Sant'Alessio* of 1631. Grassi's libretto does not employ ancient prosodic formulas, and a regular rhyme scheme is present only in certain parts of Acts II and IV. In the end, the *Apotheosis*, drawing features from both opera and Jesuit drama, is of a complex genre that cannot be determined by stylistic features alone.

So what is it? Hammond, among others, has argued for a greater sensitivity to the relationship between genre and context,[45] and an investigation along these lines suggests the description I have alluded to earlier: a *tableau vivant en musique*. The *Apotheosis* is partly a didactic tool for mounting a deep, cultivated Jesuit ideology. But it is also a visual history about the preeminence of the Catholic Church as seen through the gaze of a cohesive and insular fraternity with a specific program in mind. The *Apotheosis* does not chronicle fact. The lessons as revealed in the work create instead a fundamental myth, a *Grundmythos*, which serves an important function in any colonial history. As Jürgen Maehder has found in his examination of operas dealing with the discovery of the New World, "Mythologizing is . . . an interactive process through which historical events and protagonists are translated into cultural discourse, often subordinating the actual facts of an event to the value system of the dominant society."[46]

The *Apotheosis* was thus conceived to create an overall effect, like a ceiling fresco, but one that employs words along with images to capture the ultimate sum of various forces, a totality, "the impassioned and total integration of Tridentine faith and culture."[47] It is, in essence, a triumphant celebration of Jesuit missionary history through propaganda. Although it is not true opera, it does employ operatic conventions that serve to contemporize what is otherwise a Jesuit drama. By the 1620s the Jesuits were certainly aware of how their message and the image of the order itself could be evoked powerfully through the contemporary styles of art and music that were being cultivated in Baroque Rome. Opera was the most modern form of musical discourse available to the Jesuits, and they well understood opera's ability to make illusion shape reality, as the editors write in the introduction to the present volume. Furthermore, through its use of operatic conventions—recitative-style singing, instrumental dances, and spectacle—the *Apotheosis* profiled the Jesuits as moderns with contemporary taste, poised for a new future.

Although art historians have been cautious about validating the existence of a direct Jesuit influence on art, there is no doubt that a consistent artistic program emerges quite clearly in Jesuit-patronized art and, as the *Apotheosis* shows, music, after 1600.[48] Hibbard, for example, has convincingly reconstructed the detailed iconographic program of the Gesù,[49] and Dixon has similarly discussed the common aesthetic base of music and architecture at the Gesù during the early Baroque.[50] Although specific documentary information about the first performance of the *Apotheosis* has yet to surface, we may be able to understand the scenographic, aesthetic, and political priorities of the work by briefly examining our librettist/architect Grassi's conception for the mammoth Church of St. Ignatius, whose first stone was laid in 1626.

According to Redondi, the Church of St. Ignatius is inextricably connected to the personality of its architect. Grassi's plan was for a church, exceeded in size only by St. Peter's, that would celebrate the arching triumph and the supremacy of the Jesuits. The church does not achieve its greatness through virtuosity but through Grassi's uncompromising faith in the fundamental tenets of Jesuit education and orthodoxy. If one can ignore the stunning decorations installed in the 1680s by the Jesuit Andrea Pozzo, what remains is a sober, *terribilis* structure that conforms to what was understood as the Jesuit "style" in architecture. The facade was modeled on that of the mother Jesuit church of the Gesù, whereas the floor plan was a Latin cross as prescribed in Counter-Reformation treatises, rather than the Greek cross of Renaissance churches.[51] These same aesthetic choices guide the *Apotheosis*. Despite the spectacle involved, the work does not waver from its scholastic intent, which it pronounces in long, pontifical monologues without interruption or challenge from other characters, rather than in humanistically inspired, active dialogue, as in Florentine opera. Within the immensity of St. Ignatius, the eye is directed toward the altar of the church, which is raised by five steps. In a similar fashion, Act V of the *Apotheosis* is the climax and fulfillment of the work, in which praise for the saints is offered in the form of altar worship. Finally, the visual spectacle of Jesuit dramas and the *Apotheosis* is matched by the dazzling effect of the *trompe-l'oeil* cupola in St. Ignatius, which dramatizes the immensity of the church.[52] The visual effect of the *Apotheosis* is thus based on a coherent Jesuit iconographic program, which is drawn from traditional images used by the Jesuits, such as martyrdom and ascension, and is combined with the newer Jesuit themes of the 1620s: union with the pope, the thaumaturgic powers of the saints, the banishment of demons, and the missionary triumph over the heathen.

*The Miracles of St. Francis Xavier* by Peter Paul Rubens (Vienna, Kunsthistorisches Museum) offers an even closer look at these conventions, and in the process reveals the Jesuit aesthetics behind the visual spectacle of the *Apotheosis* (see figure 1.3).[53] Against the same backdrop as in the *Apotheosis*, a pagan temple, Xavier stands high on a short column, his right finger pointing toward heaven. The group of figures below him to the right are those in need of his miracles: a blind man (with arms outstretched), a cripple (with the beard), and a kneeling figure with a darker face who is demonically possessed and must be restrained by the two kneeling youths in front of him. Across from this group are people whose graves are being dug but who through Xavier's miraculous intercession have avoided death in the nick of time. A woman running onto the scene from the left pleads with Xavier to intervene in the imminent death of the child she is holding. The remaining group consists of Asian figures: one of them, obviously an Indian—Rubens appears to have based his images of Indians on the engravings in Linschoten's *Itinerario* of 1596 (see figure 1.4)—is lying on a bench in anguish, while another Asian (directly below Xavier's right hand) wears a ceremonial headdress. A man in armor occupies the center of the painting as a symbol of the militancy of the church. Finally, the background consists of more Indians fleeing in agony from their temple whose "pagan" idol is being dismembered by a ray from the Catholic faith, represented by the chorus of angels in the clouds above Xavier. It has apparently escaped the attention of Rubens scholars that the image used for the Indian idol is identical to the same horned demon species promoted by Varthema more than a century earlier as the Idol of Calicut (compare to figure 1.1).

The narrative in this painting of Xavier's "miracles" is very much indebted to the letters of Xavier and his autobiography, which were widely available in Europe. The destruction of idols is described in the famous letter with which this article began; the woman holding the dead child in Rubens's painting is directly inspired by Xavier's awakening of a small, dead boy in front of a crowd at Cape Cormorin[54]; and his healing of the sick was well known from his letters from the coast of Guinea in 1541.[55] The painting is identical to the *Apotheosis* in its general program of the sublimation of heathens and their conversion, and the pagan temple around which the action takes place. More specific connections between Rubens's painting and the *Apotheosis* include the gladiator in the painting, who may well represent the gladiatorial games that take place in Act V, as a mockery of Rome's "ancient customs"; even the torches aflame behind the gladiator are part of the same scene in the *Apotheosis*, in which Rome declares, "Bring together at the same time all the torches" so that the pagan temple can be set aflame. Finally in Act V, "a sudden cloud departed into the air," at which point Rome wonders, "Is not the very house of the highest heaven revealed now, where the head is already graced by divine light?" As in Rubens's canvas, the heavens open up with a beam of light as a signal for the apotheosis. Xavier's last and only words in the *Apotheosis* encapsulate the entire scene, gesture by gesture, of Rubens's painting: "This right arm of mine which once expelled the hostile band, summoned back again the bodies only recently laid in their graves that call out for the gift of eternal life, and washed countless races in the river of life [baptism]—this arm . . . is ever intent to protect Gregory and his great successors."

Although there is no actual connection between Rubens and Grassi as far as we know, their images are drawn from exactly the same sources: from Xavier's correspondence, from his highly embellished autobiography, and through the filter of Jesuit histories and their panegyrics on Xavier's death. Given the close similarity between visual images in Rubens's *Miracles* and the *Apotheosis*, the painting does suggest how the *Apotheosis* might have been envisioned as a series of tableaux. Because the work is a drama devoid

Figure 1.3

Peter Paul Rubens, *The Miracles of St. Francis Xavier*
(Vienna, Kunsthistorisches Museum).

of actual drama, dialogue, virtuosity, or tunes, it must rely on iconographic representation in the form of a *tableau vivant en musique* as the main channel through which the work is understood.

### The *Apotheosis* and Goa

Now that a new feast had been inaugurated by this work, as well as for didactic reasons, the *Apotheosis* was destined to be repeated. The canonization was celebrated yearly after 1622, and the *Apotheosis* may have survived in the Jesuit repertory for some years.[56] From 1620 to 1630 the Feast of St. Francis Xavier was the most important festival at the Church of the Gesù, and more costly than the feasts of Christmas and Easter. By 1624 the feast of the canonization had reached Jesuit outposts in India, where it was observed with the same extravagance as it was in Rome. Della Valle reports from Goa in January of 1624 that the celebration consisted of squadrons of collegians "one of which represented the *Asiaticks*, one the *Africans*, and another the *Europeans*. . . . Before the Cavalcade went a Chariot of Clouds with *Fame* on the top, who, sounding her Trumpet with the adjunction of Musick, published the news of the said Canonization."[57] A few months later, the celebrations continued, and della Valle witnessed a performance of a tragedy entitled *The Life of Santo Sciavier*, which included "Musick, gallant

Figure 1.4

Goan fisherman, from J. van Linschoten, *Itinerario* (Amsterdam, 1596).

dances, and various contrivances of Chariots, Ships, Galleys, Pageants, Heavens, Hells, Mountains and Clouds."[58]

These descriptions suggest that a seventeenth-century Goan performance of the *Apotheosis* is not unlikely. The forces required by the work— solo and choral parts of no great technical difficulty scored mainly for boys, along with brief instrumental sections—could easily have been found at the College of St. Paul. By the end of the sixteenth century, the college supported ninety Jesuits, the boys of the seminary, the choirboys, and the servants, amounting to a total of 250 persons on the payroll. Documents show that polyphony (*canto d'organo*) was being sung in Goan churches before the middle of the sixteenth century, from which we can assume that by 1622 the musical training in Goa was sufficiently developed to support such a production.[59] Feast days were celebrated in Goa with unusual opulence, particularly the Feast of 11,000 Virgins or the Feast of St. Ursula (October 21), and the Feast of the Conversion of St. Paul (January 25), in honor of the College. Masses for these days included singing (sometimes with organ) and wind instruments.[60]

Mainstream Italian or Portuguese music is not extant in Goa in the form of manuscripts or printed books, and archival sources are characteristically vague in their descriptions of sung or played music. Nevertheless, we know that a musical infrastructure capable of supporting mainstream Roman music must have been in place by 1622, because Sebastiani describes that during his trip to Goa in 1663, he heard works by Carissimi (the most famous composer at the Jesuit German College in Rome between 1629 and 1674) performed on a massive scale at Bom Jesus for the feast of St. Ignatius. Sebastiani also confirms the high musical standards in Goa by the middle of the seventeenth century:

> In that city [of Goa] I enjoyed many times listening to very beautiful music for feast days, especially that of St. Ignatius Loyola, which was celebrated with seven choirs and the sweetest *sinfonie* [instrumental pieces or sections] in the Professed House of the Fathers of the Society, where lies the body of St. Francis Xavier; and when I said that it was like being in Rome, I was told that I was not mistaken, because the composition was that of the famous Carissimi that was brought to that place. I cannot believe how musically proficient are the Canarini [Goans and Konkanis], and with what ease they perform.
>
> There is no town or village of the Christians which does not have in its church an organ, harp, and a viola, and a good choir of musicians who sing for festivities, and for holy days, Vespers, masses, and litanies, and with much cooperation and devotion. . . .[61]

Sebastiani's description is borne out by archival documents from the College of St. Paul, Goa, which show regular payments to musicians for harp and viola strings, as well as for the playing and teaching of the organ during the years 1680–1710.[62] These three instruments constitute a small but fairly typical Spanish or Portuguese continuo group, one that would be entirely appropriate for small services and everything but the instrumental numbers in a work like the *Apotheosis*. The archives also show payments for a choir of twelve, and for certain occasions, twenty-two singers. Significantly, there are frequently extra payments for music (listed with the food payments) in March for the feast of St. Francis Xavier.[63]

The *Apotheosis . . . of Francis Xavier* celebrated one of the most important events ever to take place in Catholic Rome. Its purpose was to recognize the Jesuits' historical role, to promote a Jesuit myth, and to define the theological substance of the Jesuit worldview. Through their clever synthesis of an officially sanctioned Jesuit program with operatic splendor and Jesuit drama, Grassi and Kapsberger created a living painting that is didactic and nationalistic but *imagined*. Cultural difference between east and west is bridged in the *Apotheosis* through India's willful subordination to the church. But a reading of the work from the side of the other, as I have attempted here, exposes the rhetorical strategies and images that are part of the Jesuit program to sublimate India's national identity. By freezing these deeply embedded forces of Jesuit colonialism, nationalism, and gender in the powerful genre of tableau images, the colonial imperative is made powerfully and eternally clear. *This* is how Xavier conquered India.

NOTES

1. Letter of January 27, 1545, from Cochin, India, to Ignatius Loyola about the conversion of the Mukkuvas, a fishing community on the Arabian Coast, quoted in P. Rayanna, S.J., *St. Francis Xavier and His Shrine*, 2nd ed. (Panaji, Goa: Rekha Printers, 1989), 105. The most thorough account of Xavier's activities in India is in Georg Schurhammer, S.J., *Francis Xavier: His Life, His Times*, vol. 4, *India, 1541–1545*, trans. M. Joseph Costelloe, S.J. (Rome: The Jesuit Historical Institute, 1977); for the context of the letter of 1545, see p. 470.

2. The standard book on the Roman College is Ricardo G. Villoslada, *Storia del Collegio Romano dal suo inizio (1551) alla soppressione della Compagnia di Gesù (1773)*. Analecta Gregoriana 66 (Rome: Pontificae Universitatis Gregorianae, 1954), 84–115.

3. Joseph Wicki, ed. *Documenta Indica*, vol. 10 (1575–1577): *Missiones Orientales* (Rome: Institutum Historicum Societatis Iesu, 1968), 330. For a study of political and cultural implications of Western music in Goa, see Victor Coelho, "Cross-Cultural Repertories and the Politics of Music in Renaissance Goa," in *Encomium Musicae: A Festschrift for Robert Snow*, ed. D. Crawford (Stuyvesant, N.Y.: Pendragon Press, 1997).

4. See Charles J. Borges, "Foreign Jesuits and Native Resistance in Goa, 1542–1759," in *Essays in Goan History*, ed. Teotonio de Souza (New Delhi: Concept Publishing, 1989), 77.

5. For a summary of Jesuit chronicles of India from approximately 1545–1600, see Donald F. Lach, *India in the Eyes of Europe: The Sixteenth Century* (Chicago: University of Chicago Press, 1968), 427–66.

6. On the Jesuit letters and their statistics, see Lach, *India in the Eyes of Europe*, 438ff.

7. Pietro Redondi, *Galileo: Heretic* (Princeton: Princeton University Press, 1983), 69.

8. The other canonizations were for Filippo Neri, the founder of the Oratorians and Teresa of Avila, both Catholic reformers, and the twelfth-century Isidore "the Worker" of Madrid, a saint for veneration by the lower classes.

9. *Apotheosis sive consecratio SS. Ignatii et Francisci Xaverii.* The work survives in two manuscript sources only: (1) Paris, Bibliothèque Nationale, Rés. F. 1075 (in Kapsberger's own hand); and (2) Vienna, Nationalbibliothek, Cod. 16013; there is at present neither a modern edition nor a facsimile. The *argomento* was published in *Argomento dell'apotesi de' Santi Ignatio Loiola e Francesco Saverio rappresentata nel Collegio Romano nelle feste della loro canonizzazione* (Rome, 1622). The *Apotheosis* has received surprisingly little critical study. The earliest examination of the piece is in Wilhelm Ambros's *Geschichte der Musik* (Leipzig: F. E. C. Leuckhart, 1909), 4:469–89. The most detailed but relatively noncritical examination of the work is by James Forbes, "The Non-liturgical Vocal Music of Johann Hieronymus Kapsberger," Ph.D. diss., University of North Carolina, Chapel Hill, 1978, 245–451. In 1991 the *Apotheosis* was revived at Boston College as part of its Ignatian year celebrations.

10. A detailed account of Kapsberger's life is in Victor Coelho, "G. G. Kapsberger in Rome, 1604–1645: New Biographical Data," *Journal of the Lute Society of America* 16 (1983): 103–33. On Kapsberger's operatic output, see Victor Coelho, "Kapsperger, Giovanni Girolamo," in *The New Grove Dictionary of Opera*, ed. S. Sadie (London: Macmillan, 1992), 2:949–50. Kapsberger was not a Jesuit.

11. See Redondi, *Galileo: Heretic*, 179–202.

12. From documents quoted in Villoslada, *Storia del Collegio Romano*, 283–84.

13. Verzellino, quoted in Redondi, *Galileo: Heretic*, 69. The Vienna manuscript source of the *Apotheosis* states that the work was performed five times.

14. On Jesuit dramas, see Per Bjurström, "Baroque Theatre and the Jesuits," in *Baroque Art: The Jesuit Contribution*, eds. Rudolf Wittkower and Irma Jaffe (New York: Fordham University Press, 1972), 99–110.

15. The English translations are by the author and George V. Coelho, with occasional recourse to the translation printed for the Boston College performance of the *Apotheosis*, prepared by Frank T. Kennedy, S.J.

16. Edward Said, *Orientalism* (New York: Pantheon Books, 1979), 3.

17. Ibid., 222.

18. See Sara Suleri, *The Rhetoric of English India* (Chicago: University of Chicago Press, 1992), 16.

19. Maynard Solomon, *Beethoven Essays* (Cambridge: Harvard University Press, 1988), 69.

20. The version consulted was Cesare Ripa, *Iconologia*, ed. Piero Buscaroli (Milan: Editori Associati, 1992), 297–98, based on the 1603 edition.

21. Lach, *India in the Eyes of Europe*, 439, lists relevant documentary evidence.

22. See Partha Mitter, *Much Maligned Monsters: A History of European Reactions to Indian Art*, 2nd ed. (Chicago: University of Chicago Press, 1992), 18–19.

23. Historical Archives of Goa, Livro Morato da Relação, f. 120v, letter of Antonio da Cunha: "e nos ditos bailos e ensaios delles metem muitas cousas torpes, e cantigas ruins, e outras cousas que só por arte diabolica as podem fazer, nas cantigas metem seus pagodes e idolatrias, o que tudo he contra o bem commum da republica christã e contra a boa crição. . . ."

24. This theme is treated in Eve Kosofsky Sedgwick's *Between Men: English Literature and Male Homosocial Desire* (New York: Columbia University Press, 1985), 94–96.

25. *Nationalism and Sexualities*, eds. A. Parker, M. Russo, D. Sommer, and P. Yaeger (London: Routledge, 1992), 6.

26. Shiva is also representative of the dance, which can bring ecstasy.

27. The elephant god Ganesha, the remover of obstacles, has phallic associations; see Mitter, *Much Maligned Monsters*, 78.

28. The *Discorso* is printed in Angelo Solerti, *Le origini del melodramma* (Turin: Fratelli Bocca, 1903), 148–79.

29. *The Travels of Pietro della Valle in India*, 2 vols., ed. Edward Grey (London: The Hakluyt Society, 1892; reprint, New Delhi and Madras: Asian Educational Service, 1991), 1:235.

30. See Heinrich Zimmer, *Myths and Symbols in Indian Art and Civilization*, ed. Joseph Campbell (Princeton: Princeton University Press, 1946), 126–30.

31. See S. S. Desai, "An Ethnological Study of Goan Society," in *Goa: Cultural Trends*, ed. P. P. Shirodkar (Panaji, Goa: Casa Packmaster, 1988), 34–45. On the roles of Brahmins in Portuguese Goa, see M. N. Pearson, *Coastal Western India: Studies from the Portuguese Records*. Xavier Centre for Historical Research Studies Series 2 (New Delhi: Concept Publishing, 1980), 93–115.

32. *The Travels of Pietro della Valle*, 2:266–76.

33. I have borrowed this term, the "voiceless," from the Goan scholar Teotonio de Souza; see his "The Voiceless in Goan History," in *Indo-Portuguese History: Sources and Problems*, ed. John Correia-Afonso S.J. (Bombay: Oxford University Press, 1981), 114–31.

34. R. Radhakrishnan, "Nationalism, Gender, and the Narrative of Identity," in *Nationalism and Sexualities*, 84.

35. Ibid., 91.

36. Ibid.

37. See Coelho, "G. G. Kapsberger in Rome," 121.

38. *Operas for the Papal Court, 1631–1668* (Ann Arbor: UMI Research Press, 1981), 175.

39. Ambros, *Geschichte der Musik*, 476.

40. Forbes, "The Non-Liturgical Vocal Music," 297.

41. Frederick Hammond, *Music and Spectacle in Baroque Rome: Barberini Patronage under Urban VIII* (New Haven: Yale University Press, 1994), 185.

42. On *Delectare et docere*, see ibid., 199–254. For a comprehensive study of Roman operas by Rospigliosi, see Murata, *Operas for the Papal Court*.

43. See ibid., 221–434. Hammond has placed these operas within the program of Barberini patronage in *Music and Spectacle*, 183–98.

44. See Margaret Murata, "Classical Tragedy in the History of Early Opera in Rome," *Early Music History* 4 (1984): 111–22.

45. Hammond, *Music and Spectacle*, 189.

46. Jürgen Maehder, "The Representation of the 'Discovery' on the Opera Stage," in *Musical Repercussions of 1492: Encounters in Text and Performance*, ed. Carol E. Robertson (Washington, D.C.: Smithsonian Institution Press, 1992), 258. For an extended treatment of the use of myth within scientific and musical discourse of the early seventeenth century, see Victor Coelho, "Musical Myth and Galilean Science in Giovanni Serodine's *Allegoria della scienza*," in *Music and*

*Science in the Age of Galileo*, ed. V. Coelho (Dordrecht: Kluwer Academic Publishers, 1992), 91–114.

47. Redondi, *Galileo: Heretic*, 120.

48. See Rudolf Wittkower, "Problems of the Theme," in *Baroque Art: The Jesuit Contribution*, 1–14.

49. Howard Hibbard, "*Ut picturae sermones:* The First Painted Decorations of the Gesù," in *Baroque Art: The Jesuit Contribution*, 29–50.

50. Graham Dixon, "Musical Activity in the Church of the Gesù in Rome During the Early Baroque," *Archivum Historicum Societatis Iesu* 49(1980): 323–37.

51. See Redondi, *Galileo: Heretic*, 123–26.

52. On the relationship of the *Apotheosis* and previous Jesuit dramas, see Forbes, "The Non-Liturgical Music," 443–44.

53. This large canvas, along with its companion, *The Miracles of St. Ignatius of Loyola* and a cycle of thirty-nine other paintings, was executed by Rubens around 1617 for the Jesuit Church in Antwerp. The works remained there until the fire of 1718, which destroyed all but the two *Miracles* paintings, which were relocated to Vienna. For a history and analysis of the cycle, see John Rupert Martin, *The Ceiling Paintings for the Jesuit Church in Antwerp* (London: Phaidon, 1968).

54. See Schurhammer, *Francis Xavier*, 389–90.

55. Ibid., 16–27.

56. On the Vienna manuscript version it is written that the work was performed five times, in a hand that is undoubtedly later than Kapsberger's autograph in Paris.

57. *The Travels of Pietro della Valle in India*, 2:402.

58. Ibid., 411

59. On the introduction of polyphony in Goa, see Coelho, "Cross-Cultural Repertories. . . ."

60. See Wicki, ed., *Documenta Indica*, vol. 12 (1580–83), 881.

61. Joseph di Santa Maria (Giuseppe Sebastiani), *Seconda speditione all'Indie Orientali* (Venice, 1683), 3:105: "Godei più volte in quella città con occasione di feste assai belle musiche, particolarmente in quella di S. Ignazio, che si celebrò a sette cori con suavissime sinfonie nella Casa Professa dei Padri della Compagnia, ove si trova il corpo di San Francesco Saverio; e dicendo, che mi pareva di stare in Roma, mi fi risposto che non m'ingannava, perché la composizione era del famoso Carissimi portata in quelle parti. Non può credersi quanto rieschino nella musica quei Canarini, come ci si esercitino, e con quanta facilità.

"Non v'é aldea, o villaggio di cristiani, che non abbia nella chiesa organo, arpa, e viola, o un buon coro di musici, cantandovisi nelle feste, e nei sabbati, vesperi, messe, e litanie, e con molto concorso, e devozione. . . ."

62. Historical Archives of Goa (HAG): Jesuitas 2088, *Receita e despeza dos Jesuitas, 1684–1692*, f. 113: "De consertar, ensinar os orgaos dous x.e e meyo-002.2.37"; HAG Jesuitas 2570, *Lembranças dos artigos recebidos do Reino pelos padres jesuitas, 1664, Registo de efeitos*, f. 28v: "Tres macos Cordaduras de Arpa-003" / "Tres macos de Cordas de Violla-003."

63. HAG, Jesuitas 2088, f. 106v, *Despesa domes de Majo de 1685:* "De muzica da festa de S. Fran.^{co} X^e. . . ."

## CHAPTER TWO

*The Italian (Castrato) in London*

Todd S. Gilman

'Tis neither for man nor for woman, said she,
That thus with lamenting I water the lee;
But 'tis for a singer so charming and sweet,
Whose musick, Alas! I shall never forget.—*Henry Carey**

The leading Italian castrati were among the most famous and most highly paid musicians in Europe; yet examination of their reception in London between roughly 1710 and 1740 immediately reveals that they were loathed as much as they were admired. Thomas McGeary has shown that the abhorrence manifested itself in Augustan satirists' notions that these "effeminate" songsters and the "feminized" and "senseless" Italian opera in which they sang constituted a palpable threat to a myth of British identity that valorized manliness and "rational" music and drama.[1] Gary C. Thomas has elaborated the point: detailing the "nexus of music, gender/sexuality, and nation" in eighteenth-century London, Thomas notes that "the castrato [prompted] highly ambivalent and conflictive reactions: as an exotic spectacle it seduced and entertained; as a gender-bending image of mutilated and sodomized Italian (non) masculinity it repulsed and threatened."[2]

Although McGeary and Thomas have identified a similar conflict between desire and disgust in the reception of the castrato and both have connected the conflict to British nationalism, I believe the model they use (attraction vs. repulsion) risks limiting our understanding of the reception itself and thus of the relationship between that phenomenon and British nationalism. The reception of the castrati can indeed be separated into the large categories of desire and disgust, but the attacks manifesting disgust are themselves further divisible. Disgust with the effeminate and sodomitical qualities of the castrati is countered by an equally palpable disgust (partly masking envy) emanating from their sexual prowess with women and thus with their presumed hypervirility. The attacks, then, embody a compelling and thus far unexplored paradox.

*T. S. Gilman*

I shall survey the British attacks on the castrati with a view to furthering our understanding of what such criticism demonstrates about early eighteenth-century British attitudes toward gender, sexuality, opera, and nation. First, I shall explore the paradoxical satirical representation of the castrati, arguing that this representation originates in and reveals the satirists' (and presumably their audience's) discomfort with a growing awareness of the ambiguous, contingent nature of gender and sexuality, an awareness triggered in part by the emergence of the castrati. Second, I shall relate this discomfort surrounding gender and sexuality to a nascent British national ideology, arguing that this ideology, which depended for its viability on a stable equation between manliness and heteronormative sexuality, was thrown into doubt by the castrati. Finally, to explain how and why the castrati came to mean what they did among Britons, I shall attempt to situate the singers in relation to two other liminal groups in eighteenth-century London with whom they shared essential attributes: male actors and mollies, or sodomites.

## Paradoxical Attacks

As constructed in the writings of Augustan satirists and polemicists, the castrati transgressed a normative gender and sexuality at once insofar as their feminine beauty, cultivated deportment, and sirens' voices were believed capable of turning men into sodomites *and* because their popularity among the fair sex rendered them more sexually viable and thus more virile than British men. So broad and consistent were the constructions and criticisms of the castrati from Augustan pens between 1710 and 1740 that one need scarcely treat the singers as individuals; let it suffice to note that those regularly invoked in the period were the most famous: Nicolini (a.k.a. Nicolo Grimaldi, 1673–1732), Senesino (a.k.a. Francesco Bernardi, d. 1759), and Farinelli (a.k.a. Carlo Broschi, 1705–1782).

A connection between the castrati, womanishness, and sodomy emerges as early as 1653, in John Bulwer's censorious treatise *Anthropometamorphosis*. Bulwer argues that castration is degrading to manhood and, insofar as it interferes with the "propagation of Posterity" and makes men look and sound like women, unnatural.[3] The singing castrati are prime examples of this violation of nature: their "Voices scandalize their breeches . . . the Testicles being taken away, and so the heart affected, the Voice and very form becommeth womanish" (355–56). Bulwer ends by asserting that many eunuchs become catamites for debauched heathens, serving "as men of their Chambers, in a foule and unlawfull acquaintance . . ." (360).

By about 1700 the notion that Italy was the home of sodomy was well established by means of anticlerical or anti-Catholic propaganda. In one collection of slanderous letters, purportedly by a genteel traveler to Italy, the author confides to his reader that all the monks and priests he met are "addicted to the abominable Sin of *Sodomy*."[4] Similarly, in his satirical poem *The True-Born Englishman*, Daniel Defoe proposes a country of origin for each of the sins that now inhabit England, noting that "*Lust* chose the Torrid Zone of *Italy*, / Where Blood ferments in rapes and Sodomy."[5] An anonymous Juvenalian satire makes a similar charge: "In *Italy*, Poor *Sodom*'s fatal Vice / Of Loving Smock-Fac'd Boys, first took it's [sic] Rise."[6]

By 1706, after the first Italianate operas had come to England, John Dennis published a pamphlet condemning the foreign works. He reveals his fears (and those of others as well) in response to the operas—and to the support for such opera he perceived among London theater managers—that Italian opera would take over the English stage. Dennis's vilification rests on four interrelated points:

1. the Italian opera is comprised of "soft and effeminate Musick" that subordinates sense to sound and exemplifies "the reigning Luxury of modern *Italy*."[7]
2. "Musick may be made profitable as well as delightful, if it is subordinate to some nobler Art [i.e., legitimate drama], and subservient to Reason"; otherwise it becomes "a mere sensual Delight" (385).
3. Thus Italian opera, as an entertainment of "mere Musick," threatens to "banish Poetry," the chief moral good of English drama (387).
4. Italian opera is as "unnatural" as the sodomitical acts Italy's inhabitants enjoy (392).

A few years later, when Nicolini's astounding successes in such Haymarket operas as *Pyrrhus and Demetrius* and Francesco Mancini's *Hydaspes*, or *L'Idaspe Fedele* (the extravagances of which Addison parodied in the well-known *Spectator* 13) had established the castrato as a staple of Italian opera in London, Dennis went so far as to warn the public of the opera's ability to make sodomites of British men and lure them from women: "The more the Men are enervated and emasculated by the Softness of the *Italian* Musick, the less will they care for [women]. . . . I make no doubt but we shall come to see one Beau take another for Better for Worse. . . ."[8]

The same year an anonymous Irish broadsheet proclaimed Nicolini's ability to charm his listeners.[9] It begins with a paean to the general seductiveness of the eunuch's voice, but soon we learn that Nicolini can seduce women and men—nay, soldiers—alike:

The dripping Fair, distills from ev'ry Pore,
Gods 'tis too much! she cryes, and I can hear no more,

. . .

Ev'n the rough Soldiers mov'd, the dusty Field,
And the big War to softer Pleasures yield.                    (314)

The poem suggests that even Odysseus, who succeeded in resisting the Sirens, would have succumbed:

> When the fam'd Greek to native Shoars design'd,
> Had left in Flames unhappy Troy behind,
> T'unbend his Mind the sweetest Syrens fail'd,
> His Nobler Arts o'er all their Pow'rs prevail'd;
> Had sweeter Nic. been in the Syren's Place,
> And fond of Conquest shone in ev'ry Grace,
> Th' unguarded chief had on his Accents hung,
> And fall'n the noblest Triumph of his Song;
> His Eyes no more, had seen the Graecian Coast,
> But tristful Pen. had mourn'd her Hero lost. (314)[10]

Women need not worry, however, for Nicolini will bring them no scandal in the form of pregnancy:

> Ye blooming Nymphs who warily begin
> To dread the Censure, but to love the Sin,
>
> . . .
>
> From Scandal free, this pretty Play-thing meet,
> Cool as May Dew, and as it's Butter sweet. (315–16)

In 1718 the notorious publisher Edmund Curll issued an English translation of Charles Ancillon's French treatise on the castrati. *Eunuchism Display'd* promised to "Describ[e] all the different Sorts of Eunuchs"; to determine "whether they are capable of marriage, and if they ought to be suffer'd to enter into that State."[11] Most extraordinarily, it proposed to compare "Signior *Nicolini* and the Three celebrated Eunuchs now at *Rome*" in response to an interest "Occasion'd by a young Lady's falling in Love with *Nicolini*." The treatise begins with a disparaging definition of the eunuch (8), followed by a quotation purportedly by St. Basil:

> Eunuchs [are] an abominable Tribe, who are past the Sense of Honour, who are neither Men nor Women. . . . They are jealous, despicable, fierce, effeminate, Gluttons, covetous, cruel, inconstant, suspicious, furious, insatiable. They cry (like Children) if they are left out of an Entertainment. . . . The Knife indeed has made them chaste, but this chastity is of no Service to them, their Lust makes them furious, which yet is impotent, sterile, and unfruitful. (9–10)

By the 1720s the satires of the castrati became as childish as *Eunuchism Display'd* claimed the castrati themselves were. In "An Epistle To the most Learned Doctor *W[oo]d[war]d*; From a PRUDE, That was unfortunately Metamorphos'd on Saturday December 29, 1722," a former prude (she signs herself "Prudentia") asks the doctor, a physician/paleontologist, to tell her to what gender she should now be assigned, for she has recently sprouted a penis after watching Senesino lose *his* while singing at the opera.[12] She describes the sequence of events as follows: "Chast Senesino" is himself first transformed into a prude by means of a "fatal song" he sings in Rolli and Bononcini's *Crispo*, and this metamorphosis causes the audience to burst into laughter (5). Prudentia suppresses her own laughter; yet the laughter's "vapours" cause turmoil in her body, so that by the time she is home in bed they cause her simultaneously to have an orgasm ("matrimonial Pangs") and to grow a penis ("force out something—I ne'er felt before") (5–6). Prudentia begs the doctor to determine whether she "in Love must Bridegroom prove or Bride" (8). She becomes increasingly alarmed by her new appendage, which, despite her efforts to ignore and modestly hide it, becomes erect and bothers her with sexual feelings: "By Female Dress it's Boldness I oppose, / In Petticoats the Monster bolder grows, / And bears aloft my Hoop—'spite of my Nose—" (8). Finally, in desperation—"These horrid Pangs no longer I'll endure"— she asks the doctor to "cut if off—or bring some other Cure" (8).

Senesino is chaste, and so it is fitting, the satirist implies, that his woman-ish singing should cause him physically to lose his penis and become a prude. Indeed, by the same token, Prudentia's suppressed laughter appo-sitely inspires not only sexual feeling, but an actual penis—perhaps the one that Senesino lost—with the result that she and Senesino switch roles. Her new penis leaves her no more chaste than "chaste" Senesino's did him: Prudentia becomes a sexual freak—a nymphomaniac and a hermaphro-dite—like the castrato she was foolish enough to admire. She even seems to be a molly, given her preposterous/camp "Maiden Name."[13] Thus willful or hypocritical ignorance of the castrato as a sexual being ironically results in the unnaturally chaste woman being forced at once to see that having a penis means having sexual feelings and thus to forego her own chastity as punish-ment, and to become a hermaphroditical sodomite like (or in place of) the castrato himself.

A series of verse "epistles" purportedly exchanged among London's opera stars followed between 1724 and 1727—a period coinciding with the height of the success of Handel's Royal Academy of Music. In 1724 "An Epistle from S[enesin]o to A[nastasi]a R[obinso]n" appeared; here Senesino tries to mollify an offended English diva. Because she is a prude, Robinson resents their last stage embrace, during which the castrato was too forward with her. Senesino reminds her that because he is impotent and thus physi-cally incapable of responding sexually to her, his "Transports" are pure show—"My Flames and Darts are nothing all but Art."[14] The most the two can do together, he says, is excite others' passions through their "chast Endearments" (2). Despite this defense, by the end of the poem Senesino's apology turns to insult as he implies that her anger in fact emanates not from what she imagines is his lust, but from his inability to satisfy her (3).

Similarly, "An Epistle From S[ignio]r S[enesin]o to S[ignior]a F[austin]a," which features a frontispiece engraving of Senesino and Faustina where the diva sings lovingly to the castrato in the final moments of Handel's *Admeto*, exhibits a fictitious prurient background.[15] The poem itself depicts Senesino complaining that Faustina's applause-mongering by means of "feign'd Transports" during their scenes together causes him "real Pain," for he suspects that he is either being made the butt of a joke or being pressured into responding tenderly but insincerely (6). He wishes that Faustina's "Heat cou'd alter Nature's Law! / And bless what's frozen with a kindly Thaw" (6).

The *British Journal* of March 25, 1727 announced that the response to this satire was so lewd they refused to reprint it.[16] Here Faustina replies indignantly that her advances have been rebuffed by "a Castrate Wretch" (A2r). She speaks of how many men she has rejected to save herself for Senesino, but we quickly learn that her interest in him has been self-serving:

> To keep my Character, my Shape, my Voice
> I fix'd on Thee, cold Slave, my prudent Choice,
> Well knowing safe with Thee I might remain,
> Enjoy Loves Pleasures, yet avoid the Pain;
> By Thee caress'd, continue yet a Maid,
> Nor of a Tell-tale B[ab]y be afraid. . . .          *(4–5)*

She goes so far as to accuse him of using impotence as an excuse to hide his lack of desire: "Want of Desire, not want of Power plead, / Unwilling Souls are Impotent indeed!" (5).

She threatens and goads him, arguing that he can surely satisfy her, that he does not need to be able to ejaculate; indeed, ejaculation has proven a hindrance in her prior relations with men. She speaks of the other castrati who have satisfied women:

> Did not fat N[icoli]ni though a Clown,
> Enjoy the finest Creatures in the Town:
> And little B[enedit]i's Weazel Face,
> No nor his Voice had e'er got him a Place,
> Without some farther Merit in the Case[?]          *(6)*

Moreover, she alludes to her own and Senesino's ability to excite both men and women to same-sex lust: "The Fair have wish'd their Lovers warm as me, / The Men themselves caress'd instead of Thee" (7). Finally, she vows never to touch Senesino again, and to get even by inviting the men she has formerly spurned to woo her. These men will ensure that she is the reigning diva of London:

> . . . Prostrate Eunuchs shall before me fall,
> With Hatred and Disdain I'll treat 'em all;
> But much more Thee, for why, 'twill be my Pride,
> That thou shalt daily ask to be deny'd.          *(8)*

With the arrival of London's next great castrato, Farinelli, the verse satires resumed, especially at his apex, between 1735 and 1737. In 1735 "The Rake's Progress" appeared, a hudibrastic poem keyed to the prints of William Hogarth's *Rake's Progress*. The second canto, corresponding to the famous engraving of the Rake in the company of Farinelli, implies that the Rake's preoccupation with the eunuch is queer:

> But Music most his Bosom warms,
> And heavenly *Farinelli* charms.
> One God, one Songster he'll confess,
> But of the two thinks the first less.[17]

The Rake's own admiration and lust for Farinelli give way to an envious reflection on the castrato's sexual prowess with his female fans:

> See him [the Rake] amidst the admiring throng,
> Forego all Pleasures for a Song.
> No wonder that the Ladies pay,
> They take it out another Way.
> Who would not be unmann'd to gain
> What they [the castrati] with so much Ease obtain.          *(17–18)*

The poet finally consolidates the irony of the castrato's ability to please more than the manly British man, not despite, but because of, his missing testicles: "Strange that the Loss of all our Store / Should make us able to do more" (18).

James Miller's Horatian imitation "upon such VICES and FOLLIES, as are either above the Reach, or without the Verge of the LAWS" satirizes the castrato's paradoxical sexual appeal to all of London, again in spite of his lack of the manliness embodied in testicles:

> ASK *Fa[rinel]li*, please your Grace, to sing.
> No, the cram'd Capon answers—no such Thing.
> Shall I, who, being less than Man, am more;
> Whom Beaux, Belles, Peers, and Senators adore;
> For whose sweet Pipe the City's so forsaken,
> That, by *Excisemen*, it might now be taken,
> And great Sir *Bob* [Robert Walpole] ride thro', and save his Bacon;
> What! shall I sing when *ask'd?*—I'm no such Elf:
> Not I, by Jove, tho' ask'd by *G[eorg]e* himself.[18]

The satirist condemns Britain for allowing the castrati to carry off their women, making dupes of British men:

> Sleep, *Britain*, in thy State of Reprobation,
> Thou mere *Milch-cow* to ev'ry foreign nation.
> *Heaps* upon *Heaps* thy Fair expire, alas!
> Slain by the *Jaw-bone* of a warbling Ass.          *(3–4)*

Constantia Phillips addresses Farinelli next in a long satire mostly copied without acknowledgment from the earlier "F[AUSTI]NAs Answer to S[ENESIN]Os Epistle." She begins by contrasting "real men" and castrati, to the former's disadvantage:

Men, filthy Fellows! poison to my Sight,
Shock to my Senses, and my Soul's affright;
Rough-bearded Monsters, scrubbing Brushes, Saws!
What is a tender Woman in their Paws?[19]

Like the author of "The Rake's Progress," she then rhapsodizes about the true reason women lavish gifts on Farinelli: " 'Tis not for thy sweet Voice and warbling Tongue, / But that thou'rt handsome, vigorous and young" (5). Again, women's safety from pregnancy is asserted, as is his ability to conquer manly British men and women alike:

The well-drest Warriour, with the Lady gay,
At ev'ry Trill shall faint and die away;
And 'stead of facing Cannon, or his Foes,
Shall hold a Smelling-Bottle to his Nose;
And he that would not start at Death, or Fire,
Shall like a Girl at thy soft Trill expire.                                   *(13)*

Henry Fielding takes up the castrati in his ballad opera farce *Eurydice, or the Devil Henpeck'd*, performed at Drury Lane Theatre on February 19, 1737, as an afterpiece to Addison's *Cato*; *The Historical Register for the Year 1736* followed this at the New Theatre in the Haymarket in May 1737. *Eurydice* trades on the by now familiar notion of the castrato's indeterminate gender. Orpheus, seeking Eurydice in the underworld, speaks with Charon about being ferried across the river Styx:

CHARON [*to Orpheus*]. I wish you would be so good . . . Master, to give us one of your *Italian* Catches.
ORPH. Why, dost thou love Musick then, Friend *Charon*?
CHARON. Yes, fags! Master, I do. It went to my heart t'other day, that I did not dare ferry over Signior *Quaverino*.
ORPH. Why didst thou not dare?
CHARON. I don't know, Sir; Judge *Rhadamanthus* [a judge in the classical underworld] said it was against the Law: for that no body was to come into this Country but Men and Women; and that the Signior was neither the one nor the other.[20]

Farinelli is later connected with sodomy in the figure of Orpheus himself, the legendary musician, originator of pederasty, and popular subject of opera. A shrewish Eurydice provokes Orpheus to denounce all women: "*Ungrateful, barbarous Woman! Infernal* Stygian *Monster!*" (147). Indeed, Bertrand A. Goldgar has noted that this passage echoes Ovid's account of the origin of pederasty.[21] The sexual inadequacy of the castrati then comes into play, as the Author, a metadramatic personage typical of "Rehearsal" plays of the period, comments that the idea of the castrati as sexual beings is as senseless as Italian opera itself: "[F]or an *English* People to support an extravagant *Italian* Opera, of which they understand nor relish neither the

Sense nor the Sound, is heartily as ridiculous and much of a piece with an Eunuch's keeping a Mistress . . . " (148).

In Act 2 of *The Historical Register* a group of women speak of Farinelli:

FOURTH LADY. He's everything in the world one could wish!

FIRST LADY. Almost everything one could wish!

. . .

FIRST LADY. Well, it must be charming to have a child by him.

THIRD LADY. Madam, I met a lady in a visit the other day with three! . . . All Farinellos, all in wax.

FIRST LADY. Oh Gemini! Who makes them? I'll send and bespeak half a dozen tomorrow morning.[22]

The "children," then, we learn, are dildoes, the means by which Farinelli satisfies the women.

Henry Carey, in one of his verse satires (c. 1737), describes a woman crying over Senesino's departure from England. The speaker hears the woman moaning and asks her who has caused her such pain. She responds with the epigraph to this essay.[23] In another satire Carey symmetrically insinuates Farinelli's sexual appeal to men. The speaker himself might even be a sodomite, wandering the parks of London and stumbling on to a partner in crime[24]:

As saunt'ring I rang'd in the park all alone
A sparkish young fellow was making his moan;

. . .

For his dear Farrinelli had flown into Spain,
And he never should hear the sweet creature again.[25]

In 1738 Thomas Gilbert seconds this motion; on the one hand, the castrato is a successful ladies' man: "without benefit of propagation, / Gay *Farinelli* cuckolds half the nation."[26] On the other, his name becomes a synonym for sodomy:

For now the syren is the taste of *Spain*,
No more will *Spaniards* plunder o'er the main;
But ravish'd with his song enchanted lie,
While our rich merchants sail unheeded by:
No more shall lust of gold their sons entice,
But *Farinelli* be the reigning vice.                    *(127)*

Finally, in still another verse satire of this time, a sodomite called Lord Epicœne is shocked and disappointed to discover that Farinelli, with whom he has been having intercourse, assuming the castrato was a man, has revealed his true biological gender by becoming pregnant:

How does *Lord Epicœne* his Loss Lament!
His Sighs, his Pray'rs, and all his Jew'ls mispent?

"Have I," crys he, "'fore Swine been casting Pearls
And lavish'd so much Treasure on a Girl?"[27]

These early eighteenth-century British attacks on the castrato are not, then, reducible to the stereotype of the effeminate sodomite roundly denounced by all who addressed him in print—whom Randolph Trumbach identifies and McGeary and Thomas both implicitly agree the castrato basically was or was thought to be.[28] Although the castrato is to a degree characterized in this manner, he is constructed as a more complex figure; he becomes also the (excessively) manly heterosexual and the unmanly (excessive) heterosexual—for lack of a less anachronistic term—all by virtue of the confusion he creates through the overlap of his various significations. The only permutation not ascribed explicitly is that of the manly sodomite, a category of identity that seems not to have gained wide popular currency.[29] Thus we should see the reception of the castrato, his status as a signifier, as embodying a more general fear: the fear that the castrato's excessive, uncontainable gender exposed the contingent nature of gender and sexuality.

## The Attacks and British Nationalism

The attacks on the castrati also reveal how these singers were used to define an emergent British nationalism. Thus the signifier of the castrato can indeed be placed in Thomas's "nexus of music, gender/sexuality, and nation." Still, the paradoxical nature of the attacks suggests that we cannot take the castrato's threat to British nationalism to be embodied unproblematically in manliness or its absence. The castrato was not simply a scourge to a heteronormative British manliness, as Thomas and McGeary argue; rather, if the castrato was simultaneously a sodomitical failure, a sodomitical success, and the ultimate British-woman pleaser, the supremacy, even the viability, of the manly British man becomes doubtful. In other words, because we can equate the signifier of the castrato with the more general fear that his gender exposed the contingent nature of gender and sexuality, what British nationalism risked with the emergence of the castrato is also necessarily altered. British nationalism risked the ability of the construct of the manly Briton to signify unproblematically and tenaciously among Britain's constituents. The manly Briton was potentially no longer the ultimate man and, by virtue of that exemplary status, the ultimate Briton.

Moreover, the fact that Italian opera was gaining popularity in London at the very moment that British nationalism was emerging helps explain another line of attack in the satires. The ridicule of the castrati was not confined to matters of gender and sexuality but became conflated with attacks on Italian opera itself, the foreign (Hanoverian) British aristocracy who supported that art form, and popery—in short, with attacks on the "luxury" and "corruption" against which British nationalists (especially Tories) fought in this "period of financial revolution."[30] As John Sekora notes, "Throughout English history the disturbance of any kind of national equilibrium was likely to be followed by fresh condemnations of luxury."[31] To put the matter another way, the accident of the contemporaneity of the rises of Italian opera in London and British nationalism in the early eighteenth century contributed to British nationalism's becoming defined not as an ideology narrowly constructed solely on the basis of political desiderata—public virtue, hierarchy, and necessity in general[32]—as it might otherwise have been, but as one that aligned these desiderata with prescribed norms of gender and sexuality.

The connection between the accusations of gender and sexual excess and "luxury" and "corruption" finds its strongest underpinnings in what J. G. A. Pocock and Linda Dowling have identified as the classical republican ideal of the virtuous citizen as manly warrior.[33] Dowling notes that sexual love between men was associated with "luxury," "corruption," and "effeminacy" by a "classical republican discourse that had exercised a powerful hold over the English cultural imagination" since the late seventeenth century, a "body of political theory always identifying the health of the polity as a whole with the *virtus* or virility of an ancient warrior ideal."[34] This particularly potent, if unconscious, ideal was the basis of the British psyche's nationalist pride. The castrato, in stark contrast and thus threatening to this ideal, was an emblem of the *effeminatus*—a category of person so physically enfeebled and morally emasculated as to be unfit for citizenship in the commonwealth of virtue-as-manliness. The *effeminatus* has to do not with femaleness in any modern sense but with an absence of value, deriving from an obsolescent notion of effeminacy.[35] Thus what the early eighteenth century often condemned in effeminacy is not what the twentieth century thinks of as homosexuality; effeminacy "has to do not with sexual but with civic incapacity, the dissolution of social categories which occurs when community itself has begun to dissolve into an aimless and self-regarding egoism" (9). The category of the *effeminatus* was large, "defined by the entire sphere of social existence populated by the nonwarrior or not-warrior: boys, girls, slaves, eunuchs, hermaphrodites, and all others perceived as unsuitable to or incapable of discharging the martial obligation to the polis" (8).

The castrato, then, separate from and in addition to his being condemned as a freak of gender and sexuality, as we have seen, becomes the perfect emblem of "luxury" and "corruption," the folly and excess that led John "Estimate" Brown to characterize his age as one of "a vain, luxurious, and selfish EFFEMINACY."[36] The distinction is obvious in that Brown does not object to musicians and, especially, to music per se, "that divine Art"; rather, he laments that music is "at length dwindled into a Woman's or an Eunuch's effeminate Trill. . . . The Question now concerns not the Expression, the Grace, the Energy, or Dignity of the Musick . . . but the *Tricks* of the *Performer*; who is then surest of our ignorant Applause when he runs through the compass of the Throat . . ." (45–47).

This objection to the castrato as one of the nefarious concomitants of opera itself had been explicit as early as 1711 in John Dennis's essay quoted earlier as an example of opera's connection with sodomy. Here the castrato served as an emblem of Italian opera's base, unnatural, unmanly sensuality, which Dennis opposed with more morally righteous British arts and British public virtue.[37] Dennis further objected that if Italian opera is not quelled presently, it will eventually debase and emasculate the British virtue of courage in the way it had already done to the manly/virtuous British drama; he ended by implying that British aristocrats who supported the opera were nearly traitors to England (395).

In strains similar to Dennis's, Richard Steele bid a sardonic good-bye to Nicolini when the singer left England in 1714:

> Back to thy own unmanly *Venice* sail,
> Where Luxury and loose Desires prevail;
>
> . . .
>
> Hence with thy Curst deluding Song! away!
> Shall *British* Freedom thus become thy Prey?[38]

As late as 1727 Henry Carey was still sounding the luxury–corruption–effeminacy alarm.[39] Still, as I have argued, the castrato does not serve simply to challenge the classical republican warrior ideal of manliness, for he is himself manly in his reputation for rampant cuckoldry. Thus if the castrato is at once the *effeminatus*—that is, a threat to virtue-as-manliness—*and* a Don Giovanni potentially more virile than British men, the threat he poses is finally to the stability of *the equation among* manliness, heteronormative sexuality, and civic virtue that the British citizen aspired to for identity/orientation in his sociopolitical milieu. The castrato may have been "effeminate" in all possible senses of the word—unmanly, sodomitical, self-regarding, even feminine in the modern sense—but he was also a hero, even a warrior hero at times, in opera, and men and women alike took him seriously in this role. J. J. Quantz, for example, said of Senesino, "His countenance was well adapted to the stage, and his action was natural and noble. To these qualities he joined a majestic figure; but his aspect and deportment were more suited to the part of a hero than of a lover."[40] Steele had similarly praised Nicolini's acting and deportment in the *Spectator* in 1709: "He performs the most ordinary action in a manner suitable to the greatness of his character, and shows the prince even in the giving of a letter, or despatching of a messenger. . . ."[41] The condemnation of the castrato as a British nationalist project, then—in spite or perhaps because of the songster's merits—may best be accounted for as Thomas suggests:

> Operating as loose correspondences in a relation of opposition . . . [musicality, Italianicity, and homosexuality] stand ready for their social and ideological appropriation: musicality as an "effeminizing" and "indeterminate" property to be controlled and channeled; Italianicity, constructed from the I/eye of the English as a "confusion" of attraction and loathing, in need of a firm, anglicizing hand from

above . . . ; homosexuality . . . linking the musical, the effeminate, and the Italian/pagan, stands in need of disciplined suppression, if not total erasure. . . . The ideological work performed through these discursive operations serves [above all to maintain] Anglopatriarchal authority and control.[42]

## Castrati, Actors, Queers

Why the castrati signified as complexly as they did might be traced to two developments in the period that independently engendered similar paradoxical fears. Kristina Straub has identified an increasingly problematic connection among theatrical specularization, gender, ethnicity, and sexuality among eighteenth-century dramatic actors, a connection that might be applied instructively to the castrati. Like the eighteenth-century male actor, the castrato can be seen, in Straub's terms, as a commodified spectacle. Both the actor and the castrato were at once the object of a "feminizing" gaze and the male subject—the public figure and professional—who claimed a certain control over that gaze, appropriating it through social power; and thus they became contradictorily gendered.[43]

The contradiction became further entrenched in the case of the castrato. He was not simply a male subject by virtue of this public stature; his international celebrity consolidated his socially defined masculine prowess in Britain. Still, the combination of his lack of secondary sex characteristics brought on by a lack of androgen, his generally "freakish" appearance,[44] and his Italianness imbued him with a palpable sense of unmanliness. Moreover, although he was typically the male hero of *opera seria*, he was also often travestied to play female roles. Margaret Reynolds has noted that the castrato often played the female simply because he was the singer of choice for *all* high-voice roles.[45] For example, in the first performance of Monteverdi's *Orfeo* (1607), the parts of La Musica, Eurydice, and the Messagiera were all sung by castrati (137). Enid and Richard Peschel observe that actual women on the stage further complicated signification, especially when they sang in a lower tessitura than the castrati:

> For instance, the male roles of Nero and Ottone in Monteverdi's *Incoronazione di Poppea* (1642) were composed for soprano voices and were sung by castrati, whereas Ottavia and Poppea were performed by (female) contraltos. . . . [I]n Cavalli's *Eliogabalo* the male parts of Eliogabalo, Alessandro, and Cesare are for sopranos, while Zenia (a woman) is written for the tenor voice. In Cavalli's *Didone* the part of Jarba, Dido's rejected lover, is for a [castrato] who sings higher than Dido herself.[46]

Reynolds recuperates the practice, arguing that only relatively recently has it been perceived as unusual: "in the early days of the opera virility, authority, and power were not incompatible with a high voice. Quite the contrary."[47]

Still, as was the case with the cross-dressed boy actor on the Renaissance stage, the practice was inevitably queer-friendly:

> this willingness to make the demands of gendered naturalism entirely subservient to the requirements of musical fitness [resulted in] . . . an awareness of the sexual ambiguity that might arise when the audience looks upon women dressed as men or men dressed as women. Several of Handel's operas (*Alcina, Partenope, Siroe, Serse*) include scenes where sexual complications arise because of this practice. Neither does Handel seem to be averse to exploiting the presence on stage of a castrato singer to allow for teasing questions of sexuality and potency. . . . [T]here was sexual anarchy on stage.          (137–38)

In light of Thomas's investigations into Handel's own sexuality, Reynolds's assessment becomes scarcely less convincing than it is appealing. In any case, the truth of the castrato's gender is that he was not simply the "luxurious" *effeminatus* that Dowling brings to light, but was simultaneously as "womanish" as the mythical eunuch of Bulwer. The French traveler Charles de Brosses, visiting Italy in 1739–1740, commented that the castrato Porporino was "as pretty as the prettiest girl"; when Horace Walpole met Senesino in March 1740, returning to Siena in a chaise, he wrote, "We thought it a fat old woman; but it spoke in a shrill little pipe, and proved itself to be Senesini."[48] The castrati themselves were not only aware of but exploited their excessive gender; as Heriot reports, a certain Consolino "was able to carry on an affair with a society woman under her husband's nose, by the simple expedient of arriving in one of his stage costumes; and it was not uncommon for castrati to go about in women's clothes all the time."[49]

A second reason for the castrato's peculiar signification, his status "beyond" gender, can be traced to the growing public awareness of another set of liminal figures in early-eighteenth-century society: the mollies. Not only were the practices of these figures widely believed to have come to England from Italy, as noted, like the castrati and opera themselves, but the reception of the mollies evinced a similarly paradoxical relationship to gender. As Ned Ward observes in his satirical pamphlet *The Secret History of Clubs*, the "Mollies Club" is most noteworthy for its members' scandalous relationship to heteronormative gender and sexuality:

> The Mollies . . . are so far degenerated from all masculine Deportment, or manly Exercises, that they rather fancy themselves Women . . . affecting to Speak, Walk, Tattle, Cursy [sic], Cry, Scold, and to mimick all Manner of Effeminacy, that ever has fallen within their several Observations; not omitting the Indecencies of lewd Women, that they may tempt one another . . . to commit those odious Bestialities, that ought for ever to be without a Name. . . .[50]

Two related antisodomitical tracts issued at key moments in Italian opera's London progress explicitly attribute the growth of sodomy to the growth of the opera: "How famous, or rather how infamous *Italy* has been in all Ages, and still continues in the odious Practice of *Sodomy*, needs no Explanation. . . . [S]ince the Introduction of Italian Opera's here, our Men are grown insensibly more and more *Effeminate*. . . ."[51]

The author of the later of these, *Satan's Harvest Home*, appends a poem, "The Petit Maitre," to his tract—a thoroughly malicious portrait of the sodomite.[52] It begins, "Tell me, gentle hob'dhoy! / Art thou Girl, or art thou Boy? / . . . I stand amaz'd, and at a Loss to know, / To what new Species thou thy Form dost owe" (62).

Finally, we can adduce more than a modicum of evidence to suggest that at least some castrati were queer. Angus Heriot remarked that

> there were admittedly homosexual castrati, as Casanova's accounts bear witness. In 1745 he writes: ". . . an abbé with an attractive face walked in [to a café]. At the appearance of his hips, I took him for a girl in disguise, and I said so to the abbé Gama; but the latter told me that it was Bepino della Mamana, a famous castrato. The abbé called him over, and told him, laughing, that I had taken him for a girl. The impudent creature, looking fixedly at me, told me that if I liked he would prove that I was right, or that I was wrong."[53]

McGeary adds that "in Rome, [Casanova] describes sexual orgies involving castratos and reports 'We then went to the theatre, where the *castrato* who played the prima donna was a great attraction. He was the favourite pathic of Cardinal Borghese, and supped every evening with his Eminence.' "[54] Casanova continues:

> In a well-made corset, he had the waist of a nymph, and, what was almost incredible, his breast was in no way inferior, either in form or in beauty, to any woman's; and it was above all by this means that the monster made such ravages. . . . When he walked about the stage during the *ritornello* of the aria he was to sing, his step was majestic and at the same time voluptuous; and when he favoured the boxes with his glances, the tender and modest rolling of his black eyes brought a ravishment to the heart. It was obvious that he hoped to inspire the love of those who liked him as a man, and [who] probably would not have done so as a woman. Rome the holy city, which in this way forces every man to become a pederast, will not admit it, nor believe in the effects of an illusion which it does its best to arouse.[55]

Daniel Heartz has recently elucidated the correspondence of Farinelli and Pietro Metastasio, the greatest opera librettist of the time. Heartz presents their relationship as an affectionate rivalry initiated by their debut on the same occasion in 1720[56] and later focused on their amateur musical settings of Metastasio's famous *Canzonette a Nice*, a long, amatory epistle in three installments. However, although of their "voluminous and unceasing"[57] letters only those to Farinelli survive, their erotic character is unmistakable.[58] Indeed, as other evidence suggests, *pace* Heartz, I suspect Farinelli and Metastasio were in love.

Farinelli sent Metastasio his setting of one of the Nice poems from Madrid in 1747, to which the poet responded: "Your music to my Nice is worthy of you. . . . I readily give way to you, or rather am proud of being vanquished by you; and who would be ashamed of being surpassed in music by my incomparable Farinelli?"[59] Another topic in this letter is Farinelli's request for a portrait of his *caro gemello*, to which the poet responds: "The patience necessary to serve as a model to the indiscretion of a painter, is to me the most difficult of all virtues to attain. . . . But who can resist the solicitations of a beloved twin brother? At my return from the country, I shall undertake this business as a penitence for my sins, and try to indulge your *longing* in such a manner as may prevent a miscarriage" (359, emphasis in original). Even Metastasio's flirtation with Teresa Castellini in 1749 seems directed equally to Farinelli:

> What is the beautiful Castellini doing; and is it true that, she is so pleased with my salutations that she means to honour me with her correspondence? Ah! if you love me, let not my friendship be put to so great a trial. After the alluring description which you have given of this amiable person, the violent temptation of a letter would precipitate me into the commission of some mental infidelity [to Farinelli?], for which I should be inconsolable. Tell her, however, that, as a twin, I can only receive the emotions of your heart at the rebound; that when I hear your name, I feel a certain tingling sensation which incommodes me . . . and tell her—No Sir, tell her nothing. The road is too slippery, and it is easier to keep out of it, than when entered, to avoid falling.      *(361)*

When Metastasio set the third installment of the *Canzonette*, he inspired Farinelli to set it as well; the librettist acknowledged receipt of this in a letter of June 13, 1750:

> Your music to my canzonet is expressive, graceful, and the legitimate offspring of one arrived at supremacy in the art. I thank you for communicating it to me, particularly as a testimony of your love; but if it was maliciously sent, as a critique of mine, I shall take care to revenge myself on the first poetry that you send to the press. Yet, if the devil should tempt you to become a poet, who knows but you may *unsheath* some other latent talent? Oh nothing is wanting to complete my ruin, but to have you for a rival. . . .      *(361, my emphasis)*

In a famous portrait of Farinelli by Jacopo Amigoni,[60] the castrato holds a copy of Gaetano Latilla's setting of an aria by Metastasio for the *primo uomo* in *Zenobia*; this inclusion reveals, according to Heartz, the "air of passionate, amorous longing by which [Farinelli] wanted to be remembered by posterity" (364). Could the song be Farinelli's synecdoche for Metastasio himself, with whom the castrato appeared in another portrait by Amigoni of the same period?[61]

Heartz further argues, "that [Farinelli] should choose such a piece for a musical emblem is not out of keeping with what we know from other sources about his *affettuoso* nature. When [Charles] Burney first met him in 1770 he reported: 'Upon parting he took hold of both hands and in English said *kiss me*? —The men here, who are intimate, always kiss the cheek at meeting and parting'" (365). He adds in a footnote that, "Burney left this detail, which is in his manuscript journal, out of his printed tour of 1773" (366, n. 18). Is it possible that Burney knew of Farinelli's proclivities and felt that even his disclaimer ("the men . . . always kiss") would not be sufficient to distance himself from suspicions of queerness?

John Rosselli characterizes the relations of librettist and castrato with obtuse modesty.[62] By contrast, George Rousseau has noted that

> Joseph Spence [in his *Observations*, II, 56] records that he came upon the "real history" of Metastasio . . . while in Italy. According to Spence, Gravina, the unequivocally homoerotic Italian poet-critic . . . adopted [Metastasio] as "son" and lover; nine years later he left the now twenty-year-old Metastasio a small fortune to set himself up as a librettist. Metastasio recognised his own sexuality; he gravitated to the court not only because of his vocation, but also because the court offered him economic security and sexual licence. Apparently by choice he spent the next fifty years as court-poet in Vienna, enjoying the favours of younger men who now courted him.[63]

According to Rousseau, Burney is also silent on the affair with Gravina.[64]

Despite his fitful reticence concerning the loves of Metastasio and Farinelli, Burney is aware of Farinelli's man-pleasing charms. He reports the following anecdote about the first time Senesino and Farinelli sang together, in a performance of the pasticcio opera *Artaserse* (c. 1734): "Senesino had the part of a furious tyrant, and Farinelli that of an unfortunate hero in chains; but in the course of the first air, the captive so softened the heart of the tyrant, that Senesino, forgetting his stage-character, ran to Farinelli and embraced him in his own."[65]

We can thus perhaps see Heriot's characterization of Farinelli, like Heartz's and Rosselli's, as a direct descendent of Burney's—as equally if not more notable for what it does not say than for what it does: "[Farinelli] was known as 'Il ragazzo'—'the boy'—and, being handsome as well as a phenomenal singer, he was a particular success with the female part of his audiences; yet amorous intrigue does not seem to have been among his interests, and not a single anecdote of gallantry is attributed to him."[66] As Thomas winningly observes in a discussion of "closet knowledge," the knowledge that we have about our own and others' sexualities but do not admit:

Closet knowledge depends on silence, an "absence" out of which is generated a discursively elaborated "presence," the secret. Then, as in Freud's "negation" or Foucault's "spiral"—mechanisms by which an object to be denied, repressed, or disciplined gains more, rather than less, presence and power—the secret is by the logic of "reverse discourse" further constituted and elaborated in a procession of alibis, justifications, or explanations: the "repressed," to put it in Freudian language, "returns." . . . a lack becomes an "excess"—knowledge is produced in "excess" of what is spoken, i.e., in its interstitial and subtextual spaces—everywhere, that is, except in the open. The closet is that space where silences speak, obfuscations reveal, absences signify, and negations posit.[67]

In the case of the castrati, though, the silences sing.

NOTES

*Henry Carey, "A Sorrowful Lamentation for the Loss of a Man and No Man."

1. Thomas McGeary, " 'Warbling Eunuchs': Opera, Gender, and Sexuality on the London Stage, 1705–1742." *Restoration and 18th Century Theatre Research* 7, no. 1 (1992): 1–22.

2. Gary C. Thomas, " 'Was George Frideric Handel Gay?': On Closet Questions and Cultural Politics," in *Queering the Pitch: The New Gay and Lesbian Musicology*, eds. Philip Brett, Elizabeth Wood, and Gary C. Thomas (New York: Routledge, 1994), 186.

3. John Bulwer, *Anthropometamorphosis* (London, 1653), 354.

4. [Gabriel D'Emiliane], *The Frauds of Romish Monks and Priests* (London, 1691), 403. Dennis Rubini, "Sexuality and Augustan England: Sodomy, Politics, Elite Circles and Society." *Journal of Homosexuality* 16, no. 1 (1989): 381, reprints "Jenny Cromwell's Complaint Against Sodomy," an anti-Williamite satirical poem from the late 1690s in which sodomy is again attributed to monasteries.

5. Daniel Defoe, *The True-Born Englishman* (London, 1700), 6.

6. Anonymous, "The Town Display'd, in a Letter to Amintor in the Country" (London, 1701), 4. As Ozell's translation of Henri Misson's *Memoirs and Observations in His Travels over England* (London, 1719), 24, makes plain in its entry on buggery / sodomy, the myth had become legend two decades later.

7. John Dennis, "An Essay on the Opera's [sic] After the Italian Manner," in *The Critical Works of John Dennis*, ed. Edward Niles Hooker (Baltimore: Johns Hopkins University Press, 1939), 1:384.

8. John Dennis, "An Essay upon Publick Spirit," in *The Critical Works of John Dennis*, ed. Edward Niles Hooker (Baltimore: Johns Hopkins University Press, 1943), 2:396.

9. "The Signior in Fashion: Or the Fair Maid's Conveniency. A Poem on Nicolini's Musick-Meeting," in T. J. Walsh, *Opera in Dublin, 1705–97* (Dublin: Allen Figgis, 1973), 313–16.

10. A theoretical treatise on music by the castrato Bontempi had earlier likened the powers of song and semen. G. A. Angelini Bontempi, *Historia musica* (Perugia, 1695), 239–40.

11. [Charles Ancillon], *Eunuchism Display'd* (London, 1718).

12. Anonymous, "An Epistle to ... Doctor *W–d–d*" (London, 1723), 4.

13. The heroine states explicitly, "(as undetermin'd what I am) / I venture to subscribe my Maiden Name—PRUDENTIA" (8). Mollies, as sodomites were known in the eighteenth century, frequently referred to themselves and each other by means of such affectionate Maiden Names, or camp appellations. Indeed, some of these names were "prestigious"—such as Princess Seraphina and the Countess of Camomile—whereas others were suggested by physical characteristics, occupations, place of origin, or personality. Rictor Norton, *Mother Clap's Molly House: The Gay Subculture in England, 1700–1830* (London: Gay Men's Press, 1992), 92–93. That this practice would have been known to the reading public is suggested by two earlier publications. In John Dunton's *The He-Strumpets: A Satyr on the Sodomite Club* (London, 1707) the author notes that his subjects address one another as "*Sukey* (for so 'tis said you greet / The Men you pick up in the Street)"; in a letter to *The Tatler* of June 9, 1709, a writer complained of a group of Pretty Fellows calling one another Betty and Nelly who frequented such popular haunts as White's Chocolate-house and St. James's Coffee-house. Norton, *Mother Clap*, 50–51; 11.

14. Anonymous, "An Epistle from S—o to A—a R—n" (London, 1724), 2.

15. Anonymous, "An Epistle From S—r S—o to S—a F—a" (London, 1727). The plate is reprinted in Lowell Lindgren, "The Staging of Handel's Operas in London," in *Handel Tercentenary Collection*, ed. Stanley Sadie and Anthony Hicks (Ann Arbor: UMI Research Press, 1987), 101.

16. Anonymous, "F[AUSTI]NAs Answer to S[ENESI]NOs Epistle" (London, 1727).

17. Anonymous, "The Rake's Progress; or The Humours of Drury Lane" (London, 1735), 17. The plate on which the poem is based is reprinted in Daniel Heartz, "Farinelli revisited." *Early Music* 18 (1990): 439.

18. [James Miller], "Seasonable Reproof, A Satire in the Manner of Horace" (London, 1735), B1r.

19. [Constantia Phillips], "The Happy Courtezan, or, the Prude demolish'd" (London, 1735), 2–3.

20. Henry Fielding, *Eurydice, or, the Devil Henpeck'd*, in *Miscellanies by Henry Fielding, Esq.*, ed. Hugh Amory; introduction and commentary by Bertrand A. Goldgar (Middletown, Conn.: Wesleyan University Press, 1993), 2:146.

21. Ibid., 147n. The passage occurs in *Metamorphoses*, X, 79–84.

22. Henry Fielding, *The Historical Register for the Year 1736 and Eurydice Hissed*, ed. William W. Appleton (Lincoln: University of Nebraska Press, 1967), 24–25.

23. Henry Carey, "A Sorrowful Lamentation for the Loss of a Man and No Man," in *The Poems of Henry Carey*, ed. Frederick T. Wood (London: The Scholartis Press, 1930), 109.

24. On London's eighteenth-century cruising grounds see Norton, *Mother Clap*, chapter 4. That such places were known to contemporaries is owing chiefly to the tracts published by the societies for the reformation of manners between approximately 1690 and 1738. Dudley W. R. Bahlman, *The Moral Revolution of 1688* (New Haven: Yale University Press, 1957); Norton, *Mother Clap*, 44–52. Also, Laurence Senelick, "Mollies or Men of Mode? Sodomy and the Eighteenth-Century London Stage." *Journal of the History of Sexuality* 1 (1990): 42, notes that "The 1730s, a period of intensive legislation against the theatre's outspokenness, also happened to be a high-water mark of English newspaper reporting on sodomitical arrests and on the Dutch executions of seventy men for sodomy."

25. Henry Carey, "The Beau's Lamentation for the Loss of Farrinelli," in *The Poems of Henry Carey*, 110.

26. Thomas Gilbert, "The World Unmask'd," in *Poems on Several Occasions* (London, 1747), 126.

27. Anonymous, "An Epistle to John James H[ei]dd[e]ger, Esq; on the Report of Signior F[a]r[i]n[e]lli's being with Child," 5, quoted in McGeary, "Warbling Eunuchs," 13.

28. See, for example, Randolph Trumbach, "London's Sapphists: From Three Sexes to Four Genders in the Making of Modern Culture," in *Body Guards: The Cultural Politics of Gender Ambiguity*, ed. Julia Epstein and Kristina Straub (New York: Routledge, 1991), 112–141. See also McGeary, "Warbling Eunuchs," 7–8; Thomas, " 'Was George Frideric Handel Gay?' " 186.

29. Norton, *Mother Clap*, 93, however, argues that many of the mollies were neither feminine nor sexually passive—even those with extremely feminine "Maiden Names": "For example, Fanny Murray was 'an athletic Bargeman,' Lucy Cooper was 'an Herculean Coal-heaver,' and Kitty Fisher was 'a deaf tyre Smith.' " John Dunton, "The He-Strumpets: A Satyr on the Sodomite Club," sees sodomites as emerging because so many female prostitutes were infected with venereal disease. He refers to them as He-Strumpets and He-Whores given to He-Lechery and He-Lust. He even adds that, "Girls they hate," but does not state or imply that they are effeminate. See Norton, *Mother Clap*, 50–51. For nuanced treatments of male effeminacy in the period see especially Senelick, "Mollies or Men of Mode?" and Susan Staves, "A Few Kind Words for the Fop." *Studies in English Literature* 22 (1982): 413–28; see also Susan C. Shapiro, " 'Yon Plumed Dandebrat': Male 'Effeminacy' in English Satire and Criticism." *Review of English Studies* n.s. 39 (1988): 400–12.

30. John Sekora, *Luxury: The Concept in Western Thought, Eden to Smollet* (Baltimore: Johns Hopkins University Press, 1977), 68, uses this term to refer to the years from 1688 to 1756, which saw the growth of the newer commercial Britain from an older agrarian England. Richard Leppert, in "Imagery, Musical Confrontation and Cultural Difference in Early 18th-Century London," *Early Music* 14 (1986): 330, observes that early Italian opera in London was connected with political differences between certain Tories, who opposed it—to them it represented a decline in national virtue—and certain eminent Whigs, who supported it.

31. Sekora, *Luxury*, 72.

32. See ibid., 53–57; 68–72.

33. J. G. A. Pocock, *The Machiavellian Moment: Florentine Political Thought and the Atlantic Republican Tradition* (Princeton: Princeton University Press, 1975), especially chapters 13 and 14; Linda Dowling, *Hellenism and Homosexuality in Victorian Oxford* (Ithaca, N.Y.: Cornell University Press, 1994), especially chapter 1.

34. Ibid., xv.

35. Ibid., 8.

36. [John Brown], *An Estimate of the Manners and Principles of the Times* (London, 1757), 29.

37. Dennis, "An Essay upon Publick Spirit," 393–94.

38. Richard Steele, "On Nicolini's Leaving the Stage," in *Poetical Miscellanies* (London, 1714), 44–45. Donald Bond has suggested that Steele did not pen this poem; see *The Spectator*, ed. Donald Bond (Oxford: Clarendon Press, 1965), 1:514n. Indeed it seems strange Steele would write this given his earlier praise of Nicolini in the *Spectator* noted later.

39. [Henry Carey], "Faustina: or the Roman SONGSTRESS, A SATYR ON THE LUXURY AND EFFEMINACY OF THE AGE" (London, 1727).

40. Quoted in Angus Heriot, *The Castrati in Opera* (1956; reprint, London: Calder and Boyars, 1975), 94.

41. Richard Steele, quoted in ibid., 125–26.

42. Thomas, "'Was George Frideric Handel Gay?'" 188.

43. Kristina Straub, *Sexual Suspects: Eighteenth-Century Players and Sexual Ideology* (Princeton: Princeton University Press, 1992), 39, chapter 8.

44. Enid R. Peschel and Richard E. Peschel, "Medicine and Music: The Castrati in Opera." *Opera Quarterly* 4, no. 4 (1986): 27.

45. Margaret Reynolds, "Ruggiero's Deceptions, Cherubino's Distractions," in *En Travesti: Women, Gender Subversion, Opera*, eds. Corinne E. Blackmer and Patricia Smith (New York: Columbia University Press, 1995), 137. Dorothy Keyser, "Cross-Sexual Casting in Baroque Opera: Musical and Theatrical Conventions." *Opera Quarterly* 5, no. 4 (1987): 49, 51, notes that "the castrato is at the center of the most unlikely of all the baroque opera conventions—the virile heroic or romantic male lead who sings soprano or alto. The practice, which arose during the first half of the seventeenth century, became so popular that these treble heroes virtually monopolized leading male heroic and romantic roles until the end of the eighteenth century"; that in a production of *Il ratto delle Sabine* in 1680 the Roman raptors (Romolo, Ostilio, Appio, and Tazio) were all played by male trebles; and that Jacopo Peri's *Euridice*, which premiered in 1600 at the Palazzo Pitti in Florence, featured one castrato in the roles of the goddesses Venere and Proserpina and two others as the allegorical Tragedia and the male Arcetro; similarly, Keyser adds, in 1637 the first public opera house, the Teatro San Cassiano in Venice, featured Francesco Manelli's *L'Andromeda* with the goddesses Venere and Astrea sung by castrati.

46. Peschel and Peschel, "Medicine and Music," 22; moreover, Roger Covell, "Voice Register as an Index of Age and Status in Opera Seria," in *Vivaldi and Opera*, eds. Michael Collins and Elise K. Kirk (Austin: University of Texas Press, 1984), 209, notes that women played four male roles in Alessandro Scarlatti's *Pompeo* in Naples in 1684; Winton Dean, *Handel and the Opera Seria* (London: Oxford University Press, 1970), 14–15, notes that Handel's London operas feature at least twenty-six male roles written for women, and eight or nine others, originally for castrati, that the composer assigned to women in revivals.

47. Reynolds, "Ruggiero's Deceptions," 135; John Rosselli, "The Castrati as a Professional Group and a Social Phenomenon, 1550–1850." *Acta Musicologica* 60 (1988): 148, notes that the high voice perhaps derived its prestige from its association with superiority: "'Soprano' means 'higher,' a notion not taken lightly by a society that was at once intensely hierarchical-minded and accustomed to displaying hierarchical order in forms readily perceived by the senses."

48. Charles de Brosses, quoted in Peschel and Peschel, "Medicine and Music," 30; Horace Walpole, quoted in Winton Dean, "Senesino," in *The New Grove Dictionary of Music and Musicians*, ed. Stanley Sadie (London: Macmillan, 1980), 17:130.

49. Heriot, *The Castrati in Opera*, 27.

50. [Ned Ward], *The Secret History of CLUBS* (London, 1709), 284–88.

51. Anonymous, *Satan's Harvest Home: Or the Present State of Whorecraft . . . Sodomy, and the Game at Flatts* (London: 1749), 55–56. This and other passages are copied from *Plain Reasons for the Growth of Sodomy in England* (London, 1729), and

nearly the entirety of the remainder of the tract is lifted without acknowledgment from [Father Poussin's] *Pretty Doings in a Protestant Nation* (London, 1734).

52. Not surprisingly, the anonymously reprinted poem was the work of Henry Carey, originally entitled "The Effeminate." It is included in *The Poems of Henry Carey*, 111.

53. Heriot, *The Castrati in Opera*, 54. Keyser, "Cross-sexual Casting," 50, quoting a more recent translation, lends the anecdote still greater cogency: "He gives me a bold look and says that if I will spend the night with him he will serve me as a boy or a girl, whichever I choose."

54. McGeary, "Warbling Eunuchs," 13.

55. *The Memoirs of Jacques Casanova de Seingalt*, quoted in Heriot, *The Castrati in Opera*, 54–55.

56. Farinelli made his debut in Nicolo Porpora's serenata *Angelica e Medoro* in Naples, the libretto of which was the first musico-dramatic work of Metastasio; thus the two called themselves twins [*gemelli*]. Daniel Heartz, "Farinelli and Metastasio: Rival twins of public favour." *Early Music* 12 (1984): 358–59.

57. Heriot, *The Castrati in Opera*, 96.

58. Heartz, "Farinelli and Metastasio," 358–366. Heartz is silent on the question of homoeroticism. Heriot, *The Castrati in Opera*, 96, notes only that "their friendship was immediate, and lasted with increasing warmth throughout their lives."

59. Pietro Metastasio, quoted in Heartz, "Farinelli and Metastasio," 359. The translations are Charles Burney's.

60. Reproduced in Heartz, "Farinelli and Metastasio," 360.

61. Reproduced in ibid., 358.

62. Rosselli, "The Castrati as a Professional Group," 175–76.

63. George S. Rousseau, "The Pursuit of Homosexuality," in *Perilous Enlightenment: Pre- and Post-Modern Discourse, Sexual, Historical* (Manchester: Manchester University Press, 1991), 25.

64. Ibid., 41, n. 80.

65. Charles Burney, quoted in Heriot, *The Castrati in Opera*, 99.

66. Heriot, *The Castrati in Opera*, 97.

67. Thomas, " 'Was George Frideric Handel Gay?' " 167.

## Part II

## Nationhood and Sexual Difference

Romantic friendship: Adalgisa (Elena Obraztsova) and Norma (Shirley Verrett) swear eternal loyalty in Bellini's *Norma*. (Courtesy of Winnie Klotz, Metropolitan Opera.)

## CHAPTER THREE

# Farinelli's *Electronic Hermaphrodite and the Contralto Tradition*

Felicia Miller

Gender bending is hot. In academic discussions we see the rise in importance of gender and queer studies, but at a broad cultural level there is a lot of "gender trouble" in the contemporary spate of plays and films that present a sexually ambiguous character as spectacle: *Victor/Victoria*, *The Crying Game*, *Farewell My Concubine*, *M. Butterfly*, and *Farinelli*, the 1994 film about the eighteenth-century castrato. This melodrama merits interest both for the musical and cultural antecedents it recapitulates and for its extraordinary electronic facsimile of a castrato voice. The discussion here focuses on the musical traditions that subtend the film's simulation of a castrato voice as they draw from another historical curiosity, the nineteenth-century fascination with the hermaphrodite.[1] Specifically, I consider how the figure of the hermaphrodite can be linked to the phenomenon of the pleasure of an ambiguously gendered voice. In the French cultural context the never-well-received castrato voice gave way to the female voice with bel canto, the imported music that, ironically enough, played a role in opera's contributions to the sense of national identity. With this music rose the fortunes of the contralto voice. The voice of Pauline Viardot as Orpheus and the dually gendered voice in *Farinelli*, operatic hermaphrodites both, exemplify culturally confounded positions that offer a particular pleasure between and across gender definitions and boundaries.

# The Hermaphrodite

F. Miller

The exhibition of photographs by the nineteenth-century photographer Nadar held recently in Paris and New York takes the visitor through a rogue's gallery of legendary personalities such as Balzac, George Sand, and Baudelaire. The photograph seems to offer the truth of character, a notion pursued in the medical and legal discourses of Nadar's time. From the 1860s on, experiments with photography to determine criminal type would find their place in the medicalization of criminology. This was the period of Lombroso's photographic atlas of criminal types and of Charcot's theatrically posed hysterics.[2] Likewise, Daniel Arasse, in discussing photographs of guillotined heads at this time, links the guillotine with the camera as Foucauldian apparatuses of social control and analysis.[3] The first photographs in the catalogue are a series of studies in electrically induced facial expressions with titles such as "Pain," "Displeasure," "Terror," that illustrated Dr. Duchenne and Nadar's *Mechanism of Human Physiognomy* (1854).

The last rooms of the Nadar exhibition offer documentation of a different sort in the photographs of the Paris sewers and catacombs, models for helicopters, and the final surprise of the "crotch shot" of a hermaphrodite. The subject's muscular legs are spread, double genitalia exposed by another's hand in a vulnerable close-up. As if to hide his/her shame or identity, the subject's face is averted, covered by a protecting arm. In "Beyond the Portrait, Beyond the Artist" Sylvie Aubenas notes that Nadar took a series of nine photographs of this hermaphrodite sometime before 1861. Little is known about the series, but Aubenas suggests it was commissioned by Armand Trousseau, head of clinical medicine at the Hôtel Dieu. Aubenas indicates that Nadar owned books about hermaphroditism and was interested in Saint Wilgeforte, a bearded woman martyr. Androgyny was a fascination for many of the time, most famously for George Sand, and for Gautier in *Mlle de Maupin* and in the poem "Contralto."

In "Le Vrai Sexe," Foucault speaks of the nineteenth-century conception of truth as found in "sex," or, as we would say, gender.[4] In his introduction to the *Journal of Herculine Barbin*, Foucault writes of Alexina's pleasure in "her" own ambiguous state in the paradise of a girl's convent, a condition that turned to painful exile after she came under the control of the medical gaze with its demand for a fixed truth. Judged to be male, Alexina took the name Herculine, attempted to live as a man, and eventually committed suicide. Foucault points here to the nineteenth-century insistence that sex be singular. The clinical gaze joins forces with the camera to seek a single truth, with sexual identity seen as key to the truth of identity itself. The relative tolerance for sexual ambiguity of earlier times was lost. Sexual irregularity was now perceived to belong to "the world of chimerae," a notion that would persist.[5] Foucault remarks in conclusion that the late nineteenth century was haunted by the theme of the hermaphrodite, as the eighteenth century had been by that of travesty.

## Farinelli, Il Castrato

Focusing on opera, the film *Farinelli, Il Castrato* refers to eighteenth-century travesty in its story of the famous castrato while creating an electronic hermaphrodite on the soundtrack. Together with historical elements drawn from the singer's life, the script engages in free inventions of Farinelli's relations with his older brother, the composer Riccardo Broschi, and Handel. The film harnesses the qualities of excess associated with the castrati so as to present Farinelli as a sexy, tormented character in the service of a plot that obeys Hollywood codes offering predictable narrative closure in the creation of a heterosexual couple (seen joyously expecting a baby at that). The historical Farinelli, Carlo Broschi, was quite different. Unlike most castrati, he came not from an impoverished family, but from an aristocratic and musically educated one. According to Patrick Barbier, Salvatore Broschi, the boy's father, took a calculated risk for his son's career when he decided to have him castrated. He knew the dangers, both physically and musically, because most castrated boys lost the beauty of their voices anyway. The father also saw, however, the stellar opportunities castration could open to musical talents.[6]

In the film the castration is dramatized for modern audiences as a horrifying event to the boy, who resists it and then keenly experiences his loss as a source of permanent trauma. A common excuse at the time for the operation was "a fall" that "required" it to save a boy's life. In the film the image of a white horse recurs in flashbacks as Carlo's nightmare; his brother had told him the story of a boy who rides too close to Helios and falls (Icarus?) to comfort him in his opium-induced delirium after the operation. The film binds the brothers in a nearly incestuous closeness, professionally, Riccardo writing only for Carlo's voice, and sexually, for they share women: "C'est le pacte, Madame." The drama turns on Farinelli's break with his brother on learning (from Handel, no less) that the responsibility for his castration belongs to Riccardo, seen as parasitically attached to the talented Carlo. The film symbolizes Riccardo's mediocrity in his inability to complete an *Orpheo*, intended to be their "joint masterpiece." In fact, Carlo frequently helped his struggling brother, sending him money, making him guardian of his estate, and occasionally singing his compositions. The portrayal of Handel in the film ascribes to him a fictional contempt for the castrato voice, dramatized as an eroticized struggle for power, represented by the composer's withheld esteem. Their struggle ends when, in eroticized surrender, he breaks out in a sweat and faints away while Farinelli performs "Lascia qu'io pianga" from Handel's *Rinaldo*.

Barbier's account of the conduct and temperament of the historical Farinelli little resembles the turbulent character presented in the film, whose frustration makes him an opium addict, prone to fits of pique and imperious behavior, but also a sexual artiste. Contrary to the stereotype of the male prima donna, Carlo Broschi seems to have been a dedicated professional. The very delicacy of his manner and his exaggerated modesty may have

75

*Farinelli*'s
Electronic
Hermaphrodite
and the
Contralto
Tradition

contributed to his success. He was unfailingly generous to his colleagues, courteous to all, and conscientious in his commitments, able to negotiate the social intricacies of life among theater people and aristocrats alike, among whom he lived and worked. Although he worried about his health, he withstood a demanding schedule of frequent travel and extended engagements, more workhorse than temperamental prima donna. While in London he wrote in a letter: "The life I lead since setting foot in London consists in keeping my mouth open all the time, so that I amaze myself and wonder how I manage to keep going."[7]

The portraits of Farinelli in Barbier's book and contemporary descriptions show a man of almost feminine delicacy of mien. Paintings of him render his features with the pink and white beauty favored by eighteenth-century tastes. As Todd Gilman shows in his article in the present volume, some women found castrati to be extremely attractive[8]; Barbier notes that aristocratic women in particular appreciated this delicacy and the built-in sexual freedom the castrati offered. The operation did not necessarily interfere with sexual function, and some castrati were kept from marrying only by the church's injunction against sterile unions. Gilman cites a poem by Constantia Phillips that refers to Farinelli's "sweet beardless chin" and "rosy cheeks," the "agreeable and melodious sweetness" of his speaking voice. The historical Farinelli exploited this quality of a Jungian *puer eternus*, using the picture of an angel as a signature stamp for his letters throughout his life. He was a solitary figure, moreover. Barbier notes his extreme *pudeur* and the impression of solitude that emerges from his letters, finding little in the way of possible liaisons: a crush he shared with a ballerina in 1733, which produced some frustration to which he refers obliquely, and what Barbier calls his "more than friendly" attachment to his student, Teresa Castellini, at the court of Madrid.

Tracing the association of the castrato in the English mind with the "effeminate sodomite," Gilman contends that the castrato is constructed as a more complex figure: "he becomes also the (excessively) manly heterosexual and the unmanly (excessive) heterosexual—for lack of a less anachronistic term—all by virtue of the confusion he creates through the overlap of his various significations. . . . Thus we should see the reception of the castrato, his status as a signifier, as embodying a more general fear: the fear that the castrato's excessive, uncontainable gender exposed the contingent nature of gender and sexuality."[9]

The film translates for modern heterosexual tastes the femininized yet hypersexual quality attributed to the castrato. The Farinelli it presents is very tall (as the castrati sometimes were), with dark, wavy hair left unbound to fall to shoulder length, a handsome yet fine face by modern standards often whitened with greasepaint, full lips pinkened, even offstage. Farinelli's dress is feminized too: he is shown wearing white scarves and pink vests. His musical conquests are paired with sexual ones. At one performance an imperious Farinelli halts everything in order to force an aristocratic *précieuse*, reading a book and clinking her teacup, to pay attention. Such a demand is, of course, anachronistic, since audiences of the time were neither quietly attentive nor expected to be. It was not until the nineteenth century that respectful silence became part of what James Johnson calls the audience's "horizon of expectations."[10]

77

*Farinelli*'s

Electronic

Hermaphrodite

and the

Contralto

Tradition

In the film the embarrassed countess listens, moist-eyed (as his listeners are often shown), experiencing what she later calls her "first musical orgasm." She sends him the present not only of an expensive necklace, but of the maid who places it around his neck. Farinelli takes the provocative visitor to bed, where he artfully excites her to orgasm, whereupon his brother enters the room, wearing the token of the brothers' "pact," the often seen red velvet robe. Carlo rises and puts on the robe and watches while Riccardo, who takes his place in the bed "completes" the act with his reproductively potent ejaculation. The latter's "Italian" sexuality and musical style are underscored by the casting of Riccardo: the actor Enrico Lo Verso has strongly marked Italian features and usually speaks Italian, whereas Stéphano Dionisi, who plays Farinelli, more often speaks French. Blue rings worn by both brothers link them visually, and Riccardo makes explicit to Handel the fact that "music unites us, better than lovers." As the countess puts it, "Farinelli procures *la jouissance* [orgasm, pleasure], Riccardo provides *la sémence* [semen], together the brothers Broschi are entirely formidable." The *Sight and Sound* review remarks, "Farinelli turns out to be a bit of a stud, who, it is true, can't plant the seed, but nonetheless ploughs the field satisfactorily beforehand."[11] The film demands that sex lead to the biological end of reproductive possibility. Thus the film is heavily invested in the theme of a very (hetero)sexual yet frustrated Farinelli, wounded particularly by his inability to have children and irked by his bonds, sexual and musical, with his brother. *Farinelli* insistently recuperates the sexuality of the castrato figure to a normative heterosexual model, linking it to his liberation from the florid, highly ornamented style of Porpora and Riccardo.

The general shock of Farinelli singing Handel's music in public during this time of intense competition between Porpora and Handel is paired in the film with Farinelli's personal shock on learning the "truth" of his castration. Next seen in Spain, Farinelli has formed a couple with an ardent admirer, Alexandra, who has given up everything for "this senseless love." Presumably, her love is *irraisonable* because of Farinelli's sterility, which the narrative logic of the film corrects by closing with the brothers' reconciliation, sealed by their temporary resumption of the pact in order to inseminate Alexandra. The film ends with Farinelli seen ecstatically kissing her pregnant belly while a voice-over by Riccardo, intercut with shots of him riding off through a desert Spanish landscape, bids him a fond farewell, "having restored to you your share of humanity." By emphasizing the horror of castration and spicing up the story with titillating scenes of sexual threesomes, the film provides suitable closure. Apparently, the end justifies the means on several levels in what *Sight and Sound* calls the film's "pure old Hollywood" melodramatic embroidery.[12]

The film beautifully conveys artifice, however, in its use of theatrical *mise-en-scène* to re-create the extravagance of Baroque staging. Artifice as theme and device dominates this film about a castrato, whose artificial voice exploits the display of technical virtuosity. The camera lovingly displays Farinelli in performance as he descends from a gloried empyreum in a chariot as a god to gasps and acclaim from the audience, or sings "Son qual nave qu'agitata" ["Like a boat tossed"] against a moving sea, shown in countershot from behind as stage machinery: painted wooden paddles rotating on a wheel. Richly costumed, heavily made up in white paint and red lipstick, wearing enormous multicolored plumed headdresses in orange and gray, or black, blue, and silver, Farinelli resembles nothing more closely than a gorgeous bird.

The film's use of the spectacular theatrical machinery of the period reinforces the subtext of the singer's voice as artifice itself, employing bird imagery to convey this idea. Porpora had, in fact, taught Carlo Broschi to imitate bird song as part of his musical training; and bird song, like storms and battles, was a referent audiences looked for and recognized in operatic singing. The familiar topos of the singer as exotic bird underscores the exotic and artificial strangeness of the castrato's trilling voice. Farinelli is shown at one point with a painted bird's wing mechanically opening and closing behind his head, releasing a dove while singing Rinaldo's "Cara sposa" ("Dear wife"). A huge peacock slowly unfurls its brilliant tail as he sings "Lascia qu'io pianga" ("Let me lament"), Almirena's song from the same opera. Farinelli thus sings in turn love arias by both parties of *Rinaldo*'s separated couple.

The scene shows him turning away from the excessive ornamentation in Porpora and his brother's music to embrace Handel's stylistically restrained but emotionally intense music. The film condenses its preoccupation with artifice in a series of shots that cut from Handel fainting with emotion ("you will be the greatest of singers if you can evoke any emotion from me, what none of your kind has ever been able to do") to a "flashback" of Carlo as a drugged boy, sitting in a tub of milky ice water, Salmacis's pool, as it were (a shot seen often throughout the film as the sign of his trauma). Blood visibly upwells in the white water (perhaps a sign of the semen Carlo cannot produce). The film then cuts to a close-up of Farinelli on stage, face whitened with greasepaint, red lips opened in song.

Handel's *Rinaldo*, though, far from being exemplary of music as in some way natural or simple, turns on the Baroque spectacle afforded by the tale: the sorceress Armida makes mischief key to the story, producing a magic boat, sirens, a bewitched wood, monsters and spirits.[13] The opera exploits her supernatural powers of trickery to generate its plot, justify marvelous effects in staging, and provide a number of bravura pieces. Farinelli sings one such set piece in the film: "Venti, turbini" ["Winds and storms"].

The film writes into its version of the rivalry between Porpora and Handel in London a false rejection by Handel of the castrato voice. In fact, he wrote regularly for castrato voice, albeit for the contraltist rather than the sopranist voice typified by Farinelli. Nonetheless, the film distills in this rivalry the actual shift in taste taking place away from excessive ornamentation during Farinelli's time. As Barbier notes, the historical Farinelli himself embraced this stylistic turn. As a young man he had dazzled audiences with his tremendous range, his easy passage between extremes in register without *portamento*, his perfectly even trills. To his sure technique he added carefully prepared and original cadenzas and tastefully placed ornamentations. One of his patrons was Emperor Charles of Austria, who offered the criticism the film ascribes to Handel, urging Farinelli to go beyond vocal fireworks, to adopt a more simple and tranquil method in order truly to "ravish hearts." Barbier notes that Farinelli took the lesson and afterward used a more simple, supple technique, privileging pathos, tenderness, and feeling in general. He notes, moreover, that, "After the years 1740–1750, many castrati followed this route in any case, as the purely 'baroque' period . . . yielded to classical moderation: Guadagni, Pacchiarotti, Rauzzini, Rubinelli would famously exemplify this new art of singing during the second half of the century."[14] The musical sea-change the film attributes to the genius of Handel belongs more accurately to the stylistic departure of Gluck's reforms, inaugurated in his *Orpheus*, written for Guadagni. Farinelli remains, however, the most famous exponent of the castrato voice and its remarkable fluidity.

The voice of Farinelli in the film was painstakingly constructed through an elaborate electronic manipulation and fusion of recorded tenor and soprano voices. Terry Nelson gives an account of how the Belgian director Gérard Corbiau undertook to re-create the effect of a castrato voice electronically with the help of musicologist Marc David, conductor Christophe Russet, and recording engineer Jean-Claude Gaberel. The filmmaker proposed "the slightly crazy project . . . [requiring] lots of work and lots of patience" of recording a Baroque orchestra with two separate voices, countertenor and coloratura soprano. The recordings were then to be re-edited to form the playback for the shooting of the film. The initial effort of multitracking was not sensitive enough to the interplay of voice and orchestra, so Gaberel effected the recording eventually by having both soprano Ewa Mallas Godlewska and countertenor Derek Lee Ragin record the arias individually, then edited them together electronically. On the computer the engineers modified the timbre of the soprano parts through audio "morphing." They selected for the "boyish" quality of the voice through global modifications, attenuating the higher frequencies to reduce breathiness and "brighten" the spectral envelope.[15] After seven months of intensive editing at the Institut de Recherche et Coordination Acoustique/Musique (IRCAM), the engineers attained the desired vocal qualities for "Farinelli," allowing them to turn at last to a final mix with the orchestral tracks.

79

*Farinelli*'s

Electronic

Hermaphrodite

and the

Contralto

Tradition

Why go to such effort? Why give the voice of Farinelli the Industrial Sound and Magic treatment? The castrato voice, with its legendary range and suppleness, its power to sustain phrases longer than 200 notes, which adapted it to the virtuosic *fiorituri* demanded by the eighteenth-century music of Porpora, Handel, and others, no longer exists; much of the castrati's repertoire is now considered unsingable. In its historical focus, the film recalls, albeit distortedly, the importance of the castrato in opera generally, the rivalry between Porpora and Handel in London, and Farinelli as a figure in particular. A key part of this film's interest, however, lies in its play upon our fascination with gender ambiguity at the theatrical site of opera.

## The Contralto, the Hermaphrodite, and Gender Ambiguity

As a late-twentieth-century product, *Farinelli* attests to our continuing interest in the ambiguously gendered voice.[16] At the same time, the film obliquely reflects the eventual demise of the castrato, superseded by the female voice in the nineteenth century. Its double-gendered role was taken over by the contralto voice associated with Pauline Viardot, who embodied this hermaphroditic voice of the nineteenth century.

In a recent radio interview Marilyn Horne spoke of how this tradition derived from the castrato voice. Referring to the travesty roles she often sang, Horne cited the roles Rossini specifically wrote for a woman singer in travesty. His aim was to achieve a certain effect in duets between such a singer and a soprano: their interwoven trills produced a textural effect he and his audiences found particularly pleasing. Later he relinquished that style, but in our century, bel canto was revived by Maria Callas and taken up by Joan Sutherland, who sought partners capable of singing such roles. To some extent Horne attributes her professional success to her ability to occupy this niche. She also referred to the song of the grieving lady from Handel's *Rinaldo* as among the most beautiful and stately songs ever written. The reference can only be to Almirena's "Lascia qu'io pianga," which Farinelli sings in the film.[17]

Pauline Viardot was a key figure in the development of the female contralto voice. One can trace a musical filiation through her to Porpora, Farinelli, and Horne: the young Carlo Broschi studied with Porpora for five years in his home, as was the usual practice.[18] As a performer Broschi assumed the stage name Farinelli, the traditional diminutive of his master's name, Porporino, having already been assumed by another student. Years later, Viardot's father, Manuel García, himself a singer, furthered his musical training as an adult in Italy by seeking out the remaining proponents of the Porpora school. While in Italy he created the role of Almaviva in Rossini's *Barber of Seville*, possibly composing his own bravura arias. In the imagination of nineteenth-century writers Porpora remained an emblem of Italian art in song. (George Sand and Gérard de Nerval both evoke Porpora in their fiction.[19])

A harsh master, García trained his own children musically: the legendary, short-lived María Malibran; his son, who became known as a singing teacher and recorded his father's method; and Pauline. Although Pauline initially studied piano with Liszt, after María's death Pauline's mother told her she would be a singer, not a pianist. This instruction apparently provoked nothing more than a slight *moué* from the even-tempered young woman. Viardot herself would later be known as a knowledgeable proponent of "antique Italian song" and performed arias by Handel and other eighteenth-century composers in Paris as part of the contemporary revival of such music. Appearing with her rival, Jenny Lind, at a series of concerts in Coblenz in 1844 in honor of Queen Victoria, Viardot sang an aria from *Rinaldo*, perhaps one sung by Farinelli in the film.

81

*Farinelli*'s

Electronic

Hermaphrodite

and the

Contralto

Tradition

Despite her acknowledged fine musicianship, praise of her genius in reviews by Gautier and Musset (who compared her art with that of Rachel), and the high regard of Liszt, Berlioz, and many others, Viardot did not achieve success initially in Paris. She sought to avoid the trap of the contralto niche, because her extraordinary range also suited her for the starring soprano parts. But she could not do so at the Paris Opera, where these roles went first to the well-established Grisi and Persiani and later to Rosine Stoltz, mistress of Léon Pillet, director of the Opera.

As a young woman, Viardot was criticized for being plain. The Parisians may have preferred prettier heroines, but resistance to Viardot was also political, at least after 1841. Her husband's collaboration with George Sand and Pierre Leroux in creating the journal *La Revue Indépendante* damaged her politically, and she was subsequently shut out of the Opera by cabals or was harshly reviewed. Attributing her bad reviews to this cause, Louis Viardot defended her in a letter to the editor: "There are some generous-hearted people who strike a woman in order to injure a man."[20] Consequently, Viardot built her career mainly abroad, first in London, then in St. Petersburg, Madrid, Vienna, and Berlin; she returned to France to rest and occasionally to do concerts. She sang in *Othello* at the Odéon as a result of her husband's work in establishing the Théâtre-Italien there. She also sang *La Cenerentola*, but not until 1848 did she work again at the Paris Opera. The height of Viardot's Parisian success came for her as Orpheus in the revival of Gluck's first "reform" opera, the work originally written for a contralto castrato voice and intended, in the simplicity of its writing, to lead away from the highly ornamented, florid style typified by Farinelli.

Michel Poizat has noted the importance[21] in the history of opera of the castrato voice as the angelic voice, heard as uncannily *hors sexe* ("beyond sex").[22] In France, however, the castrato was never well received, even in works by Gluck, and by the nineteenth century its privileged place was divided between the (newly codified) tenor and soprano voices, with the female voice granted preeminence in bel canto. Although Viardot's repertoire changed over the course of her long career, her debuts were associated in particular with Rossini's music. Like Farinelli, she had an extraordinary and sure range, noted by Gautier in his review of her debut performance.[23] Dulong writes:

> Pauline Viardot's voice was first striking for its expressive intensity. . . . One was immediately moved, conquered, possessed. And then one noticed the exceptionally extensive resources of her vocal organ. Music critics measure pedantically the extremes. . . . Three and a half octaves, one says, carried away by enthusiasm. . . . Let us accept . . . Berlioz['s assessment], according to [which] Pauline's voice had as its limits low F and high C, say, two octaves and a fifth . . . her voice was, as Berlioz says, "equal in all registers, true, vibrant and agile."[24]

This description closely resembles the descriptions of Farinelli's voice as Barbier cites them: "One found his voice surprising, because perfect, efficient, and sonorous in quality and rich in its range from the deepest notes to the highest, the equal of which one has never heard today."[25] Dulong quotes critic Ludwig Rellstab's characterization of Viardot's voice as "a blend of soprano and tenor, such that the low register has an affinity with the cello and the high with the piano."[26] This quality of a dually gendered voice impressed Gautier, who wrote a poem entitled "Contralto," which initially appeared in the *Revue des Deux Mondes* in 1849 and was included in *Emaux et Camées* in 1852.

The poem takes as its point of departure a visual evocation of the statue *Sleeping Hermaphrodite* in the Louvre, which Gautier calls "an enigmatic statue of disquieting beauty." He wonders whether it is a man or a woman, but attributes to it the beauty of each sex. The poet praises the "multiple beauty" of the "charming monster," "the ardent chimera"), and avows, "you have preoccupied me for many nights." "Modulating" to the auditory register, he finds both girl and boy in its metamorphosis and praises the contralto:

> How you please me, oh strange timbre
> Double sound, at once man and woman!
> Contralto, bizarre melange
> Hermaphrodite of the voice!

Gautier then adduces a list of contralto roles, almost all, except for Zerlina, from Rossini operas: Cinderella, Tancredi, Arsace, Malcolm. These roles match those that Gautier imagined for Viardot in his review of her debut.

Commenting on Nerval's "Sylvie" and the contralto voice in *The Writing of Melancholy*, Ross Chambers asks astutely:

> The question . . . is whether, with respect to the categories of male and female, or feminine and masculine, the contralto quality Nerval attributes to the female voice that figures his own suicidal writing signifies a *neither/nor* consequent on the attenuation of gender difference, or whether it means rather, as Gautier's poem certainly suggests . . . a both/and that maintains and enforces gender difference by

grounding it in the supposed biological givens of sexual differentiation. Does the hermaphroditic quality of the contralto voice affirm
the fungibility of gender difference and maintain that difference by
affirming a sexual *coincidentia oppositorum*?[27]

Chambers cautions that despite the possibility of imagining this voice as a
site of gender indeterminacy that:

83

*Farinelli*'s

Electronic

Hermaphrodite

and the

Contralto

Tradition

> *[S]exual* difference is maintained, as in Gautier's interpretation of the
> contralto, and with it—by virtue of the sex-gender system—gender
> distinctions as well. . . . A feminization of the male subject productive
> of a hermaphroditic *coincidentia oppositorum* . . . does not deny him his
> maleness. [emphasis in text]

Yes or no? True or false? Chambers's reading of Nerval that delicately places
the shimmering balance of the "both/and" within a system that enforces an
"either/or" opposition is congruent with Louis Marin's discussion in "Sex
Neither True nor False, Or, Hermaphrodite Seized by the Neuter."

Starting from the myth as told in Ovid's *Metamorphoses* (IV, 358–394),
Marin suggests that the myth "traverses with a refined grace the whole axis
of the relation of masculine and feminine, and covers the whole field of the
relations of opposition and of complementarity that the generic term of sexual difference deploys, to end in the hybrid man-woman: Herme-(es)-
aphrodite."[28] Marin proposes that this body "operated on" by the violence of
love and a linguistic imprecation, by the adding together of the two sexes and
their secondary characteristics, "operates" simultaneously the synthesis of
contraries. The tale seems to show the "secret work of the neuter." Neither
concept nor category, the neuter emerges out of the reversal of concepts,
within the relation's "gap" [*écart*].

Ovid names Hermaphroditus only after the nymph violates the boy,
forcing him into a coitus that costs him his virility. The *puer* becomes *vir* at
the expense of his *virilitas*. Reading Hermaphroditus etymologically, Marin
notes how Hermes and Aphrodite mutually penetrate and nullify each other
in their offspring's name. The metamorphosis effected in the medium of the
"indifferent water," the nymph's pool, figures this indifference: the water,
bearing no mark of memory, neither true nor false, is the opposite of
Narcissus's pool. Showing no sign, trace, or memory—impotent—the
water is yet pure sign, trace, and memory, creating the "half-man," part boy,
part nymph, who leaves it, doubly neutralized. *Neutrumque et utrumque
videntur*: they seem neither one nor the other, both one and the other.

Not the dream of plenitude symbolized by the sphere of reunited opposites, Hermaphrodite is the forced grafting of two forever unfulfilled opposites. Marin explores the notion that Hermaphrodite embodies the destruction of both masculine and feminine as categories in an "indefinite abyssal
space," Kant's "indeterminate."[29] This is "the space of infinity of the unnameable zero, of the 'neither true nor false,' compelled to displace it cease-

lessly in the apparatuses of representations of sexual difference."[30] In this gesture of Derridean *différance*,[31] Marin finally reads Hermaphroditus not as figuring the abolition of difference, the creation of an unthinkable third sex, but as dramatizing the oscillation of difference in a space of negativity bound by its semantic definitions.

In *Gender Trouble* Judith Butler discusses gender within the binary frame. In her argument that gender is performative not substantive, she takes up the figure of the hermaphrodite, specifically Herculine Barbin as read by Foucault. Butler asserts that "[h]is analysis implies the interesting belief that sexual heterogeneity (paradoxically foreclosed by a naturalized 'hetero'-sexuality) implies a critique of the metaphysics of substance as it informs the identitarian categories of sex."[32] For her Foucault does not go far enough: to undo the regime of gender it is necessary to dispense with "man" and "woman" as abiding substance and locate the production of gender in performative repetition. Butler finds that in failing to interrogate "sex" as a category, Foucault reinscribes the regulatory system he seeks to expose.

A look at Foucault's 1980 version of this piece, published as "Le Vrai Sexe" in *Arcadie*, does not entirely support this interpretation. After discussing the medical preoccupation with sexuality in 1860–1870, he states:

> I know perfectly well that the medicine of the 19th and 20th century has corrected many things in this reductive simplism. No one would say today that all hermaphrodites are "pseudo," even if one limits considerably a domain in which one placed earlier many diverse anatomical anomalies. The possibility is also admitted—with much difficulty besides—for an individual to adopt a sex that is not biologically his own.[33]

Such statements do not seem to reflect a reified model of sexual singularity.

Some of Butler's criticism of Foucault may lie in a problem of translation: the word *gender* as we understand it in English does not work in French: *genre* means "category"; it usually suggests literary genre to French speakers. This problem of translation may account for some of the difficulties American gender theorists have had among French-speaking feminist writers. In *Nomadic Subjects* Rosi Braidotti historicizes the "stalemate" in discussions between continental and Anglophone feminists during the 1980s, noting the "increasing awareness of the culture-specific forms undertaken by feminist theory." She points out that "the notion of 'gender' is a vicissitude of the English language, one that bears little or no relevance to theoretical traditions in the Romance languages. As such, it has found no successful echo in the French, Spanish, or Italian feminist movements. For example, in French *'le genre'* can be used to refer to humanity as a whole . . . it is a culture-specific term and consequently untranslatable."[34] Braidotti argues on this basis that the sex/gender distinction on which Anglophone feminist theory relies does not make sense, epistemologically or politically. In non-Western, non-Anglophone contexts, notions of "sexuality" and "sexual difference" are used instead. If Foucault does not interrogate sexuality from Butler's standpoint, he may not be falling into the biological reductivism that Butler ascribes to him, for the language in which he thinks itself renders it difficult to articulate gender separately from "sex."

In her reading Butler argues that it is the conventions of female homosexuality that underpin Herculine's story, that stories of forbidden loves "produce" this seemingly unconventional sexuality. Butler reads in the text "an irresolvable ambivalence produced by the juridical discourse on univocal sex. . . . we fail to discover multiplicity, as Foucault would have us do; instead, we confront a fatal ambivalence, produced by the prohibitive law, which for all its effects of happy dispersal nevertheless culminates in Herculine's suicide."[35] She appropriates Herculine for female homosexuality and pinpoints Foucault's use of the term of nonidentity as a move that refuses to Herculine a female homosexual discursive position. According to Butler, Foucault would thereby be obliged to engage the category of sex, which he in fact wants the narrative to move us to reject. She reads in this "nonidentity" the work of the prohibition of homosexuality that produces apparently transgressive pleasures. With regard to Herculine's self-characterization as a "usurper" of masculine prerogative, she writes that this language suggests:

> a participation in the very categories from which s/he feels inevitably distanced, suggesting also the denaturalized and fluid possibilities of such categories once they are no longer linked . . . to the presumed fixity of sex. Herculine's anatomy does not fall outside the categories of sex, but confuses and redistributes the constitutive elements of those categories.[36]

Interestingly, Butler refers to the hermaphrodite as Herculine, the adopted male name, whereas Foucault uses the original female name Alexina. In its confusion of categories, the hermaphrodite seems ready-made to be read through each reader's particular preferences. Butler asks:

> If homosexuality produces sexual nonidentity, then homosexuality itself no longer relies on identities being *like* one another; indeed, homosexuality could no longer be described as such. But if homosexuality is meant to designate the place of an *unnameable* libidinal heterogeneity, perhaps we can ask whether this is, instead, a love that either cannot or dare not speak its name?[37] [emphasis in text]

Butler reads in Foucault the desire for a utopian space of sexual multiplicity that she has earlier ascribed to him. The passage recalls Marin's "unnameable zero," an impossible-to-articulate third gender in a negative space, here placed under cover of a denied homosexuality. Thus Butler herself seems unable to resist claiming for Herculine a feminine marking. In discussing Irigaray's articulation of the false binary logic of phallagocentrism, she notes the unrepresentability of the female sex in this economy, and goes on to say that "[i]t is not 'one' in the sense that it is multiple and diffuse in its

85

*Farinelli*'s
Electronic
Hermaphrodite
and the
Contralto
Tradition

pleasures and its signifying mode. Indeed, perhaps Herculine's apparently multiplicitous pleasures would qualify for the mark of the feminine in its polyvalence and in its refusal to submit to the reductive efforts of univocal signification."[38] Quickly stepping back from this claim, to return to the surer ground of ambivalence, Butler concludes that the hermaphrodite cannot finally step outside the law. Nevertheless, her desire to frame this narrative within a female homosexual reading parallels Foucault's own use of it as she reads him.

At the end of *Gender Trouble* Butler argues on behalf of parodic play with gender as a performative mode that may create an emancipatory space. Along with the intriguing practices of gender crossing in theatrical travesty and the pleasures of drag performance that Butler discusses, one might add opera, which incorporates both. Her theory makes a suggestive frame for a discussion of opera as a performative site that often seems to serve as an escape from gender. Although this theory of gender performativity may account for some of the fascination with the performed ambiguity of travesty, as of the hermaphroditic voice, the theory cannot be applied wholesale to opera. It is necessarily limited by the caveats and difficulties posed when the materials are taken in a historical context. Film theorists who have tested melodrama as a space for the expression of female desire found this possibility to be ultimately qualified by its place within the Hollywood paradigm. Opera is a public art, a very expensive and officially sanctioned entertainment. As a sanctioned site of artifice and transgression, it offers certain transgressive pleasures with seemingly little risk. As Gilman argues, however, this license is liable to be sharply contested.

## French Opera and Nationality

Music cannot be viewed as separate from its ideological and social functions.[39] Along with Herbert Lindenberger and others, Jacques Attali notes that opera in the nineteenth century, no longer an aristocratic property, was directed toward a bourgeois public.[40] The stakes were not merely aesthetic or about the prerogatives of the nouveaux riches; they were highly political. In *The Nation's Image: French Grand Opera as Politics and as Politicized Art*, Jane Fulcher details the public and contested role played by opera as a focal point for political emotion and imagery, a situation fraught with conflict as the difficulties of opera's reception were compounded by the effects of revolution and reaction. Ironically enough, the national image that the Paris Opera sought to project was dominated by international opera, namely, the imported music of Rossini and the bel canto style in the 1830s and, later, the crowd-pleasing formulas of Giacomo Meyerbeer, a German.

Pauline Viardot, the singer whose career is emblematic of the fortunes of the contralto voice, reentered the Paris scene in the context created by the events of 1848, when the Paris Opera became the Théâtre de la Nation. Viardot's biographer, Gustave Dulong, believes that the progressive couple followed the political events of February with "an ardent sympathy." Viardot associated herself with the new Republic, participating in a competition of "national song" instituted shortly after the establishment of the provisional government. Her *Cantate pour la Jeune République* was performed on April 6, 1848, with words by Pierre Dupont at the Théâtre Français, renamed the Théâtre de la République. Written for tenor, it also featured a chorus of fifty young girls dressed in white muslin with tri-colored sashes. Dupont's name is firmly associated with Republicanism: Siegfried Kracauer writes that of the worker-poets who appeared in 1845, "[T]he best of them was undoubtedly Pierre Dupont, who sang of country life, the poverty of the people, and the beauty of the social revolution."[41] Viardot's use of Dupont's lyrics for the cantata thus underscores her political stance in 1848.

87

*Farinelli*'s

Electronic

Hermaphrodite

and the

Contralto

Tradition

Viardot returned to London to sing in Meyerbeer's *Huguenots*; Dulong writes, "In London, people declared that the old Italian repertoire was finished."[42] In 1849 she performed at the Opera in Paris to acclaim as Fidès in Meyerbeer's *The Prophet*. The circumstances surrounding this production were turbulent, for the public read the drama allegorically. Fulcher notes that although government intervention at the Opera of 1848 had been "a brief aberration from an otherwise commercial institution," the Opera's efforts to project a particular national image fell subject to confusion and contradictions, becoming in 1849 the "nexus for the contestation of class" opened by the revolutions of 1848.[43]

Strategic choices in subject matter and composer backfired because of the effects of delay and "unforeseen modes of construal and the Republic's political shifts." Fulcher argues that the Second Republic's manipulation of the Opera continued in the production of Meyerbeer's *The Prophet* in 1849, which became "the matrix for a heated political debate that in turn brought about a change in direction in operatic policies and intent."[44] Despite attempts by the Opera to control with care the meaning of the production at its premiere, *The Prophet* proved controversial because of the parallels with contemporary events the public read into the drama. Dulong emphasizes the highly politicized reception of the drama, which focuses on John of Leyden and the Anabaptist revolt, an uprising interpreted by many as an allegory of contemporary political and class conflicts.[45] Fulcher writes:

> The choice of symbols . . . now involved not only the problem of expressing an anonymous, collective, depersonalized and "desacralized" power, but also that of communicating directly with a new, unsophisticated electorate. . . . Images were charged with communicating political ideas and thus entered into a complex counterpoint with other modes of discourse. . . . Once again, the problems of artistic and political definition were integrally intertwined as the nation attentively awaited the new regime's symbolic self-definition.[46]

Social and political crises surrounded the production of *The Prophet*. On the day of the premiere, the Assemblée Nationale began a debate over the expeditionary force sent to protect French republicans in Rome. An outbreak of cholera in the city during an unusually hot summer nearly bankrupted the theaters. But Viardot benefited: in the role of Fidès, she shone, in contrast to the bland prophet. Her musicianship impressed all and offended no one.

Despite her success, Viardot's contract with the Opera was revoked in 1851. The political winds had shifted enough to the right for the political associations of those active in the 1848 actions to become a liability. In 1849, reports Dulong, a rightist journal, *La Patrie*, published hostile remarks, to which Louis Viardot responded in a letter to the editor in which he defended his hospitality to political exiles and insisted on his wife's detachment from politics.

But Viardot was not simply an artist abstractly absorbed in her art. An old friend of George Sand, she shared her political convictions, as publicly evidenced by her *Cantate pour la Jeune République*. Before retiring from the Opera in 1851 she had a short run in an opera that Gounod wrote for her, *Sapho*, which received bad press, even before its premiere, because she was associated with it. *La France Musicale* sneered at Gounod as a "humanitarian composer."[47] After the massacres of December 2, Viardot's daughter Louise recalled how their home was searched by the police. They found little, missing the compromising packet of correspondence from Sand. (In writing to them, Sand signed as "Ninon.") The Viardots left for Scotland in December soon after Pauline's contract was terminated.

## Orpheus as Hermaphrodite

Viardot did not appear at the Paris Opera again until 1859, when, her reputation established, she starred in a revival of Gluck's *Orpheus*, transcribed for her by Berlioz. After 1850, musical tastes had shifted. Viardot participated in a series of festivals in London, the "Evenings of ancient classical music," revivals of music by Handel and Gluck. In the mid-1850s she performed some pieces from Handel oratorios and arias from Gluck operas in Paris, where interest in this music was awakened through a series of programs sponsored by the Société des Concerts du Conservatoire.

Wendy Bashant declares *Orpheus* to be the "queerest opera I know." She argues that gender confusion is written into the myth itself, that Orpheus becomes "not-man and not-woman," and that Gluck's setting evokes a world where procreation and sexual difference are irrelevant, for the drama begins after Eurydice's death. Thus Orpheus's sexual identity becomes irrelevant to his role as sexless singer.[48] I agree with her reading as qualified in light of Alexander Doty's notions about queer

> positions, queer readings and queer pleasures . . . [as] part of a reception space that stands simultaneously beside and within that created by heterosexual . . . straight positions. [They] also suggest that what happens in cultural reception goes beyond the traditional opposition of homo and hetero, as queer reception is often . . . beyond the audience's conscious "real-life" definition of their sexual identities and cultural

positions—often, but not always beyond . . . sexual identities and sexual politics. . . . [For] queer reception doesn't stand outside personal and cultural histories; it is part of the articulation of these histories.[49]

The figure of Orpheus offers a position of identification to those who do not think of themselves as queer, despite the opera's boundary-crossing effects. Emphasizing the castrato heritage, Bashant observes that Orpheus was perceived as both asexual and suprasexual. The second part of her analysis of the opera is also important in that it traces the gender shifts in the history of the role of Orpheus. Gluck was compelled to transpose it for male tenor and to alter the libretto to make it acceptable to the Parisians in 1774. Berlioz restored the work later to a more authentic version and transcribed the role specifically for Viardot.

89

Farinelli's

Electronic

Hermaphrodite

and the

Contralto

Tradition

Gluck had originally written Orpheus's role for the castrato Gaetano Guadagni, who performed it in Vienna in 1762. As is well known, Gluck had begun to turn away from the bravura technique characteristic of *opera seria* that Farinelli's virtuosity typified. Barbier speculates how during Gluck's visit to the octogenarian Farinelli, they may have spoken of "the ever more worrisome fate of the castrati, at a time when their decline was becoming evident."[50]

Although Bashant notes that all-female productions of *Orpheus* became commonplace later on, Viardot had to steel herself to undertake this role, previously sung in France only by male singers. Dulong writes of her hesitation at taking it on but notes that the public of the time was familiar with such travesty roles, and particularly with Viardot in them. The cover of Dulong's biography shows Viardot in an 1860 portrait as a laurel-crowned Orpheus gazing somberly heavenward, arms bared, biceps visibly tightened, to hold aloft a lyre in hands that are by no means small or delicate. As a forty-year-old Viardot made a handsome and convincing Orpheus. She was a huge success, and the production was a hit, drawing large audiences and universal praise. Usually reserved, Viardot wrote to her friend Rietz after the premier that each word, each phrase had been understood by an intelligent public made up of *le tout Paris*—musicians, amateurs, pedants, young lions. Her inventive interpretation of the thrice-repeated theme of "J'ai perdu mon Eurydice" sent those in the hall into ecstasy.

In a sense, Gluck effected his reform a second time in this performance. In his analysis of the opera Alfred Einstein writes of the moment when Orpheus sends the chorus away, wishing to be alone to grieve, in a *ballo*. More than an exit for the chorus, it is a "consolation and transfiguration, a deeply affecting spiritual reflection of heaven such as may on occasion illuminate the most cruel pain." Einstein says of the strophic song that follows that it was "one of Gluck's greatest notions to have made a eunuch's voice the vehicle for the part of Orpheus," but that it was his most "deplorable" compromise to have rewritten it for tenor for the Paris performance later: "For his Orpheus is not merely a plaintive human being, but a symbol of the singer's most exalted art, transcending all that is personal, wherever it finds expression in regular forms. Thus Orpheus's lament on having his wife torn from him is no wild outburst of woe, but a reflection of his loss seen in nature's acoustical mirror—the echo."[51]

Einstein traces the heightening of effect in the three strophes by figuration and "color" of wind instruments, whereas the "echo orchestra on the stage consists of strings and the primitively natural chalumeau." The text itself writes this echo parenthetically into the lines of Orpheus's song, for the recitatives and arias that follow repeat the echo after every two or three lines, sixteen times in all.[52] In its figuration of Orpheus expressing the experience of wrenching loss, it is not surprising that the orchestra emphasizes the echo. Orpheus joins with Echo to appeal to the psyche's deep articulation in loss. The audience watching the spectacle of Orpheus keening over his bride's corpse witnesses a public ritual of death and mourning.

All music, even when it dramatizes grief, is not so affecting, however. As Einstein points out, a key aspect of the song's affective power lies in its attribution to a voice that reaches beyond gender. Bashant puts it well by saying that the role "encompasses all realms of gendered desire."[53] Orpheus's "simple chalumeau" conceals its own artifice to communicate the universality of loss. The move is similar to that of Farinelli in the film when he sings Almirena's "stately" song of grief from *Rinaldo*, "Lascia qu'io pianga," a gesture that marks his rejection of virtuosity for the rich affect of Handel's music. There, too, the emotion of overwhelming loss is communicated by an artist whose gender is transgressed in the part.

*Orpheus* as performed by Viardot offered a complex, prismatic subject position to its listeners, not only encapsulating its own history of gender doubling in the role itself, but dramatizing the archetype of the lyric at the moment of Orpheus's loss of love, embodied for nineteenth-century audiences by a woman singer, in a role created in the eighteenth century for a castrato.

Like Viardot's *Orpheus*, the film *Farinelli* encapsulates its own tradition. Its twentieth-century audiences listen to the voice of an electronic hermaphrodite, a modern simulation of the hermaphroditic voice of Carlo Broschi, handed down musically to his contralto heir, Pauline Viardot. This nineteenth-century singer embodied the hermaphroditic voice triumphantly in Berlioz's revival of *Orpheus*. Through the tradition she exemplified and helped develop, this dually gendered voice has come down to the ears of modern audiences. The transgression of gender that haunted the eighteenth century as travesty, becoming the nineteenth-century preoccupation with the hermaphrodite, continues to resonate for us today.

NOTES

1. Thanks to Bertrand Augst, who brought the Foucault and Marin articles to my attention and to Ross Chambers and Nelly Furman for their useful comments.

91

Farinelli's

Electronic

Hermaphrodite

and the

Contralto

Tradition

2. Georges Didi-Huberman, *Invention de l'hystérie: Charcot et l'iconographie photographique de la Salpêtrière* (Paris: Macula, 1982).

3. Daniel Arasse, *La Guillotine et l'imaginaire de la terreur* (Paris: Flammarion, 1987).

4. Michel Foucault, "Le vrai sexe," in *Dits et écrits, 1954–1988*, eds. Daniel Defert and François Ewald (Paris: Editions Gallimard, 1993), vol.4, 1980–1988, 115–23.

5. Foucault, "Le vrai sexe," 118.

6. Patrick Barbier, *Farinelli, castrat des Lumières* (Paris: Bernard Grasset, 1994).

7. Quoted in ibid., 86. The translations from French in this article are my own.

8. Todd S. Gilman, "The (Italian) Castrato in London," in the present volume.

9. Ibid.

10. James H. Johnson, *Listening in Paris: A Cultural History* (Berkeley: University of California Press, 1995).

11. Peter Matthews, "*Farinelli, Il Castrato*," *Sight and Sound* (November 1995): 41.

12. Ibid.

13. George Friedrich Handel, *Rinaldo*. Compact disk recording, Teatro La Fenice di Venezia. John Fisher, conductor. Libretto trans. Timothy Alan Shaw, 1991, 12–13.

14. Ibid.

15. Terry Nelson, "Farinelli." *Studio Sound and Broadcast Engineering* 37, no. 7 (July 1, 1995): 38–40.

16. See *En Travesti: Women, Gender Subversion, Opera*, eds. Corinne Blackmer and Patricia Juliana Smith (New York: Columbia University Press, 1995).

17. Radio interview with Marilyn Horne on "The Diane Rehm Show," WAMU, American University, Washington, D.C., December 25, 1995.

18. Barbier, *Farinelli*, 27–28.

19. See George Sand, "Consuelo," in *La Comtesse de Rudolstadt*, 3 vols, eds. Leon Cellier and Leon Guichard (Paris: Editions Garniers-Frères, 1959); and Gérard de Nerval, "Sylvie," in *Les Filles du feu* (Paris: Gallimard, 1972).

20. Quoted in Gustave Dulong, *Pauline Viardot, Tragédienne Lyrique* (Paris: Association des Amis d'Ivan Tourgueniev, Pauline Viardot et María Malibran, 1987), 45.

21. Michel Poizat, *L'Opéra ou le cri de l'ange* (Paris: A. M. Métaillé, 1986). English translation by Arthur Denner, *The Angel's Cry* (Ithaca, N.Y.: Cornell University Press, 1992).

22. See Felicia Miller Frank, *The Mechanical Song: Women, Voice, and the Artificial in Nineteenth-Century French Narrative* (Stanford: Stanford University Press, 1995).

23. Ibid., 67–68, 201, *n*. 11.

24. Quoted in Dulong, *Pauline Viardot*, 18–19.

25. Barbier, *Farinelli*, 52

26. Dulong, *Pauline Viardot*, 19.

27. Ross Chambers, *The Writing of Melancholy: Modes of Opposition in Early French Modernism*, trans. Mary Seidman Trouille (Chicago: University of Chicago Press, 1993), 111–12. With the exception of chapter 4, published as *Mélancholie et opposition: Les débuts du modernisme en France* (Paris: José Corti, 1987).

28. Louis Marin, "Le Sexe ni vrai ni faux, ou hermaphrodite saisi par le neutre." *Traverses: ni vrai ni faux* (Paris: Editions du Centre Nationale d'Art et de Culture George Pompidou, 1989), 41, 90–98.

29. See Miller Frank, *The Mechanical Song*, chapter 6.

30. Marin, *Le Sexe ni vrai ni faux*, 95.

31. Nelly Furman, in conversation, Chicago, December 27, 1996.

32. Butler, 24.

33. Foucault, "Le Vrai Sexe," 117.

34. Rosi Braidotti. *Nomadic Subjects: Embodiment and Sexual Difference in Contemporary Feminist Theory* (New York: Columbia University Press, 1994), 150.

35. Ibid., 99.

36. Ibid., 101.

37. Ibid.

38. Ibid., 105.

39. Jacques Attali, *Noise: The Political Economy of Music*, trans. Brian Massumi (Minneapolis: University of Minnesota Press, 1985), 59.

40. Herbert Lindenberger, *Opera, The Extravagant Art* (Ithaca, N.Y.: Cornell University Press, 1984).

41. Siegfried Kracauer, *Orpheus in Paris* (New York: Alfred Knopf, 1938), 100.

42. Dulong, *Pauline Viardot*, 98.

43. Jane Fulcher, *The Nation's Image: French Grand Opera as Politics and as Politicized Art* (Cambridge: Cambridge University Press, 1987), 122.

44. Ibid., 122–23.

45. "Meyerbeer's new work had the [dubious] merit of exciting contradictory passions of which the real motives seem often to have been fairly extraneous to the work's intrinsic value. It was already enough that one could recognize 'sixteenth-century socialists' in these ruffians who, 'in the name of evangelical *égalité* and *fraternité*' raised up the poor classes against the lords and castles, for the rightist journalists to be inclined to judge the *Prophet* more favorably than their leftist colleagues, even from the musical point of view." (Dulong, *Pauline Viardot*, 99.)

46. Fulcher, *The Nation's Image*, 123–24.

47. Ibid.

48. Wendy Bashant, "Singing in Greek Drag," in *En Travesti*, 218–19.

49. Alexander Doty, *Making Things Perfectly Queer* (Minneapolis: University of Minnesota Press, 1993), 15.

50. Barbier, *Farinelli*, 212.

51. Alfred Einstein, *Gluck*, trans. Eric Blom (New York: McGraw-Hill, 1964), 72–73.

52. Christoph Willibald von Gluck, *Orpheo*. Janet Baker, mezzosoprano; Elizabeth Gale, soprano; Elisabeth Speiser, soprano; Richard Leppard, conductor; Glyndebourne Chorus; London Philharmonic Orchestra. Recorded 1982. Libretto to compact disk recording (London: Erato, 1992), 39.

53. Bashant, "Singing in Greek Drag," 222.

## CHAPTER FOUR

# "O Patria Mia": Female Homosociality and the Gendered Nation in Bellini's Norma and Verdi's Aida

Patricia Juliana Smith

Vincenzo Bellini's *Norma* (1831) and Giuseppe Verdi's *Aida* (1871), two of the perennial standards of the Italian opera repertory, share the trope of romantic triangulation in which one man is the shared object of desire between two women. In both cases this configuration is complicated by the backdrop of nations at war, resulting in each of the women, either literally or metaphorically, sleeping with the enemy. Accordingly, romantic love, the mainstay of Italian opera plots, finds itself in conflict with another significant plot motif, that of national politics. As we observe the characters' inner turmoil arising from their psychomachia, the question of exactly *who* the enemy is arises and, to some extent, mitigates actions that would otherwise be regarded as nothing less than treasonous. Less noticeable, however, is the tacit yet significant aspect of homosocial and homoerotic desire that, as critics such as René Girard and Eve Kosofsky Sedgwick have posited, is almost inevitably a part of such triangulation.[1]

The similarities between the two operas end here. The forty years that separate their production are among the most tumultuous in modern Italian history, a period during which the concept of nation drastically changed for most Italians and during which many assumptions about sexuality and gender began to come under the "scientific" scrutiny of medical sexology. Accordingly, although what Anthony Arblaster has defined as the "central conflict between love and public duty" (82) in *Norma* is central in *Aida* as well, relative values in the battle between the private loyalties to self and romantic love and traditional public loyalties to the gods, country, and family are considerably realigned, as are notions of appropriate conduct and loyalty in relationships between women.

In Bellini's opera, Norma and Adalgisa, Druid priestesses, both love Pollione, the Roman proconsul, despite the fulminating rebellion of the Druids and the Gallic people against the Roman invaders. Rather than allowing this rivalry to divide them, however, the two countrywomen renounce the colonizing male, pledging their mutual and undying fidelity and affection in what would seem, both musically and verbally, an extravagant love duet. Thus although Norma must ultimately offer herself as a sacrifice to appease the angry god Irminsul, female homosociality—or what Lillian Faderman has deemed "romantic friendship"—functions as the medium through which the integrity of the Druid nation (as it were) and its religious hierarchies are preserved.[2] Four decades later, Verdi's opera drastically reconfigures female homosociality and homoeroticism. The Egyptian princess Amneris and her slave, the captured Ethiopian princess Aida, partake in a relentless sexual rivalry for the love of the Egyptian captain Radamès—a cause to which matters of state, although significant in the positioning of the animosity between the women, are decidedly secondary. While Amneris clearly exploits her power over her deracinated counterpart, she covertly deploys the stratagems of a quasi-erotic mode of "female bonding"—augmented by an ample dose of sexually pathological behavior—to gain her objective. Amneris's tactics nevertheless fail and unadulterated heterosexuality wins the day—even if it literally loses the battle. Consequently, all three principals become, in varying degrees, traitors to their fathers/fatherlands. If female homosociality might be said to preserve the nation in *Norma*, heterosexuality and a lack of affectional ties between women surely compromise national security in *Aida*.

These conflicts have for the most part gone unremarked by opera critics; not, I believe, because they are unapparent, but because their very apparentness makes them too dangerous to comment upon. Yet to isolate the personal sexual and affectional issues from their setting of national struggle and "public duty" would be to distort the intricate structures of these operas. A crucial concept with which to begin this analysis, then, is that curious Italian word *patria*, the cause from which these operatic conflicts arise. A cognate of the Latin *pater* (and, by extension, *patriarchy*), the Italian noun for *fatherland* is nonetheless gendered as feminine. The concept of the nation as feminine is carried over, particularly in the context of war and invasion, to the binary oppositions of conqueror and conquered, victimizer and victim, colonizer and colonized, even rapist and raped. Thus in these operas even the gendering of patriarchal nations becomes, in a macrocosmic sense, a matter of ambiguity. Simultaneously, on the microcosmic level, a more specific gendering of the respective nations is symbolically indicated through the biological sex of the characters representative of those nations, a matter made even more complex by the relative sympathy with which each character is delineated.

*Norma* is about the personal and public psychomachia Arblaster describes, not only that peculiar to the eponymous heroine, but also that afflicting the two other principals involved with her in erotic triangulation. That *Norma* might be about the Druids of ancient Gaul and their struggle for freedom from Roman incursion is merely coincidental, a by-product of romanticism's fascination with ancient Celtic peoples. It could just as well be set in any historical and spatial setting in which an ethnic or religious group lacking the structures of a permanent central government of their own chafes under the rule of a more powerful imperial force. In essence, it could just as well be the fragmented Italy of the 1830s, in which Risorgimento was little more than an idea gathering force in urban areas, still waiting to strike a significant blow against the occupying foreign powers.[3]

The internal and external conflicts are almost immediately set forth in the first scene. Led by Oroveso, the Druids await the rising of the moon for the ritual of divination over which Norma herself will preside, and they indulge in war-mongering fantasies of their god liberating them and creating chaos *nella città dei Cesari*. Such fanciful bloodlust is gendered behavior of an undoubtedly "masculine" sort, almost parodically so. Yet although Oroveso is a patriarch—the leader of the priesthood and Norma's father—these daydreams must be set aside when vetoed by Norma's prophecy. Accordingly, the Druid patriarchy and *patria* are emasculated under the sway of her "feminine," indeed "feminizing" declamation.

That Norma is a woman in possession of tremendous powers and that she is completely aware of this is clear from the moment of her entrance. Speaking of herself in grandiose third person, she rebukes the *sediziose voci* among those assembled before her who would "presume to dictate answers to the prophetess Norma, and to hurry the secret fate of Rome."[4] This pronouncement leads to a brief stand-off with her father, who, acting as the voice of the colonized, insists that the swords of the Gauls "cannot remain idle." Quite remarkably, Norma, conceivably the Freudian phallic mother of the Druids, not only silences but effectively castrates her own father by destroying, through her premonitory metaphor, that most phallic of symbols, the sword. It will, she says, "fall in pieces . . . if any of you dares to unsheathe it before time." Subsequently, none dare to dictate to the prophetess Norma, for by the second verse of her ensuing aria "Casta diva," her hymn of praise to the chaste female deity who stands in contradistinction to the fierce and hypermasculine Irminsul, the Druids all follow her lead in begging the goddess to "spread upon the earth that peace which you cause to reign in heaven."

The aria itself is a masterpiece of what can only be called the rhetoric of bel canto. In terms of actual content it says very little. Rather, Norma seems to feminize the gathering through style and form. As if to demonstrate the extent to which music might indeed have the charm to soothe the savage *barbari*, Norma affects a reversal of the call to arms that only a moment before seemed so overwhelming. But although this gesture forestalls the seething insurrection—and in so doing provides the first and perhaps most extraordinary of the many moments of aesthetic pleasure the opera possesses—it does not remedy the deep internal and external divisions that inform the actions of the principals and the crowd. Once Norma's aria and her ritual are concluded, Oroveso and the Druids return to their dreams of the Gauls' "day of vengeance," merely delayed by the gods' will. Norma, on the other hand, reveals through her own musical soliloquy the basis of her own division—her amorous involvement with Pollione, who she senses has lost interest in her. Through her role as prophetess she has the power to punish him, a power she vows to use when expedient; yet no sooner does she enunciate this than she admits, "my heart will not let me."

Norma is thus presented as an atypical operatic heroine; she is, as Edward J. Dent observes, the "exciting lady" of Romantic opera (170), the descendant of such sorceresses as Alcina, Armida, and Medea. Unlike her own goddess, she is not chaste, nor does she abide by the beliefs she ostensibly serves. Despite the beauty of her oration, she is nonetheless a type of the charismatic false preacher who uses the pulpit for self-gain. She is not wrong, for example, in foretelling the fall of Rome "consumed by her own vices," but she neglects to tell her audience that this event is still three centuries away. She preaches peace yet is prone to violent emotions and, we discover, can raise a clarion call to war when it suits her purposes. From a purely political point of view, she is a collaborator or native informer, betraying the freedom of her own people for purely personal motives.[5] Indeed, in the first scene the idea of *patria* is evoked only once, not by the nationalistic Druids, but by Norma herself. Her concept of *patria*, however, has nothing to do with the ambitions of her father or her fatherland: *e vita nel tuo seno e patria e cielo avrò* ("and in your breast I shall find life and fatherland and heaven"),[6] she declares in her apostrophe to the absent Pollione.

Characteristic of Dent's "exciting ladies," Norma can entice men but cannot retain their love, for she is, above all, a most inconvenient woman. Although such a character is intriguing, what can be done with her is inevitably problematic: "Italian opera often . . . enlisted the sympathies of the audience on her side, but it was difficult to make suitable matrimonial arrangements for her at the end, so . . . it was generally found more convenient to let her die"; her lover, meanwhile, is left "to enjoy comparative happiness in the arms of some less exciting lady" (170).

The supposed hero and the "less exciting lady" are not long in appearing. Between Oroveso's assembly of the militants and Norma's declamation, Pollione intrudes upon the scene. A relatively uncomplicated and unconflicted character, he lacks any mechanism of self-criticism and bases his actions on emotional whim. His discourse is punctuated by threats to destroy the "barbarous" Gauls and their religion, as is his "right" as a civilized

Roman. Arblaster aptly and sardonically describes his manner as being in the "best imperial style" (83). His imperial "right" extends, moreover, to the sexual appropriation of the native female population, supported by the will of his god, Eros/Amor. Accordingly, he can presume to discard Norma, who has secretly borne him two sons, because "the old passion has died in my heart, and a god extinguished it." Likewise, he can persuade Adalgisa to forsake her "terrible, cruel god" and country for his vastly superior god, one unlike Irminsul, "who is opposed to your wishes and mine": "Love is the god you must invoke." In manipulating the gods to do his will, he is the reflection of Norma as false religionist.

By contrast with both Norma and Pollione, Adalgisa embodies honor and integrity. This makes her, perhaps inevitably, a "less exciting lady" than Norma; yet she is hardly simple or bland. Unique among the characters, she is capable of true faith, both in the religious and interpersonal senses. Unlike Norma, she is yet virginal, but her infatuation with Pollione has offended her god, to whom she perceives herself, like a Catholic nun, "vowed to espouse." If she is to take leave of him by eloping to Rome with Pollione, she feels compelled to do so in an upright if emotionally wrenching manner by seeking dispensation from Norma, who, to extend the nun analogy, functions as her mother superior. To extend the analogy even further—for surely the vows that bind Norma and Adalgisa resemble those of Catholic nuns more than any putatively historical Druid priestesses—Adalgisa is also capable of the latently erotic female homosociality so often associated with the convent. This becomes the key factor not only in maintaining her fidelity to her religion—here inseparable from her national allegiance—but also in restoring and redeeming the unfaithful Norma.

Adalgisa's doing right for its own sake brings the three principals together in the same place, apparently for the first time. The setting itself bespeaks the enormity of Norma's powers, as she is able to dwell apart from the other Druids in a habitation, replete with Roman furnishings, with the sons known only to herself and her "confidente" Clotilde.[7] Indeed, that their prophetess could carry on an affair with the enemy leader and bear him two children without arousing public suspicion illustrates how much Norma is inaccessible to and out of touch with her own people.

Adalgisa petitions Norma to release her from her vows. Her rhetoric in doing so presents the various facets of her own psychomachia; her potential pleasure in the marriage she is to enter is adulterated by her breaking faith with all her previous loyalties: she has promised her yet unnamed lover "to flee the temple, to betray the altar to which I am bound, to abandon my country [la patria]" (translation mine). Although this statement demonstrates the vast difference between Adalgisa's ethical perspective and Norma's, the latter sees only the similarities of their predicaments. Accordingly, she engages Adalgisa in an act of metanarrative by requesting her to relate the history of the emotional state that has led her to this impasse. As Adalgisa details her distracted feelings in encountering her mysterious suitor, Norma responds with what Bellini's contemporaries would have identified as empathetic sensibility and recalls the early stages of the liaison she wishes to revitalize with Pollione. As long as Norma sees only the parallels of situation and not of person, she engages Adalgisa in a fantasized exchange of men, analogous in many ways to the exchange of women Sedgwick sees between men who, because of social taboo, cannot act upon their repressed desire for one another. In effect, Norma, who already senses Pollione's withdrawal, derives a certain erotic *frisson* from Adalgisa's narration of her own sensual bewilderment. Their mutual emotionality gives rise to the duet "Oh! rimembranza!"—the first instance in the opera of what might be called "homovocal" *jouissance* between the two women, or what Elizabeth Wood has termed Sapphonics (27).[8]

All this comes to an abrupt end, however. Before Adalgisa can do more than indicate that her intended is not "one of us," Pollione enters and, through the mutual accusations that create the vocal fireworks between the former lovers, Adalgisa learns what had heretofore been occluded. Her response, tellingly, is one informed by neither fury nor sensibility but rather by a stunningly pragmatic sense of honor and a gynocentric alliance with Norma in the face of their now mutual enemy. She is immediate in her denunciation of the perfidious Pollione and in her renunciation of a love about which she has clearly been of more than one mind; so immediate that the mercurial Norma, who has already displaced her own romantic predilection onto the young woman's situation, cannot quite comprehend this reconfiguration of the triangle.

Thus Norma remains convinced that Pollione will have his way with Adalgisa, and so, having failed in her Medealike attempt at infanticide, she summons her putative rival and addresses her as the children's prospective stepmother, her own suicidal martyrdom already being foreshadowed. Adalgisa, however, rejects Norma's plan; and, just as Norma had used Adalgisa's narrative for her own erotic ends, so now Adalgisa constructs a metafiction regarding a rejuvenated passion between Pollione and Norma, one that she aspires to arbitrate. In this manner she can become the agent of the otherwise inaccessible Norma's pleasures and desires through the mediation of Pollione, whose erotic attentions she now spurns but to whom she nonetheless remains linked. That Norma does not quite grasp this plan, or its alternative, is understandable:

NORMA: Oh, my dear girl! What do you want to do?
ADALGISA: To give you back your rights
　　or else I swear by heaven and men
　　to stay concealed with you forever.

If Adalgisa cannot realize her fiction of a renewed heterosexuality for Norma, the least she can do is construct a new, occluded homosociality between the two of them—forever. Norma, heretofore fixated on her own thwarted desires, is unexpectedly moved by the notion; the result is the second instance of homovocal *jouissance*, the conclusion of the duet "Mira, o Norma," when the two women together sing of their mutual love:

> Yes, you will have me as your companion
> until your last hour;
> the world is large enough
> to be a shelter to both of us together.
> With you I shall set my face
> firmly against the shame which fate may bring,
> as long as I feel your heart
> beating on mine.[9]

There are few instances in opera, save those when one woman is *en travesti*, of such passionate declamation of feeling between women. This mutual avowal, with its climactic musical structure, feels as if it is—or should be—a final resolution, even a happy ending: both women will forget Pollione and start anew together. But if the opera were to end at this point, it would mean the ultimate triumph of female romantic friendship over the ever dominant institution of heterosexuality, a condition as likely in nineteenth-century opera as the ultimate triumph of the Gauls over Imperial Rome. The duet, then, is the end of the opera for Adalgisa. Although her actions inform the events in the two ensuing scenes, she is conspicuously absent from the stage; her "love duet" with Norma stands as her final word.

In the final scene, after Pollione is captured in the temple attempting to abduct Adalgisa, he and Norma are alone for once in the opera. Engaged in an extended duet of mutual sadomasochism, they make the absent Adalgisa their term of negotiation: Norma will spare Pollione's life and relinquish her claims to him if he will vow to leave Adalgisa alone, an offer he refuses. Norma then threatens to accuse Adalgisa of complicity and thus hand her over as a sacrificial victim, but at last recalls Adalgisa's love for her. When the moment comes to announce the name of the "perjured priestess" who has consorted with the Roman colonizer, she astonishes all with her self-revelation. Pollione, his love for this "wonderful woman" perversely reawakened, joins her in the flames.

But what resolution can this ending bring about? A traditional (i.e., heterocentric) reading would conclude that this is simply one more example of love conquering all. Yet the relentless desire that takes both parties to a fiery death would seem more a case of erotic obsession overwhelming all in a struggle that no one wins. A romantic reading, moreover, fails to take into account that Norma, in her final scene, never returns Pollione's declarations of love. If there is no satisfactory resolution in this opera, it may well be because the political context that gave birth to the opera had no solutions to offer. Nor does only one area of politics inform this opera; a satisfactory solution in terms of national politics here would not necessarily be satisfactory in terms of sexual politics, or vice versa.

Catherine Clément perceives this multilayered dilemma; Norma, in her never resolved psychomachia, symbolizes the colonized nation: "Completely hemmed in by endlessly involved betrayals, she ends up surrendering before rebelling. With all her heart she embodies defeated Gaul, ready to become Roman; and *Rome*, the terrible magical word, is the embodiment of every oppression" (104). At the same time, though, Norma the prophetess, a woman able to subvert the male-dominated structures of religion, embodies all that misogynistic European Christian civilization fears: she is the priestess and denizen of "a Gaul dreamed up by Felice Romani and Bellini; a Gaul where romantic Italy fantasizes the fierce, feminine resistances surrounding its Eternal City. Vanquished she will be, but at least she will drag the Roman down with her" (102). The Roman pagan is, in this regard, merely supplanted by the Roman Catholic, leaving the subjugation of women intact. Accordingly, Clément adds, Norma "prefigures the diabolical popesses, still titillating cardinals in the Curia" (105). As such, she cannot be allowed to win, even if she is the symbol of the colonized nation. Even so, in her defeat there is a subversive victory: "From betrayal to betrayal, Norma could no longer waver between Rome and Gaul, between love and defeat. The only one able to save her is the pagan god Irminsul, even if it is at the cost of her life. Rome bows before the god of the people it is colonizing" (Clément, 105). The only resolution available to her is a purely symbolic one; she becomes the symbol of the colonized—and therefore feminized—nation, just as Pollione remains in the end a symbolic representation of hypermasculine imperialism. Norma saves herself inasmuch as she saves her nation, for only when she announces her own guilt does she reconnect Gaul with the concept of *patria*, her own feminized fatherland: *Una spergiura sacerdotess i sacri voti infranse, tradi la patria e il Dio degli offese* ("A perjured priestess has broken her vows, betrayed her country and offended the god of our ancestors"). In this rediscovery of *patria*, along with her destruction of the enemy in her own destruction, she is redeemed as an icon of resistance.

She can be so, however, only as a result of that romantic friendship "surpassing the love of men." Because Adalgisa is willing to give all for Norma, Norma is able, in the end, to sacrifice herself for Adalgisa as well as for Gaul and Irminsul. In this manner the absent Adalgisa is at least metaphysically present at the opera's end. Her physical absence is nonetheless troubling; Bellini and Romani give us no hint of what will become of the most compelling "less exciting lady" in opera. Clément notes that when all is done, "A young forsaken woman remains. Adalgisa, young and alive—something else, no doubt, will happen to her" (106). No doubt, but precisely what is unknown, left up to the individual observer's imagination.[10] In one sense, she must stay young and alive as a message of hope to any colonized people, as a symbol of an honorable continuance that bespeaks a future without betrayal or complicity. On the other hand, perhaps it is appropriate that her "love duet" with Norma is her final word. This other love, the one that goes unnoticed, can never be realized; yet it is thus never betrayed but remains itself "young and alive" in the realm of what might have been. Here, then, the aspirations of those subjected to gender oppression as well as of those subjected to national oppression endure until a better day arrives.

For Bellini's Italian nationalist contemporaries, unlike *Norma*'s Gauls, that better day was not centuries off. If *Norma* was a product of the early stirrings of the Risorgimento, then *Aida*, "the end of Verdi's great line of political, or partially political dramas" (Arblaster, 144), appeared just as the last vestige of foreign domination, the French troops of Napoleon III, withdrew from Italian soil, allowing Rome to become part of a unified Italy.[11] Thus, as Edward W. Said has noted, Verdi, long the cultural spokesman for the aspirations of a divided and subjugated Italy, could at last compose an opera that was not primarily concerned with his own nation's struggles: "Whereas it had been Italy and Italians (with special force, paradoxically enough, in *Nabucco*) who were addressed in Verdi's earlier operas, despite the often exotic or *outré* subject matter, in *Aida* it was Egypt and Egyptians of early antiquity, a far remoter and less engaging phenomenon than Verdi had ever set to music" (114). The result of this "remoter and less engaging" subject matter may well be that, as Arblaster observes, "apart from Amneris . . . the characters are not especially complex or subtly drawn" (141).

At a remove of more than a century, it is easy to lose track of what *Aida* is "about," particularly given the ensuing events through which we must filter our present-day perceptions. That this opera is, as Said argues, a cultural artifact of nineteenth-century European imperial adventurism and represents a highly imaginary Egypt from a thoroughly European perspective goes almost without saying. Indeed, since Verdi's time it has become even more so. Italian imperialist adventurism in Ethiopia inevitably projects its ignominious shadow across the work; so much so that during Mussolini's regime, an Italian production of the opera could hubristically present "a Blackshirt Radames triumphing over the barbarous Africans" (Arblaster, 142). The oppressed and divided nation that gave birth to the operas of Bellini and Verdi had itself swiftly become an oppressor.[12] Conversely, and at the opposite end of the political spectrum, the opera has taken on new meaning for American and European audiences alike since the 1960s, in the wake of the American civil rights movement and the identification of the title role with African-American soprano Leontyne Price. Although it is doubtful that Verdi and his librettist Antonio Ghislanzoni (or, for that matter, their French sources Auguste Mariette and Camille Du Locle) had the recently abolished American institution of slavery in mind when creating *Aida*, parallels with the conditions of black women in the antebellum South nonetheless exist in the libretto, particularly in terms of the relationship between slave and mistress.[13] But *Aida* is not, as some would suggest, about Italian imperialism in the aftermath of nationhood. Nor, for that matter, can it be accurately said to be about race; unlike the heroes of Verdi's *La Forza del Destino* and *Otello*, Aida's race is never directly mentioned within the libretto, nor is it attributed as a causal factor in her slavery.[14] Rather, like

*Norma*, *Aida* is about the psychomachia that ensues when two women are engaged in erotic triangulation with the same man and when that triangle is divided by the nationalities of its parties when their nations are at war.

The dynamic forces at work in *Norma* are present in *Aida* as well, but they are drastically reconfigured. The central story is typically simple and "operatic"; reduced to absurdity, it is the story of "a tenor and a soprano who want to make love but are prevented by a baritone and a mezzo" (Said, 114). Indeed, but the baritone happens to be the king of Ethiopia and the mezzo the daughter of the king of Egypt, just as the soprano is the daughter of the baritone king. The tenor, moreover, is the commander of the Egyptian army, which happens to be engaged in combat with the Ethiopian army. Religion and priesthood play a substantial part in *Aida* as well, but whereas the Druid priesthood functions in *Norma* as intercessor between an oppressed people and its deities, the ruthlessly theocratic Egyptian priests of "*Immenso Fthà*" are the sole instigators of microcosmic and macrocosmic strife in Verdi's opera.

This sacerdotal malevolence is, no doubt, a protest on Verdi's part against the temporal powers of the Roman Catholic Church, one made far less subtly in the earlier *Don Carlo*. In this sense, it is the only remaining vestige of Risorgimento politics to be found in *Aida*. In 1861 Pope Pius IX published his *Syllabus of Errors*, indicating his unwillingness to engage in any form of contemporary liberal thought. In 1870, by means of the First Vatican Council, he had himself declared infallible, and, within the same year, in response to being stripped of his temporal rule over Rome, threatened with excommunication all those who partook in Italian national politics. (Verdi himself had been a member of Italy's first parliament.) If religion and its ministers take on a thoroughly sinister role in *Aida*, as opposed to their relatively benign role in *Norma*, it is surely a reflection of the strife arising from the church's continued attempts to obstruct the success of the new and long-sought Italian nation.[15]

Yet the reconfiguration of religious and national power structures and dynamics over four decades is not the only cause of the significant differences between the ethos of *Norma* and that of *Aida*, nor were the unified Italian state and papal infallibility the only significant elements in the zeitgeist of the early 1870s. By mid-century, feminism was gaining momentum in Europe and America; in Italy the movement was associated with the " 'illustrious women' of the risorgimento" (Käppeli, 485). This revolution within a revolution inevitably met cultural resistance. The mid-nineteenth century, writes Judith R. Walkowitz, "produced the historic moment when middle-class women gained access to public space to speak about sexual matters, thanks to the new mass media and political networks available in a redefined public domain" (371). Moreover, as Regina Barreca suggests, the period "saw itself as wrestling equally with the forces of nature and technology, with theories of natural selection and unnatural acts, with the drive to triumph over the evils of passion while passionately arguing for the triumph of fecundity and creation" (xii). As a result, forces in opposition to feminism—forces that appropriated the cultural and social authority of science and religion to justify their dictates—were also at work; by the 1870s, German medical sexologists were beginning to publish their findings on "deviance" and "degeneracy," while Italian phrenologist Cesare Lombroso was already accumulating the "evidence" that would eventually lead to his classification of female criminal types. Among the worst of the "female offenders" these men of science defined was the virago, a woman who usurped masculine prerogatives as her own and who acted upon her own passions. If not stopped, such women, they warned, would undo two and a half millennia of Judeo-Christian civilization in their quest for equality and self-assertion.[16] Amneris, the willful and manipulative Egyptian princess, might well be seen as such a woman.

As the fear of the virago grew, so did the need to promote her antithesis, the virtuous "natural" woman. In Italy, where the Catholic Church retained cultural, if not temporal or even spiritual power, the educated or public woman needed to strike some balance between her feminist aspirations and traditional Catholic self-effacement if she was to retain respectability.[17] Without directly invoking this historical dichotomy, Catherine Clément sees the antipathetic contrast between Aida and Amneris as one constructed upon religious differences: "Aida is more a Christian than a Nubian. Her chivalrous Radamès is Christian as well. The only Egyptian is the lofty Amneris, the pharaoh's daughter. Her violence, her dignity and her anger are Egyptian" (116). That the self-sacrificial Aida and her equally self-sacrificial lover are somehow, if anachronistically, "Christian" is evident from their romantic European sense of love and honor; that they are in some contextual sense pagans merely makes them "noble savages," those who would be Christian if they only could. It is in this sense that their struggle to reconcile the personal and the political, to reconcile the erotic and the nationalistic must be understood. Amneris, in contrast, is the savage noble, having not only the self-centered will of the heathen aristocrat, but every quality that the century regarded as unwomanly and therefore feared in the feminist virago. Her aggressive desires set her apart from the other characters; Arblaster's observation that she is the opera's only complex or subtly drawn character is surely analogous to Clément's assessment of her as "Egyptian." Her "Egyptianness," moreover, makes her problematic to European audiences a priori. As the pharaoh's daughter, she is an embodiment of the biblical enslavers from whom God's Chosen People were delivered; thus the enslaved Aida is automatically analogous to Jewish people of the Old Testament and therefore sympathetic—and, in light of nineteenth-century European anti-Semitism, possibly more sympathetic than the original type. Moreover, although the opera does not specifically address race, Amneris's Egyptianness could be construed (albeit anachronistically) along nineteenth-century lines as, paradoxically, "Semitic," thus linking her with all the negative traits attributed to the people the Egyptians once enslaved. Accordingly, Amneris embodies much of what Lombroso would soon classify as "degenerate" in Jews and female criminals alike.[18] All such attribution is, of course, utterly illogical, but nonetheless characteristic of the zeitgeist in which *Aida* was created.

If love between women could save the integrity of the Gallic nation in *Norma*, such homoaffectional relations are nowhere in sight in *Aida*. Rather, the oppositionality of the two women becomes emblematic not only of the nineteenth-century polarities of the good/Christian/natural woman and the evil/heathen/unnatural woman, but also of the antipathies between their respective nations. Set between these two extremes of female characterization is the often curiously simplistic Radamès, who, as a result of his own psychomachia between his duty to the "sacred soil of Egypt" and his love for the Ethiopian slave, eventually finds himself compromised and thus, ironically, feminized.[19]

The peculiar gendering of roles in this triangle is revealed in the first scene of the opera. Radamès prefaces his aria "Celeste Aida" by citing his reasons for wanting to lead the Egyptian army to victory against the Ethiopian onslaught—which, ironically, is coming to rescue Aida from captivity. His dreams will be fulfilled if he can return "crowned with laurels" to tell Aida, "for you I fought, for you I conquered!"—not thinking that she might be grieved by the slaughter of her countrymen. Yet even in conquering the forces of her nation, he would imaginatively grant her the royal powers in her own land that, unknown to him, she once possessed: "I would return you your lovely sky, the gentle breezes of your native land; a royal crown on your brow I would set, build you a throne next the sun." This is, of course, merely a faux Egyptian version of castles in the air. Radamès, subject to whims of the pharaoh—and, more pointedly, those of the pharaoh's daughter—possesses no such power to confer sovereignty. His relative lack of power becomes obvious once Amneris enters. Her words, directly addressed to Radamès, frankly bespeak her desire and admiration for the young officer; his response, however, is one of trepidation lest she discover "the hidden love that burns in my heart." That Amneris not only reveals her erotic longings forthrightly but also threatens "woe" should the object of her desires desire another immediately establishes her as a dangerous and emasculating usurper of male prerogative. That Radamès quite obviously fears her not only confirms her status as the virago but indicates the extent to which he is reduced to a feminine status and mode of response in her presence, despite his selection as commander of the army.

Although Amneris's lust surely bends the established paradigms of gendered behavior, it is nonetheless heterosexual; yet she is not above presenting a simulacrum of homosocial affection to suit her needs. Speculating that her slave could be her rival, she intercepts her with a pretense of sorority and equality in language that is redolent of seduction: "Come, my dearest, come hither; you are neither slave nor servant here where in sweet enchantment I called you sister. . . . Reveal the secret of your tears to me." Although her ostensible purpose is to discover their liaison, she is also demonstrating to Radamès that Aida is *hers*, not his. Even if she is merely enacting an affectional relationship with another woman, such an action had become, by the latter half of the nineteenth century, yet one more characteristic of the virago's degeneracy.

In contrast, Aida is constructed as one who loves and suffers; given her sex and her enslavement, she is not granted the agency to do much else. Once left alone, she reveals in the lengthy aria "Ritorna vincitor!" the depth of both her love and her suffering and the psychomachia that arises therefrom: "The sacred names of father, of lover, I cannot utter, nor yet recall. For the one, for the other, confused, trembling, I would weep, I would pray. But my prayer changes to a curse, for me tears are a crime, sighs a fault. In the dark night my soul is lost, and in this cruel anguish I would die." To wish victory on one is to wish destruction on the other. Utterly disempowered, she perceives there is nothing she can do but weep and pray—and wish for death. Although her exotic setting and situation make Aida's dilemma extraordinary, she is not much different from the average nineteenth-century European woman who, although not a de facto slave, was reduced to a similar condition by church and society through the ideological construct that a good woman is a loving and suffering woman. Clément's specification of Aida's "Christianity" is thus apt; more precisely, Aida is a type of a much-honored Catholic woman, the virgin martyr. Indeed, this notion is linguistically present in her reprise of her aria in the second act: "Numi, pietà del mio martir." And just as hagiography provides the virgin martyr with an extremely limited range of narrative possibilities, so does the opera provide few to its heroine. If it is the fate of the martyr to love, suffer, and pray until she at last dies, then such a narrative is certainly imposed upon Aida by the opera's "interesting lady."

Quite aware that the Egyptian army has conquered its foe and that Radamès is returning the victor, Amneris "sets up" Aida rhetorically. There is no logical reason for her need to discover Aida's secrets of the heart, for there is little Aida can do to prevent a union between the princess and the hero. Rather, it would seem that Amneris indulges in the rhetoric of the virago for its own sake, for the pleasure of seeing the suffering she inflicts on the other woman—as well as the vicarious and thus monstrously homoerotic pleasure of witnessing the passion of the other woman for the man *both* desire. Thus she moves from declaring her respect for the sorrows of the "daughter of the vanquished" and offering sisterly comfort to teasingly assuring her that the loss of her people will someday be assuaged by *amore*. Upon seeing the captive's agitated response to her suggestion that the powers of erotic love can obviate all else, Amneris probes Aida with a tormenting question that lays bare her psychomachia and filial guilt, a question designed at once to evoke the greatest possible pain and allow Amneris a voyeuristic enjoyment of Aida's desire: "Among the warriors who fought for the downfall of your country, one, perhaps, has aroused sweet anguish in your heart?" Subsequently, she taunts Aida with a false report of Radamès's death, only to retract it so that Aida will betray herself; then she orders her to witness the spectacle of his return—and her espousal to him.

This scene can leave little doubt of the depth of Amneris's depravity. She is, in this sense, the harbinger of the decadent women who would make the operatic stage "one of the major stalking grounds of the headhuntress, as well as of temptresses of every comparable sort" (Dijkstra, 376) by the end of the century. But although she exists in *Aida* primarily to provide a contrast to the virtuous heroine and to function as the instigator of her virtuous suffering, Amneris's monstrosity is so overwhelming that Radamès would forfeit the crown of Egypt proffered him and desert the army he has led rather than marry her.

Although relatively uncomplicated, Radamès displays considerable incongruity in his motivations and actions, symptomatic of the gender duality of his public and private subject positions. His outward political role as a military leader in the service of the theocratic state is unquestionably masculine; yet although he commands the slaughter of the Ethiopian host (for the love of an Ethiopian woman), he is not a zealot for his own nation's cause. Rather, he is the "good soldier" who simply does his duty and does not question its causes and effects. His ambitions, although grandiose, are limited; he has no interest in the prospect of ruling Egypt as Amneris's consort: "Ah no, the throne of Egypt . . . the soil of Egypt . . . the kingship of Egypt is not worth Aida's heart." Preferring traditionally "feminine" and private romantic concerns, he lacks the patriarchal interests by which masculinity is defined in a male-dominated society. But the Egypt represented in *Aida* is partly dominated by a masculinized woman—surely Amneris has far more to say in the opera than does her father—and Radamès fears her. Thus faced with the prospect of being, for all intents and purposes, her "wife," he chooses the ostensibly cowardly option of flight, one traditionally employed in romantic texts by women seeking to avoid sexual violation. In planning to elope with Aida to Ethiopia, he assimilates her disempowered feminized condition and eschews the masculine patriarchy for the feminine *patria*.[20]

Their projected flight to *la patria* is, ironically, aborted by the intrusion of *il padre*. Amonasro, by contrast with Radamès, is not a feminized man; rather, as a defeated king held captive in a hostile nation, he fights the emasculation of his state and plots his revenge. Unlike the traditional *senex*, he does not attempt to obstruct young love, but rather would utilize it as a means to his political and military ends. Thus when he discovers his daughter contemplating suicide—for "O, patria mia" could be considered Aida's suicide note, so to speak—he bids her to live by promising love and freedom and the restoration of their native land—if only she will extract the secret route of attack from Radamès. But if Radamès does not necessarily believe in his nation's cause, he does believe in honor, which, significantly, has long served as the ultimate talisman of the sexually besieged woman. Aida initially rejects her father's plan, refusing to play the "masculine" role of dishonoring (thus symbolically violating) her love. Amonasro, then, pressures her into compliance by appealing to her worst female fears while giving her an alternative and more luridly masculine role: "Remember the Egyptian has cruelly profaned our homes, our temples and our altars, bound the ravished virgins in chains; murdered mothers, old men, children." If she will not comply, the ghosts of her slaughtered fellow Ethiopians, including that of her own mother, raising her "fleshless arms," will point to Aida, crying, *Per te la patria muor!* ("Through you the homeland perishes!"). If she cannot or will not respond to those most basic threats to women, rape and murder, then she will become, in effect, the rapist and murderer of *la patria*.

So effective is Amonasro's rhetoric that Aida emulates it in convincing Radamès to flee with her when all other arguments fail: "Go, go, Amneris awaits you at the altar." By invoking the name of the dreaded virago, she appeals to his threatened violation and secures both his cooperation and his military secret. Amonasro's triumph lasts for barely a minute, but his last action on stage before he flees (to fall not gloriously in battle but abjectly in exhaustion) is a pointed one. When discovered by Amneris and the high priest Ramfis, he turns his dagger not on the theocrat who has precipitated the war but on his daughter's rival. Radamès, conceivably motivated by a death wish, throws himself between them. Amonasro escapes and his motives thus remain unexplained in the confusion of the moment. Yet the assassination of a princess seems a curiously ungallant and dishonorable action for a king, particularly when more suitable male targets are available. Perhaps Amonasro recognizes her as being more masculine than any of the men present, or he may see the virago not as a woman but as a usurper of male prerogative and thus an abomination more deserving of death than any male foe.

Death is not, however, the virago's fate. Instead she has yet to fulfill a curious role, one that might even evoke sympathy for the she-devil, for if there is anyone worse than a virago, it is a theocrat. With Amonasro dead and Aida vanished, she offers the imprisoned Radamès mercy if he will put the past behind and begin a new life with her; but he has already resolved to emulate Aida in the role of martyrdom. Left alone for the first time, Amneris at last has her soliloquy (not quite an aria) in which she engages in self-reflection and acknowledges her responsibility for the needless suffering she has caused, citing a putatively feminine trait, *atroce gelosia*, as the cause. Thus self-chastened, she rails against the unyielding priests who pronounce the sentence: "Oh, the criminals! They are never sated with blood, and they call themselves ministers of heaven!" Her protests and curses are in vain; she is a mere woman after all, and even a princess, *la figlia dei Faraon*, cannot gainsay the dictates of those who arbitrate the will of the gods. Radamès goes stoically to his death, buried alive in the crypt and joined secretly by Aida, who had merely postponed her own martyrdom/suicide. But it is to Amneris, whom Verdi denied so much as a grand aria, that the final word is given. After the lovers hail their approaching beatific vision and expire in their ecstatic farewell to earthly abjection, Amneris mournfully intercedes with the gods and, by extension, everyone else: *Pace t'imploro, pace, pace, pace!* ("Peace, I beg, peace, peace, peace!"). Not only is this an incredibly novel idea in this opera, but these are, perhaps, the only words of good sense uttered by any of its characters.

No, Verdi and Ghislanzoni, unlike Bellini and Romani, did not kill off their "interesting lady," for it would diminish the glory of the heroine's romantic martyrdom. Instead, the virago is granted a conversion of sorts. She is put in her place; she is only a woman, no match for the sinister homosocial institution of the priesthood. There is no Norma, no Adalgisa here to save the integrity and honor of the nation through mutual love; love between women was, by 1871, well on its way to becoming too suspect for that. Nor, for that matter, can the heterosexual love of Radamès and Aida save either of the respective nations; indeed, it would seem to undermine the cause of the oppressed Ethiopians and violate the national security of the oppressive Egyptians. In the end, the Egyptians hold a military and political advantage, but they are divided among themselves. No cause is served, except that most solipsistic one of heterosexual romance for its own sake.

This unfortunate end is indicative of the future of Italian opera. After Verdi, the political would be secondary to the personal (as in, for example, *Tosca*), if present at all. Desire and passion—specifically *heterosexual* desire and passion—would be all that mattered.[21] And then, after the reign of Verdi's putative heir Giacomo Puccini, the tradition of Italian grand opera would simply fade away, perhaps because it had nothing significant left to say. But how did Verdi's last "political opera" come to this? Perhaps, with the completion of Risorgimento, there was no need to continue the line of nationalist operas focusing on *la patria oppressa* (Arblaster, 63). Perhaps, as several critics have suggested, *Aida* was really of little interest to Verdi; what mattered was the honor of the commission and the remuneration.[22] Or, even worse but more likely, this ending may represent a glimpse into the heart of darkness of the modern world of the late nineteenth century, a truth that not even the triumph of Risorgimento could obviate, a truth still pertinent today: "What we find here is the absolute triumph of a system over all those individuals and groups who oppose or deviate from it. . . . It is a terrible, despairing conclusion, mitigated only by the mutual devotion of Radames and Aida" (Arblaster, 141).

That opposition or deviation, I would suggest, applies to gender as well as to politics. *Aida* is an opera in which everyone—with the possible exception of the priests—is in some state of gender dislocation, a fearful if latent response, perhaps, to the growing fear of women asserting their rights and challenging gender roles in the late nineteenth century. Even so, Aida may well be the last purely honorable female victim, the last great sacrificial virgin of the operatic stage. In the hands of Puccini and his lesser colleagues, such women would lack her nobility; they would become decadent, tainted, and without any greater cause than *amore*.

But no, Verdi and Ghislanzoni did not kill off Amneris. Though defeated and supplicant at the end of *Aida*, she lives all the same. And as the twentieth century dawned, the virago, the latter-day configuration of the Romantic "interesting lady," would yet have her day on the operatic stage.

NOTES

This essay is dedicated to Anne K. Mellor.

1. Girard, while demurring on the homosexual aspect of such triangulation, is nonetheless the pioneering critic in the analysis of various forms of "triangular desire" and fascination with the rival in narrative (1–52). Sedgwick, in turn, explores the elements of male homoerotic desire in such configurations, which she terms "homosociality," and the extent to which it is a major factor in narrative structure, specifically in nineteenth-century English literature (*Between Men*, 1–5, 21–27). Subsequently, she has examined male homosociality in larger cultural contexts (*The Epistemology of the Closet*, 182–212). More recently, Terry Castle (67–91) has provided a particularly female homoerotic reconfiguration of this paradigm.

2. Faderman uses the term *romantic friendship* to denote an intense yet platonic same-sex love relationship. In *Surpassing the Love of Men* (65–143), she demonstrates the extent to which such relationships flourished since the early modern period and argues that they once were regarded as positive and ennobling.

3. This is not to force an intentional or causal connection between the settings, but to indicate the extent to which sympathetic analogies might be created. The opera's libretto, by Felice Romani, is based on a contemporary French play, Louis Alexandre Soumet's *Norma, ou l'Infanticide*. Romani himself had written, some years earlier, a libretto for an opera by Giovanni Pacini entitled *La Sacerdotessa d'Irminsul*, set in eighth-century Saxony (which certainly illustrates the historical inauthenticity of the Druid's god "Irminsul"). On Bellini and Romani's sources, see Weinstock (275–76, 525 n. 26, 526 n. 28). On the highly imaginative and ahistorical treatment of the Druids in Romantic literature and art, see Piggott (131–81). On the possible origins of the name Irminsul, see Dent (170); as a source of historical information, however, Dent must be taken with a grain of salt; in the same paragraph he mistakenly sets the opera in the British isles, presumably mistaking "ancient Wales" (170) for ancient Gaul, and states that the clearly male-gendered Irminsul (Oroveso calls him *terribil Dio*) "is described in the opera as a goddess" (170). Finally, while Bellini is often considered one of the least political composers of nineteenth-century Italian opera, it is worth noting that he was, some ten years prior to the composition of *Norma*, a member of the Carbonari, a nationalist secret society that participated in an insurrection against foreign rule in Naples. On the Carbonari, see Holt (44–66); on Bellini's participation, see Arblaster (87–88) and Weinstock (18–20).

4. All citations of the libretto are from the Italian text and the English translation by Kenneth Chalmers, both included in the booklet that accompanies the 1989 compact disc reissue of the 1964 London recording, unless otherwise specified.

5. Arblaster, while making an effective case for seeing Norma as a traitor (albeit a redeemed traitor by the end of the opera), suggests that it is "worthwhile imagining how *Norma* might have been received in France or in the Netherlands or Czechoslovakia during World War Two" (82). Perhaps, although I must wonder if audience reception of any opera is ever really that simple. This is to construct the

opera's meaning based solely on the perceptions of the audience and the political ideologies and subject positions of the members of that audience. Conversely, we might find it "worthwhile to imagine" what the reception to *Norma* might have been in the 1960s (when such *Norma*s as Joan Sutherland, Montserrat Caballé, and Beverly Sills were at the height of their powers and the opera was frequently performed) in the context of popular protest against the Vietnam War. In such a context *Norma*, at least at this point in the opera, might be construed, quite sympathetically, as one who promoted the then popular message, "Make love, not war." *Norma* has, nonetheless, been utilized historically to support nationalist causes; for examples of this see Rosselli (165–67) and Dent (173).

6. Translation mine.

7. Although Clotilde remains a mere *comprimaria* with neither identity nor motive in Bellini's opera, she is considerably more complex and vocal in Soumet's original. Her complicity in this incredible cover-up is given a relatively logical basis; she is not a Druid but a Christian who advises Norma's children (who have speaking roles in the play) that her god is more powerful than those of either the Romans or the Druids. As such, she has no reason to fear Irminsul's wrath. This possibility is obviated in the opera, however, as it is set in the first century BC. See also Weinstock (526, *n.* 28).

8. In this article Wood also discusses (38–39) how the opera *Norma* and its music were used by modernist lesbian authors Kate O'Brien and Willa Cather as a covert signifier of love and desire between women.

9. Although I use Chalmers's translation here, I have substituted *companion* (*compagna* in Romani's libretto) for Chalmers's *friend*. In Italian, *compagna* suggests "life companion" or "spouse"; these meanings are not found in *amica* ("friend"), the term by which Norma calls Adalgisa immediately before this duet. I thank Carole Gallucci for clarifying this.

10. And we can be sure that whatever is left in the opera to the individual imagination will surely find its expression in a new production of that opera. As an indication that I am not the first to notice the homosocial (if not homoerotic) relationship between Norma and Adalgisa, in a recent British production of the opera, Adalgisa returned in the last scene to accompany Norma to the pyre. I thank Margaret Reynolds for this information.

11. The historical conditions leading to the Risorgimento might be said to begin with the French invasion of Italy under Napoleon I in the 1790s and the division of Italy between various victors of the Napoleonic Wars as a result of the Congress of Vienna in 1815; Italy was, however, divided into multiple jurisdictions long before the eighteenth century. After several failed plots in the first two decades of the nineteenth century and early uprisings, such as those of the Carbonari in which the young Bellini participated in the 1820s (see note 1), the most serious stirrings of the movement began with Giuseppe Mazzini's organization of "Young Italy" and the Este Conspiracy, both in 1831, also the year in which *Norma* was first performed. After three decades of intermittent armed conflict, a united Kingdom of Italy was proclaimed in 1861, with Vittorio Emanuele II of Piedmont as its ruler, primarily as a result of Giuseppe Garibaldi's military campaigns; Vittorio Emanuele II of Piedmont was its ruler. In 1870, with the withdrawal of French military forces, Italian troops seized Rome from papal rule, thus uniting the Italian peninsula under a central government. For a brief overview of the causes and effects of the Risorgimento, see Riall; for a more comprehensive chronological history, see Holt.

12. Italian colonialism in Africa began in the late 1880s during the premiership of Francesco Crispi, who had earlier been a Risorgimento leader. By 1889 Italy claimed Eritrea, a region of northern Ethiopia bordering on the Red Sea, as a colony, as well as most of present-day Somalia. In 1896 the Ethiopian army, which was well armed by Britain and France, repelled Italian attempts to conquer Ethiopia, the only independent African nation, at the Battle of Adowa. The Italian defeat was the first in colonial history inflicted on a European army by Africans and resulted in the downfall of Crispi's government and ensuing social unrest in Italy. Italy nevertheless retained control over much of the Horn of Africa until World War II, and, in 1935, Mussolini's forces succeeded in invading Ethiopia and deposing Emperor Haile Selassie. Accordingly, Italian audiences in the 1930s may have been able to identify with the political aspects of the production of *Aida* Arblaster describes, at least in terms of the Triumphal March of Act II, Scene 2. How such an audience would reconcile a "Blackshirt Radames" with his love for a woman who is the princess of these "barbarous Africans" or his subsequent planned desertion and divulging of military secrets remains unexplained.

Possibly because of—rather than in spite of—the aforementioned simplicity of its major characters, *Aida* can touch many deeply felt concerns for a wide range of audiences; therefore the opera is susceptible to a wide range of political and cultural interpretations—often at odds with one another. For a provocative interpretation of a 1981 Frankfurt Opera production that appropriated the opera as a commentary on European class struggle, see Weber (107–26).

13. It is probably not too great an exaggeration to say that for a whole generation of opera listeners (which includes the author of this essay), Leontyne Price *is* Aida. Price herself is quite candid on her reappropriation, as it were, of this role as a vehicle of nascent African-American pride—and quite rightfully so: "As a black soprano, it was the only time I got to sing a black character. Normally being black is of no artistic significance [in opera] whatsoever. But in this case it said things about where I was as a woman and a human being, about the life and progress, or lack of it, of millions of people at home in the States—things I could not have said as eloquently in other ways." Yet Price is quick to add that Verdi's heroine must not be taken out of context in this sort of identification: "I think that sometimes the notion that Aida is truly a princess has been lost sight of " (Matheopoulos, 163).

14. It must be obvious to any audience that the Ethiopian Aida is, perforce, black (although, as historical photographs from the 1870s to the 1950s reveal, she was not necessarily performed as such by generations of European sopranos). To assign a race to Aida's Egyptian captors (particularly along the lines of a black–white dichotomy), however, must inevitably, given the current climate of academic discourse, open a can of worms that is well beyond the scope or intentions of this paper. Let it suffice to say that Verdi and Ghislanzoni do not assign racial labels in the opera; those who wish to explore this avenue (or those seeking an overview of the debate on race and antiquity) would be well advised to consult Martin Bernal's *Black Athena* for a thoughtful "Afrocentric" perspective and Mary Lefkowitz's *Not Out of Africa* for a considered opposing view. I would merely add that *Aida* is not, as long supposed, a story that originates with French Egyptologist Auguste Mariette. Rather, as numerous scholars have noted, it has an Afro-Grecian source in the second-century *Aethiopica* (*The Book of the Ethiopian Women* or *Ethiopian Things*) of Heliodorus of Emesa. On the *Aethiopica* as a source for Verdi via Mariette, see Phillips-Matz (571–72).

15. Lucy Riall, commenting on the actions of the church during the period in which *Aida* was composed, defines the impact these rulings had on the ordinary Italian: "When Pope Pio IX obliged Italians to choose between their loyalty to the Church and their support of the new state, he dealt a devastating blow to the legitimacy of Liberal Italy. Pio IX, unlike the new state, possessed both the moral and the institutional power to enforce his instructions. The beliefs, rituals and language of the Catholic Church united Italians . . . in ways that a sense of secular nationhood did not" (79). On the obstructive role of the papacy in Italian reunification, see Holt (279–82, 292–99) and Riall (15–25, 76–80 passim). On Verdi's political career, see Phillips-Matz (425–39).

16. For a concise historical overview of medical sexology, see Bullough (9–60). For an examination of the effects of medical sexology and antifeminism on nineteenth-century European art and culture, see Dijkstra; on the effects of medical sexology on nineteenth- and early-twentieth-century women and literature, see Faderman (239–53).

17. For a summary of the conditions of nineteenth-century Italian women and their struggle to reconcile feminism and Catholicism, see DeGiorgio (166–97).

18. For a compelling examination of Lombroso's work, particularly as it stigmatized women and Jews, and its implications for subsequent Italian literature, see Harrowitz.

19. All citations of the libretto are from the Italian text and an uncredited English translation, both included in the booklet that accompanies the 1987 compact disc reissue of the 1962 London recording.

20. It is noteworthy that although the word *patria* occurs frequently in the libretto—indeed, it is the focus of Aida's second aria—it is primarily used to signify defeated Ethiopia. Its only use in signifying Egypt occurs after Radamès is accused of treason; this would seem to suggest that what is defeated or betrayed is feminized. In their more imperialistic moments, however, the Egyptian characters use the masculine phrase *il sacro suol dell'Egitto* ("the sacred soil of Egypt"), which connotes both divine privilege and the essential nature of "Egyptianness."

21. For an examination of such "opera[s] without politics" that took "late Romantic opera so far from contemporary reality and contemporary concerns" (261), see Arblaster (245–61).

22. See, in particular, Arblaster (141–43). See also Phillips-Matz (567–98) on Verdi's attitudes and actions during the period of composition.

WORKS CITED

Arblaster, Anthony. *Viva la Libertà!: Politics in Opera.* London: Verso, 1992.

Barreca, Regina. Introduction. *Desire and Imagination: Classic Essays in Sexuality,* ed. Regina Barreca. New York: Meridian, 1995:xi–xxiii.

Bellini, Vincenzo. *Norma.* Libretto by Felice Romani, trans. Kenneth Chalmers. Performed by Joan Sutherland, Marilyn Horne, John Alexander, and Richard Cross. Conductor, Richard Bonynge. London Symphony Orchestra and Chorus. London 425 488–2, 1964, reissued 1989.

Bernal, Martin. *Black Athena: The Afroasiatic Roots of Classical Civilization,* 2 vols. to date. New Brunswick: Rutgers University Press, 1987–.

Bullough, Vern L. *Science in the Bedroom: A History of Sex Research.* New York: Basic Books, 1994.

Castle, Terry. *The Apparitional Lesbian: Female Homosexuality and Modern Culture*. New York: Columbia University Press, 1993.

Clément, Catherine. *Opera, or the Undoing of Women*, trans. Betsy Wing. Minneapolis: University of Minnesota Press, 1988.

DeGiorgio, Michela. "The Catholic Model." In *Emerging Feminism from Revolution to World War*, eds. Genevieve Fraisse and Michelle Perrot, vol. 4, *A History of Women in the West*, gen. eds. Georges Duby and Michelle Perrot. Cambridge: Harvard University Press, 1993:166–97.

Dent, Edward J. *The Rise of Romantic Opera*, ed. Winton Dean. Cambridge: Cambridge University Press, 1976.

Dijkstra, Bram. *Idols of Perversity: Fantasies of Feminine Evil in Fin-de-Siècle Culture*. New York: Oxford University Press, 1986.

Faderman, Lillian. *Surpassing the Love of Men: Romantic Friendship and Love Between Women from the Renaissance to the Present*. New York: Morrow, 1981.

Girard, René. *Deceit, Desire, and the Novel: Self and Other in Literary Structure*, trans. Yvonne Freccero. Baltimore: Johns Hopkins University Press, 1965.

Harrowitz, Nancy A. *Antisemitism, Misogyny, and the Logic of Cultural Difference*. Lincoln: University of Nebraska Press, 1994.

Holt, Edgar. *Risorgimento: The Making of Italy 1815–1870*. London: Macmillan, 1970.

Käppeli, Anne-Marie. "Feminist Scenes." In *Emerging Feminism from Revolution to World War*, eds. Genevieve Fraisse and Michelle Perrot, vol. 4, *A History of Women in the West*, gen. eds. Georges Duby and Michelle Perrot. Cambridge: Harvard University Press, 1993:482–514.

Lefkowitz, Mary R. *Not Out of Africa: How Afrocentrism Became an Excuse to Teach Myth as History*. New York: Basic Books, 1996.

Matheopoulos, Helena. *Diva: Great Sopranos and Mezzos Discuss Their Art*. Boston: Northeastern University Press, 1991.

Phillips-Matz, Mary Jane. *Verdi: A Biography*. Oxford: Oxford University Press, 1993.

Piggott, Stuart. *The Druids*. New York: Praeger, 1968.

Riall, Lucy. *The Italian Risorgimento: State, Society, and National Unification*. London: Routledge, 1994.

Rosselli, John. *The Opera Industry in Italy from Cimarosa to Verdi: The Role of the Impresario*. Cambridge: Cambridge University Press, 1984.

Said, Edward W. *Culture and Imperialism*. New York: Knopf, 1993.

Sedgwick, Eve Kosofsky. *Between Men: English Literature and Male Homosocial Desire*. New York: Columbia University Press, 1985.

——. *Epistemology of the Closet*. Berkeley: University of California Press, 1990.

Verdi, Giuseppe. *Aida*. Libretto by Antonio Ghislanzoni. Performed by Leontyne Price, Jon Vickers, Rita Gorr, and Robert Merrill. Conductor, Georg Solti. Orchestra and Chorus of Il Teatro dell'Opera di Roma. London 417 416–2, 1962, reissued 1987.

Walkowitz, Judith R. "Dangerous Sexualities." In *Emerging Feminism from Revolution to World War*, eds. Genevieve Fraisse and Michelle Perrot, vol. 4, *A History of Women in the West*, gen. eds. Georges Duby and Michelle Perrot. Cambridge: Harvard University Press, 1993:369–98.

Weber, Samuel. "Taking Place: Toward a Theater of Dislocation." In *Opera Through Other Eyes*, ed. David J. Levin. Stanford: Stanford University Press, 1994:107–46.

Weinstock. Herbert. *Vincenzo Bellini: His Life and His Operas*. New York: Knopf, 1971.

Wood, Elizabeth. "Sapphonics." In *Queering the Pitch: The New Gay and Lesbian Musicology*, eds. Philip Brett, Elizabeth Wood, and Gary C. Thomas. New York: Routledge, 1994:27–66.

*P. J. Smith*

---

## CHAPTER FIVE

## Structures of Identity and Difference in Bizet's Carmen

Susan McClary

The first act of Georges Bizet's opera *Carmen* opens with a chorus of soldiers who are killing time watching people pass by in the street. The dragoons are ostensibly part of a Spanish army, yet they are of a significantly different class, ethnic, and even—by implication—national constituency from those they observe. They emphasize their difference in their refrain, which they sing repeatedly with accents of mock surprise: *Drôles de gens que ces gens là!* ("What funny people these are!"). This chorus introduces the audience into the terrain upon which the opera will unfold, and it explicitly legitimates distanced, objective, voyeuristic observation. It invites us, the spectators, likewise to gaze unabashedly at these "funny people": a sideshow of women, exotics, and grotesques. Without necessarily noticing how, we enter into the opera's dramatic events from the soldiers' point of view.

For Bizet's original audience, this identification would have been easily made, for the soldiers' music resembles that of light Parisian entertainments of the 1870s: it is French, in other words—unmarked by characteristics used by Bizet in the opera to signal "Spain." The chorus poses no barriers for comprehension: it sounds utterly familiar, yet flatters the ear with its vaguely sophisticated nuances. The soldiers are calculated to sound like "us." In fact, we may not even notice them. (Theirs is not the music we go away humming.) As our stand-ins, they are transparent; we listen past them to the exotic spectacle they offer for our delectation. They both naturalize spectatorship and situate us as part of the dominant (French) social group that watches the colorful antics of the local (Spanish) inhabitants from the safety of the sidelines. But as the opera proceeds, questions of identity and difference become increasingly perplexing. Who precisely are the "funny people" we are supposed to be observing? And with whom are we to identify, once the stick soldiers disappear?

Prosper Mérimée's novella *Carmen*, for all its artful ambiguities, is much more forthright on these matters.[1] He begins his story with a Greek epigraph: "Woman is bitter as gall, but she has two good moments: in bed and dead." And he concludes it with a pseudoscientific ethnography of the gypsy people in which the story's narrator attempts to distance himself from and purge the contagion that fatally infected his acquaintance Don José and that might well have contaminated him as well. These overemphatic framing devices leave little doubt that this narrative concerns threatening encounters with the other: the other primarily understood as woman and as gypsy. However, we learn in the course of the novella that several other varieties of alterity are at stake here besides gender and racial or ethnic difference, including class, nation, religion, culture, legal status, and language. Still, identity is anchored securely in the voice of the narrator, even though his own sense of self is severely shaken during the course of the novella.

Our narrator is a French archaeologist who has gone to Spain for field research. As a scholar, he prides himself on his superior skills in objective observation and his abilities as a wordsmith. Along the way, he has a fleeting encounter with an outlaw renowned for his violence. He protects himself by befriending this desperate criminal who seems so radically different but who bears the traces of an upper-class background in his name, Don José. Like the narrator, José is of a cultivated and privileged class; he is white, Christian, of northern rather than southern origin; we even learn that he is a sensitive musician. Yet in behavior, appearance, and reputation he has taken on the characteristics of the most brutal strata of humanity— same, yet other. The narrator can only wonder how such a thorough transformation can have occurred.

After parting company with José, the narrator makes his way into Cordoba, where he learns that the local pastime is watching working-class women bathe in the river at dusk. Confident in his skills of disinterested observation, he eagerly joins the assembled group of men to gaze. But his gazing is interrupted by a charming young woman who engages him in conversation. She is dark in complexion, and he casts about for her proper classification, taking her variously to be Andalusian, Moorish, or Jewish (a word he cannot bring himself to utter). He finally must be told she is a gypsy. Against his better judgment, he goes home with her to have his fortune told. But before they can get down to that or any other kind of business, the door bursts open and Don José rushes in. He is on the brink of murdering the narrator in a fit of jealous rage when he recognizes his traveling companion and spares his life. The narrator flees to the safety of his archaeological pursuits.

On passing back through Cordoba several months later, the narrator learns that Don José has killed Carmen, the gypsy to whose exotic charms he himself had submitted without resistance. He visits José in prison and is told more or less the story we know from the opera: how he was an officer in the military who fell in love with Carmen and consequently (in a kind of Domino Theory of morality) was sucked into the downward spiral of degradation that led eventually to her murder. It is after the narrator has learned of these events that he is compelled to write his hysterical ethnographic essay. For if José had not interrupted his encounter with Carmen and saved him, he might well have found himself in José's predicament.

The narrator therefore attempts to eradicate from himself those inclinations that made him vulnerable to Carmen's charms. He argues in his concluding essay that gypsies are filthy, superstitious, treacherous, and hideous in appearance—especially the women. He seeks by means of a barricade of words to hold at bay the dangerous other and finally focuses on language itself. For Carmen, a colonial subject who has learned of necessity to maneuver within the imposed languages of imperialism, remains fluent in her native tongue. By contrast, the narrator, who eloquently wields the cultural discourses of privilege, has no access to gypsy speech. He is linguistically transparent and vulnerable; she is multilingual, possesses the verbal currency necessary to slip in and out of all social contexts, whether organized by ethnicity, nationality, class, or gender. As he tries to fix her and her people in his analytical writing, his masterful, cultivated words drop impotently into a confused heap. He finishes cryptically with a gypsy adage: "Between closed lips no fly can pass."

Translating a text this convoluted and deliberately conflicted onto the stage was no easy matter, and some critics have complained that Bizet and his librettists betrayed Mérimée's celebrated novella. Indeed, if one locates Mérimée's ingenuity in *Carmen* in its structural and narratological virtuosity rather than in the lurid story, then the linear tracking of the opera may seem unspeakably pedestrian. The most drastic alteration in the adaptation of the novella for purposes of opera involves the elimination of the French narrator—the omniscient voice that guided us through the story, that situated us with respect to subject position, that interpreted what we were permitted to see and hear. Nor is Don José's narrative voice present in the opera: his is simply one of several competing for attention in what appears to be an unmediated presentation of the events themselves. In other words, we move from the monologic conventions of fiction to the polyvocal (and apparently far more democratic) conventions of drama.

This elimination of narrative control was potentially quite perilous. In Mérimée's novella, the figure of Carmen was always multiply mediated: through José's recollections, through the French narrator, through Mérimée's self-consciously literary language. Yet she had been regarded as lethal nonetheless. Not even Don José's knife contains her: the narrator lunges to erect a moralizing scholarly text about gypsy women, hoping thereby to contain the contagion spread through ill-advised contact with the exotic. And in their turn, French bourgeois critics condemned the unleashing of such a monster onto the literary terrain. Three decades later, the scandal still remained alive. Thus when Bizet and his collaborators first proposed setting *Carmen* for the Opéra-Comique, the producers were aghast: how could this infamously sordid woman be represented in the theater that was a favorite site for family outings? Halévy, one of the librettists, promised that they would tone the character of Carmen down and balance her with a proper girl.[2] But they did intend to present Carmen: not through mere verbal descriptions, but in spectacular enactment and with her treacherous utterances heard directly, rather than filtered through three layers of male narrators.

In casting aside Mérimée's complex framing devices, Bizet and his collaborators risked creating a simplistic reduction of the novella. But they also risked unleashing a monster far more dangerous than his, insofar as this operatic Carmen would appear to speak for herself without the constant intervention of narrative voices. Given the sensitive, even sensationalistic nature of this story's subject matter—the humiliation and degradation of male, white authority at the hands of a woman of color—this was a problem the collaborators could scarcely afford to overlook. But their strategies of containment had to be radically different from those of Mérimée's novella, given the nature of their medium.

The most obvious counterweight added by the librettists is the character promised by Halévy, Micaëla—a girl from José's home who has been sent to him as a messenger and potential bride by his mother. Mérimée had no such figure: his is a world in which desperate men circle warily around Carmen as though she were the only woman on earth and compete to the death for her favors. However, the dramatic stage—especially the family-oriented stage of the Opéra-Comique—was regarded as a more influential site of social formation than the novel. Because the lifelike representations enacted there were more likely to be perceived by impressionable viewers as real than the creatures of fiction, the guidelines surrounding theatrical works were considerably more strict. Micaëla was offered up explicitly as a foil to Carmen: as the normative good girl who stands as the ideal against which Carmen is to appear all the more monstrous. With Micaëla aboard they hoped to receive a PG rating rather than an R or an X.

But the most intricate restructuring of the novella for purposes of this opera—the delineation of relative subject positions and points of view—is the work of Bizet alone, and it takes place within the music itself. Although the opera involves only Spanish characters, Bizet articulates the narrative tensions of the story in such a way as to reinforce but also to destabilize the foundations of French national identity. It is he who creates vivid images of the other—Carmen's frank sexuality, her indicators of racial and class difference—just as he constructs Don José's presumably more cultivated utterances. And he locates all these within a delicate web of cultural associations, thematic correspondences, and subtle affective commentaries that match or surpass in complexity the framing devices engineered by Mérimée, even though they operate on the basis of entirely different premises—the formal premises of musical procedure.

We have already seen that the beginning of Act I situates us in the comfortable position of the dragoons, the military presence that sings in the latest Parisian fashion while practicing surveillance over the native Andalusian population. A number of amusing spectacles are presented to them (and us) in untroubled succession: a shy provincial girl, a procession of street urchins pretending to be soldiers, and a group of languorous women who work at the local cigarette factory. The characters who will become prominent in the drama are casually introduced through the "B" sections of the symmetrical ABA formula that governs most of the numbers: Micaëla is interpolated into the soldiers' chorus, Don José into the street urchins' march, and so forth. Musical well-roundedness and plot advancement thus proceed along together, apparently without strain.

Most of Bizet's music during the first several numbers can be justified either as music that is to be heard within the context of the action itself (such as the bugle call that announces the changing of the guard) or as the accompaniment that supports and psychologically amplifies the singers in turn. It seems, in other words, objective. But there is one extremely interesting editorial moment in the first number that subtly situates the listener in a male subject position. The dragoons have just concluded their first full presentation of "Drôles de gens" when Micaëla comes onto the stage. At this point neither they nor (ostensibly) we in the audience know who she is. Bizet might have cued us that this is a sweet girl from home by having the orchestra play one of her guileless motives. Instead, Micaëla is marked by her musical creator as a femme fatale, for her entrance is accompanied by the kind of slinky chromaticism that later will mark Carmen's dangerous sexuality. As Don Giovanni would say, she exudes (at least at this initial moment) an *odor di femina*, and the rising bassline that undergirds Morales's description of her movements leaves little doubt as to the prurient interests of her spectators. Of course, we and the dragoons find out soon that we have misread the signs: she will be sanctioned many times over during this scene and the rest of the opera as a model of modest bourgeois femininity—indeed, precisely the kind of French bourgeois femininity characteristic of the Opéra-Comique. If the plot acknowledges Micaëla as Spanish, she sings in the unmarked discourse that identifies her, like the dragoons, as one of "us" with respect to nation.

Yet for all her modesty, Bizet goes out of his way to slant the piece in the direction of male address through his slight four-bar commentary. Given that this is a piece often taken to be about an innocent young soldier and a temptress, the politics of this first encounter between the sexes are most interesting. In this opera, women are by definition other—even good girls. Micaëla manages to escape the clutches of the aroused soldiers, and they retreat frustrated and bored to their chorus of "Drôles de gens." She provides a diversion—a mere passing dissonance that momentarily enlivens the action before the security of the inevitable return to the beginning. She is the B section that makes the reprise of A meaningful in this ABA structure.

The multivalent dissonance of Carmen herself, of course, proves to be not so easily resolved or contained; when she enters, the confident ABA procedures that had organized the earlier numbers in Act I suddenly lose their certainty. Nevertheless, in a composition in which the listener is so conditioned to expect formulaic returns to opening materials, one might expect that the frame of the quasi-French soldiers will eventually step back in for the sake of structural balance and closure. And we would be correct in anticipating some kind of reprise. But the formal return that ultimately rounds out the opera as a whole involves music we have not yet discussed: the Prelude, which actually occurs prior to the raising of the curtain, prior to the occupying army that would seem to be in control in Act I.

For this opera has two frames competing for the privilege of formal closure. In contrast to the familiar discourse of the dragoons, which invites automatic identification, the Prelude establishes the exotic setting we have presumably come to the theater to sample. I hesitate to call it Spanish, for most of Bizet's writings in this and many of his other works are products of his own synthesized, all-purpose mode of exoticism.[3] If his exotic passages succeed in convincing listeners that they are hearing "the very soul of Spain," it is not because they are ethnographically accurate; he seems not to have been interested in reproducing the traits of any particular ethnic music in his compositions so much as the aura of exoticism itself. Thus when he recycled materials among some of his other works, he occasionally would resituate a piece that was originally supposed to sound Russian in Brazil or in the Orient. Bizet did some small amount of research for *Carmen* and used a couple of snippets of authenticated folk music and some stylistic patterns resembling flamenco. But he also happily incorporated an African-Cuban popular song that became the "Habañera." His success was in large part a result of his uncanny ability to draw upon common assumptions about what the "other" (of whatever stripe) should sound like. Like so many of his contemporaries in French literature and painting, Bizet's imagination only came to life when it engaged with Orientalism: many of his nonexotic compositions were left incomplete or were viewed as quite ordinary by both him and his critics.

Edward Said has written extensively about the appeal of Orientalism for the nineteenth-century artist.[4] On the one hand, the exotic held out the promise of supplementing the increasingly dreary, restrictive world northern Europe had become: it was an imaginary zone where whatever was lacking in the everyday world could be supplied, where behaviors held to be taboo could be indulged in freely, where tedious rationality (the white man's burden) was replaced with its opposite. Nietzsche, for instance, writes:

> This music [of *Carmen*] is cheerful, but not in a French or German way.
> Its cheerfulness is African; fate hangs over it; its happiness is brief, sud-

den, without pardon. I envy Bizet for having had the courage for this sensibility which had hitherto had no language in the cultivated music of Europe—for this more southern, brown, burnt sensibility. —How the yellow afternoons of its happiness do us good! We look into the distance as we listen: did we ever find the sea smoother? —And how soothingly the Moorish dance speaks to us? How even our insatiability for once gets to know satiety in this lascivious melancholy![5]

On the other hand, these projected characteristics and imaginary constructions were often confused with reality itself and were taken to demonstrate the essential inferiority of the other. This "free zone" became a compensatory space for weary, bored northern Europeans (once again, their/our interest in watching these "funny people") and, at the same time, a site for ideological reproduction of the most lethal variety. Moreover, as imperialist expansion began to reach its limit and people from the colonies started to make their way onto European soil, the insulated, all-white context within which exoticism had served merely as colorful, escapist entertainment became increasingly riddled with the social consequences of French nationalist engagements with the "Orient."[6]

The Prelude opens with bright, festive music. It is flashy, especially when the cornets that have already been heralded by the fanfarelike motive finally enter the ensemble. Such an opening might be regarded as in bad taste if it were not marked as other, but its exotic pretenses justify it. Moreover, its syntax is gaily irrational: each four-bar phrase is stable within itself, but each pivots harmonically at the last moment under a flamboyant trill to the next segment, which sets out a contrasting key area. In sequence the keys established are A major, D major, A major, and C major, with an abrupt return to A major for the conclusion. The Prelude exhibits a high degree of certainty, with the constant reassuring returns to tonic. But the harmonic destabilizations under the flourishes give at least the illusion of risk, and the emergence of the irrationally related key of C major offers the momentary thrill of the unexpected, even if it is pulled back immediately under the control of the tonic. The effect is bold and colorful, though ultimately stable. It also serves as a rapid portrait of the world of the other. It does so not by drawing on exotic materials, but by acting out against the restrictions of "rational" and well-behaved northern European conventions. "Spain" is gaudy, flamboyant, irrational, static (i.e., not progressive), unpredictable, potentially treacherous. So is Carmen.

Even more than the opening scenes of Act I, the Prelude is obsessed formally with nested symmetries: ABA structures that may incorporate contrasting materials but that inevitably loop back for closure. The tiny section we have just considered operates that way with respect to its brave excursions away from and back to A major; the section as a whole is the A segment in a small ABA complex that comes back dutifully to round off; and the entire ABA complex in turn becomes the A part of a larger structure that incorporates the F major "Toreador Song" as a B section before returning intact. If the Prelude flirts with a wide assortment of keys, it easily pulls them all back to home base. Formally, the Prelude resembles Freud's game of *fort–da* in which a child experiments with feelings of separation and identity by tossing a spool on a string away (*fort*), then triumphantly retrieving it (*da*). But the Prelude's final toss of the spool destroys this illusion of control.

Following what sounds like the confident final cadence of the Prelude, the orchestra plunges into D minor with a quaking, fortissimo string tremolo. The contrast could not be more dramatic. Time itself (which had been fastidiously meted out in four-bar units until this point) seems to stand still. Under this sustained tremolo, a new, somber motive emerges. It is characterized by the interval of the augmented second: an interval traditionally associated in Western music either with exotic others (Jews, Orientals, gypsies, depending on context) or with anguish. In *Carmen*, both connotations are crucial, and they continually play off of one another as a kind of grim and deadly pun. For the motive will later be linked explicitly both with Carmen and with Don José's fatal, anguished attraction to her.

Another important referent operates here as well: the diminished-seventh tremolos and the foreboding strokes on the timpani that greet each statement of the motive reproduce the signs of horror and suspense first developed in one of Bizet's favorite operas, Weber's *Der Freischütz*. In that earlier context, this cluster of signs had been deployed to stand for pure evil—the evil of the demon Samiel in the Wolf Glen. Now, with the mere addition of the augmented second, the cluster warns us of the Oriental and the femme fatale, which to the late nineteenth century were far more diabolical forces than Samiel ever was.

After writhing its way to two temporary points of rest, the motive rises through increasing intensification to a crisis on a diminished seventh, only to break off onto another diminished seventh followed by silence. After all the cushioned protection of regular phrases and reliably returning opening materials, we find ourselves disgorged into a tonal, rhythmic, and structural void. The *fort–da* game is violently ruptured, and it is within the breach that thereby opens up that the dramatic action of the opera takes place; the unresolved dissonance that concludes the Prelude casts its shadow across the events as they unfold. Given the conventional constraints of formal process (especially as they have been established in this piece), such a gaping wound must eventually be healed or corrected, whatever the cost.

It is here, of course, that the curtain rises on our quasi-Parisian dragoons, confident in their ability to observe these "funny people" as a sideshow, to channel them as the B units of nicely symmetrical ABA forms. But in context, their authority is considerably undermined. It could be argued that the "funny people" have already staked out this terrain, that the soldiers represent but a blip within a far more stringent symmetry. And we don't have the security of Mérimée's narrator to situate us. The Parisian soldiers may manage to erase temporarily the memory of the Prelude, but its claim to being the determining element of the piece becomes increasingly clear as the opera progresses. For unlike any of the materials introduced by the soldiers or their first few tableaux, the various themes of the "Spanish" prelude return to mark significant occurrences in the drama: its final segment (often referred to as "fate") signals critical moments in the relationship between Carmen and Don José; the "Toreador Song" becomes the theme song of Escamillo, José's principal rival; and the festive march of the opening finally reenters in the final act to celebrate the anticipated bullfight and to indicate the beginning of the end—the return of the entire repressed Prelude complex for its postponed closure. In other words, a high tide of exoticism washes up, gradually obliterating the fragile "unmarked" (i.e., French) presence asserted by the dragoons at the beginning of Act I.

Thus far I have said little about the principal characters of this piece, Carmen and Don José, largely because they are part of this much larger set of issues. Most readings of the opera focus exclusively on their personalities and their relationship. But like most love stories we care about, this one has far more baggage attached than the mere matching or mismatching of two individuals. Although in another context I might lavish considerable attention on the details of Bizet's psychological portraits, here I am interested in Carmen and José as discursive types.

Carmen belongs both to the flashy exotic world already introduced in the Prelude and to the succession of women who have been ogled by the dragoons (and presumably by the spectators) since the curtain went up. She is doubly cast as other—as woman and as Oriental, with all the characteristics both entail. Her music is heavily marked both as grounded in the body (unlike Micaëla, Carmen lives up to her slinky introduction) and as treacherously chromatic and exotic.

But there is another kind of alterity projected onto Carmen: that of popular music. With rare exceptions, Carmen sings what are to be construed—even within the terms of the opera itself—as cabaret song-and-dance numbers, not "real" utterances. Thus the "Habañera" was lifted expressly from the Parisian cabaret scene, where exoticism was no less of a box office draw than in high art. And Bizet encountered the flamenco that flavors several of Carmen's other tunes through contact with gypsy night spots of ill repute on the rue Taitbout. In other words, even the most "Spanish" components of the score—those associated with Carmen—resonate with growing cultural tensions within France itself. Institutions such as the Opéra-Comique were designed expressly as wholesome alternatives to these more nefarious forms of entertainment. Thus to have the leading lady in an opera singing the very cabaret songs that opera was supposed to displace was extremely shocking to its bourgeois clientele. Early reviews often refer to Carmen's songs as vulgar and to Célestine Galli-Marié's performance style as obscene.[7] Because Carmen's songs have always been "opera" to us, the transgression is not quite so apparent today. In response to such reviews, musicologist Winton Dean likes to protest that Carmen sings not a vulgar note in the whole opera.

But Carmen's music is *deliberately* vulgar. Bizet draws on practices that were guaranteed to offend his audience, and he knew this in advance. We have often scoffed at listeners who were so narrow-minded that they overlooked the beauty of these tunes. But it was not simply a matter of a prudish bourgeoisie misreading the opera before finally learning that the "Habañera," too, qualifies as great art. The vulgarity of Carmen's tunes (or at least their association with popular urban culture) is crucial to the workings of the opera's dramatic structure.

Andreas Huyssen, in his "Mass Culture as Woman: Modernism's Other," has examined the antagonism between high and low culture from the nineteenth century into the twentieth.[8] To an increasing extent, serious artists took as part of their mission the necessary warding off of the advance of mass culture, which was associated with the working classes, with appeals to sentimentality and sexuality, and thus with the feminine. The move toward abstraction in the modernist painting, poetry, and music of this time was designed expressly as protection against this rising tide of what was regarded as trash.

*Carmen* was written just as these movements were gaining momentum. Like Orientalism, popular music provided a space where the elite could slum, could satisfy the kinds of pleasures that imperious official culture denied itself. Bizet confessed in a letter in 1867: "I am German by conviction, heart and soul, but I sometimes get lost in artistic houses of ill fame." And it is no accident that the music we remember from *Carmen* is precisely this ill-famed material: the more typical operatic numbers with which it is juxtaposed offer little to compete with its vitality and sensuality. But by the same token, its seductiveness demands that it be regarded (along with Carmen and the gypsies) as a polluting influence, that it be purged.

Purged in favor of the musical discourse of Don José, for it is Don José who bears the Germanic burden of Bizet's split personality. Although some critics recoiled in horror from the pop-culture obscenity of the opera, at least as many despised its moments of confusing Teutonic learnedness, its Wagnerian obscurity: it was heard as aping the difficult symphonic style that was acquiring the status of "universal" music during this period—even (despite the efforts of nationalist critics) in France. The features of complexity singled out by such critics are, in fact, Don José's principal characteristics: his long, impassioned melodies that avoid regular phrasing and cadences for the sake of postponed gratification, his rages in which both his utterances and his psychological amplification in the orchestra threaten to wreck all sense of order. As Winton Dean has pointed out, "The Paris Bourgeoisie liked its music broken up into small watertight compartments set in a framework of ordinary speech."[9] And by those French standards, Don José behaves at least as badly as Carmen.

To those of us who still accept nineteenth-century German style as the universal norm, José's intemperate excesses may not be readily apparent. Indeed, compared with Carmen's insistence on the body, José's visionary spans may seem like a relief. Carl Dahlhaus, for instance, writes approvingly of what he calls José's "lyric urgency," and he sees Bizet's principal challenge in the opera as the problem of how to write for Carmen, a character who is "incapable of lyric urgency."[10] To the extent that we regard both types of utterances—Carmen's and José's—as transparent, we are likely not only to misconstrue contemporary complaints that the piece lacks stylistic unity, but also to underestimate both the essential incompatibility of these two characters and the tensions within French culture they embody.

In an eclectic assemblage that could only have arisen in cosmopolitan (if culturally fragmented) Paris, Don José is a creature of high German style who somehow finds himself on the stage of the petty bourgeois Opéra-Comique playing opposite an exotic cabaret performer. She is contented with the intoxicating grooves of her dance numbers—with the body, sensuality, pleasure. He continually wants to make their encounter into an endless melody of yearning, unquenchable desire—a through-composed drama in which all is sacrificed for the sake of climactic transcendence. And the Opéra-Comique audience and critics found both parties to be distasteful; only Micaëla, Escamillo (whose music Bizet referred to as trash), and the Parisian-style crowd scenes of the opening act were received favorably.

To view José as the discursive norm (as Dahlhaus does) obscures an important point. His high-minded denial of sensuality, his incessant push for something other than the pleasure of the moment cause him to be musically violent. He whips himself up into frenzies that cannot be satisfied except through destruction. Even within the "Flower Song," he cannot attain climax except by establishing musical ceilings and then forcibly penetrating them. For it is not pleasure or sensuality he seeks, but rather control and possession. This is clear to Carmen by the conclusion of the "Flower Song," where she quietly undermines his protestations of love with "Non, tu ne m'aimes pas." And she is right. He loves the narrative trajectory she has induced him to imagine (for this, not her, is what the "Flower Song" is about); but he has no concept of love as it involves other sentient human beings. That is why the tiny exchange between Carmen and Escamillo in the final act—when they sing to each other with the same music and then together in harmony—is so poignant. Such mutuality is impossible for Don José.

In this he follows faithfully his Germanic models, which likewise cannot accommodate pleasure or dialogue and which increasingly find it difficult to believe in the adequacy of the cadence to ground their huge narratives of tonal desire. The more intensively the contradictions between desire and compensation are pursued (say, in Beethoven or Brahms), the more violent the attempts at forcing belief. Compositions such as Mahler's *Resurrection Symphony* reach closure only after apocalyptic explosions and then only through imposition. In each of the last three of four acts of *Carmen*, Don José resorts to charging with his knife. And his final thrust attains closure.

Which brings us back to the question of frame. As was mentioned earlier, two parallel but conflicting framing devices appear at the beginning of the opera: the "Spanish" music of the Prelude and the unmarked soldiers' discourse of the beginning of Act I. Throughout the opera each of these vies for the right to claim ownership over the proper conclusion of the piece. The Prelude's claim rests on two factors: first, its extraordinary symmetries that suddenly are ruptured, thus demanding return and closure; and second, the significant appearances of its various elements to register key moments in the drama. But if the Prelude were to succeed in rounding itself off at the end of the opera, it would mean that the other—the exotic stuff that was supposed to provide the terrain for mere entertainment—had won. A paranoid tale indeed.

The case for the unmarked side is far more complicated, for unlike Mérimée's novella, the opera offers no obvious authorial voice to guide us through the piece. The voyeuristic soldiers provide grounding for a while, but then they fade into the woodwork, leaving us to contend with the polyphony of the various voices on stage. Moreover, Acts II and III take place on terrains established not by our bourgeois stand-ins but by the gypsies themselves, first at Lillas Pastia's tavern and then in the smugglers' hideout. In both these contexts it is José who is positioned as the outsider, the other. The return to Seville for the festival in the final act reintroduces the funny street people we encountered in the opening act, and they now dwarf the dragoons, who had first offered us this scene for purposes of distanced amusement.

Identity in this opera, then, would seem to be pinned on the character of Don José himself. Winton Dean writes, "José is the central figure of *Carmen*. It is his fate rather than Carmen's that interests us."[11] This, of course, might be contested, especially in this age when the classics are being reread from the vantage points of race, class, gender, and nation. For instance, in Catherine Clément's and Nelly Furman's readings of the opera, Carmen herself is the central figure.[12] Social assumptions regarding proper feminine behavior or the entertainment value of ethnic others that used to be taken for granted and that helped to anchor this piece are no longer reliable. To the extent that Bizet could count on French, white, Christian audiences and the "universality" of male address, he did not need to articulate quite so explicitly that side of the argument.

Yet I think Dean is correct in suggesting that the piece as it is written means to be about Don José. But it is the music itself (rather than the libretto) that subtly makes this case. Bizet accomplishes this through a variety of strategies, the most important of which is his use of what I will call "movie music"—the background music that tells the listener how to feel about the action, whether dread, pathos, or anxiety. In its original Opéra-Comique version there were extensive sections of unaccompanied spoken dialogue. Thus the passages that might otherwise seem to be most prone to instrumental inflection and commentary were not generally available within this genre. Bizet does, however, take advantage of a few important moments.

For example. We have to wait for a very long time in the opera to hear Don José actually sing. He enters during the second number—the children's march—and is present throughout the cigarette chorus and the "Habañera," but he only speaks in the course of this entire sequence. His subjectivity is, however, registered in the music itself. After Carmen has insolently thrown the flower at him and the women have repeated their mocking refrain from the "Habañera," the orchestra bursts out in passionate display of lyric urgency. This is unmistakably José's characteristic idiom, and it conveys his powerful feelings long before he has put words to them. Unlike the other characters in this opera, all of whom operate more or less straightforwardly in the social domain, José is presented as having interiority and deep emotions that he can put into words only with great effort. He resists singing and can be compelled to give voice to his private thoughts only in extreme situations. The first of these is when Micaëla tells him that she comes from his home, to which he replies with effusive passion *Parle-moi de ma mère!* The second occasion for his bursting into lyric expression occurs in the "Seguidilla" where Carmen has suggested to him that they might become lovers. (Significantly, he sings back dutifully the phrase Carmen has fed him: her one strategic use of lyric urgency demonstrates that she is fluent enough in this discourse, but like Mérimée's Carmen she deploys it only when necessary.)

From that point on, José is like a loose cannon: his passion, once aroused, can have only one conclusion. And the orchestra supports him in this. The violent rage that bubbles up in the last two acts to overflow the generic boundaries expected in the Opéra-Comique is his: his subjectivity motivates the push for closure at the end and persuades the listener of the necessity, the inevitability, and even the desirability of the murder. If the other characters have more memorable tunes, José possesses the musical techniques of narrative drive that propel the opera toward its bitter end.

But if he can finally demand closure, he apparently has no control over how that closure is articulated. The most brilliant stroke of the opera involves what awaits José at his moment of truth: namely, the thematic materials from the Prelude. The "fate" complex had already returned when Carmen and José met in the first act; the "Toreador" segment returns with Escamillo's entrance in the second. With the return of the very opening of the Prelude for the bullfight procession in the final act, all elements are present, working their way inexorably to their own long-delayed closure. They process by in order as Carmen and José have their final encounter, punctuated with the "fate" materials that failed to reach their conclusion at the outset of the piece. Just before he kills Carmen, José explains that he cannot let her go because she would laugh at him in Escamillo's arms. But it is precisely with Escamillo's signature tune that José's triumph is celebrated. José has no tune—he is identified solely through his goal-oriented techniques, his urgent articulation of subjective passion. And we get one last pathetic glimmer of this before the concluding triad when he sings: "It is I who have killed her, O my beloved Carmen!"

Despite the finality of Carmen's death and the power of the drama that brought us to this moment, it is difficult to unravel with certainty what Bizet's opera (or any given part of it) means. I have deliberately presented a decentered account of the piece—focusing on odd details, tracing its constituent parts back into the social and music worlds that informed them—in part to get away from the kinds of simple love-story synopses that proliferate around *Carmen*. But my decentered account also results from my lack of conviction that a thoroughly coherent, consistent reading of the opera is possible or even desirable.

It could be argued, for instance, that José too is just one of the funny people the soldiers and audience have come to observe—in which case, the spectator (who has perhaps been lured into transferring identification from the distanced soldiers to José) may feel the need to step back at the end and erect an explanation that reestablishes difference. This would, in fact, recreate some of the moves of Mérimée's narrator, who also finds himself implicated in a slippery slope that begins with responding to the charms of a beautiful gypsy and ends in mayhem. And the irony of Bizet's conclusion assists one in achieving distance, for the "movie music" dimension of the piece that had represented José's subjectivity no longer operates in isolation at this point. Its confrontation with Escamillo's fight song can help us disengage ourselves from José's plight.

But like Mérimée's novella, Bizet's *Carmen* raises issues that are insoluble, at least given the premises from which they begin. Both are powerful documents precisely to the extent that they lay bare central faultlines of nineteenth- and twentieth-century French culture: those related to class, race, gender, and cultural hegemony. On some level, both novella and opera present something like the line in one of the more infamous songs by Guns 'n' Roses: "I used to love her but I had to kill her," and this needs to be acknowledged more than it is, whether it is sung by Axl Rose or Plácido Domingo. Yet both Mérimée and Bizet also perform (wittingly or not) a kind of cultural critique. If Don José did not experience his life in terms of lack—lack of sensuality, pleasure, freedom—he would not have been attracted to Carmen in the first place. If we in the audience did not find Carmen and her music irresistible yet somehow not quite kosher, the opera would not work for us. And if we were not still stuck in the dilemmas Mérimée and Bizet point to, we would not be witnessing the endless stream of *Carmen* productions on stage, film, and TV.

But playing the dilemma through over and over again is not sufficient. We have to begin taking apart the very structures of identity and difference that permit such pieces to make sense to us as they drive toward their awful conclusions. Paul Ricoeur has written of the anxieties of our present moment in history: "When we discover that there are several cultures instead of just one . . . when we acknowledge the end of a sort of cultural monopoly, be it illusory or real, we are threatened with destruction by our own discovery. Suddenly it becomes possible that there are *just* others, that we ourselves are an 'other' among others."[13]

If that discovery is threatening, however, it may also be our only hope. Instead of going to *Carmen* to experience the thrill of blurring the distinction between self and contaminating other before violently reimposing boundaries, I suggest that we view it as a mirror. For it is perhaps *we* who are the "funny people": the people who derive pleasure from such stories. We need to find other stories. But first we have to discover how we have organized ourselves to date. And we can learn a great deal about that from our responses to *Carmen*.

NOTES

1. Mérimée's *Carmen* first appeared in *La Revue des Deux Mondes* (October 1, 1845).

2. Ludovic Halévy reported his version of the negotiations between the Opéra-Comique management and the collaborators in "La millième représentation de *Carmen*," *Le Théâtre* 145 (1905). A partial translation of this document appears as "Breaking the Rules," trans. Clarence H. Russell, *Opera News* 51, no. 13 (1987): 36–7, 47.

3. See "The Musical Languages of *Carmen*," in my *Georges Bizet:* Carmen (Cambridge: Cambridge University Press, 1992), 44–61.

4. Edward W. Said, *Orientalism* (New York: Pantheon Books, 1978).

5. Friedrich Nietzsche, *The Case of Wagner*, trans. Walter Kauffman (New York: Vintage Books, 1967).

6. For more on the ways *Carmen* thematizes specifically French issues, see "Images of Race, Class, and Gender in Nineteenth-Century French Culture," in my *Georges Bizet:* Carmen, 29–43.

7. For more on the reception of *Carmen*, see chapter 5 of my *Georges Bizet:* Carmen, 111–29.

8. Andreas Huyssen, "Mass Culture as Woman: Modernism's Other," *After the Great Divide: Modernism, Mass Culture, Postmodernism* (Bloomington: Indiana University Press, 1986), 44–62.

9. Winton Dean, *Georges Bizet: His Life and Work* (London: Dent, 1985), 38.

10. Carl Dahlhaus, *Nineteenth-Century Music*, trans. J. Bradford Robinson (Berkeley and Los Angeles: University of California Press, 1989), 280–82.

11. Dean, *Georges Bizet*, 224.

12. Catherine Clément, *Opera, or the Undoing of Women*, trans. Betsy Wing (Minneapolis: University of Minnesota Press, 1988), and Nelly Furman, "The Languages of *Carmen*," in *Reading Opera*, eds. Arthur Groos and Roger Parker (Princeton: Princeton University Press, 1988). For another feminist critique of *Carmen*, see also "Sexual Politics in Classical Music," in my *Feminine Endings: Music, Gender, and Sexuality* (Minneapolis: University of Minnesota Press, 1991), 53–67.

13. Paul Ricoeur, "Civilization and National Culture," in *History and Truth*, trans. Charles A. Kelbey (Evanston, Ill.: Northwestern University Press, 1965), 278.

## CHAPTER SIX

*The Waters of Prometheus:*
*Nationalism and Sexuality in Wagner's* Ring

Lawrence Kramer

## Unholy German Art

Nationalism and sexuality: these very topical concerns of the twentieth-century *fin de siècle* are also the historical terms of the infamous "case of Wagner," *Der Fall Wagner*, as Nietzsche called it: the instance, medical problem, and criminal investigation of that "neurosis" (Nietzsche's term) whose "magnificently equivocal, suspect and compelling" work (Thomas Mann's phrase) makes you love what is hateful and forget what must above all be remembered, and that *keeps on doing this* no matter how shrewdly you resist it.[1]

What is left to say at this late date about the case of Wagner—about the wizard, charlatan, and Minotaur (Nietzsche again) whose music all too compellingly, all too seductively, mobilizes deeply entrenched dynamics of sexual identity and desire to promote a reprehensible end: the sentimental, anti-Semitic nationalism that would in time inexorably become the Third Reich and the Holocaust? Even as those atrocities increasingly fade from living into textual memory, changes in the way we think about music make it harder and harder to disengage Wagner's aesthetics from his politics. The argument that music as great as his transcends the dross of history is scarcely presentable in its bald form any more, especially on this topic, so such statements of it as appear tend to be ever more subtilized. Is Edward Said, for example, boxing the moral compass or indulging in wishful thinking when he bravely claims that the close of *Die Meistersinger*, with its elevation of "holy German art" as a politico-cultural sacrament, is a false patch on the truth of the larger whole:

> As for Wagner's neurotic closure . . . we can take that as the merest crude attempt to grab once and for all what has already been proved to be a possession far in excess of, therefore transgressing, the clutches of one owner, be that owner an individual, a town, or a nation. [Pierre] Boulez is quite right to say that Wagner's "music by its very existence refuses to bear any ideological message it is intended to convey." *Die Meistersinger* cannot really be reduced to the nationalist ideology its final strophes stress. It has set forth too much in the way of contrapuntal action, character, invention.[2]

The burnished tunes and gorgeous orchestration of this opera, the nobility of Hanns Sachs's renunciation of Eva, the ravishing beauty of the Prize Song—anyone moved by these musical wonders wants Said to be right. But what about Marc Weiner's demonstration that the burnished glow of this music is broadly applied with the dirty rags of anti-Semitism?[3] What about Arthur Groos's demonstration that the processional scenes of the third act conjure up a trope of medieval Nuremberg as a once and future nationalist utopia, a kind of *Wagner Welt* theme park?[4] And what about the way the nobly lyrical tunes and splendid "contrapuntal action" of the overture form a sonoric image of this utopian space, within which the listener is decisively situated for more than four bewitching hours? Can the music really refine this dross in its expressive magic fire? Or does the dross render it inescapably a music of national and "racial" supremacy—the music Nietzsche heard in the overture and described as "something arbitrary, barbaric, and solemn . . . something German in the worst and best sense of the word"?[5]

Said's impulse to contradict Wagner about the ideology of the latter's own music is genuinely tempting. When, for example, we learn that Wagner said of the third act of *Siegfried*, "That is Gobineau music . . . that is race," the claim that he is spouting nonsense seems close to self-evident.[6] What could Joseph-Arthur de Gobineau's racist theories of pure blood, which admittedly weigh heavily on *Parsifal*, have to do with the splendid love duet between Siegfried and Brünnhilde that brings *Siegfried* to an orgasmic close and gives the *Ring* cycle its consummate interlude of happiness? But perhaps, having asked this question rhetorically, it would be better to ask it in earnest.

I invoke the love duet here because, for Nietzsche at least, it marks the historical crux of the case of Wagner, the moment after which the fires of musical art cease to refine the dross of sexual and national brutality. Nietzsche is not quite explicit on this point, but his description in *The Case of Wagner* of what he takes to be Wagner's betrayal of both himself and his listeners in the *Ring* leaves little doubt of it. The part of the saga that leads upward to Brünnhilde's rock, to the love duet ringed by magic fire, compels both Nietzsche's admiration and his identification with Siegfried as a "free spirit." The ascending Siegfried is cherished as an exemplary immoralist, a breaker of ossified contracts, and a liberator of women (this, yes, from the arch-antifeminist philosopher, whose enthusiasm we might read in Derridean terms as an embrace of the putatively feminine abilities to evade morality and break contracts—and get away with it).[7]

This good Siegfried, in what proves to be a cardinal relationship, is at once pro-erotic and antinationalist. On the erotic side, his entry into the ring of magic fire initiates "the sacrament of free love; the rise of the golden age; the twilight of the gods for the old morality—*all ill has been abolished*" (FW, 163). On the nationalist side, he embodies the spirit of the French Revolution in mythic, which is to say world-historical, terms: "Half his life, Wagner believed in the Revolution as much as ever a Frenchman believed in it. He searched for it in the runic writing of myth, he believed that in Siegfried he had found the typical revolutionary." The revolutionary Siegfried is the very antithesis of a Germanic hero, almost an incarnation of universalism versus parochialism, the spirit of French Enlightenment versus that of German *Aufklärung*. Insofar as he (like his creator) is indeed a revolutionary, Siegfried is "an incarnate protest against all 'German virtues' "[8] (EH, 248).

Wagner's great betrayal, Nietzsche continues, is the reactionary substitution of ideology—nationalist false consciousness—for free thought and the cognate substitution of displaced and tormented sexuality for the simplicity of free love. When Siegfried descends from Brünnhilde's rock he blunders into the modern world, the scene of social organization rather than mythic adventure, of kinship alliance rather than glorified incest. This is a world that dupes and belittles the hero who is still somehow supposed to redeem it: the Gibichung world of rich Junkers and their nubile sisters, of corrupt Germans and crafty Jews, of bourgeois marriage and adultery. Siegfried's mind, never his strong point, becomes cloudy in this world. The clarity of utopian optimism dies into the murk of Schopenhauerian pessimism with the monstrous twin birth of the political and the sexual unconscious. On the political side, writes Nietzsche, "What did I never forgive Wagner? That he *condescended* [in the sense of lowering himself, debasing his divinity] to the Germans—that he became *reichsdeutsch*" (EH, 248). On the sexual side, this Teutonization takes the form of abjection and disillusionment: "So he translated the *Ring* into Schopenhauerian terms. Everything goes wrong, everything perishes, the new world is as bad as the old: the *nothing*, the Indian Circe beckons" (FW, 164).

Nietzsche's construction of the good versus the bad Siegfried constitutes a classic nineteenth-century *doppelgänger* narrative, a type that regularly personifies and opposes the socially acceptable and unacceptable forms of masculine personality. As a reading of the *Ring*, this narrative is suspect both because it fits Nietzsche's own philosophical agenda too comfortably and because it is obviously ripe for deconstruction; who would be surprised to learn that the good Siegfried is always already the bad one, that Wagner the reactionary is always already inscribed on the text of Wagner the revolutionary? But Nietzsche's reading is powerful, too, and has a great deal to

133

The Waters of
Prometheus:
Nationalism and
Sexuality in
Wagner's *Ring*

offer, including some important clues to the case of Wagner, if we decline to deconstruct it prematurely. (One might say that deconstruction, like stand-up comedy and good sex, requires a keen sense of timing. The point is to deconstruct an opposition only after one has learned what it has to teach, so that its undoing can teach something, too.) Accordingly, I want to entertain for a while the notion that the *Ring* cycle pivots on the strange transformation by which the revolutionary lover who is Siegfried in the eponymous *Siegfried* becomes the social-climbing philanderer who is Siegfried in *Götterdämmerung*. And I want to entertain, too, the broader implication that this transformation uncovers a real antithesis between nationalism and eroticism—an antithesis, moreover, with its own keen sense of timing. The erotic, in this structure, first inhibits or defers the advent of the national, then becomes appropriated to the national, and finally undoes the appropriation to undo the national.

Siegfried, then, becomes a nationalist hero only when he becomes vain, stupid, brutal, and lecherous. This is not a joke. Only in the world of *Götterdämmerung*, where political consciousness is mystified and sexual desire never recognizes its object, can the national hero come to be, and even then only on the condition that he come to grief. The national hero is born to be a martyr. Wagner probably thinks of this as a cautionary tale; Siegfried is, after all, brought down by the machinations of the saturnine Hagen, the half-caste and half-breed, the parasite whose relation to his hosts replicates the fantasmatic relation posited between Germans and Jews by the racialist anti-Semitism that Wagner embraced. Siegfried's fate foretells what will happen to Germany if the race is not kept pure.[9]

From another perspective, however, this compulsory default in the national hero is the source of his authenticity. The hero does not incarnate national identity by what he is, but by what someone else imagines him to be. The Siegfried of *Götterdämmerung* is debased on stage but ennobled in Brünnhilde's fantasy; the bad Siegfried becomes good again when desire and misrecognition install him in the place where she lacks him, the place where he has always already betrayed and abused her. This Siegfried does not appear until after the "real" Siegfried's death. And although this final Siegfried is strangely still capable of action—his dead hand rises up to prevent Hagen from taking the ring—he has no voice except, belatedly, Brünnhilde's voice in mourning for him. He becomes present, to her and to us, only in the music that expresses Brünnhilde's love and grief for him, music always tuned to absence rather than presence, whether at the beginning of *Götterdämmerung*, with its love duet marking the parting of the lovers, or at the end, with its double threnody of funeral music and immolation scene.

But do Brünnhilde's acts of mourning and fantasy really bring back the good Siegfried or merely idealize the bad one? When she conjures the hero up is she a revolutionary herself, uncontainable by the constraints of her sacrifice, self-betrayal, and abjection, or has she, too, become *reichsdeutsch*, no longer a Nietzschean–Derridean figure of truth truly evaded but only a kind of hapless *Mädchen* in Valkyrie uniform?

These questions particularly beset me when I listen to the funeral music, although I will dwell more here on the subsequent immolation scene. My first experience of this music, more than thirty years ago, remains unforgettable, and traces of it persist even in my canniest moods of resistance. I placed a scratchy monaural LP casually borrowed from the library on a cheap record player and was physically staggered by what I heard. (Nothing had taught me yet to hear these sounds in the spirit of the Third Reich and of the dread that had hovered namelessly over my childhood in questions my parents wouldn't answer, neighbors with tattoos that couldn't be explained, leaflets imprinted with old German script left in doorways and hurriedly snatched away.) I was stunned by the music's combination of ferocity and solemnity, by its power to turn its climactic drumbeat figure into the pounding of the blood at my temples, and to turn this impact on my body into a ritual of heroic mythopoeisis. But was I really hearing a transfigurative threnody for a solar hero, a world-historical Promethean figure ultimately consumed by his own gift but soon to rise again, phoenixlike, in the song about him sung by the loving enemy who is preparing to share his funeral pyre like an Indian widow? Or was I just hearing the most sublimated possible form of the *Horst Wessel* song?

Perhaps we need to consult a fiery revolutionary to get some sort of answer. Nietzsche's good Siegfried is a late-blooming instance of Romantic Prometheanism, a figure who defies authority by ringing himself with magic fire. Perhaps we should search the runic writing of myth for him, eventually including the runes of modern myth, which is to say, of theory.

## Magic Water Music

Prometheus, thief of fire—"[Hephaestus'] flower, the brightness of fire that devises all," says Aeschylus. In the Aeschylan version of the myth the gift of fire is what enables humanity to make the epochal transition from nature to material culture. Prometheus finds human beings "liv[ing] like swarming ants in holes in the ground, in the sunless caves of the earth"; fire, as if putting the sun in human hands, "[becomes] the teacher of each craft," culminating in metalwork.[10] In classical terms, Prometheus the fire-bringer is a personification of Bronze Age technology. Only much later, in the Promethean texts of European Romanticism, does the emphasis shift from material to symbolic culture, from technique to value. (Another example, here, of oppositions to be deconstructed—but not prematurely, and therefore not in this context.) Only then does Prometheus become a culture hero in the full sense. Byron's Prometheus gives "precepts" that "strengthen Man with his own mind," thus grounding human identity in a putatively unalienated self-consciousness. Shelley's champion of humanity explicitly subordinates the material to the ideal; though he has taught the uses of the fire and the other elements, in his culminating act, "He gave man speech,

135

The Waters of

Prometheus:

Nationalism and

Sexuality in

Wagner's *Ring*

and speech created thought, / Which is the measure of the Universe." Goethe's Prometheus, somehow with impunity, his virile outrage somehow transmuting itself to creative–procreative sexual difference, sits in inspired solitude and fashions the human race in his own image "to suffer, to weep, / To enjoy and rejoice, / And pay [the Thunderer] no heed."[11]

Yet something strange happens at this turning point in the mythography of Prometheus. For some reason the fire becomes expendable. Byron does not so much as mention it, and in all the vast bulk of *Prometheus Unbound*, Shelley can manage it only the one perfunctory nod as a technological convenience. More revealingly, Goethe displaces the fire into Prometheus's "holy glowing heart," a prototypical gesture of internalization that refigures a material agency as a symbolizing power. It is as if the advent of culture in the symbolic sense coincided not with the gift of fire but with the gift of fieriness as a character trait of the heroic rebel and lover. It is this fieriness, moreover, that establishes him as universal, primordial, and therefore transnational: an elemental, not a historical hero.

When the good Siegfried ascends to Brünnhilde's rock, the first thing he discovers is his own Promethean fieriness. His relation to fire, like that of his archaic precursor, marks his defiance of divine authority, but he is not the figure who gives fire; he is the one who masters it. He takes it as his element and thus takes it into himself, and in so doing turns it into a symbol. The passage from technique to value is enacted through his crossing of the fiery threshold: what Brünnhilde has proposed as a practical device to keep cowards from taking sexual advantage of her, Siegfried turns into a sign of the enveloping, protecting passion that he will consummate with her.

Reflecting on this prospect, Siegfried states that he will "bathe" in the fire to win his bride:

> *Ha! Wonnige Glut! Leuchtender Glanz!*
> *Strahlend nun offen steht mir die Strasse.*
> *Im Feur mich baden!*
> *Im Feur zu finden die Braut!*

> Ah, marvelous glow! radiance gleaming!
> Shining now the road stands open before me:
> To bathe in the fire!
> In the fire to find my bride!

It is a curious metaphor. Curious, because it identifies fire with the water that extinguishes fire, and curious because it identifies mastery over fire with the bodily pleasure of *not* extinguishing it. The bad Siegfried will be consumed, if also redeemed, by fire, but the good Siegfried will be cleansed and refreshed by it, like some primordial Tamino whose ordeals by fire and water occur simultaneously and in the form of pleasure rather than pain. But what does it mean, this water of Prometheus?

One answer, traced in the runes of myth, can be found in Freud's *Civilization and Its Discontents*. To be sure, this is one of Freud's looniest ideas; even he admits that, but the more you think about it, the harder it is to dismiss out of hand. Freud says that "primitive man" gained control over fire when one man, one day, resisted the homosexually tinged desire to put out a fire by urinating on it. Thus that man became Prometheus, the thief because not the murderer of fire, the godfather of the arts and sciences.[12] One becomes the first culture hero by renouncing the "pleasurable struggle" (Freud's phrase) to which the fire beckons with its phallic flickering.

This theory is itself a piece of mythmaking, part Promethean and part Rabelaisian. Meant to inscribe, with a certain polemical gusto, the humble bodily beginnings of high cultural forms, it is of a piece with Mikhail Bakhtin's near contemporary theorization of the grotesque body in both carnival and the text of Rabelais: the "open," oriface-studded body that, in its frank connection to the material world through the passage of fluids and substances, opposes the dead—and deathly—seriousness of official culture.[13] (One might say that opera especially is the art of the open body insofar as operatic voice so palpably courses from the body's depths into the breadth of theatrical space, and that this is particularly so with Wagner, whose vocal extremity is a matter not of roulades and high notes but of singing at high pressure so that the voice bursts as if from within the notes in streams of suffering or pleasure.)

It is tempting to underscore Freud's point by taking note of the boyish romance of firemen and their red trucks—from Walt Whitman's erotic fascination with "The march of firemen in their own costumes, the play of masculine muscle through clean-setting trowsers and waist-straps"[14] to William Carlos Williams's notation of a phallic pictograph, "The Great Figure," piercing the nocturnal depths of the city in *jouissant* rhythm:

> Among the rain
> and lights
> I saw the figure 5
> in gold
> on a red
> firetruck
> moving
> tense
> unheeded
> to gong clangs
> siren howls
> and wheels rumbling
> through the dark city.[15]

But something is amiss with Freud's formulation. There is something he misses because as usual he errs on the side of severity; he pits abjection against supremacy, all or nothing, the stakes of a scene of castration. His

137

The Waters of
Prometheus:
Nationalism and
Sexuality in
Wagner's *Ring*

version of taking mastery over fire posits a psychological relation of sublimation between bodily urge and cultural form. Partially renounced, the urge achieves partial satisfaction in the substitutive embrace of form. But what if the relation between these terms is as much tropological as it is psychological, a question not only of the body denied and symbolization affirmed, but also of the body affirmed precisely as a field of symbolization? Certainly, one way to take power over fire is not to put it out: I can endure the answering fire in my body and choke off the instinctual impulse. But another way is to *perform* the impulse rather than either restraining or releasing it: to find a liminal zone between tension and release in which the impulse can produce meanings and feelings in tandem with a fire that it does not altogether put out, at least not all at once. I can approach the fire with Promethean assurance if I make the bodily impulse exquisite, playful, rhythmic, ritualistic . . . artistic.

Yes: if I do that, if I trace my impulse cursively in the shape of the fire, I don't extinguish the fire at all. Rather I defer its extinction, I shape and inscribe and finally perpetuate the fire in the form by which it's extinguished: fire unkindled as water. If this is a Rabelaisian gesture, most suitable to Gargantua's legendary act of pissing *Par ris* [for laughs] on a great city, thus endowing the city with its name,[16] it is a gesture that can also be invested with lyricism, pathos, tender irony, and mythopoeic force—effects all present when James Joyce has recourse to it in the "Ithaca" chapter of *Ulysses*.

Like the *Ring*, *Ulysses* centers on a woman who emblematically reaches her sexual peak on a high rock and confers identity by purely imaginary means on the wandering hero who loves her. Here, then, are Leopold Bloom, a cosmopolite like the good Siegfried, accompanied by Stephen Dedalus, a sectarian like the bad one, contemplating, from the garden of the Bloom house at no. 7 Eccles Street, Dublin, the "visible luminous sign" denoting the mystery of an "invisible person" in the bedroom window of Molly Bloom, singer extraordinaire and "flower of the mountain": "At Stephen's suggestion, at Bloom's instigation both, first Stephen, then Bloom, in penumbra urinated, their sides contiguous, their organs of micturition reciprocally rendered invisible by manual circumposition, their gazes, first Bloom's, then Stephen's, elevated to the projected luminous and semi-luminous shadow."[17]

Between the two men, between their gazes of unspoken desire, between the shadowy penumbras of their Promethean waters, a mute duet unfolds, something suggestive of those irridescent Baroque duets between two high voices intertwining with each other regardless of sameness or difference of sex, the contralto–soprano couple presenting an ideal both parallel with and counter to the pederastic ideal implied by the combination of the older and younger man, as if Molly Bloom's unheard operatic voice were taking both parts in its approving silence.

Admittedly, any link between Siegfried and the lyrical Rabelaisianism in the Blooms' garden exists only in theory. And no doubt Siegfried's mastery over fire has only the most vestigial relationship to his ability to hold his water—though let it be recalled that Wagner must have valued this ability as a test of acculturation: in his day there were no facilities for relieving oneself at the *Festspielhaus* in Bayreuth. ("Mercilessly denying the fact of human bodily needs," writes Beat Wys in an analysis of the architecture of Wagner's Bayreuth, ". . . Wagner's dictatorial art cancels the public as corporeal fact. . . . The Wagnerian stage corresponds to the historicist idea of cultural formation, wherein the claim of culture withdraws to an interior 'soul' while on the outside, the unsightly material circumstances are tolerated as necessary evils."[18]) Only in theory, then: the good Siegfried, with all due qualifications entered, to some degree acts as a Freudian Prometheus when he first passes the ring of fire and emerges on Brünnhilde's rock. Having bathed in the fire, Siegfried discovers the bodily pleasures, and becomes the conduit for the musical pleasures, of controlled, ritualized impulsiveness as he slowly discovers that the nature of his relationship to Brünnhilde is mutual desire. Having bathed in the fire, he finds it reproduced as the liquid radiance of the sun in Brünnhilde's awakening words—*Heil dir Sonne! Heil dir Licht! / Heil dir, leuchtender Tag!*—and bathes anew in the same fire now transfigured as the purifying waters of eros: *ich selbst, wie ich bin, / spring' in dem Bach: / O dass seine Wogen mich selig verschlängen* ("Hail to you, sun! / Hail to you, light! / Hail to you, radiant day! . . . I myself, as I am / will leap in the stream: / O that its waves devour me in bliss!")

This nuptial baptism by fire is both the prelude and the form of the freespirited bliss that Nietzsche celebrates. *Contra* Wagner, the "immoralist" philosopher hears the fire-punctuated love duet as the very antithesis of Germanic "race music"; any racial or national character the music may seek (even in its composer's retrospect) is drowned in sexual fire. But is it?

This question arises with exemplary acuteness near the start of the scene, just after Brünnhilde has been awakened by Siegfried's kiss. The hero, who has had his mother much on his mind while musing over the sleeping bride, and who will soon misrecognize Brünnhilde herself as his mother, responds to the miraculous awakening with a maternal invocation that Brünnhilde at once echoes, the musical phrases of the couple overlapping and intertwining:

SIEGFRIED: *O heil der Mutter, die mich gebar,*
[Hail to the mother that bore me]
BRÜNNHILDE: *O heil der Mutter, die dich gebar,*
[Hail to the mother that bore you]
SIEGFRIED: *Heil der Erde, die mich genährt!*
[Hail to the earth that nursed me!]
BRÜNNHILDE: *Heil der Erde, die dich genährt!*
[Hail to the earth that nursed you!]

The music for these lapped phrases is remarkable for the way it vaults beyond the stilted machinery of the epic hail to express the "sublimest ecstasy" [*erhabenste Entzückung*] (see example 6.1). Each phrase begins at full cry with

139

The Waters of
Prometheus:
Nationalism and
Sexuality in
Wagner's *Ring*

jagged, leaping melody, then eases a little into something smoother and more continuous. As each partner finishes an utterance, the other bursts forth to mirror that utterance. In a cycle of reciprocations, the melodic movement of each voice from intensity to repose rekindles the spark of intensity in the other voice. The cycle itself intensifies as the second pair of phrases compresses the first, complicates the mirroring effect, and adds harmonic breadth. Once complete, the cycle calls forth an ardent closing passage celebrating the mutual gaze of discovery, during which the voices shift freely between caressing counterpoint and shared melody, and finally coalesce in one of Wagner's rare perfect cadences.

The vocal interchange of the *Heil der Mutter* passage couples Siegfried and Brünnhilde in sexual desire and pleasure long before either one of them recognizes the fact. It propels them immediately from maternal to erotic love (or, if you prefer, from pre-Oedipal to Oedipal sexuality) in apparent disregard of the maternal imagery of the text. This imagery, however, is not there just to be disregarded. It also enhances the radical, "free-spirited" character of the

Example 6.1

Wagner, *Siegfried*, Act III: love duet ("Heil der Mutter").

Example 6.1 (page 2)

Wagner, *Siegfried*, Act III: love duet ("Heil der Mutter").

incipient lovers' desire by recalling the transgressive desire of Sieglinde, Siegfried's incestuous mother and the alter ego for whose sake Brünnhilde defied Wotan's law. A transgressive link of this sort is basic to Nietzsche's claim that free sexuality is antithetical to the production of race music.

The only trouble is that the maternal invocation is also the very thing that *establishes* the love duet as race music. At the crudest level, the presentation of an epic genealogy that Wagner—foolishly, according to Nietzsche—thought was *echt*-Teutonic, the invocation can always be denationalized by the kind of Nietzschean hearing I have just proposed for it. But Wagner's introduction of the mother at this point has a deeper resonance. The displacement of heroic genealogy from the father's line to the mother's is not only a way of taking a position beyond and against the compacts of paternal law, but also a way of establishing Siegfried's racial purity, which is to say, his identity as a German, not a Jew. In context, the maternal invocation is just as much a test as the magic fire is.

That context is intricate, twisting through a lifelong preoccupation with the nature of maternity; I will single out just two strands. First, in reading the works of Ludwig Feuerbach while developing the libretto of the *Ring*, Wagner (as Jean-Jacques Nattiez has shown) discovered something highly congenial to him: an association between the sexual love of man and woman and the realization of universal human being through the annihilation of the ego, ultimately in death. This association would come to have an obvious bearing on the love duets of *Die Walküre* and *Siegfried*. The same association, however, also had a third, "racial" element. Since the Jews (for Feuerbach) are characterized by a refusal to surrender their individuality, since "their principle—their God . . . [is] egoism, or, more specifically, *egoism in the form of religion*," it follows that the loving, transcendental union of man and woman must coincide with the negation of all that is Jewish.[19]

Second, at about the same time that Wagner, having read Gobineau, identified the music of the love duet with "race," he was much preoccupied with the question of contaminated bloodlines. Here again a coincidence of sexual and racial themes emerges. Racially, the problem is miscegenation: Jewish blood is impervious to it. "Let Jew or Jewess intermarry with even the most foreign of races; a Jew will always be the result."[20] (Jewish law, as Wagner may or may not have known, would half agree, in terms with some pertinence to our topic: regardless of the father, anyone born of a Jewish mother is considered a Jew.) Sexually, the source of danger in the crossing of bloodlines is (unsurprisingly) feminine: "In the mingling of races, the blood of the nobler male is corrupted by that of the less noble female: the male suffers, character is destroyed, whereas women gain so much as to take over from men."[21] It follows that the worst possible racial impurity would issue from the union of a man of noble (that is, Germanic) race and a Jewish woman.

When Siegfried spontaneously cries out *Heil der Mutter* at the sight of the newly awakened Brünnhilde, he signifies his readiness to enter into a transcendentally loving union by recognizing that he is the offspring of one. In the act of invoking his mother, he intuits her ability to sustain such a union; in intuiting her ability, he discovers and validates his own. In racial terms, what Siegfried discovers is his mother's purity: the fact that she could transmit her beloved's noble blood without taint, and the cognate fact that she could annihilate her ego, along with her beloved's, in a way that annuls egoism, and therefore Judaism, as a principle. These racial terms, of course, are not the only ones that apply here; we have already seen some of the others. But they do apply; they must be applied. By insinuating them, Wagner provides the audience (and no doubt himself) with a reminder, and a reassurance, of which Siegfried has no need. In her own love duet in *Die Walküre*, Sieglinde anoints herself, along with Siegmund, as a member of a pariah race, the Wälsungs, a clan chosen by (a) god for sufferings and greatness. But any resemblance between this race and another chosen people is purely coincidental. The Wälsungs are not Jews.

So, at any rate, Wagner would like to believe, or at least to pretend. But as Thomas Mann showed trenchantly in his short story "The Blood [*Blut*: blood, bloodline, race] of the Wälsungs," the racial ideology of nineteenth-century Germany made an identification of the Jews and the Wälsungs the most obvious thing in the world—and the most anti-German. Mann's Siegmund and Sieglinde, Jewish twins from a wealthy family, attend a performance of *Die Walküre* shortly before Sieglinde's arranged marriage to a German—a wooden, maladroit figure, a travesty of Hunding, the original Sieglinde's thuggish husband. (The basis of the marriage is predictable: his name for her money.) Once home, the twins live up to their names by making rapturous love on a Wagnerian bearskin. Ordinarily arch and petulant, they achieve an unaccustomed gravity through their incest, which they haltingly understand as a form of "revenge." Mann's irony here spares no one, certainly not Wagner, but the racial link between the two sets of twins holds firm, if only because it, too, is ironic. The pleasure of incest is the revenge of the Other. Mann's twins make explicit the racial fantasies of which Wagner's twins are partially the product. (Jews, runs the anti-Semitic bromide, care only for other Jews; they incarnate endogomy.) Wagner's twins, however, do more than stumble unwittingly across the imaginary position of the Jewish Other. Rather, in the love duet that is the primal scene of *The Ring*, they impel the listener to identify unreservedly with the subjectivity of the Other. Their love, too, is a revenge, the object of which is the very medium of its expression. They fulfill the erotic imagery of medieval Germanic *Minnesang* from a self-conscious racial position of alienation, defiance, and transgression.

The mother test, then, or something like it, would be necessary because Siegfried, as a Wälsung, cannot avoid being racially suspect. He is even doubly suspect because his origins are tainted with the pleasures of otherness and "free love" that must in part be reenacted in the ecstasy on the rock. Wagner's matrilinealism is a means of resolving these racial uncertainties by

143

The Waters of
Prometheus:
Nationalism and
Sexuality in
Wagner's *Ring*

disavowing them, and, like disavowals generally, it works none too well. In the very act of quelling racial anxiety, the mother test underscores the possibility that Siegfried's status as pariah and Nietzschean immoralist risks turning the figure who will be (but is not yet) a German national hero into a *Judenbube*—or, to make the point more circumspectly, risks installing Siegfried originally in the Jewish subject position of the nineteenth-century German symbolic order.

That position is above all the place where Siegfried cannot be: not only because it is the pariah position par excellence, beyond revocation or redemption, but also because, in terms of nineteenth-century Germany's conceptualization of the "Jewish question," it is precisely the position from which national identity is refused, declared impossible, thrown implacably into dispute. "The Jew," wrote the Young Hegelian Bruno Bauer in his *Der Judenfrage* (The Jewish Question), "can only adopt a Jewish attitude, i.e., that of a foreigner, toward the state, since he opposes his illusory nationality to actual nationality, his illusory law to actual law." "We discern in Judaism," wrote Karl Marx, ". . . a universal *antisocial* element of the *present time*, whose historical development, zealously aided in its harmful aspect by the Jews, has now attained its culminating point."[22] "The Jew," writes Wagner more pungently than either, ". . . strikes us first and foremost by his external appearance, which, no matter which European nationality he may belong to, has something about it that is foreign to that nationality and that we find insuperably unpleasant."[23]

Thus the free-spirited bliss that Nietzsche saw in the love duet of *Siegfried* dances, in true Nietzschean fashion, on the edge of a nationalist–racialist abyss. At the height of Wagnerian immoralism there is a pivot, a hinge, that swings the other way.

Nietzsche, pretty plainly, would have liked the *Ring* to end with the ecstasy on the rock. In a sense, he even made it do so fantasmatically by taking as his favorite work by Wagner the instrumental poem "A Siegfried Idyll," which draws largely on the music of the love duet. In this piece Wagner himself might be said to have recomposed the *Ring* without *Götterdämmerung*, to have given Siegfried and Brünnhilde (or himself and his wife Cosima, to whom the work was given as a birthday present) an idyllic alternative world immune from the catastrophe of modernity. The ecstasy on the rock, however, was also destined to be replayed in *Götterdämmerung* itself in debased form, by a Siegfried who adopts a debased form for the purpose: the physical form of his shady blood brother Gunther, a form assumed by magic so that Siegfried can abduct Brünnhilde in order to enact a primitive bride exchange with the other man, who will hand over his own sister in return. We will have to reckon, too, with that. And we will have to reckon with the torsion of gender in the utopian sexuality of the love duet, which, for all its free-spiritedness, is still distinctly, not to say egregiously phallogocentric. The price of the ecstasy on the rock is Brünnhilde's abjection—

an abjection that is perversely understood to be her normality, her natural decline from godhead to womanhood.

## Much Ado About Nothung

Why, indeed, is the bad Siegfried of *Götterdämmerung* so willing to go pimping for Gunther? Or more exactly, why does he desire to? For the magic potion that impels him, like Tristan and Isolde's, only uncovers a real desire in the guise of imposing a deluded one. Isn't it that Brünnhilde has now become the vehicle for the bad Siegfried's erotic union with Gunther, a classic vehicle of sexualized homosocial—in other words, of disavowed homosexual—love? I ask this question rhetorically because the insight it embodies, drawn from the influential work of Luce Irigaray and Eve Sedgwick, is no longer surprising in itself.[24] It is important to specify, then, that what Siegfried finds desirable in Gunther is not only the generic aura of masculinity, but in particular the virile spirit of *Heimat*, the national rootedness that he, Siegfried, may embody but cannot possess himself in his role as itinerant hero. Gunther represents social rather than mythic masculinity, secure patrilineal legitimacy rather than transgressive maternal suffering and pleasure. Gunther needs no mother test to establish his lineage; he passes muster as the scion and symbol of normal community even though his actual mother, Grimhild, has borne a child to the loveless, greedy Nibelung, Alberich, the mythological equivalent of a Jewish banker. Siegfried, it turns out, harbors a secret burning desire to condescend to Germans.

To do that he has to enter the corrupted modern world, where free spirits are turned into Teutonic poster boys, the world that each noble (but stupid) Gunther must always share with a base (but ingenious) half-brother (Hagen, Alberich's son, whose "base," basso profundo voice sticks out in *Götterdämmerung* like the Jewish nose of anti-Semitic caricature, or its cognate, the supposedly croaking Jewish voice that, according to Wagner the anti-Semite, brings the true German to instinctive, immediate recoil.)[25] The modern world, in turn, reveals that the sexuality on which the free spirit staked so much is no longer either simple or unambiguous, and indeed never was, not even during the ecstasy on the rock. The discovery of Brünnhilde is not as heterosexual as it may seem at first—though this is not to say that its homosexuality can be reduced to the bad Siegfried's furtive, bad-faith misalliance with Gunther. When the good Siegfried bridges the fire, he sees something quite remarkable:

> *Ha! In Waffen ein Mann!*
> *Wie mahnt mich wonnig sein Bild!*
> *Das hehre Haupt drückt wohl der Helm?*
> *Leichter würd ihm, löst ich den Schmuck.*
> *Ach! Wie schön!*
> *Schimmernde Wolken saümen in Wellen*

145

The Waters of
Prometheus:
Nationalism and
Sexuality in
Wagner's *Ring*

*den hellen Himmelssee;*
*leuchtender Sonne lachendes Bild*
*strahlt durch das Wogengewölk!*

Ha! A man in the armor!
How delighted I am at the sight!
Does the Helmet constrict his noble head?
It would be lightened for him if I loosened the catch.
Ah! How lovely!
Shimmering clouds cluster in waves
on the shining lake of heaven;
the laughing sun's radiant face
gleams through the billowing clouds!

Brünnhilde, sleeping beauty in armor, is an image of lovable maleness before the good Siegfried's discovery of her breasts makes him cry out—comic, naive, amazed—*Das ist kein Mann!* ("That's no man!") The discovery of sexual difference, and more particularly of a masculine sexuality oriented around a feminine counterpart, is what makes it possible for Wagner to represent Siegfried's union with this figure initially limned by sexual likeness.

This heterosexual turn neither falsifies its homosexual impetus nor is falsified by it; the sexual formation arises in the dynamism that mediates the two modes of desire. The concomitant indeterminacy is viable, even vivifying, in the world of *Siegfried*, but it is fatal in the world of *Götterdämmerung*. When the bad Siegfried goes back, a new-minted Perseus, to the nuptial rock, his nonrecognition of Brünnhilde's body constitutes an announcement that, *from the perspective of the modern social and symbolic order*, he has never really known her in the first place. That knowledge will not be forthcoming from this new rendezvous, either—which is why, betrayed, Brünnhilde hates Siegfried so fiercely: not that the good Siegfried was false to her, but that the bad one did not know her, and never had. (Between *Siegfried* and *Götterdämmerung*, Brünnhilde slides from misrecognition to misrecognition down a slippery Oedipal slope, from the postures of motherhood and virile youth to that of another man's bride.) Muddled in mind as well as body, Siegfried knows no one now but Gunther, the blood brother whom *we* know as the tarnished mirror image of both the hero's identities: Siegfried's "good" Gunther, the ideal friend, the fellow hero, and Hagen's "bad" Gunther, the effete aristocrat corrupted by the blandishments of the Nibelung's son, the supposed pillar of the Reich befooled by an assimilated Jew, by a Leopold Bloom with attitude. Siegfried's sexual ignorance of Brünnhilde is the medium for his sexual knowledge of Gunther.

Not that he knows this, either. Wagner's libretto swears that punchdrunk Siegfried and ravished Brünnhilde slept with the sword, *Nothung*, between them, in a classic case of heroic bundling. But the music, vintage Hollywood *Begleitungsmusik* before its time, says that they did something else that could not be shown. (Siegfried confirms this later, if confirmation were needed, by making double entendres about it to his fiancee Gutrune.) The need (*Not*) signified by the sword is not only that of a proof of the unity (*Vereinung*) of blood brotherhood but that of an emblem of denial (*Verneinung*): the need to say that what happened was nothing—nothing at all. But the music puts this nothing at naught. In the tumult of the music, Siegfried now sleeps *for the first time again* with Brünnhilde. In the hidden depths of the cave, the counterpart to the theatrical hollow in which the audience at Bayreuth sits and dreams the *Ring* (as Hagen dreams, with eyes wide open), Siegfried relives in darkness the sexual act that he consummated in light on the open heights of the rock. He transforms the woman who was the author of his mythic identity into the medium of his social identity. He acts as a sexual surrogate for Gunther so that when Gunther repeats the sexual act on the official wedding night the two men can meet in the medium of the woman's body.

In this surrogation what was once the discovery of mutual desire between man and woman becomes a contest of wills. In other words, it becomes rape, which is something that the music also avows beyond the libretto's disavowal; glowering brass fanfares of doom and a recurrent two-note bump-and-grind figure leave the ear in little doubt. We are not, of course, supposed to like this. We are even invited to feel it from Brünnhilde's perspective, as a savage violation. Nothing in the opera, however, suggests that the ugliness of this violation is inherent in Siegfried's behavior as such. Aryan blood brothers do these things for each other; the problem here is that Gunther is cheating and lying, violating a code that itself goes unquestioned but is unable to withstand the corrupted modernity it is ultimately meant to redeem. In the logic of this code the consolidation of national identity in masculine identity requires the sexualizing of the homosocial. That sexualization, in turn, requires not only the interposition but also the violation of the woman's body. Brünnhilde's rock thus becomes the symbolic birthplace of German confraternity precisely to the degree that it becomes the site sacred to, made sacred by, a woman's body on which adoration and abuse are inflicted by the same man in identical sexual acts.

Sublimate this compact a little more, wrap it in the odor of sanctity, and the result will be *Parsifal*, Wagner's veiled anticipation of Freud's thesis that social feeling has its origin in homosexual libido, and by far the thorniest problem in the whole case of Wagner. "In the art of seduction," writes Nietzsche, "*Parsifal* will always retain its rank as the *stroke of genius* in seduction. —I admire this work; I wish I had written it myself. . . . Never before has there been such a *deadly hatred* of the search for knowledge! — One has to be a cynic in order not to be seduced here; one has to be able to bite in order not to worship here" (FW, 184). It should go without saying that this seductiveness has nothing to do with Kundry, who as a femme fatale is the most spectacular (and grateful) failure in all opera. Wagner's last stroke of genius was to realize that the nexus of physical suffering, sin and repentance, and sacred ritual, could elevate German confraternity like

147

The Waters of

Prometheus:

Nationalism and

Sexuality in

Wagner's *Ring*

a host and place it at the center of a translucent closet: translucent, not transparent, because Kundry's body is still required to unite Parsifal and Amfortas, a process that immolates her—she is the real sacrifice here, her speech and her will the burnt offerings on this pyre—but that, burning at the core of the *Bühnenweihefestspiel*, allows the translucent chamber to fill with a soft, steady glow.

## Redaction for the Redeemer

Nothing in the *Ring* is as vindictive as this. Brünnhilde, however abject she must become to fulfill the contrary logics of free and national spiritedness, is never deprived of voice as Kundry is, and, though cruelly deprived of agency by both father and lover, she recovers it in a literal blaze of glory at the close. The importance of this recovery lies less in its welcome resistance to the kind of unlimited, self-sanctifying phallogocentrism on offer in *Parsifal*—something of the sort can even be found in *Parsifal* itself—than in its formulation of the logic, the inner dynamic, of that resistance.

The dynamic begins in the love duet of *Siegfried*, where Brünnhilde's regrettable maidenly vulnerability (regrettable, anyway, in long retrospect) forces Siegfried, that wild child, to embark on a civilizing process under her tutelage. In Wagner's Germany, such tutelage was understood to be maternal.[26] Here, in the wake of the *Heil der Mutter* passage, its maternal character is absorbed into an eroticism that, among other things, frees Brünnhilde to retrieve some of her earlier godhead in the figurative embrace of *leuchtende Liebe, lachende Tod* ("radiant love, laughing death"). Even though the retrieval is, for the time being, figurative and no more—Brünnhilde is still chained to her rock—it sets the terms for its more than figurative realization in the immolation scene of *Götterdämmerung*.

Meanwhile, Brünnhilde's sexuality gives her the power to intervene in the symbolic order. At the same time as this sexuality requires the sacrifice of her autonomy and turns her into a mere sign of Siegfried's mastery, it endows her with mastery of the signifying process itself. The result is to lay a foundation for the transcendent act of interpretation by which she will ultimately right the wrongs of the entire *Ring*. When the good Siegfried enters the ring of magic fire, he receives from Brünnhilde an identity that the bad Siegfried, thug and shill in the same place, cannot wholly revoke. She makes him a bard, the oral historian of his own exemplary saga, over before it begins but never over at all. Sculpted in her mind, he arrives as a male Galatea and leaves as a young Prometheus molded by the discovery of her body. She receives and sanctions him as his destined Molly Bloom, as she who alone can bear true witness to his story; without her nothing can happen, nothing have meaning. Brünnhilde's rock, ratio of fire and water, is literally the bed-rock of Siegfried's legend as he knows it—and as he comes to sing it, to venture down the Rhine to sing it, to die singing it. On this rock is founded the circle of myth that Wagner's national culture claims as its universal origin; from this rock spring the arts—as fire? as water?—that flush with voice and proclaim their return to that origin on the mytho-graphic–fantasmatic stage at Bayreuth.

This return, however, is "magnificently equivocal." As soon as Siegfried descends from the rock, the legend with which Brünnhilde endows him must be reiterated in order to endure. It must be signified in the leitmotifs of the Rhine Journey music, narrated in fragments by Hagen and Siegfried at the Hall of the Gibichungs and in toto—the fragments now stitched together in a bizarre semipsychoanalytic dialogue between Hagen/Freud and the Wolf Man/Siegfried—in the forest during Siegfried's death scene, and renarrated by the combined voice of Brünnhilde and Wagner's orchestra in the closing double threnody. But with each reiteration except the last, the legend draws closer and closer to sentimental nationalist rant. The only countervailing force, in terms of the Nietzschean allegory I am enfranchising here, is the radicalized sexuality that emerges in the ecstasy on the rock and that really belongs to Brünnhilde, not Siegfried.

Far from merely reinscribing the cliches of nineteenth-century feminin-ity (from which, admittedly, it is by no means free), this sexuality is an impossible, indecipherable formation. It is conceived in sympathy with incest and awakened only insofar as Brünnhilde is a woman whose body arouses homosexual desire for her—literally for *her*—in a boy who through knowing that desire becomes a man. It is a sexuality, also, con-sumed by its one and only consummation and thereupon redirected entirely into Brünnhilde's imaginary register, her construction of Siegfried as hero, whether as free spirit or nationalist shill. The result is that the most erotic moment in the *Ring* is the nuptial conclusion of the immolation scene, an imaginary reversal of the abduction scene and an imaginary reprise of the original ecstasy on the rock:

> *helles Feuer das Herz mir entfasst,*
> *ihn zu umschlingen, umschlossen,*
> *in mächtigster Minne vermählt ihm zu sein. . .*
> *Siegfried! Siegfried! Sieh!*
> *Selig grüsst dich dein Weib!*

> bright fire grips my heart,
> to embrace him, be enfolded by him,
> to be wed with him in the mightiest love! . . .
> Siegfried! Siegfried! See!
> Blessedly greets you your bride!

The musical eros that arises from and envelops this cry transforms the unmistakably false consciousness of the immolation scene, the dialectical reclamation of the bad as the good Siegfried, into something we—I—could wish to believe.

The origin of this transformation predates even the ecstasy on the rock, though Brünnhilde's rock is indeed where it starts. The origin lies at the

149

The Waters of
Prometheus:
Nationalism and
Sexuality in
Wagner's *Ring*

close of *Die Walküre*, in which Brünnhilde, resisting her own Promethean punishment of helpless exposure on the mountain peak, proposes the magic fire. In so doing, she constitutes the man who will be Siegfried as a Promethean figure, he who takes control over a fire struck by a god. Crucial here is the fact that the idea originates with Brünnhilde, not with Wotan. Even in abjection, Brünnhilde, firebrand to Valhalla, is the wellspring of moral agency in the *Ring* cycle. (Abjection, indeed, may at one level be little more than the raw material of her own Promethean creativity, which is merely displaced onto the more conventional figure of the masculine hero.) The fire, limned so pictorially in the music, can be taken to symbolize all the cardinal aspects of the heroic but terrible destiny that Siegfried–Prometheus will find in and through entering this other Ring, Brünnhilde's Ring: desire, ordeal, betrayal, immolation:

> The only hope, or else despair
>> Lies in the choice of pyre or pyre—
>> To be redeemed from fire by fire.[27]

At this point a certain deconstruction is no longer premature: the magic fire music already has its full symbolic density long before Siegfried masters it and renders that symbolism active, explicit, present, just as Wotan's deeply lyrical threnody of farewell to Brünnhilde contains a moving eroticism, as unactable as a dream, that can be enjoyed only by the free spirit who awakens Brünnhilde. The close of *Die Walküre* indicates that Siegfried is always already an imaginary form, projected out of a woman's defiance and desire.

No longer Wotan's instrument but a human subject, half woman and half phoenix, the Brünnhilde of the farewell scene usurps Wagner's place as Siegfried's librettist and composer, and she never relinquishes it. Her fantasy of a fire-fangled Promethean hero becomes Siegfried's destiny. When the magic fire music first flickers to life in the orchestra, it rings her with the power of her own thought. In the farewell scene it haloes her body to prepare her once-in-a-lifetime union with the man her thought has sculpted. Later, in the immolation scene that closes *Götterdämmerung*, it reignites to prepare her fiery reunion with the man her thought has doomed.

The return of the magic fire music begins the immolation scene's long climax. The renewed flickering of orchestral flames impels Brünnhilde to sing her redemptory signature motive by Siegfried's pyre (see example 6.2). This motive is not a familiar strand in the melodic web of the *Ring*. Sung only once before, by Sieglinde to Brünnhilde in *Die Walküre*, it reappears in the orchestra during the immolation scene with its significance, even its identity, still undetermined. Brünnhilde virtually plucks the motive out of the air, claims it as her own, and endows it with the meaning it lacks. Her unconditional melodic action corresponds to the unconditional interpretive action by which she reclaims the bad Siegfried as a free spirit. Both actions, moreover, gain credibility (more exactly, suspension of disbelief) from another feature of the redemptory motive. Although it is almost a nonpareil, the motive bears some resemblance to a more familiar one used elsewhere to mantle Brünnhilde in lyrical pathos (see example 6.3). When she claims the redemptory motive, Brünnhilde also disclaims the pathetic one. Her claim is not only that she has moved from low to high, from pathos to sublimity, but that all of her former abjection has been burned away.

The words sung to the motive say just this, that Brünnhilde is on fire, that she is the fire: *Fühl meine Brust auch, wie sie entbrennt, / helles Feuer das Herz mir erfasst* ("Feel my breast, too, how it flames up, bright fire seizes my heart"). The focal point of this supreme act of self-recognition, by which Siegfied is consumed without remainder, even more fully than by the pyre on which he burns, is the key word *entbrennt*. When Brünnhilde sings her redemptory motive, she does so only twice. *Entbrennt* solders these two motivic statements together, beginning the second by ending the sentence otherwise given in the first. The signifier of flaming up, of catching fire, often used in the sense of becoming inflamed with love, thus becomes identified with the continuation of the melodic process that Brünnhilde has kindled with her motive. Brünnhilde herself soon entrusts that continuation to the orchestra. She goes on to seek a final, irrevocable, ecstasy, urging her voice upward along a chromatic chain of climactic high notes to a high A at *vermählt ihm zu sein* ("to be wed with him"). The orchestra, which has meanwhile begun braiding the most intense segment of her motive into a rising sequence reminiscent of Isolde's Transfiguration (the so-called *Liebestod*) in *Tristan and Isolde*, breaks through this pitch ceiling even as Brünnhilde reaches it.[28] The orchestral process validates her longings, not by satisfying them, but by projecting their satisfaction beyond her voice and her life. Brünnhilde responds decisively. After a brief apostrophe to Siegfried, her voice descends toward a climactic cadence that accompanies her leap into the last ring of magic fire and, in so doing, releases the all-consuming tongues of flame in the orchestra.

151

The Waters of
Prometheus:
Nationalism and
Sexuality in
Wagner's *Ring*

A great singer can invest this cadence with enormous authority, but it is important to recognize that she cannot invest it with closure. The cadence is of the kind technically known as deceptive, involving the resolution of melody but not of harmony; Brünnhilde's immolation falls just short of fulfilling her desire. Fulfillment, it turns out, must wait until her imaginary relationship to Siegfried has been replicated in the listener's relationship to her; the fulfillment can occur only in someone else's conception of it. The music offers to model that conception some moments after Brünnhilde's death, when the orchestra, now singing for her (on her behalf, in her voice) as well as about her, reprises her redemptory motive in counterpoint with the water music of the Rhine that emerges from murky depths of the *Rheingold* prelude at the very beginning of the *Ring*. The annulus of aesthetic closure thus becomes the metaphorical equivalent of Brünnhilde's bridal consummation—not a mere sublimation (though one can choose to hear it that way) but an expansion, a reinscription, a redaction. Her wedding band becomes a ring of fire mirrored in a ring of water.

Didn't Wagner lose faith in his national and social ambitions in the virtual *jouissance* of scenes like this one—and like Wotan's farewell and the ecstasy on the rock? Might it have been for the sake of these moments that he took such care to excise his anti-Semitism (meticulously restored by modern scholarship) from his musical theater? Here, if anywhere, is an answer to the case of Wagner: not that the music surmounts or falsifies its dire ideologies, but that it yields on our behalf to their allure—an allure often cached, a guilty secret, in the psychical back pockets even of those who most passionately reject it. Having yielded, the music carries the logic of that allure to the point where it shatters, and in shattering releases an even stronger allure than the dire one lost. We do not have to forget the direness to enjoy the music; we enjoy the most when we best and most cunningly

Example 6.2
_____

Wagner, *Götterdämmerung*, Act III: immolation scene ("Fühl' meine Brust auch").

remember. We discover that we can solve, if not resolve, the case of Wagner by learning to hear how one of his most famous formulas, the line "Redemption for the redeemer" that concludes *Parsifal* and was blazoned on a wreath at Wagner's funeral, is continually subjected to travesty variations. The music-drama compels us as it does because it ultimately betrays its own betrayals: seduction for the seducer. . .

Redaction for the redeemer: the wordplay is an act of ironic negotiation with Wagner's ghost, but it is also more. As the word's prefix indicates, a redaction is never simply the production of something in textual form, but always a re-production. For that reason what the redaction fashions is not simply a text in the sense of an inscription, but always a text in the Derridean sense of a network of differential traces. The redaction is always the *différance* of the legend, narrative, image, or precursor text that it re-renders, and vice versa.[29] Wagner's *jouissant* scenes, especially the concatenation of the funeral music and the immolation scene in *Götterdämmerung*, are redactions of the music-dramas that supposedly embed them. They resignify the dra-

153

The Waters of
Prometheus:
Nationalism and
Sexuality in
Wagner's *Ring*

Example 6.2 (page 2)

Wagner, *Götterdämmerung*, Act III: immolation scene ("Fühl' meine Brust auch.")

matic action so that its erotic, ideological, and narrative components fly in different directions, their official or subtextual meanings disseminated toward unexpected and barely articulable regions. This process, moreover, seems to ground itself in next to nothing, a mere quivering in the air: in the power of the music to invoke beautiful figures we know to be false because we have seen the ugly truth of them: figures like the loving father Wotan, Siegfried "the free-spirit and immoralist" (Nietzsche), and above all the transcendental Siegfried who returns from the dead in Brünnhilde's final conception.

Nor is it an accident that the sequence of these *jouissant* scenes, each of them ringed by, bathed in, fire, traces a vocal passage from depth to height, a transcendental passage that also runs from masculine to feminine. First there is Wotan's baritone apostrophizing the sleeping Brünnhilde, then the commingling of Siegfried's tenor with Brünnhilde's awakened soprano, and finally the apostrophe to Siegfried by Brünnhilde's soprano alone. The descent of the bad Siegfried is countered by the ascent of Brünnhilde's voice.

This ascent, however, cannot settle the case of Wagner all by itself. Everything depends here on the agency of the listener, on the intervention of the act of hearing. It is more than possible to hear Brünnhilde in the immolation scene voicing a nationalist promise that if modernity will only discorrupt itself, the next Siegfried will not have to die in squalor. Part of Wagner relied on an uncritical form of this hearing. It is equally possible to hear the final Brünnhilde voicing an ostensibly philosophical pessimism that turns out to be a thinly veiled form of sentimental nationalism. That is what Nietzsche heard; Brünnhilde, who was "initially supposed to take her farewell with a song in honor of free love . . . now gets something else to do. She has to study Schopenhauer first" (FW, 164). The Schopenhauerian Brünnhilde produces a false profundity, a "counterfeiting of transcendence" (FW, 183) that flatters the narcissistic German penchant for "the idea" (FW, 178). The immolation scene monumentalizes the spirit of the first (1876) Bayreuth festival at which

Example 6.3

---

(A) Brünnhilde's lyrical motive (transposed to E major). (B) Brünnhilde's redemptory motive.

the *Ring* was unveiled and at which Nietzsche made the dismayed discovery that "Wagner had been translated into German!" (EH, 284) and thereby into complicity with "[the] most *anti-cultural* sickness and unreason there is, nationalism, this *névrose nationale* with which Europe is sick" (EH, 321).

But it is also possible to hear something more, not something that supplants these critical hearings, but something that burns through and partly consumes them. It is possible to claim that the final Brünnhilde preserves and enhances what Nietzsche himself recognized, but not for publication, as the power of Wagner's music to "persuad[e by a] secret sexuality [wherein] one found a bond for a society in which everybody pursued his own *plaisirs*" (EH 285n). Consummating the scenes of fire-fringed voice that precede it, Brünnhilde's voice at the peak of its intensity in the immolation scene burns through the scheme of calculated redemption that Nietzsche excoriated. Conjoined with the funeral music and orchestral peroration, this voice constructs a Siegfried utterly at odds with the boorish *farceur* depicted in *Götterdämmerung*; it apostrophizes the partner of a desire even less subject to rationalization than the one that prompts the ecstasy on the rock. It shrills and croons, this voice, from within a zone of untranslatable, uncompromising, unredactable pleasure—a zone for free spirits:

> Fire and foam. Music, veerings of chasms and clash of icicles against the stars.
> O bliss! O world! O music! And forms, sweat, eyes and long hair floating there. And white tears boiling, —O bliss!—and the feminine voice reaching to the bottom of volcanoes and the grottoes of the arctic seas.
>
> —*Arthur Rimbaud, "Barbare"*[30]

The woman's voice in extremis rends the veil of our subjectivity, the veil that *is* subjectivity. We become subjects sometime in childhood by simultaneously identifying ourselves with the symbolic order of language and hiding our genitals: subjectivity arises between the logos and the fig leaf. If the hidden real of art is so often sexual, that is because sexuality is the prototype of reality in hiding. And if singing, especially operatic singing, is the most sexually real of the arts, that is because the singing voice, naked beneath its words, throbbing, sinking, soaring, assaulting, caressing, half understood, half not needing to be, the unconstrained singing voice simultaneously sexualizes utterance and utters forth sex.

Always feminine whether a man's or a woman's, that utterance at its peak shatters the mirror in which nationalist or other ideologies reflect, and so support themselves upon, sexual desire—the mirror in which such ideologies thereby constrain and normalize sexual desire. Nietzsche's betrayed utopia revives, if only for a little while, in what always seems the once-only sound of this voice, and above all in the genuinely once-only sound of Brünnhilde's self-immolating voice and its orchestral counterpart or continuation. The

155

The Waters of

Prometheus:

Nationalism and

Sexuality in

Wagner's *Ring*

voice opens an invisible breach through which all "wayward and unproductive" sexualities (Foucault's phrase)[31]—sexualities otherwise policed, idealized, or disavowed—pour forth and are heard. The sexuality that once upheld and suffused national identity now scatters both itself and it.

Of course this is not the only possible outcome. Indeed, the opposite is equally likely, perhaps even more so; one can find it realized in such latter-day Wagnerian artworks as Leni Riefenstahl's *Triumph of the Will*. But in Wagner himself the process goes in one direction only: an ignited eros burns out the thanatos of nationhood, even at the cost of becoming the thanatos of itself. The further that sexuality—or feminine sexuality, here Brünnhilde's—moves from conventionality (the bedroom farce of *Götterdämmerung*) to free love (the ecstasy on the rock, its reenactment on the pyre), the more the narrative movement is utopian rather than redemptive, universalizing rather than nationalizing.

At this point a caution is in order. I do not want to identify uncritically with this mode of hearing and in so doing to mystify sexuality as a source of liberation from the oppressions of culture. Rather, I want to recognize that Wagner, or Wagner heard via Nietzsche, is able to mobilize a trope of sexuality capable of disrupting all normalizing structures, including its own— a trope that, placed at the climactic moments of the *Ring*, can disseminate that disruption though and across the entire body of the opera, pleasurably shattering the nationalist ideologies that have otherwise found in a certain sexuality a far less pleasurable support. What I'm imagining for Wagner is a kind of anti-Foucaldian deployment: not a putting of sexuality into discourse, but a putting—a casting—of ideologically loaded discourse out of sexuality, the production of a counterdiscourse of eros that successfully masquerades as pre- and postdiscursive.

Not wanting to turn a deaf ear to this sonoric *jouissance*, I decided to embody, not merely to recommend, a course of listening. I began to construct a "musical," expressive text in place of a sober linear statement of a thesis. (The case of Wagner requires thinking through, but the thought must be personal, figurative, and associative as well as conceptual.) If statues, I wanted to ask, if statues in fountains could talk, or, better, sing, wouldn't they tell us that the shape of the waters of Prometheus circulating around and through them was the ever-returning presence of the sensibility—desiring, contingent, material, vulnerable—denied by and to their marble bodies? Wouldn't their song proclaim that the shape of the waters was not a sublimation of that sensibility but a channel for it running all aglitter without walls? Nor could such a shape stand as a monument to hero, statesman, soldier, or nymph; the politics of exclusion would drown in the shimmer of unabatement. So I delight to imagine Brünnhilde as Molly Bloom, Molly as Brünnhilde, kindling and quenching the great pyre with her indelible dying voice. We need to hear more from the garden of the Blooms:

> The trajectories of their, first sequent, then simultaneous urinations
> were dissimilar: Bloom's longer, less irruent, in the incomplete form

of the bifurcated penultimate alphabetical letter who in his ultimate year of High School (1880) had been capable of attaining the point of greatest altitude against the whole concurrent strength of the institution, 210 scholars; Stephen's higher, more sibilant, who in the ultimate hours of the previous day had augmented by diuretic consumption an insistent vesical pressure.                                (703)

The light in the window is doubled by the celestial fire of a falling star, the trajectory of which is again doubled by the double trajectories of Bloom's and Stephen's streams of urine. Each man proves an artist in water, and side by side the two make art together, love together, each in liquescent calligraphy intimating a letter in space, Y and S, respectively, and thereby forming together an alphabetic couple that Molly Bloom will conjoin with an E to produce the *jouissant* last word on which the novel ends: "and then he asked me would I yes to say yes my mountain flower . . . and his heart was going like mad and yes I said yes I will Yes" (783). The parabola of each Promethean stream traces the curve of its author's history, Bloom's with a positively Siegfriedlike reminiscence of parabolic splendor, and, like the track of the meteor from Vega in the Lyre (for the poet Stephen) to the constellation Leo(pold), the parallel streams preserve as form the fiery energies they consume as material. Could it be that this glittering urinary epiphany traces the fulfillment of that most Wagnerian of ideals, the total work of art, in which the fusion of signifying media configures the audience into a single and, despite itself, a denationalized polity, whose united and divided halves, Adam and Eve, Siegfried and Brünnhilde, Leopold and Molly, Jack and Jill, continually live and die in each other's fiery streams of song?

157

The Waters of
Prometheus:
Nationalism and
Sexuality in
Wagner's *Ring*

NOTES

Two or three paragraphs of this essay have been adapted from my "The Real in Embers, the Arts Enflamed," *Modern Language Quarterly* 54 (1993): 285–94.

1. Friedrich Nietzsche, *The Case of Wagner*, bound with *The Birth of Tragedy*, trans. Walter Kaufman (New York: Random House, 1967), 166 (subsequently cited in text as FW); Thomas Mann, "Sufferings and Greatness of Richard Wagner," *Essays*, trans. H. T. Lowe-Porter (New York: Knopf, 1957), 197.

2. Edward Said, *Musical Elaborations* (New York: Columbia University Press, 1993), 61.

3. Marc A. Weiner, *Richard Wagner and the Anti-Semitic Imagination* (Lincoln: University of Nebraska Press, 1995). See also Paul Lawrence Rose, *Wagner: Race, Revolution and Redemption* (New Haven: Yale University Press, 1993).

4. Arthur Groos, "Constructing Nuremberg: Typological and Proleptic Communities in *Die Meistersinger*," *19th-Century Music* 16 (1992): 18–34.

5. Friedrich Nietzsche, *Beyond Good and Evil*, trans. Marianne Cowan (Chicago: Regnery, 1955), sec. 240.

6. *The Diaries of Cosima Wagner*, trans. Geoffrey Skelton (New York: 1978–80), 17 October 1882.

7. See Jacques Derrida, *Spurs: Nietzsche's Styles*, trans. Barbara Harlow (Chicago: University of Chicago Press, 1979).

8. Friedrich Nietzsche, *Ecce Homo,* bound with *On the Genealogy of Morals,* trans. Walter Kaufman (New York: Random House, 1967), 248 (subsequently cited in text as EH).

9. It is important to stress the exact terms by which I link Hagen to anti-Semitism here. Simply to identify Nibelungs like Alberich and Mime as "Jews," and Hagen as "at least a half-Jew," as does Jean-Jacques Nattiez in his *Wagner Androgyne: A Study in Interpretation,* trans. Stewart Spencer (Princeton: Princeton University Press, 1993), 60, 70, 87, too bluntly overrides the obliquity of Wagner's practice and its deeply ambivalent motives. Similarly, Theodor Adorno's statement that "all the rejects of Wagner's works are caricatures of Jews" is only a half-truth, if a powerful one (Adorno, *In Search of Wagner,* trans. Rodney Livingstone [London: Verso, 1981], 23). Although the only appropriate response to Wagner's anti-Semitism is merciless critique, the critique loses its edge when it becomes too easy.

10. Aeschylus, *Prometheus Bound,* trans. David Grene, ll. 6–7, 111, 449–50, 500–502, from *The Complete Greek Tragedies: Aeschylus II,* ed. David Grene and Richmond Lattimore (Chicago: University of Chicago Press, 1956).

11. Byron, "Promethus," ll. 36, 38, from *Poetical Works,* ed. John Jump (Oxford: Oxford University Press, 1970); Shelley, *Prometheus Unbound,* act II, scene iv, 72–73, from *Shelley's Poetry and Prose,* ed. Donald B. Reiman and Sharon B. Powers (New York: Norton, 1977); Goethe, "Prometheus," ll. 54–56, from *Gedichte. Versepen* (Frankfurt am Main: Insel, 1970).

12. Freud, "The Acquisition of Power Over Fire," *The Collected Papers of Sigmund Freud: Character and Culture,* ed. Philip Rieff (New York: Macmillan, 1963), 294–300; *Civilization and Its Discontents* (New York: Norton, 1961), 37n.

13. Mikhail Bakhtin, *Rabelais and His World,* trans. Hélène Iswolsky (Bloomington: Indiana University Press, 1984), 303–67.

14. "I Sing the Body Electric," l. 28, from *Leaves of Grass,* ed. Sculley Bradley and Harold W. Blodgett (New York: Norton, 1973).

15. William Carlos Williams, *Selected Poems,* 1909–1939, vol. 1 (New York: New Directions, 1938). Copyright 1938 by New Directions. Reprinted by permission of New Directions.

16. François Rabelais, *Gargantua and Pantagruel,* trans. J. M. Cohen (Baltimore: Penguin, 1955), bk. 1, ch. 17.

17. James Joyce, *Ulysses* (New York: Random House, 1961), 702 (subsequently cited in text).

18. Beat Wys, "Ragnarok of Illusion: Richard Wagner's 'Mystical Abyss' at Bayreuth," trans. Denise Bratton, *October* 54 (1990): 72.

19. Nattiez, *Wagner Androgyne,* 123–25; Feuerbach quoted (by Nattiez) from *Das Wesen des Christenthums* (1841), in *Sämtliche Werke,* ed. Wilhelm Bolin and Friedrich Jodl (Stuttgart, 1903), 2: 137.

20. Wagner, "Ausführungen zu 'Religion und Kunst.' 1. 'Erkenne dich Selbst.'" [Continuations of Religion and Art. 1. Know Thyself], 1881. Quoted in Nattiez, *Wagner Androgyne,* 167.

21. Wagner, *Das Braune Buch: Tagebuchaufzeichnungen 1865 bis 1882* [The Brown Book: Diary Entries, 1865–1882], October 23, 1881; quoted by Nattiez, *Wagner Androgyne,* 170.

22. Both quotations from Karl Marx, "On the Jewish Question" (1843), in *The Marx-Engels Reader,* 2nd ed., ed. Robert C. Tucker (New York: Norton, 1978): Bauer, 27; Marx, 48.

23. Wagner, "Das Judenthum in der Musik" [Judaism in Music], *Gesammelte Schriften und Dichtungen*, 10 vols., 2nd ed. (Leipzig: E. W. Fritzsch, 1887–88), 5:69.

24. Luce Irigaray, "Women on the Market," *This Sex Which Is Not One*, trans. Gillian C. Gill (Ithaca: Cornell University Press, 1985), 170–91; Eve Kosofsky Sedgwick, *Between Men: Homosocial Desire and English Fiction* (New York: Columbia University Press, 1985).

25. For the nose, with other bodily markers of Jewish difference, see Kristin M. Knittel, "'Ein hypermoderner Dirigent': Mahler and Anti-Semitism in *Fin-de-Siècle* Vienna," *19th-Century Music* 18 (1995): 259–65, and Sander Gilman, *The Jew's Body* (New York: Routledge, 1991). For Wagner on the Jewish voice, see "Das Judenthum," *Gesammelte Schriften* 5: 71.

26. See Friedrich A. Kittler, *Discourse Networks, 1800/1900*, trans. Michael Metteer with Chris Cullens (Stanford: Stanford University Press, 1990), 26–69.

27. T. S. Eliot, "Little Gidding," IV, ll. 5–7, from *Collected Poems 1909–1962* (New York: Knopf, 1963).

28. The resemblance to *Tristan* is more than fortuitous. Isolde's transfiguration and Brünnhilde's immolation enact the same cultural trope, one in which the death of the beloved man releases a kind of libidinal flood that washes away, even falsifies, the distressing truths of the dramatic action. For a discussion of this process in *Tristan*, see my *Music as Cultural Practice: 1800–1900* (Berkeley: University of California Press, 1990), 135–66. The most important difference between Isolde and Brünnhilde in this connection is that the latter must overcome a far greater weight of resistance in order to reach her goal. Isolde is visionary, Brünnhilde heroic.

29. See Jacques Derrida, *Positions*, trans. Alan Bass (Chicago: University of Chicago Press, 1981), 26–27; and "Différance," *Margins of Philosophy*, trans. Alan Bass (Chicago: University of Chicago Press, 1982), 1–27.

30. From *Illuminations*, trans. Louise Varese (New York: New Directions, 1957).

31. Michel Foucault, *The History of Sexuality*, vol. 1, *An Introduction*, trans. Robert Hurley (New York: Random House, 1980), 44.

159

The Waters of
Prometheus:
Nationalism and
Sexuality in
Wagner's *Ring*

## CHAPTER SEVEN

*Constructing the Oriental "Other": Saint-Saëns's* Samson et Dalila

Ralph P. Locke

## Dichotomies Invoked and Reinterpreted

Opera is rich in works that construct visions of the non-Western world and its inhabitants. Many of these reenact in fairly routine ways standard stereotypes of how distant peoples in fabled lands think and act.[1] But other works, such as Rameau's *Les Indes galantes*, Mozart's *Die Entführung aus dem Serail*, Bizet's *Pêcheurs de perles*, Verdi's *Aïda*, Strauss's *Salome*, or Puccini's *Turandot*, offer representations that are—in the cumulative opinion of generations of sophisticated operagoers and attentive critics—more imaginative or engaging, more affecting or nuanced. This is not to say that such operas are notably more accurate (historically, ethnographically) in their depictions than are more routine works. Quite the contrary, for the richness in these works often derives from their creators' willingness to exploit familiar stereotypes but in new ways (e.g., by giving a timeworn convention a new twist, by allowing one character to shift back and forth between two sides of a dichotomy basic to the plot, or by aligning several different stereotypes in such a way that they sometimes reinforce each other and sometimes conflict fascinatingly). Camille Saint-Saëns's long-popular *Samson et Dalila* provides an opportunity to explore this process in some detail with reference to Europe's nearest and most continuously important others: the inhabitants of the Middle East.[2]

*Other*, in the sense used here, is defined primarily by geographical and ethnic and religious difference from the West. But the term, as generally understood in cultural and critical theory today, may apply equally to women (especially in genres and traditions in which the primary agent is normatively the male "hero"), men who neglect their national-patriotic duties, male homosexuals, or any other individual or group understood as not inviting identification on the part of the viewer imbued with the proper values of mainstream (patriarchal) society. As we shall see, several of these categories of others are also actively at work in exotic operas, overlapping with and often reinforcing the basic dualism of West and East. This is most easily demonstrable at what we might call the foundational or plot premise level of an opera, conveyed in various ways through prose summary, set design, costuming, and stage movement and gesture. The discussion becomes more interesting when one considers how this dualism of self and other is supported or undermined (or some perhaps unsettling combination of the two) by the artfulnesses of the libretto, including shifts of tone and topic, a character's declarations and poetic flights, and his/her loaded words and no less powerful silences—and of course the artfulnesses of the music—including vocal lines and orchestral passages that may be by turns resplendent or touching, mystery laden or spine chilling.[3]

The question can be explored with particular profit in regard to Saint-Saëns, a composer who was creatively obsessed with the Middle East (e.g., *Suite algérienne* for orchestra). This obsession takes on a nearly prismatic range of glints and colors in *Samson et Dalila*, the opera that was dearest to him and that, in part because of its Biblical plot, had the longest road to acceptance on the operatic stage.[4] (Begun in 1868, the work was not performed until 1875—in Weimar, Germany—and did not reach the Paris Opera until 1892.)[5] In this opera various accepted dichotomies of national style (European vs. Oriental—a dichotomy figured as Hebrew vs. Philistine—but also French vs. German/Wagnerian) are almost systematically engaged, elaborated, reformulated, and challenged.

The work's negotiation of the French/German stylistic dichotomy (or perhaps "struggle") will be suggested from time to time in this essay (especially as seen in a parallel dichotomy: opera vs. oratorio) and relates to a basic creative tension in Saint-Saëns between an archetypally French suavity and talent for amusing, and a devotion to more sober musical values, as embodied in the works of composers he admired, such as J. S. Bach, Mozart, and Liszt.[6] My major concern, though, is to explore the work's other main dichotomy-of-nation: Europe vs. Orient (and specifically the Middle East). In the process we will see how this dichotomy interacts with other dichotomies, notably (1) male (or, in a woman, masculine or independent) vs. female (or, in a man, effeminate or dependent) and (2) appropriate (self-controlled) sexual desire versus inappropriate (hysterically needful, manipulative, perverse) desire. Such dichotomies are very much present at the foundational (prosaic/visual) level of this work, thanks largely to the Bible story upon which it is based. But a closer look at what the characters sing—and how the orchestra comments—deeply enriches and destabilizes these apparently simple dichotomies, to the point that a listener may feel a disturbing yet compelling mixture of sympathy and antipathy toward nearly all the characters and their actions: a yearning to "identify" yet also a nagging desire (or is it a proto-Brechtian invitation?) to critique.[7]

The outline set forth in the previous three paragraphs—a hierarchy moving upward from plot summary and stage sets to imaged verse and shimmering music—may seem to slight the importance of that first, "prosaic" level (including highly conventionalized visual markers), subordinating it to the more "poetic" ones (including music). My intention is the opposite; I feel it crucial to start out by establishing that the work's framework of "givens" is shaped by, and in turn conveys to the audience, an ideologically driven view of the East, a view now generally known as Orientalism. (This is discussed later in "Orient: Reality and Illusion.") The poetry and music will intensify, complicate, and even sometimes contradict this basic message, but they never completely efface it.

This point about a work's "givens" is often neglected. Musicologists regularly approach the problem of "the exotic" in an opera by going right to the notes of the score and trying to sniff out the one or two most overtly "foreign"-sounding numbers (often ballets or choruses) and noting the use, in those few numbers, of unusual melodic touches or orchestrational devices. This is an important task, of course, but a severely limited one, precisely because it scrutinizes the upper, "poetic" commentaries but neglects the foundational givens upon which they comment, as if, in discussing a painting of Christ's deposition from the cross, one were to seek a religious message in the brush strokes and color without first discussing composition and iconography. Speaking more generally, an exclusive focus on musical style tends to echo an unspoken ideology of formalism, seen in the assumption that somehow the pitches and rhythms will convey all the necessary data or messages, whether or not the listener is familiar with the work's social and cultural contexts.[8] By contrast, we focus first on the larger attitude toward the East in this particular Oriental (indeed, one might say "Orientalist") opera. This will prepare us for the two passages that are most striking or anomalous (non-Western sounding): the dance numbers for the Philistines. But our preliminary focus on the work's larger attitude toward, or construction of, the East will also free us to consider many other sections of the work and to explore Saint-Saëns's handling of a broad range of operatic techniques, including distinctive orchestrational combinations, pointed contrasts of musical style, revealing manipulations of melodic motives and accompanimental figures, and dramaturgically apt structural manipulations (such as a love duet in which one of the characters dominates). These in turn will help us see how the composer has characterized the two opposing national-religious groups in the work and the individual leading roles, notably the paradoxical heroine/villainess Delilah.[9]

## The Paradigmatic Oriental Opera Plot

The paradigmatic plot for Orientalist operas, seen in whole or large part in Meyerbeer's *L'Africaine*, Félicien David's *La Perle du Brésil*, *Aida*, Delibes's *Lakmé*, and Puccini's *Madama Butterfly*, could be summarized as follows: a young, tolerant, brave, possibly naive or selfish, white European tenor-hero intrudes (at the risk of disloyalty to his own people and to the colonialist ethic with which he is identified) into mysterious, dark-skinned, colonized territory represented by sexy dancing girls and a deeply affectionate, sensitive lyric soprano, thereby incurring the wrath of the brutal, intransigent tribal chieftain (bass or bass-baritone) and the blindly obedient chorus of male savages.

The libretto for *Samson*, written by the composer and a close associate,[10] follows this scenario in the main but departs from it in three crucial respects:

1. It is set not in some modern-day colonized territory but in the Biblical land of the Israelites and Philistines.
2. Its heroine is a ripe mezzo, indeed a vile seductress, rather than a delicate soprano. Delilah's striking degree of self-mobilizing agency makes her come to seem, as the opera progresses, the central figure—dare we say the protagonist?—of the story. (Saint-Saëns's manuscript bears the revealingly simple title *Dalila*.)
3. The natives are an imperial power holding the West (the Hebrews) captive, an inverted power relationship that is set right by Samson's God-ordained act of destruction, which is also an act of national liberation.[11]

The mixture of plots enriches rather than confuses, largely because, as suggested, the added elements (Western piety, Oriental femme fatale, national liberation from Oriental tyranny) often reinforce rather than contradict the opera's underlying binary opposition between a morally superior "us" (or "collective self") and an appealing but dangerous "them" ("collective other"), who come close to causing "our" downfall.

### Orient: Reality and Illusion

This opposition, located primarily at what I have called the "foundational level" of the work, echoes a widespread worldview that flourished at the time and is now often known as "Orientalism."[12] Edward Said defines Orientalism as a "corporate institution for dealing with the Orient—dealing with it by making statements about it, authorizing views of it, describing it, by teaching it, settling it, ruling over it: in short, Orientalism as a Western style for dominating, restructuring, and having authority over the Orient."[13] The Orientalist project is reflected in and advanced by works of literature, art, and music. In particular, it reiterates certain stereotyped images of "Oriental despotism, Oriental splendor, cruelty, sensuality . . . promise, terror, sublimity, idyllic pleasure, intense energy."[14]

France was, with the possible exception of England, the most active colonial power in North Africa and the Middle East during the nineteenth and early twentieth centuries, and used all the military, economic, educational, and journalistic forces at its command to secure geopolitical leverage, access to raw materials, and other advantages of colonial domination, and to ensure public support for that system of domination. It is not surprising that some of the most familiar and historically significant instances of Orientalism in the arts are French, such as the poems of Hugo (*Les Orientales*, 1829) and the paintings of harem scenes and scimitar-wielding warriors by Ingres, Delacroix, Renoir, and—closer to our own day—Matisse.

Immediately striking in many Orientalist works are the references to local settings and customs. Poets often guided the reader's sense of place by citing easily recognized names and terms, and painters depicted opium pipes, curved sabers, Algerian and Moroccan costumes, and Turkish wall tiles. Composers, in turn, had a way of making a sense of place credible to the listener: by imitating or evoking the musics of the region in question. In this somewhat limited sense, the two most obviously exotic-evocative moments in *Samson et Dalila* are the two dances.

The "Dance of the Priestesses of Dagon" (Act I) gives the fullest glimpse of the Philistine maidens, who wave their garlands and—as the stage directions put it—"seem to provoke [i.e., not intentionally so?] the Hebrew warriors."[15] Delilah, joining in their "voluptuous gestures," provokes Samson in a more calculating manner, despite his efforts to avert his eyes from "the enchantress." Part of the demure yet intriguing effect here comes from the elusive modal language of the music: the opening phrase (see example 7.1) uses a minor third degree but a major sixth, in addition to a lowered seventh, that single most distinctive sign of temporal or geographical displacement in Western music of recent centuries. Delicate sounds from harp and *tambour de basque* reinforce the sense of Easternness or perhaps "ancientness."[16]

The music of the famous Bacchanale (Act III) gestures more plainly toward local color, in a quasi-ethnographic sense. (Throughout his mature life, Saint-Saëns stayed for extended periods in Algeria and Egypt during the winter. His letters show him intrigued by Arab musical traditions.[17]) In this ballet the Philistine princes and maidens prolong their debauched revels beyond daybreak, urged on by hypnotic rhythms in the castanets, timpani, and low strings (notably an asymmetrical ostinato: 3 + 3 + 2) and by

Example 7.1

Act I, Dance of the Priestesses.

florid melodies and garish harmonies based on the Arab Hijāz mode, which Saint-Saëns chose no doubt for its strikingly "foreign" augmented second between degrees 2 and 3. (See example 7.2a and, for comparison, example 7.2b: a North African muezzin call, likewise in Hijāz.[18]) The rhapsodic oboe solo that opens the number (example 7.3) captures something of the improvisatory freedom that Westerners find so remarkable in much Middle Eastern music, and its opening bears an uncanny resemblance to example 7.2b and other related versions of the muezzin's call to prayer available in transcription and on disc.[19]

### Point of View: The Other as Temptation and Threat

Much else in this opera links it to the Orientalist impulses of the day. As we noted earlier, the primary aim of nineteenth-century Orientalism was to "represent" the East to the West. The way of doing this varied greatly and

Example 7.2

(A) Act III, Bacchanale: melody resembling Hijāz mode.
(B) *Adhān* (muezzin call) in Hijāz mode, transcribed by Joseph Rouanet in Tunisia in the early twentieth century.

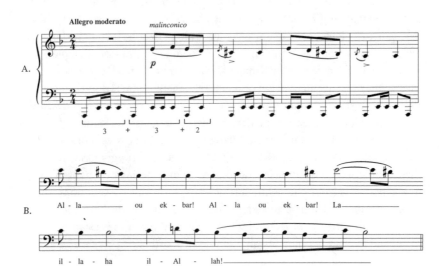

Example 7.3

Act III, Bacchanale: opening oboe solo.

did not always involve specifically non-European styles. After all, poets rarely wrote in anything like an Eastern manner, despite some passing experiments with the intellectually challenging form of the Persian *ghazal*. Similarly, Delacroix and others—to return briefly to visual art—evoked distant scenes in the most up-to-date Western manner, using virtuosic brush techniques, recent developments in color theory, three-dimensional modeling of form, and placement of figures in space and in specific, often theatrical relationships (e.g., through glance and gesture). Art historians nonetheless speak of an Orientalist attitude toward, for example, the nude or scantily dressed female figures in Delacroix's *Death of Sardanapalus*, Gérôme's *Slave Market* (fig. 7.1), or Debat-Ponsan's *The Massage*.

Figure 7.1

Jean-Louis Gérôme, *Slave Market* (early 1860s). (Courtesy of Sterling and Francine Clark Art Institute, Williamstown, Massachusetts.)

These images of woman embody what has been called the central *topos obligé* of the Western fantasy of the Orient[20]: the female figures are portrayed as objects of desire—primarily as *odalisques* (concubines) who are voluptuous, vulnerable, indolent, and sexually available to a present or implied Oriental male. Most relevant for our understanding of Delilah, these women can also be not just desirable but actively and dangerously desir*ing*. It is important to recall how little the issue of carnal desire, especially in women, was openly addressed in European high art of the middle to late nineteenth century, a direct function (and reinforcement) of male domination in the larger society.

Delilah and the dancing women in the "Dance of the Priestesses of Dagon" in Act I are presented explicitly as a seductive threat to the righteous, God-fearing Hebrews, especially Samson. The Orientalist point of view described by Said and others thus saturates the opera through the sharp dichotomies of the plot noted earlier: Delilah, chief representative of the East, is female and seeks the downfall of Samson (the male proto-European) and that of the God-chosen West. Furthermore, Samson and his people are presented, for the most part, as the dramatic "subject," the collective Self of this story, whose point of view the audience is primarily led to adopt.[21] Audiences in Saint-Saëns's day would clearly have felt in sympathy with the monotheistic Hebrews rather than with the idol-worshiping and decadent Philistines; in particular, they would have been prepared to see Samson not only as a divinely inspired Hebrew leader but also as a prefiguration of Christ and thus of Western civilization.[22] Indeed, given the increasingly anti-Semitic outlook of many educated Europeans in the late nineteenth century, it may be that an Old Testament story could *only* be acceptable if presented in a Christian (i.e., "universal") light.[23]

This partial (in both senses) reading of Samson is strengthened in the opera by some basic alterations to the Biblical tale. Samson's earlier, rambunctious exploits in war and love, including his responses to Delilah's first three attempts to learn his secret, are mentioned only obliquely. In contrast, newly concocted for the libretto (or, rather, recycled from Voltaire's own very free adaption of the Bible story, *Samson* [1732])[24] are nearly all the events in Act I, including the lament of the captive Hebrews, Samson's slaying of Abimelech, and the Hebrew revolt—all events that emphasize liberation from heathen bondage.

Saint-Saëns reinforced this privileging of the West (and, predominantly, its males, as we shall see) through basic musical and structural decisions. He opened the opera with an extended lament of the captive Hebrews rich in references to the styles and techniques of European sacred music (including a fugue), leading the listener to view the Philistines primarily through Hebrew eyes, as oppressors. Similarly, the pious chorus sung by the old Hebrew men in the middle of the act, after the Hebrews have routed the Philistine forces ("Hymne de joie, / Hymne de délivrance"), is more reminiscent of Gregorian chant than of anything recognizably Middle Eastern.[25]

But point of view in this and other Orientalist works does not necessarily function in simple, "black/white" fashion. Precisely in the portrayal of Oriental women it verges on the admiring, even the voyeuristic. We first meet the Philistine women in the middle of Act I immediately after the somber, archaic men's chorus just mentioned. The young women enter singing with exquisite sweetness and innocence of springtime, rosebuds, and love ("aimons toujours!"), while the violins evoke mild breezes, using the women's opening motive in diminution (example 7.4).[26] The women are thus allied with the beauty of nature, a feature of the Orientalist paradigm that in this case intensifies a standard Romantic preconception (woman is to nature and love as man is to civilization and war).

Delilah now speaks up, addressing suggestive phrases—about her arms, her "ebony hair," her kisses, her "sweet odor"—directly to Samson. (He has been her lover on at least three occasions before the point at which the opera begins but, to her distress, has always torn himself away and returned to the battlefield.) As she sings and glances provocatively at him, the opera audience feels Samson's anxiety and at the same time wants to keep listening, fas-

Example 7.4

Act I, chorus of Philistine women.

cinated—as earlier critics have testified—by this remarkable woman's forth-right projection of unrepressed sensuality.[27] (A photo from the Met, taken in 1915 [fig. 7.2], captures the contending dramatic vectors in this scene: a womanly Delilah seeking to enchain with garlands of flowers the hero Samson, whose face and body language reveal his deep sense of conflict, while the Old Hebrew tries vainly to warn him that the "burning flame of her glances . . . is a poison that consumes the very bones.") Delilah's opening phrases command attention by their upward leaps—frequently a sixth, extending from the fifth degree to the third above (example 7.5a)—and looping arpeggios (example 7.5b–c). Samson seems troubled by her call: in comparison to his forthright utterances in the first half of Act I, he expresses himself in anguished, descending chromatic lines. But, as the trio progresses, he begins to adopt Delilah's looping figures, as if already yielding to her stronger will or to an echoing desire within himself.[28]

Even more evocative, and plainly more effective in breaking Samson's resistance, is her aria "Printemps qui commence." This aria begins (example 7.6a, p. 172) with eight-bar periods constructed of two-bar phrases, entirely syllabic in declamation and supported by the simplest of held-note accompaniments: a syncopated dominant pedal, faintly alluding to pedal tones in Middle Eastern music. But the intensity soon builds above and below the obstinate (40-bar-long) pedal, ensnaring not only Samson but the listener in the long stretch of seductively melismatic melody reproduced in example 7.6b: the eight bars are now built of two large phrases that are themselves powerfully asymmetrical (5 + 3).

## Oriental Despots

The Philistine men are portrayed as agents of an oppressive government and a cruel, superstitious religion, consistent with Orientalist stereotypes of

Example 7.5

(A)Act I, Delilah's first words. (B)Act I trio: Delilah's beguiling invitations. (C) Act I trio: Delilah pours it on.

Middle Eastern males as smug, single-minded, intolerant, power-mad despots and fanatics, impulsive and prone to violence (when they aren't ogling their women, in a drugged haze). The Orientalist paintings of the period overwhelmingly present men as engaging in such pursuits as stabbing a lion at close range, collecting taxes at rifle point, performing military exercises on horseback, or going into a wild, disordered dance of religious fanaticism.[29]

In reality, the political leaders of the Middle East and their fighting troops—however fanatical, bloodthirsty, and highly skilled with horse and rifle—proved nearly powerless in the face of the gunboats of Western imperialism. Orientalist artworks, by insistently assigning enormous power to the archetypal Arab leaders (or their ancient stand-ins), made them easier to hate, and led the viewer to side with the innocent victim of these dangerous egomaniacs.

The High Priest of Dagon makes clear his genocidal intentions in his Act I curse: *Maudite à jamais soit la race / Des enfants d'Israël! / Je veux en effacer la trace. . . .* ("Accursed forever be the race of the children of Israel! I will wipe them out without a trace. . . .") The repulsive words are reinforced by a striking, militaristic figure that will become one of the most memorable, and most stomach churning, of the opera's many recurring motives (example 7.7, p. 173).

One might, however, wish to consider a very different but not completely incompatible political reading of the High Priest as well as of the

Figure 7.2

Scene from the end of Act I, Metropolitan Opera Archives (1915): Margarete Matzenauer (Delilah), Enrico Caruso (Samson), Léon Rothier (Old Hebrew). (Photo by White, 1915; Metropolitan Opera Archives.)

satrap Abimelech (a figure at once demonic and obtuse).[30] By such a reading the Oriental exterior of these despots is (as we noted of the sensuous priestesses) a mask or deflection, rather than a primary characteristic. Seen this way, the two characters can be taken as symbols of morally corrupt authority, much as the oppressive Egyptian priesthood in *Aida* stands for everything that Verdi detested in the politics and religion of his native Italy.[31] And if we seriously entertain this reading, we face the possibility of leaving the Orientalist paradigm behind, or at least of enriching it with other, non-Orientalist concerns.

To thus emphasize the "endotic" subtext beneath an overtly "exotic" work is not to deny that the work reflects the unequal distribution of power among the nations of the world; the very appropriation of the other for the West's own purposes of self-criticism (or whatever) in such works has probably contributed, however inadvertently, to the continued propagation of

Example 7.6

(A) Act I, Delilah's aria (opening). (B) Act I, Delilah's aria (extended phrases).

racial and ethnic stereotypes. Nonetheless, the realization that European subjectivity may persist behind these dark-skinned masks, that—to change the metaphor—the Orient may largely be a blank screen for projecting Western concerns about itself, can change in major ways a listener's or critic's response to the work.

## The Enemy

The problem of how to "read" the Philistines—whether as the "other" or as an aspect of "us"—arises more insistently in Act III, where we finally encounter the Philistine customs and religion in full dress. The chorus of Philistines taunts the blinded strongman, in a manner reminiscent of the Bach Passions, but Saint-Saëns denies his crowd any dignity. We seem, indeed, to have been thrown into a comic opera: *Sa colère est plaisante! Ah! ah! ah! ah! ah!* ("His anger is ludicrous! Ha, ha, ha, ha, ha!")

Just what the Philistines as a whole are worth is further revealed in the glitzy, slimy Bacchanale discussed earlier and most of all in the big triumphal hymn ("Gloire à Dagon vainqueur"), a fascinating mix of Bach and Offenbach. This number, the last in the opera except for Samson's brief prayer for strength and the act of destruction itself, begins with a hearty, major-mode turn-plus-scalar-descent figure that is presented in unison by the strings, suggesting festive music of the Baroque. But the instrumental forces become more shrill as the hymn proceeds (extensive melodic passages for glockenspiel!), and—at the singers' words *Dagon se révèle* ("Dagon reveals himself"), when the sacred fire flares up—the music changes into a *con brio* dance, something between a quick polka and a cancan (example 7.8). The choice of a trite hopping dance—music that is utterly philistine (with a small *p*)—for a moment of supposed religious exaltation seems, on one level, clearly conscious, a final castigation of the degenerate Philistines and the ungodliness of their religion. Again, though, an "endotic" reading is also possible: that Saint-Saëns, under the guise of castigating some safely distant other time and place, was in fact implicating the repressive French government and Catholic clergy.[32] It is no mere coincidence that Saint-Saëns was throughout his life—much like Verdi—an outspoken republican and anticlericalist.

Example 7.7

Act I, aria of the Philistine High Priest (opening).

## Reading Delilah

The problem of how strictly to read the binary opposition of West and East in this opera becomes most intense with regard to Delilah. In the main (and despite the gradual appeal to audience sympathy, to be discussed later) the portrait is misogynistic. This point needs to be stated explicitly.[33] The current tendency is to rewrite as unexpectedly strong or admirable the heroines of opera: one finds it in public comments of singers anxious to defend the heroines they portray,[34] in staging decisions of major productions, and in the elaborate argumentation of some scholarly commentators (perhaps fueled at times by the healthy impulse, typical of "first-stage feminism," to read afresh—and often more positively—certain widespread images of women in Western culture and art). But a truly critical feminism surely needs also to recognize that an opera from the 1870s, set in Biblical times, will not likely be recuperable into a modern conception of how a self-affirming woman ought to conduct herself.[35]

The libretto (unlike the Bible) has Delilah spurn the High Priest's offered bribe. Commentators going back at least to the 1890s have concurred that taking the money would have imputed a base motive to Delilah. Instead, she declares to the High Priest that she has, for patriotic reasons, pretended to love Samson in hopes of learning the secret of his strength and bringing him low.[36] What she does not say is that she is also deeply attracted to Samson. In her soliloquy just before the duet with the High Priest ("Amour, viens aider ma faiblesse"), she pleads to the pagan god of love to help her "poison" her way into Samson's heart and enslave him to her: *Samson soit enchaîné demain! . . . Il est à moi! c'est mon esclave!* ("Let Samson be in chains tomorrow. —He is mine, my slave.") But the music of the aria, and the introductory orchestral evocation of the evening breezes in the "sweet valley," emphasize the love and carnal desire—desire to "enchain" Samson to herself, for herself—that are driving Delilah, though she herself may not fully admit them.[37]

The operatic Delilah, in short, is presented as a woman who loves, or at least lusts and yearns and seeks to dominate; as we have seen, she may well

Example 7.8

Act III, Hymn to Dagon (dancelike section; shown here is the orchestral part only).

continue on some unconscious level, more in the music than in the libretto, to lust and yearn for Samson even though—or especially because—he repeatedly (before the opera begins) has cut short several love trysts with her and returned to his duties as leader of the Hebrews. But she also becomes vengeful, plainly considering her failure with Samson an affront to her beauty and to the power of the womanly arts of which she is so proud. Furthermore, she is a patriotic woman, who "abhors" and "hates" the enemy leader (words finally uttered during the course of her duet with the High Priest). Thus the word *love*, if applicable at all to Delilah, must imply not the tenderness and devotion of a *femme fragile* such as Verdi's Gilda or, later, Puccini's Cio-Cio San but the hot, scary kind of love/hate seen to varying extents in Donizetti's calculating queens; Verdi's Count di Luna, Eboli, and Amneris; and Puccini's Baron Scarpia.

A performer may disambiguate Delilah in the interests of consistency: Elena Obraztsova's recorded interpretation, despite her protests in the accompanying essay, presents a most imperious, implacable heroine, with little warmth and volatility.[38] Or the performer may revel in the sudden shifts and even add a few, as Shirley Verrett does on videotape: in the Covent Garden production, for example, she is seen grinning (aside) maliciously as Samson begins to yield just before "Mon coeur," but then she sings with an unreadable mixture of glee, passion, and anguish through to the end of the act. After betraying him, she steals out of her house, throws her body against a wall, and averts her gaze, in pain, exhaustion, and, it seems, Amneris-like remorse. Obraztsova is simpler and truer to the immediate implications of the libretto: she stands over Samson and raises her arms in brazen triumph.[39]

## The Love (or Treacherous Seduction?) Scene

All the disambiguating at the end of Act II is necessary because of the opera's most famous and dramatically "fraught" scene, which immediately preceded it. After the High Priest leaves, Delilah is alone again and waits for Samson. She moans resignedly, *Hélas, il ne vient pas!* ("Alas, he is not going to come"). Samson does finally come, "hesitantly," to bid her a "last farewell."[40] She of course plans to put his passion for her to the test one more time—at night, on her own territory.[41]

The source of their mutual attraction is most fully revealed in the middle section of their duet: an extended lyrical movement for Delilah that allows us finally to feel both the depth of her own obsession with Samson and the source of her power over him. *Mon coeur s'ouvre à ta voix, / Comme s'ouvrent les fleurs / Aux baisers de l'aurore!* ("My heart opens at the sound of your voice, as blossoms do at the kisses of dawn"), she sings flatteringly to her tenor lover, begging him to repeat the love songs he once sang to her.

This number has understandably been referred to as an aria. To be accurate, though, Samson actually does have a few echoing phrases, including a long high B-flat that, sung *piano*, reduces the hero to a state of smitten helplessness. In the climactic phrases, Delilah's vocal line leaps beyond the sixth used in Act I, expanding here to a seventh that is stated four times in a row: the first three form an upwardly surging sequence of conjoined arcs, and the third and fourth (X and Y in example 7.9), with the voice now doubled by the winds, form a descending sequence that is supported harmonically by a drop from the tonic chord to the relative minor (i.e., I-vi), a shift that adds a pang just before the cadential resolution.

Writers, disambiguating in the negative direction, have repeatedly described this aria as a "feigned" or "counterfeited" protestation of love,[42] thereby reading as entirely calculated and unfelt her closing words, *Mais, non! Que dis-je, hélas?* ("No, what I am saying?"). Solliers states outright, "Delilah does not love."[43] But such a reading seems to reduce the stature and complexity of Delilah, who is at once heroically strong and deeply needful, who indeed might be a worthy match and perhaps mate for Samson were she not twisted and dehumanized by her role as agent of the oppressor.[44] It has been argued that the return of the breeze music during the second strophe of Delilah's avowal of love proves ("warns" the audience) that she is employing a "ruse."[45] This seems too simple by far. If Saint-Saëns had wanted to give the audience a musical clue of her insincerity in this powerful passage, the master ironist could have done so; but he did not.[46]

### Since Delilah

Once we start taking Delilah's feelings at all seriously, we may begin to see in *Samson et Dalila* parallels to a story with which it has never been connected, that of Romeo and Juliet.[47] That story is useful here as an archetype of love denied or destroyed through internecine warfare (internecine in that the Montagues and Capulets are seen as warring factions of a single people). If we accept that all humanity is one family, cleft by various artificial, culturally generated distinctions—darker- and lighter-skinned, Jewish and Christian, Philistine (Palestinian?) and Western, racially "impure" and "pure"—the old story may resonate with our whole history, our present,

Example 7.9

Act II, from Delilah's "Mon coeur s'ouvre à ta voix" (slow section of the duet).

our lives. Perhaps it is no surprise if one picks up hints of this—yet another mythic paradigm, added to those discussed earlier—in *Samson*, the work of one of music's most devoted cosmopolitans, writing in an age of increasingly acrid nationalism.[48]

In short, the characteristically Orientalist binarism of this opera's plot is subverted—at various points and to varying degrees—by Saint-Saëns's music. *Samson et Dalila*, despite its polished, confident surface and its dramatically satisfying (and, to Western viewers, culturally flattering) final tableau of triumph and obliteration, leaves much unresolved and so, finally, disturbs. That, and not just its film music exoticisms, is what keeps it alive today. Something similar may be said for many other cultural products of Orientalism: they may be hopelessly outdated as any kind of statement about the non-Western regions they seem to portray, but what they have to tell us about the West's uneasy relationship to the larger world—and about the West's many internal dissymmetries: of race, religion, gender, social class—still rings hauntingly true.

## NOTES

The present study is an abridged (by more than half) and, especially in the opening pages, reformulated version of my article of the same title, published in *Cambridge Opera Journal* 3, no. 3 (November 1991): 261–302.

1. One example might be *1000 und eine Nacht* (1906), a rather lightheaded confection (freely based on music by Johann Strauss, Jr.) that once held the boards in German-speaking theaters and that bases much of its repetitious humor on fairly simple notions (e.g., Arabs are uncultured [they prefer camels to railroads] and irrepressibly, and cutely, polygamous).

2. Two gripping videos are commercially available, one traditionally staged but missing Abimelech's aria (Domingo/Verrett, San Francisco), the other complete but less traditionally staged and without subtitles (Vickers/Verrett, Covent Garden).

3. The preceding two sentences, and the present chapter, are based on the convenient assumption that words and music are always and necessarily the two most nuanced aspects of an opera. In practice, though, interpretive nuances and even major shifts of perspective can be introduced through any of the aforementioned means (e.g., through updated and freshly rethought stage direction and design, or through the creative input of individual singers). We shall deal with the latter, briefly, in the section entitled "The Love (or Treacherous Seduction?) Scene."

4. The fullest discussions of *Samson* and its musico-dramatic features are Collet, *Samson*, and the essays in *Saint-Saëns: "Samson et Dalila,"* which is issue 15 in the periodical series of introductions to operas, *L'Avant-scène opéra* (this particular issue is henceforth cited as *Avant-scène*). Collet incorporates many extensive remarks from earlier writers, notably Baumann, *Grandes Formes*. Further bibliography is listed in *Avant-scène*, 112. The question of Orientalism in this opera has been briefly examined in Quittard, "Saint-Saëns"; Marina Dubcek, "L'Orientalisme"; and Collet, *Samson*, 85, 89).

5. The most detailed account of the opera's origins, by Ratner, is printed in the booklet to the Colin Davis recording (for Philips) and is based on her article "La

Genèse." See also Saint-Saëns's long letter on the subject, in Collet, 31–44, and reprinted elsewhere; also *Avant-scène*, 8–13.

6. The opera uses the resources of Lisztian and Wagnerian chromaticism and brings certain themes and motives back in transformed versions. Yet the numbers are still quite distinct, not blended into a seamless flow, and several of the most striking are in clear-cut ABA or strophic form, suggesting a continuing influence of the French operatic *romance*. This twin aspect was perhaps what the great pianist and Wagner conductor Hans von Bülow had in mind when he said that *Samson et Dalila* was the contemporary opera that best profited from Wagner's example without descending into mere imitation (cited in Bonnerot, *Saint-Saëns*, 89).

7. As John M. MacKenzie has recently put it, the musical attractiveness of the Philistines, including their *bacchanale*, "with its apparent throwing off of all restraint, must have left its *fin-de-siècle* and twentieth-century audience in a certain emotional turmoil in terms of identity" (MacKenzie, *Orientalism*, 153). MacKenzie, a noted historian of imperialism and culture, seems to have arrived independently at similar conclusions to those in the present study and its longer version (neither of which was known to him, except through a brief excerpt in a program book).

8. In three articles I have attempted to, among other things, perform this kind of sorting operation on the largely neglected works of Félicien David, the pioneer figure in French Romantic musical exoticism: "Cutthroats," "Félicien David," and "The French Symphony."

9. On stereotypes of female characters, and the mingling thereof, see Locke, "What Are These Women Doing?"

10. Saint-Saëns himself drafted the text; it was versified by Ferdinand Lemaire, a Creole from Martinique who was a cousin by marriage of the composer.

11. In its emphasis on the East as baleful prison, *Samson et Dalila* may recall the many "Turkish Captivity" operas (ca. 1760–1830), in which a Westerner needs to be rescued from the clutches of an Ottoman despot. See Parakilas, "The Soldier."

12. My account of Orientalism is based primarily on Schwab, *Oriental Renaissance*; Behdad, *Belated Travelers*; and Said's provocative study of the writings of scholars and political commentators on the Arab world, *Orientalism*, and his *Culture and Imperialism*. Various responses to Said have been helpful (e.g., Bhabha, *The Location of Culture*; Clifford, "On Orientalism"; Harrison, "Music and Imperialism"; MacKenzie, *Orientalism*; McClintock, *Imperial Leather*; and Low, *White Skins/Black Masks*). I am also indebted to Linda Nochlin, "The Imaginary Orient."

13. Said, *Orientalism*, 3.

14. Conflated from two discussions in Said, *Orientalism*, 4, 119–20.

15. A word of caution, though: Marian E. Smith has recently reminded me that, in French ballet scenarios of the time, the verb *semble[nt]*, as in this stage direction, can mean: "is/are seen [by the audience] doing [whatever, depending on the infinitive that follows]." *Semblent* here does not in itself imply either intention or, its opposite, innocence. Still, I persist in claiming "innocence" here, taking my support largely from the music (see also Hervey's comment on the women's chorus, cited in note 16).

16. This chorus was seen as innocent by a near contemporary (Hervey, *Saint-Saëns*, 58). In our own day Abel complains that the music "sounds like the procession of a convent of nuns, not a pack of sirens" (*Opera in the Flesh*, 106). My point is, precisely, that they are not intended to sound like sirens. Indeed, the priestesses' very lack of overt seductiveness nicely illustrates the psychocultural function of

exotic eroticism for the Westerner: it offers, according to Andrew Martin, "a prolonged postponement . . . [, a] perpetually unconsummated (and therefore undi-
minished) desire" ("Occidental," 66).

17. See further discussion (regarding the Cairo dervish ceremony) in my
"Cutthroats."

18. Ex. 2b is taken from Rouanet, "La Musique arabe," 2818–19. The emphasis on
a distinctively non-Western mode here relates to McClary's concept of "fetishized
[modal] pitches" in *Carmen*, 54.

19. See examples in Oxford University Press's *History of Music in Sound*, vol. 1,
and in *Islamic Liturgy*; also Rouanet, "Musique arabe," 2820.

20. Grosrichard, *Structure*, 155.

21. Primarily, but not completely, because of the attractiveness of the Philistine
women (including Dalila) and their music; see note 7.

22. See, for example, Krouse, *Milton's Samson*, chart between pp. 68 and 69.
Readings of the Biblical Samson and Delilah are gathered and examined in Preminger
and Greenstein, eds., *The Hebrew Bible*, 549–56, and in two works by Mieke Bal:
*Lethal Love*, 37–67, and *Death and Dissymetry*, esp. 11, 27, 113–18, 135–42, 224–27.
The novelist Philip Lopate brings special insights in "Judges," 70–97. Compare the
recent TV version, as reported in Rabinowitz, "Samson."

23. Poliakov, *The History of Anti-Semitism*, esp. vols. 3–4; Zeldin, *France*, 2:
1036–39; and Sternhell, *Neither Right nor Left*, 32–65. The ramifications of anti-
Semitism for opera have been most extensively explored in Weiner, *Richard Wagner*.

24. Evidence for the libretto's reliance on Voltaire is found in the longer version
of this study.

25. Arthur Pougin noted this in his review of the first Paris performance: "dans
une tonalité de plain-chant, sans note sensible [leading tone]," p. 355. Collet, as
noted earlier, *does* hear this chant as "frais et oriental . . . aux sobres et hiératiques
harmonies" (*Samson*, 83). A New York reviewer felt that "it is plainly intended to
be a reproduction of the music of the synagogue, but is by no means successful"
(1892 review in *New York Times*, p. 4). The Hebrews' lament in Act 3 is even more
archaic: a psalmody on one tone or, later, an open fifth (cf. *Avant-scène*, 80).

26. Peter Conrad speaks of "the seditious entreaties of the Philistine women"
and claims that their music is "suggestively whispered" (*A Song of Love*, 70).
There is, though, no indication in the stage directions or the sung text that they are
directing (much less whispering) their words to the Hebrew warriors or anyone
else (as opposed to simply singing a gentle song about spring). Pougin more accurately captured this number's innocent sweetness: "plein de fraîcheur et de grâce"
(Review, 355).

27. This interest in identifying "our" (or "one's") response to the Philistine
women is not artificially imposed by a present-day reader but has its roots in
the opera's reception history. Hervey, for example, frankly admitted (in 1922)
that, after the older Hebrews' "rather monotonous psalm . . . one is not sorry to
see them go and to welcome the appearance of Delilah" and of the priestesses, the
latter singing "strains of the most irresistible charm." By the end of the act, he
adds, Delilah has "complete[d] her victory over Samson and, incidentally, of her
audience" (*Saint-Saëns*, 52–53). Cf. Roger Delage, "Saint-Saëns humaniste," 90.
On many men's need for a real or, through art, fantasy Delilah, see Lopate,
"Judges," 92.

28. Samson's yielding here is noted by Baumann, quoted in Collet, *Samson*, 87.

29. On despots in art, see Jullian, *Orientalists*, 86–91. On the transformation of the "Grand Turk" from magnificent monarch to monstrous tyrant, see Valensi, *Birth*.

30. Abimelech's revealing aria is discussed in the longer version of this study.

31. See Robinson, "*Aida.*"

32. Further readings of this scene are suggested in the longer version of the present study.

33. Saint-Saëns's painful relationships with women (and, more generally, his conflicted sexual identity) are discussed, though not sensitively, in Harding, *Saint-Saëns*, 57–58, 124, 129, 133–34, 154–56, 177, 198–202, and Faure, *Musique et société*, 45–52.

34. See the comment on Obraztsova in note 39. Other instances include Teresa Berganza's defense of the title role of Bizet's *Carmen*, in the booklet to the Abbado recording on Deutsche Grammophon.

35. Clément's aforementioned *Opera* (11, 48–53) seems to sanitize Carmen too much and, oddly, to defang her—perhaps through an excess of sympathetic identification (see my "What Are These Women Doing?"). Something similar might be said of Nelly Furman's otherwise insightful article "The Languages of Love," 168–83. Musicologists have, perhaps through greater attention to the music, generally avoided taking extreme positions on this kind of question, but the issue of how to interpret the degree of a woman character's agency and heroism when she is portrayed as facing a crushingly misogynistic social situation (e.g., are suicide, murder, or madness positive gestures of protest?) remains lively and important material for debate: see McClary, *Feminine Endings*, 56–67, 90–99, and Smart, "Silencing Lucia," 119–41. On this very question, see also the essay by feminist literary critic Carolyn Heilbrun: "Method in Madness."

36. She is thus "a kind of Philistine Judith" (review by [Joseph Bennett?], in the London *Times*, 9). On Delilah, Judith, and Salome, see Dijkstra, *Idols of Perversity*.

37. Delilah's desire and jealous love for Samson are indeed central themes in literary and visual portrayals of Delilah. For a discussion of Milton's *Samson Agonistes* (lines 790–818) and the libretto of Handel's *Samson*, and of Voltaire's *Samson*, see the longer version of the present study. An art historian finds in Rubens's Delilah "tender[ness]" and "amorous attachment even at the moment of her duplicity" (Kahr, "Delilah," 133, 135).

38. On the Barenboim (Deutsche Grammophon) recording. Cf. Blyth, ed., *Opera on Record*, 2:208–18; Conrad, *Song*, 70, 257, 258, 343, 349; and the many performance photos in *Avant-scène*.

39. Covent Garden: HBO/EMI Thorn video. Obraztsova: photo on the cover of the Barenboim (Deutsche Grammophon) recording. Verrett strikes a similar pose in the San Francisco Opera videotaped production.

40. Or perhaps to test his ability to resist her, a typical feature of stories of heroes in love: see Lopate, "Judges," 85–88.

41. On the association of woman's power and night, see Clément, *Opera*, e.g., 37–38, 88–92, 96–117; on the Orient as night, see Martin, "Occidental."

42. "Her feigned passion is expressed in strains of the most ardent nature" (Hervey, *Saint-Saëns*, 53); "a calculated show" (Conrad, *Song*, 70).

43. Solliers, "Commentaire," 47–49, echoed by Salazar, "Mythologiques," 72–75, and Delage, "Saint-Saëns humaniste," 90.

44. Lopate stresses, in the various versions of the story, the worthiness of Samson and Delilah as antagonists, hence as lovers ("Judges," 85–92).

45. Delage calls it, tendentiously, a "serpent"-like chromatic theme, "crawling and hissing" ("Saint-Saëns humaniste," 90); cf. de Solliers ("Commentaire," 49), who misleadingly labels the breeze theme "Storm"; it does not become transformed into storm music until after "Mon coeur" ends.

46. Saint-Saëns himself noted that musical irony can reveal the unspoken or indeed pointedly hidden "interior action" of an operatic character's "soul." His example is the duet from his own opera *Henri VIII* in which King Henry informs Catherine of Aragon with hypocritical sweetness of the impending arrival in England of Anne Boleyn (*École buissonnière*, 117–18). See also Ex. 13a in the longer version of this study.

47. Hence also certain similarities between this opera and *West Side Story* (and other works), noted in the longer version of this essay, and Locke, *"Four Saints."*

48. Besides his wide-ranging musical tastes, we may refer to his political views, including his refusal to indulge in chauvinist rhetoric in regard to World War I— for him, an instance of imperial nations pointlessly "exterminating" each other (see Faure, *Musique*, 64–65). He did, though, eventually compose a few marches (for piano four hands) in support of the Allies' fight against Germany.

## WORKS CITED

Abel, Sam. *Opera in the Flesh: Sexuality in Operatic Performance.* Boulder, Colorado: Westview Press, 1996.

*Avant-scène.* See *Saint-Saëns: "Samson et Dalila."*

Bal, Mieke. *Death and Dissymmetry: The Politics of Coherence in the Book of Judges.* Chicago: University of Chicago Press, 1988.

———. *Lethal Love: Feminist Literary Readings of Biblical Love Stories.* Bloomington: Indiana University Press, 1987.

Baumann, Émile. *Les Grandes Formes de la musique: L'Oeuvre de C. Saint-Saëns.* 2nd ed. Paris: P. Ollendorff, 1905.

Behdad, Ali. *Belated Travelers: Orientalism in the Age of Colonial Dissolution.* Durham: Duke University Press, 1994.

[Bennett, Joseph?]. Review of first London performance of Saint-Saëns, *Samson et Dalila.* London *Times*, September 27, 1893, p. 9.

Bhabha, Homi K. *The Location of Culture.* London: Routledge, 1994.

Bizet, Georges. *Carmen.* Carmen: Teresa Berganza. Don José: Plácido Domingo. Conducted by Claudio Abbado. Deutsche Grammophon, 1978.

Blyth, Alan, ed. *Opera on Record*, vol. 2. London: Hutchinson, 1979, 1983.

Bonnerot, Jean. *C. Saint-Saëns [1835–1921]: Sa Vie et son oeuvre.* Paris: A. Durand et fils, [1922?].

Clément, Catherine. *Opera, or the Undoing of Women*, trans. Betsy Wing. Minneapolis: University of Minnesota Press, 1988.

Clifford, James. "On Orientalism." In James Clifford, *The Predicament of Culture: Twentieth-Century Ethnography, Literature, and Art*, pp. 255–76. Cambridge: Harvard University Press, 1988.

Collet, Henri. *Samson et Dalila de C. Saint-Saëns: Étude historique et critique, analyse musicale.* Paris: P. Mellottée, [1922?].

Conrad, Peter. *A Song of Love and Death: The Meaning of Opera.* New York: Poseidon, 1987.

Delage, Roger. *L'Avant-scène opéra*, no. 15 (May–June 1978): 90–91.

Dijkstra, Bram. *Idols of Perversity: Fantasies of Feminine Evil in Fin-de-siècle Culture.* New York: Oxford University Press, 1986.

Dubcek, Marina. "L'Orientalisme dans *Samson.*" *L'Avant-Scène opéra*, no. 15 (May–June 1978): 86–88.

Faure, Michel. *Musique et société, du second empire aux années vingt: Autour de Saint-Saëns, Fauré, Debussy et Ravel.* [Paris]: Flammarion, 1985.

Furman, Nelly. "The Languages of Love in *Carmen.*" In *Reading Opera*, eds. Arthur Groos and Roger Parker. Princeton: Princeton University Press, 1988:168–83.

Grosrichard, Alain. *Structure du sérail: La Fiction du despotisme asiatique dans l'Occident classique.* Paris: Seuil, 1979.

Harding, James. *Saint-Saëns and His Circle.* London: Chapman and Hall, 1965.

Harrison, Pegram. "Music and Imperialism." *repercussions* 4, no. 1 (Spring 1995): 53–84.

Heilbrun, Carolyn. "Method in Madness: Why Lucia and Elektra Must Sacrifice Their Sanity to Preserve the Male Order." *Opera News*, 22 (January 1994): 18–19, 45.

Hervey, Arthur. *Saint-Saëns.* London: John Lane, 1921; reprint Freeport, N.Y.: Books for Libraries, 1969.

*History of Music in Sound*, vol. 1. American RCA Victor LM 6057, 1957.

*Islamic Liturgy: Song and Dance at a Meeting of Dervishes.* Folkways Records FR 8943. 1960.

Jullian, Philippe. *The Orientalists: European Painters of Eastern Scenes.* Oxford: Phaidon, 1977.

Kahr, Madlyn Millner. "Delilah." In *Feminism and Art History: Questioning the Litany*, eds. Norma Broude and Mary D. Garrard. New York: Harper and Row, 1982:119–46.

Krouse, F. Michael. *Milton's Samson and the Christian Tradition.* Princeton: Princeton University Press, 1949.

Locke, Ralph P. "Constructing the Oriental 'Other': Saint-Saëns's *Samson et Dalila.*" *Cambridge Opera Journal* 3, no. 3 (November 1991): 261–302. A short excerpt, entitled "Orientalism in *Samson et Dalila*," appeared in the Royal Opera (Covent Garden) program book for performances in 1991 and 1992.

———. "Cutthroats and Casbah Dancers, Muezzins and Timeless Sands: Musical Images of the Middle East." In *The Exotic in Western Music*, ed. Jonathan Bellman. Boston: Northeastern University Press, 1997:104–36, 326–33. Longer version forthcoming in *19th-Century Music*.

———. "Félicien David, compositeur saint-simonien et orientalisant." In *Les Saint-Simoniens et l'Orient: Vers la modernité*, ed. Magali Morsy. Aix-en-Provence: Édisud, 1989:135–54.

———. "*Four Saints, West Side Story*, and the Borderline Between 'Classical' and Broadway," in progress.

———. "The French Symphony: David, Gounod, and Bizet to Saint-Saëns, Franck, and Their Followers." In *The Nineteenth-Century Symphony*, ed. D. Kern Holoman. New York: Schirmer Books, 1997:163–94.

———. "Reflections on Orientalism in Opera and Musical Theater." *Opera Quarterly* 10, no. 1 (Autumn 1993): 48–64.

———. "What Are These Women Doing in Opera?" In *En travesti: Women, Gender Subversion, Opera*, eds. Corinne E. Blackmer and Patricia Juliana Smith. New

York: Columbia University Press, 1995:59–98. A short version appeared in *Opera Quarterly* 57, no. 1 (July 1992): 34–36.

Lopate, Philip. "Judges." In *Congregation: Contemporary Writers Read the Jewish Bible*, ed. David Rosenberg. San Diego: Harcourt Brace Jovanovich, 1987:70–97.

Low, Gail Ching-Liang. *White Skins/Black Masks: Representation and Colonialism*. New York: Routledge, 1996.

MacKenzie, John M. *Orientalism: History, Theory, and the Arts*. Manchester: Manchester University Press, 1995.

Martin, Andrew. "The Occidental Orient." In his book *The Knowledge of Ignorance: From Genesis to Jules Verne*. Cambridge: Cambridge University Press, 1985:60–121.

McClary, Susan. *Feminine Endings: Music, Gender, and Sexuality*. Minneapolis: University of Minnesota Press, 1991.

——. *Georges Bizet: Carmen*. Cambridge: Cambridge University Press, 1992.

McClintock, Anne. *Imperial Leather: Race, Gender and Sexuality in the Colonial Contest*. New York: Routledge, 1995.

Nochlin, Linda. "The Imaginary Orient." In her book *The Politics of Vision: Essays on Nineteenth-Century Art and Society*. New York: Harper and Row, 1989:33–59.

Parakilas, James. "The Soldier and the Exotic: Operatic Variations on a Theme of Racial Encounter." *Opera Quarterly* 10, no. 2 (Winter 1994): 33–56 and 10, no. 3 (Spring 1994): 43–69.

Poliakov, Léon. *The History of Anti-Semitism*, trans. Richard Howard, Natalie Gerardi, Miriam Kochan, and George Klin; vols. 1–3: London: Routledge & Kegan Paul, 1974–75; vol. 4: Oxford: Oxford University Press, 1985.

Pougin, Arthur. [Review of the first Paris performance of *Samson et Dalila*.] *Le Ménestrel* 56, no. 45 (November 9, 1890): 355.

Preminger, Alex, and Edward L. Greenstein, eds. *The Hebrew Bible in Literary Criticism*. New York: Ungar, 1986.

Quittard, Henri. "Saint-Saëns Orientaliste." *Revue Musicale* 5 (1906): 105–16.

Rabinowitz, Dorothy. "Samson, Delilah and the White House." *Wall Street Journal*, September 25, 1996, Section A, p. 16.

Ratner, Sabina. "La Genèse et la Fortune de 'Samson et Dalila.'" *Cahiers Ivan Tourguéniev, Pauline Viardot, Maria Malibran*, no. 9 (1985): 108–21.

Review of first New York performance of Saint-Saëns, *Samson et Dalila. New York Times*, March 27, 1892, p. 4.

Robinson, Paul. "Is *Aida* an Orientalist Opera?" *Cambridge Opera Journal* 5 (1993): 133–40.

Rouanet, Joseph. "La Musique arabe." In *Encyclopédie de la musique et dictionnaire du Conservatoire*, eds. Albert Lavignac and Lionel de La Laurencie, pt. 1, vol. 5 (1922). Paris: C. Delagrave, 1920–31:2676–2844.

Said, Edward W. *Culture and Imperialism*. New York: Knopf, 1994.

——. *Orientalism*. New York: Pantheon Books, 1978.

Saint-Saëns, Camille. *École Buissonnière: Notes et souvenirs*. Paris: P. Lafitte, 1913.

——. *Samson et Dalila*. Conducted by Daniel Barenboim. Deutsche Grammophon, 1978.

——. *Samson et Dalila*. Conducted by Colin Davis. Covent Garden. HBO/EMI Thorn Videotape, 1981. (Recorded 1978.)

——. *Samson et Dalila*. Conducted by Julius Rudel. San Francisco Opera. Pioneer Artists Videotape, 1981.

——. *Samson et Dalila*. Conducted by Colin Davis. Philips, 1989.

*Saint-Saëns: "Samson et Dalila." L'Avant-scène opéra*, no. 15 (May–June 1978).

Salazar, Philippe-Joseph. "Mythologiques de la femme fatale." *L'Avant-scène opéra*, no. 15 (May–June 1978): 72–75.

Schwab, Raymond. *The Oriental Renaissance: Europe's Rediscovery of India and the East, 1680–1880*, trans. Gene Patterson-Black and Victor Reinking. New York: Columbia University Press, 1984.

Smart, Mary Ann. "Silencing Lucia." *Cambridge Opera Journal* 4 (1992): 119–41.

Solliers, Jean de. "Commentaire littéraires et musicale." *L'Avant-scène opéra*, no. 15 (May–June 1978): 19–71.

Sternhell, Zeev. *Neither Right nor Left: Fascist Ideology in France*, trans. David Maisel. Berkeley: University of California Press, 1986.

Strauss, Jr., Johann. *Indigo, oder die vierzig Räuber* (1871). Conducted by Otto Dobrindt. Urania UR203, 1960s.

Valensi, Lucette. *The Birth of the Despot: Venice and the Sublime Porte*, trans. Arthur Denner. Ithaca, N.Y.: Cornell University Press, 1993.

Weiner, Marc A. *Richard Wagner and the Anti-Semitic Imagination*. Lincoln: University of Nebraska Press, 1995.

Zeldin, Theodore. *France, 1848–1945*. 2 vols. Oxford: Oxford University Press, 1973–77.

## CHAPTER EIGHT

*Fictions of the Opera Box*

Ruth A. Solie

In Paris . . . an Englishman, Howard Tempest, looked in, at the Opéra, on his cousin, Camille de Joyeuse. This lady, connected by birth with Britannia's best, and, through her husband, with the Bourbons, delighted the eye, the ear, and the palate. In appearance, she suggested certain designs of Boucher; in colouring and in manner, the Pompadour. . . .

One evening in May, Tempest entered her box, saluted her, examined the house, and, as, in a crash of the orchestra, the curtain fell, seated himself, in response to a gesture, beside her.[1]

This passage is taken from *The Monster*, a fey and histrionic novel by the eccentric and occult (and comma-loving) Edgar Saltus. Within mere paragraphs it contains all the earmarks of a scene utterly familiar in American fiction around the turn of the twentieth century, a scene set in a box at the opera. The opera box is a marker of wealth and social distinction, and it is a place for visiting. It is also a place for seeing and being seen, its primary focus being the physical appearance of a female character who is carefully set off against a background that is discovered by "examining the house." Of music there is only a vanishing trace.

What is astonishing about this example in particular is that the two characters have nothing to do with the story. Rather, Saltus employs a trope so thoroughly conventionalized by this time (1912) that the setting had itself become a picture worth thousands of words, carrying meanings far beyond those spelled out on the page and saving the author a good deal of trouble. I propose to examine the opera box trope as it is found in novels by American authors between about 1870 and 1920; that is, a period that in literary history covers the genteel tradition and—more important—the emergence of realism, and that in political history includes the aptly named Gilded Age and the progressive era.

During the nineteenth century opera gradually became detached from other aspects of the theatrical world, fixated as it was on its most extravagant and gorgeous manifestations in ways that became unfashionable in theater, literature, and the visual arts. At the same time, opera gratified the Victorian taste for theatricality in all its forms, from charades to *tableaux vivants*.[2] Its notorious reputation as a specular site marked it as peculiarly adapted to the expression of class difference and—by the century's end, after the Wagner craze was spent—resistant to modernism and social change in just the same ways that its privileged boxholders were. Since the books I will discuss are novels of manners, most of them by writers engaged in developing the realist mode in fiction, it is not surprising that they so frequently take up the opportunity that opera affords to study the morals and mores of the era, its social interactions and significations.[3]

I do not intend an act of textual criticism here; still less do I mean to interpret fictional material literally as historical information. Rather, I want to investigate aspects of the social history of opera in the United States that help to illuminate these texts and offer us a glimpse of the assumptions and interpretive strategies their contemporary readers brought to them.

## The Performance of Status

The Opera . . . plays its part as the great vessel of social salvation, the comprehensive substitute for all other conceivable vessels; the *whole* social consciousness thus clambering into it, under stress, as the whole community crams into the other public receptacles, the desperate cars of the Subway or the vast elevators of the tall buildings.—*Henry James*[4]

No doubt the most familiar of these "opera scenes," and the most frequently discussed, is the opening chapter of Edith Wharton's *The Age of Innocence*, in which we are introduced to the principal characters at a performance of *Faust* in New York's old Academy of Music. Numerous readings of the text have been offered, focusing especially on the interplay between the novel's story and that told in the opera, or on the interactions between Ellen Olenska and Newland Archer, fatefully meeting here for the first time.[5] But working outward from the details of Wharton's narrative, we can also learn much from the surrounding nimbus of social import that the setting itself would have conveyed to a contemporary reader.

Although *The Age of Innocence* was written in 1920, at the very end of the period I am concerned with, its narrative is set in the early 1870s. Just as important as the interactions that occur in the opening scene is the fact that it takes place at the opera, the quintessential site of privilege and social display. Like the original "royal box" in European court theaters, opera boxes are designed to facilitate lines of sight in all directions. That ubiquitous accessory, the opera glass, adds its iconic force as well as its optical power to an already saturated visual environment. Fictional characters use boxes just as their real-life counterparts did, both to see and to be seen. Ellen Olenska's presence in the box is, precisely, her grandmother Mingott's nose-thumbing challenge to Society to view Ellen as one of them. Boxes are also their own advertisement: those who are seen sitting in them can afford to, and in the elaborate social geography of the house they visibly do not mix with the hoi polloi in the orchestra seats.[6] Even more, "going to the opera" is a social ritual crucial to the maintenance of the urban patrician class. Etiquette books of the day include elaborate instructions for each phase of the activity: for wardrobe, for the manner of entering the box, for the promenade between acts, and for acknowledging acquaintances or not as the occasion demands.[7]

Opera is taken for granted in the world of *The Age of Innocence*; it is a common enough feature of daily life, and references to it and to the rhythms of its season are scattered almost negligently through the book. Henry James's characterization is apt: "the great vessel of social salvation" is just the one on which Ellen Olenska's reputation must ride if it is to float at all. But, in truth, James's concern was less with persons of Ellen's class than with the dreaded parvenus, the "new rich" whose money was flowing in almost uncountably fast in the sudden postwar industrial expansion and who, old Society felt, were ill equipped to spend it with appropriate dignity and taste. The contest between the two groups was felt everywhere in urban America, but nowhere more than in New York's old Knickerbocker society, proud, correct, and by this time scarcely able any longer to afford the aristocratic behaviors it had introduced into the city's social life. On his American trip in 1904–1905, his first return home from England in twenty years, James was horrified—if not particularly surprised—at what he considered the impoverishment of New York cultural life. ("Nowhere else does pecuniary power so beat its wings in the void," he observed elsewhere in the quoted passage.)

The moral earnestness of the earlier society of the 1870s, as well as its blasé habituation to its privileges, is characteristically portrayed in Elizabeth Stuart Phelps's *The Silent Partner* (1871). We are introduced to the heroine, Perley Kelso of Boston, on her way to hear *Don Giovanni*: "a young lady . . . who is used to her gloves, and indifferent to her stone cameos; who has the score by heart, and is tired of the *prima donna*; who has had a season ticket every winter since she can remember."[8] But Perley's life is changed when, in a chapter pointedly entitled "Across the Gulf," she encounters another young woman on her way to a musical entertainment. Sip Garth, a mill hand who works for Perley's father, is making her way through the January slush to the show at the "Blue Plum."

Bostonian that she is, Perley is overcome with moral confusion at the blatant class differences between them, marked so explicitly by their musical choices. She seeks Sip's friendship, and ultimately she devotes her life to the betterment of social and cultural conditions at the mill, which, as she comes to understand, pays for her gloves and opera tickets. But as crucial to Phelps's point as the stark economic and cultural differences between the young women is the commonality they share: not only the alignment with theatrical music, already feminized in American urban culture,[9] but the veiled and suggestive dangers it holds for them as well. Waiting for Perley outside the opera house after the performance, Sip challenges her: "Look here, young lady, I want to speak to you. I want to know why you tell *me* the Plum is no place for me? What kind of a place is this for you?" (29).[10]

The assiduously self-seeking Undine Spragg, heroine of Wharton's *The Custom of the Country* (1913), knows exactly what kind of place the opera box is for her and understands the process of social certification only too well. Undine, whom a contemporary reviewer called "the most repellent heroine" in American literature, is the archetype of the parvenu social climber, one of a series of turn-of-the-century heroines who ceaselessly demand everything that happens to be fashionable and who impoverish any number of men in the project of acquisition. Her gloriously mismatched name enacts her social ambition: the poetic Undine constantly at pains to camouflage the ungainly midwestern Spragg.

"The great vessel of social salvation" is an early and obvious target of Undine's rampaging cupidity, though the ferocity of her demand marks her fatally as one to whom the experience is entirely novel—a newcomer. Thorstein Veblen, the contemporary analyst of "conspicuous consumption," would have recognized without difficulty Undine's construal of the opera box as commodity, along with the dresses, hats, and accessories she purchases by the truckload.[11]

It is to the staid old Academy of Music that Ellen Olenska is brought, in an attempt to recertify her as a respectable member of Society. But Undine goes to the Metropolitan Opera, a distinction in more than chronology, and one intensely meaningful to Wharton and her readers. In the heat of the social fray between the Knickerbockers (among whom Wharton herself was raised) and the upstart robber barons of considerably greater fortune, the physical sites of spectacle themselves became game tokens. As the growing numbers of new rich—Vanderbilts, Roosevelts, Rockefellers, Morgans, Astors, Goulds, Whitneys, and their vast Victorian families—were unable to purchase boxes at the Academy, they simply built their own theater, farther uptown. The Metropolitan Opera opened in 1883, with no fewer than 122 pique-inspired boxes for which the wealthy subscribers drew lots.[12] Thus the two theaters were indelibly affiliated with warring factions of Society and, by extension, with sharply contrasting attitudes toward the seriousness of high culture. The new house, with its unprecedented and in fact grotesque complement of boxes in a "golden horseshoe," served many an author as a concrete icon of conspicuous consumption and vulgar social display.[13]

And what happens when Undine finally gets to her coveted box? Unlike *The Age of Innocence*, with its fine historical details of performer, work, and language,[14] this novel contains no music, no actual opera—and not by any oversight.

> When the curtain fell on the first act she began to be aware of a subtle change in the house. In all the boxes cross-currents of movement had set in: groups were coalescing and breaking up, fans waving and heads twinkling, black coats emerging among white shoulders, late comers dropping their furs and laces in the red penumbra of the background. Undine, for the moment unconscious of herself, swept the house with her opera-glass. . . .[15]

This, of course, is the spectacle for which she has been waiting, for which she has come. Undine is assisted in her surveillance by another operatic practice accurately detailed by Wharton, "that the numbers of the boxes and the names of their owners were given on the back of the programme" (40). For Undine the back of the program holds more meaning than anything inside it, as she peruses one of what Neil Harris has wonderfully called the period's "iconographies of possession."[16]

## Art, Business, and the Lure of Speculation

Buy May wheat. It'll beat art all hollow.—*Frank Norris*[17]

Like *The Age of Innocence*, Frank Norris's *The Pit* (1903) begins at the opera. We meet another young heroine, Laura Dearborn, with her sister and aunt, waiting for their hosts in the lobby of Chicago's Auditorium Theatre.[18] In this opening scene, as in the novel as a whole, Norris both sets up and cannily complicates a set of familiar alignments: thus male is to female as business is to culture, America to Europe, and Chicago to the older cities of the east coast, especially New York and Boston.

*The Pit*, along with *The Octopus* part of a projected but unfinished trilogy to be called "The Epic of the Wheat," is more ambivalent about these dichotomies than most novels. An unabashed celebration of the muscular energy and apparently inexhaustible natural bounty of the New World—a typical fascination of Chicago writers—the dramatic action of the book nonetheless concerns the line between sound business and irresponsible speculation. That is, investment for profit, to build the wealth and institutions of the country, is exemplary (American male) behavior, but "speculation" as technically defined—investment in anticipation of the future direction of the market—is as disreputable as any other form of gambling. The problem, of course, is that the excitement of the one lures a man irresistibly to the other.

The abstraction of the enterprise is a matter of pride for the speculators. It is the essence of risk that no actual products are being bought and sold at all, but only fictive, heroic predictions as to the rise or fall of their price.[19] The reader is caught up in this excitement, in the implication of that unspeakable fate, addiction ("worse than liquor, worse than morphine," says a minor character [p. 130])—and in the heat of the only slightly sublimated warfare between those zoological combatants peculiar to Wall Street, the bears and the bulls. In short, speculation itself is swashbuckling, amply suited to operatic treatment.

> One of those great manoeuvres of a fellow money-captain had that very day been concluded, the Helmick failure, and between the chords and bars of a famous opera men talked in excited whispers, and one great leader lay at that very moment, broken and spent, fighting with his last breath for bare existence.                                      *(34)*

Within this context the actual opera must paradoxically play two apparently contradictory roles. On the one hand, it signifies that America is capable of maintaining high culture, even on the prairie, and that Chicago's businessmen as well as New York's are able to supply even that culture's most extravagant requirements; on the other hand, the guiding vision of the novel is the historic turnabout in which the New World feeds the Old, in which American mercantile culture supersedes the old museum-life of Europe as the son outstrips the father.

And so throughout the first chapter we hear the opera—an unidentified piece minutely described but probably the invention of Norris himself—in counterpoint with whispered gossip about Helmick's failed attempt to corner the corn market.

> as the music died away fainter and fainter, till voice and orchestra blended together in a single, barely audible murmur, vibrating with emotion, with romance, and with sentiment, she heard, in a hoarse, masculine whisper, the words:
> "The shortage is a million bushels at the very least. Two hundred carloads were to arrive from Milwaukee last night—"

Laura is no social climber, no Undine, but an earnest young woman recently arrived from New England, and so she is actually listening to the music; at first she attempts to silence the whisperers, to no avail.

> While [the soprano] declared that the stars and the night-bird together sang "He loves thee," the voices close at hand continued:
> "—one hundred and six carloads—"
> "—paralysed the bulls—"
> "—fifty thousand dollars—"

The counterpoint is precisely balanced; as Laura gradually recognizes, two dramas of equal power and attractive force are vying for her attention.

And abruptly, midway between two phases of that music-drama, of passion and romance, there came to Laura the swift and vivid impression of that other drama that simultaneously—even at that very moment—was working itself out close at hand, equally picturesque, equally romantic, equally passionate; but more than that, real, actual, modern, a thing in the very heart of the very life in which she moved. *(34)*

As the principal female character, it falls to Laura to evaluate the two dramas. Sentimental Victorian reasoning would require it, on the grounds that the woman's finer moral sensibilities make her the more fastidious judge, and so Laura must finally decide how to weigh the two realms. And two men with them: true to genre, Laura in her opera box faces the choice between two suitors, the artist Corthell and the financier Jadwin.[20] Her decision represents an attempt to reach beyond her own allocated position in the aligned pair of opposites, opting for what seems at the moment a wider sphere. About Corthell she notices that "straightway he made her feel her sex. Now she was just a woman again, with all a woman's limitations, and her relations with Corthell could never be . . . any other than sex-relations."[21] But

> with Jadwin somehow it had been different. She had felt his manhood more than her womanhood, her sex side. And between them it was more a give-and-take affair, more equality, more companionship. Corthell spoke only of her heart and to her heart. But Jadwin made her feel—or rather she made herself feel when he talked to her—that she had a head as well as a heart. And the last act of the opera did not wholly absorb her attention. *(35)*

Laura's effort to escape the confines of her "sex side" must necessarily vitiate her absorption in the opera, because it disrupts the pattern of alignments as American authors used them. But other alignments are also in play: as Laura's gender stipulates that seat at the front of the opera box, so her gentility determines the sort of performance she watches. Brander Matthews's 1896 novel of financial temptation, *His Father's Son*,[22] is an intensely moralistic and old-fashioned novel in which a son "goes bad." Apprenticed in his father's investment company, Winslow Pierce suddenly realizes that the entire business of Wall Street is "getting money for nothing," and in disillusionment he turns to drink, gambling (including stock speculation), and the company of bad women. "Bad women" in this case are represented by Miss Daisy Fostelle, the soprano and principal of the Daisy Fostelle Opera Comique Company; indeed, fifty thousand of the irresponsibly gambled dollars have been invested in the troupe, "formed for the production of semi-spectacular light opera" (144). Suffering from bad conscience, Winslow takes his wife to see one of the shows—performed, irony of ironies, at the Academy of Music in its now reduced circumstances—but she is uneasy, shocked by the costumes, and worried about the company her husband is keeping (110).

Here the moral taint already evident in Winslow's crisis is both revealed and reinforced by his frequenting the wrong kind of entertainment; the virtuous woman aligns only with the highest form of cultural expression.[23] As Winslow's father tries to explain to him, great financial men like himself are different from

> the mere speculator, who is of very little account. . . . The men who rule Wall Street are the greatest benefactors of humanity the world has ever seen. They are the men who are developing this mighty country of ours, who are opening up new States to the oppressed millions of Europe, who are building the great railroads and bridging the great rivers. . . . (17)

They are also, of course, building the great opera houses in which the truly powerful have left the now déclassé Academy far behind them. Ultimately, it is unclear whether the destruction threatening Winslow Pierce is moral decay or bad taste.[24]

## Slumming

Opera has shown an endless love for those who are of foreign blood or are otherwise "outside."—*Theodor Adorno*[25]

Henry Blake Fuller's *With the Procession* (1895) dwells in that familiar territory where an older, intensely proud Society is losing both financial and fashionable ground to an upstart bevy of business titans. Truesdale Marshall, the scion of an old family just beginning to come to grips with change, has recently returned from his Grand Tour. The association with Europe and its high culture marks him as a member of his father's patrician class, but Truesdale's own vaporous artistic ambitions and the vaguely bohemian group he attempts to draw around himself upon his return signal something different. He misses the aesthetic aura of Europe.

> Mimi and Musette, the actual, the contemporaneous, once met at short range, were far, far from the *gracieuse* and *mignonne* creations of Murger and of 1830. And if disappointing in Paris, how much more so in Chicago?—where impropriety was still wholly incapable of presenting itself in a guise that could enlist the sympathies of the fastidious.[26]

Truesdale thinks operatically about slumming.

Operagoing, like other fixtures of high culture in turn-of-the-century America, encapsulated and focused an ambivalent relationship to Europe. Recognized as the source of artistic achievements that Americans had not yet matched, venerated as the reservoir of "civilized" life, and covertly eyed by ambitious mamas for those inherited titles and privileges that the American upper bourgeoisie was beginning to mourn, Europe and its artistic ways at the same time represented the effete, the effeminate, the disreputable, and—perhaps most reassuring—the commercially unsuccessful.

As a comedic turn, of course, this Philistine worldview is famously the territory of Sinclair Lewis, most especially in *Babbitt* (1922), where it is laid on with a trowel in George Babbitt's celebrated "boosting" speeches:

> In no country in the world will you find so many reproductions of the Old Masters and of well-known paintings on parlor walls as in these United States. No country has anything like our number of phonographs, with not only dance records and comic but also the best operas, such as Verdi, rendered by the world's highest-paid singers.
>
> In other countries, art and literature are left to a lot of shabby bums living in attics and feeding on booze and spaghetti, but in America the successful writer or picture-painter is indistinguishable from any other decent business man. . . .[27]

In his little-known but piquant early novel *The Job* (1917), Lewis traces the career of a small-town young woman who must move to New York to support her widowed mother and who makes her way painstakingly from typist to business owner. Una Golden's negotiation of the city and her eventual success in moving up to a slightly more leisured class (though Society is not within her grasp) require among many other things her ability to esteem cultural phenomena appropriately. She is briefly married to one of Lewis's quintessential vulgarians, Eddie Schwirtz, who momentarily distracts her with the knowingness of his aesthetic certainties:

> once I went to the grand opera—lot of fat Dutchmen all singing together like they was selling old rags. . . .
>
> Own up. Don't you get more fun out of hearing Raymond Hitchcock sing than you do out of a bunch of fiddles and flutes fighting out a piece by Vaugner like they was Kilkenny cats? . . . I notice that Hitchcock and George M. Cohan go on drawing big audiences every night—yes, and the swellest, best-dressed, smartest people in New York and Brooklyn, too—it's in the gallery at the opera that you find all these Wops and Swedes and Lord knows what-all. . . .[28]

For others less ingenuous than George Babbitt and Eddie Schwirtz, though, the "shabby bums" had a certain appeal, and in the decades just around 1900 every urban center in the United States saw the development of indigenous bohemian circles attempting to capture something of the fabled aesthetic and personal freedom of the continental artist. At the same time, curiosity was developing among the "respectable" about the life going on in the city's ethnic communities. "Little Germany" already existed in New York by the 1840s and was followed in ensuing decades by a French quarter, Chinatown, and an increasing multitude of neighborhoods whose fascination was partly what Daniel Horowitz has called their "expressive ethnic traditions" and partly simple otherness.[29] Theatrical productions—plays and musicals—about various ethnic groups as well as other "city types" became wildly popular.[30]

Urban novels naturally rely heavily on the conspicuous and well-understood social geography of cities; appropriate neighborhoods for family dwellings and permissible venues for shopping and entertainment are clearly and accurately demarcated in Wharton's New York, Norris's or Fuller's Chicago, and Howells's Boston. As cities changed, the movements of the respectable—particularly women—were increasingly restricted by their very respectability, and such restrictions chafed as much in real life as they did on some fictional characters. For the most reckless young, the slums became a tour site as suburbanization removed the well-to-do from daily contact with the poor, and new "scientific" theories of degeneracy increasingly described them in terms of various colorfully pathological behaviors.[31]

But recreational slumming expeditions were often disappointing, as Sinclair Lewis's Una Golden experiences:

> He took her to a Lithuanian restaurant, on a street which was a débâcle. One half of the restaurant was filled with shaggy Lithuanians playing cards at filthy tables; the other half was a clean haunt for tourists who came to see the slums, and here, in the heart of these "slums," saw only one another.[32]

Music critic James Huneker reports an unsuccessful evening spent in searching for authentic tango, but finding "no spoor of delirium, and absolutely nothing bacchanalian"; rather, "all that I've witnessed thus far in New York is tame and so respectable."[33]

Opera, on the other hand, offered the opportunity to engage vicariously with bohemian, foreign, or otherwise exotic lives not admitted to fastidious bourgeois circles and to experience supercharged emotions not otherwise permitted there: "In mounting fervour the aria developed, trailing, as it climbed, words such as *amore, speranza, morir*. A breath of brutality passed."[34]

Another character in *With the Procession*, the socialite Susan Bates, has triumphed over her humble origins. Her mansion includes the luxurious music room and concert grand piano that certify her arrival, and her music stand is "laden with handsomely bound scores of all the German classics and the usual operas of the French and Italian schools" (47). But Sue Bates has a secret. In a shabby upstairs room behind an office, she hides another musical life, "a small upright piano whose top was littered with loose sheets of old music" (60), on which she plays "Old Dan Tucker" and the "Java March," singing at the top of her lungs. Fortunate Sue is wealthy enough to go slumming in her own house.

## The Mating Game

On opera he doth fondly dote,
Though of its music, we confess,

He seldom hears a single note
With any real attentiveness.
From box to box he loves to float,
And there he finds us all the same;
Compared with him we promptly vote
Our favorite tenor tame.—*The Buntling Ball*[35]

It is of particular interest that so many of these fictions dwell within the sensibilities of young women and that some (*Rose of Dutcher's Coolly, The Job, The Silent Partner*) even represent that rarest of genres, the female *Bildungsroman*. To a considerable extent this peculiarity is due to the alignments discussed earlier, especially the association of women with the maintenance of high culture. But women also had, as male novelists fully recognized, much more at stake in those opera boxes than their brothers did. In an opera scene, it is a safe bet that some young woman's life course is about to be decided. Though the occasional heroine makes an obstreperous and resistant choice—perhaps under the influence of the music— much more frequently she meets or accepts her future husband in a murmured exchange in the box or during the promenade between acts. Opera boxes are for display, and most especially for the display of available young women.

Verbs of vision abound in literary opera scenes. A single page in Henry James's *Portrait of a Lady* (1909) provides *looked, scanning, perceived, recognized, appeared, seen, saw, looked* again, *watch* twice, along with several occurrences of the noun *eyes*.[36] Critics have observed that vision is a central theme in the novel as a whole, and James himself has corroborated that interpretation,[37] but that is surely not the whole story. Rather, the thematic appropriateness of sightlines to the geography and social function of the opera house suggests the suitability of the venue, with all its conventional associations, to his larger purpose.

In *Portrait* James's characters, most of whom are Americans, are in Europe—in an unnamed "large, bare, ill-lighted house" in Rome, attending an unnamed "bare, familiar, trivial opera" which is later identified as one of Verdi's, although no music is represented in the scene. His doomed heroine, Isabel Archer, has come to the opera in a group that includes Gilbert Osmond, whom she has recently met and will disastrously marry. The insistence upon vision—candid or covert, insightful or morally blind—informs the tension of the scene and signals many of its consequences. Lord Warburton, a failed suitor, visits Isabel in her box when he notes that she has seen him enter the house; when the opera resumes after intermission, he hears nothing of the music and can see "nothing but the clear profile of this young lady defined against the dim illumination of the house." Watching Isabel, he finds that she "had, in operatic conditions, a radiance, even a slight exaltation. . . ." Osmond, by contrast, is prevented by his own self-involvement from observing much about others. " 'What's the character of that gentleman?' Osmond asked of Isabel after he had retired. 'Irreproachable—don't you see it?'" Isabel herself, the reader notes, has not been seeing character particularly clearly. It is a sinister scene, on the whole, and we gather from it what is characteristic of these episodes: somehow a die has been cast, and Isabel's fate is *en train*.

Henry James's own discussion of this novel has become notorious to a degree and makes clear why the opera setting is so appropriate. He began, he says, with "a certain young woman affronting her destiny" but then wondered, what next?

> By what process of logical accretion was this slight "personality," the mere slim shade of an intelligent but presumptuous girl, to find itself endowed with the high attributes of a Subject? . . . Millions of presumptuous girls, intelligent or not intelligent, daily affront their destiny, and what is it open to their destiny to *be*, at the most, that we should make an ado about it?

To make an ado about Isabel, James considers, is an "extravagance," but a problem not without "charm."[38] The setting, as a response to the problem, may have taken on an increased zest for him after his American sojourn. In the original version of the novel (1881) Warburton only notices "that Miss Archer looked very pretty; he even thought she looked excited."[39] It is only in the 1909 revision that Isabel is fully realized in the "radiance" and "exaltation" of the "operatic conditions" in which she is set.

The situation has a certain prurience. In an opera box, as in James's novel, a young woman becomes the center of attention and the focus of all eyes, but her "charm" is that her destiny is firmly in the hands of others. Hamlin Garland acknowledges the ploy forthrightly—one might even say he exposes it—in *Rose of Dutcher's Coolly* (1895), in which a young woman from rural Wisconsin comes to Chicago and is brought to a performance at the Auditorium. Garland entitles the chapter "Rose Sits in the Blaze of a Thousand Eyes."

> [Mrs. Harvey] gave Rose the outside seat, and before she realized it the coolly girl was seated in plain view of a thousand people, under a soft but penetrating light.
>
> She shrank like some nocturnal insect suddenly brought into sunlight. She turned white, and then the blood flamed to her face and neck. She sprang up.
>
> "Oh, Mrs. Harvey, I can't sit here," she gasped out.
>
> "You must! . . . The public welfare demands that you sit there. . . ."
>
> Rose sank back into her seat, and stared straight ahead. She felt as if something hot and withering were blowing on that side of her face which was exposed to the audience. She wished she had not allowed the neck of her dress to be lowered an inch. She vowed never again to get into such a trap.[40]

In novels as in life, the opera box was singled out as one of very few appropriate sites of heterosocial interaction for the offspring of the wealthy and respectable. The increasingly threatening urban environment and the apparent spread of questionable and "alien" moral values prompted high Society to retrench and circle its wagons; social historians have observed that rituals of etiquette became more elaborate during this period, and practices of chaperonage that had fallen by the wayside were resumed with ferocious intensity. The identification of "the 400," the legendary list of approved insiders who could fit into Caroline Astor's ballroom, was less an amusing foible of the self-important than a frightened, rather desperate attempt to control the circles in which one's sons and daughters would associate and intermarry.[41]

The opera box seems an ideal site: paradoxically both private and public—private in that access to it is strictly controlled, but nonetheless in public view—it functions as a glorious jewel-box to set off its prize. At the same time it is a sort of luxuriously upholstered trap; many a girl, like Rose Dutcher, must have experienced the opera box as cul-de-sac.

New York diarist Philip Hone, explaining the situation in a rather genteel manner, described

> a beautiful *parterre*, in which our young ladies, the flower of New York society, are planted and flourish, not to "waste their sweetness on the desert air," but to expand in a congenial soil under the sunshine of admiration; and here also our young men may be initiated into the habits and forms of elegant social intercourse, and learn to acquire a taste for a science of the most refined and elegant nature, better—far better—than diving into oyster-cellars, or even in consuming night after night in the less exceptionable coteries of the clubs.[42]

Both young men and women are appropriately socialized in the parterre boxes, and there they are trained to prefer one another to any alternative companions. It stands to reason, then, that the box becomes a conventional site, and a literary topos, for the rituals of courtship.[43]

Let us return to Henry James and to another American character in a European opera house. *The American* (1877) recapitulates many themes we have visited already, in particular the contest between American and European cultural attitudes, here presented in most excruciating form. Christopher Newman—whose name, of course, signifies a new Columbus setting out this time upon a voyage of discovery to the Old World—is a Westerner, "the superlative American,"[44] a man of self-made wealth who, at the age of forty-two, considers that he has amassed a sufficient fortune and prepares to spend it. He travels to Paris in a fit of cultural acquisitiveness that is only just this side of caricature; he wants to "see first-class pictures" and to "hear first-class music"; most significantly, he seeks a wife. "I want a great woman . . . the best article in the market" (49).

It soon becomes clear, though, that Newman is a serious and sympathetic character. His exposure to these "first-class" items quickly reveals him as one with genuine sensitivity to them; the woman he finds, Claire de Cintré, is not only "the best article in the market" but, alas, too far upmarket for the pretensions of any declassed American. Though she falls in love with him and agrees to marry him, her ancient and thoroughbred family, the Bellegardes, cannot be won over: "we really can't reconcile ourselves to a commercial person," Newman is told (371). James's American is a man of thoroughly American convictions, besides having sufficient fortune to purchase whatever he fancies, and he hears this verdict with disbelief; but James himself is under no such illusions. *The American* is one of his harshest stories; when Claire's father shows some sign of weakening and permitting the match, her mother in effect kills him to prevent it. A chastened Claire ends in a Carmelite convent.

The opera scene in this novel is unusual in that Claire does not attend. Newman takes an orchestra seat—where he now seems to belong, in relation to the Bellegardes, although we are pointedly told that a box was his usual venue[45]—at a performance of *Don Giovanni*. In the family box he sees Claire's brother Urbain, the marquis, and his wife; visiting them at intermission, he is asked by the marquise to take her to the students' ball in the Latin Quarter—slumming, that is—where her husband will not go. "I'm bored to death. I've been to the opera twice a week for the last eight years. Whenever I ask for anything my mouth is stopped with that: Pray, madame, have n't you your *loge aux Italiens?* Could a woman of taste want more? In the first place my box was down in my *contrat*; they have to give it to me" (343). The first-act drama, then, is the tensions in the marquis's marriage—a marriage in which opera was transacted as part of the dowry—and indeed in the entire Bellegarde household, which have been exacerbated by Newman's arrival among them and the ensuing contretemps.

At another level of the theater's social geography, "in that obscure region devoted to the small boxes which in French are called, not inaptly, bathtubs" (335),[46] Newman spots Claire's younger brother Valentin, in the company of a young woman of dubious social origin to whom Newman has introduced him against his own better judgment, and another man. More extended and more sensational drama ensues from this triangle, which eventually leads to a duel and to Valentin's death.

The choreography of the scene is laid out impeccably. The two women are literally positioned at a vertical distance metaphoric of their discrete social orbits, and all the men perambulate from box to *baignoire* to promenade, watching the women and one another and circulating status and information. Newman can see only too well the havoc he has wrought in the Bellegarde family, but he cannot see Claire, who is too respectable even for the opera box. In her absence the reader becomes uneasily aware that Christopher Newman will not, finally, fit into her world, that the marriage will not occur.

# Wagner and the Souls of Women

*It is not possible to go to an opera in any of our large cities without seeing more of the representatives of the highest type of female beauty than can be found in months of travel in any part of Europe.—George M. Beard*[47]

The alignment of women—women of a certain economic class and social pretension—not only with culture and social maneuvering but with emotional and aesthetic susceptibility drives these fictions of the opera box. Doctor Beard is not, of course, speaking of the women on the opera stage, but of those on display in the boxes. His observation, in a book on the parlous state of American health, is provocative because it combines themes not obviously germane to one another in precisely the way they are often found entwined in novelistic opera scenes. The trope upon opera as specular site—one goes to the opera to see young women, not necessarily to hear anything—accompanies the boastful yet anxious challenge to Europe just as usual. The insistence upon the "highest type" of beauty is easily decoded as an allusion to Anglo-Saxon racial superiority, an interpretation quickly verified by further reading in *American Nervousness*.

The most evolved human types, according to Beard, unfortunately must pay for their advanced condition through a "fineness of organization" that makes them especially vulnerable to nervous disease. Revealing his empirical observations to be somewhat under the sway of his belief system, Beard explains that the "nervous temperament," which also suffers increased susceptibility to stimulants and narcotics, can be identified by physical traits such as fine hair and "chiseled" features. "It is the organization of the civilized, refined, and educated, rather than of the barbarous and low-born and untrained—of women more than of men" (26).

Beard was especially intrigued by young women: "The phenomenal beauty of the American girl of the highest type, is a subject of the greatest interest both to the psychologist and the sociologist, since it has no precedent, in recorded history, at least; and it is very instructive in its relation to the character and the diseases of America" (65).

We should be clear that Beard's ideas were not in the least unusual but perfectly typical of the era,[48] in which the state of science encouraged a strong commitment to racial essentialism that is visible in virtually every cultural context. The social fallout of Darwinian theory and the first glimmerings of a Freudian construction of the psyche combined with an ideologically charged understanding of human reproduction to yield an image of the well-born young woman so extreme in her fragility that one marvels that she ever lived to adulthood without falling into madness or moral depravity.

Given this extraordinary susceptibility, the increased chaperonage and surveillance to which young women were subjected in the last decades of the nineteenth century come as no surprise. But for just the same reason the social sanction by which the opera box was selected as a "safe haven" exposed them to a potentially greater danger: music. In fiction it is just these young women of the "highest type" who prove most vulnerable to it; their "finer organizations" respond strongly, as indeed they must to prove their gentility and feminine sensibility.[49]

The particular state of American culture in these decades, along with the preoccupations of contemporary medical science, combined to form an atmosphere perfectly primed for the emotional "Wagner craze" that hit at the end of the century, as Joseph Horowitz has recently detailed: "Wagner offered an avenue of intense spiritual experience, a surrogate for religion or cocaine, a song of redemption to set beside Emerson and Whitman. It was both intellectually and emotionally vitalizing. It spoke to America's women."[50]

Not only to the women, of course: Horowitz describes the general effects of the mania in the bourgeois population, along with such responses as critic Henry Krehbiel's "warnings against surrendering to Wagnerian narcosis" (110). But it was primarily, and most alarmingly, women who fell victim to it and at the same time drew from it a certain subversive sustenance.[51] While Horowitz is reporting on the impressions of actual women, many of them "of a certain age" and experiencing Wagner as "a consuming alternative to a world of marriage and men,"[52] the novelists naturally are more interested in the youngest and most "morbidly suggestible" of women, women whose sensibilities are yet to be tested in the crucible of opera. Often we find ourselves eavesdropping at virgin operatic excursions, and the titillation of these first Wagnerian swoons is too riveting a spectacle for authors to pass up. Thus Rose Dutcher:

> The voice of Wagner came to her for the first time, and shook her and thrilled her and lifted her into wonderful regions where the green trees dripped golden moss, and the grasses were jewelled in very truth. Wistful young voices rose above the lazy lap of waves, sad with love and burdened with beauty which destroyed. Like a deep-purple cloud death came, slowly, resistlessly, closing down on those who sang, clasped in each other's arms. . . .
>
> When she rose to her feet the girl from the coolly staggered, and the brilliant, moving, murmuring house blurred into fluid color like a wheel of roses. *(235)*

Rose is observed, in her box, by Warren Mason—whom she will marry—and after watching her in the throes of this spasm, "he began to comprehend the soul of the girl" (239).

Charles Dudley Warner's *A Little Journey in the World* (1889), part of a trilogy, tells the story of a young New England woman whose soul is lost through the acquisition of a fortune. Margaret Debree is a bluestocking, something of a feminist, and devoted to good works; she is loved and admired in a great circle of acquaintances. She scrupulously turns down an offer of marriage from the visiting John Lyon, an Englishman next in succession to an earldom, at least in part because she fears her own interest in his future title. But in New York at the opera, alas, Margaret is introduced by her friends to Curtis Henderson, and her fate is sealed.

Warner is a sophisticate concerning opera and its uses by novelists of the period, as his narrator (impersonating one of the circle of Margaret's friends) alerts us:

> In youth, as at the opera, everything seems possible. Surely it is not necessary to choose between love and riches. One may have both, and the one all the more easily for having attained the other. . . . It was in some wholly legendary, perhaps spiritual, world that it was necessary to renounce love to gain the Rhine gold. The boxes at the Metropolitan did not believe this. . . . For was not beauty there seen shining in jewels that have a market value, and did not love visibly preside over the union, and make it known that his sweetest favors go with a prosperous world?[53]

This is a delusion, to be sure, that Margaret Debree had seen through perfectly well before she was introduced into the world of the opera box.

As ever, opera glasses and sight lines diagram the play of recognition and relationship throughout the episode.

> The scene was brilliant, of course with republican simplicity. The imagination was helped by no titled names . . . but there was a certain glow of feeling, as the glass swept the circle, to know that there were ten millions in this box, and twenty in the next, and fifty in the next, attested well enough by the flash of jewels and the splendor of attire, and one might indulge a genuine pride in the prosperity of the republic. As for beauty, the world, surely, in this later time, had flowered here. . . . Here and there in the boxes was a thoroughbred portrait by Copley—the long shapely neck, the sloping shoulders, the drooping eyelids, even to the gown in which the great-grandmother danced with the French officers. *(97–98)*

Henderson is spotted in an opposite box, with Mr. Lyon and the beautiful Carmen Eschelle, a young woman of faintly sinister nature who will play a significant role throughout the trilogy. Henderson is brought to the box in which Margaret sits, takes a seat beside her, and is "quite content while the act was going on to watch its progress in the play of her responsive features. How quickly she felt, how the frown followed the smile, how she seemed to weigh and try to apprehend the meaning of what went on . . ." (101). Margaret's responsiveness is a healthy sign, a sign of her feminine competence and appropriate aesthetic susceptibility; to the knowledgeable reader, however, it also portends suggestibility to other influences.

And so it proves. Margaret marries the financier—and railroad speculator—Henderson and becomes intimate with the stylish Carmen. Her decline is long and slow, sometimes almost imperceptible, and is punctuated by her strenuous efforts to retain her original integrity. Eventually, the inevitable transformation has been completed and even her friends sadly conclude that "she was valuing people by the money they had, by the social position they had attained" (342).

In these scenes, then, we might go so far as to say that women lose their souls; more precisely, they and we first see how they are destined to be lost in the course of their stories. Isabel Archer, Laura Dearborn, and Margaret Debree are just about to enter upon their dark nights of the soul. May Welland and Ellen Olenska are embroiled in a tragedy from which neither emerges unscathed. Claire de Cintré is sacrificed—or, rather, is forced through the inexorable logic of blood to sacrifice herself. Even Olive Chancellor, Henry James's brahmin feminist, ponders her next move in the terrible struggle for the soul of Verena Tarrant at a performance of *Lohengrin*, about which Verena speaks "only of Wagner's music, of the singers, the orchestra, the immensity of the house, her tremendous pleasure."[54] Their stories have a certain operatic quality, conforming to Catherine Clément's characterization of opera itself as "the undoing of women."[55]

But, very occasionally, a woman comes along who escapes the common fate through sheer purity, Parsifal-like. In *That Fortune* (1899), the third of Warner's trilogy, the narrative contortions necessary to create such a woman and to keep her credibly up to the task are remarkable: readers understood the stakes. Evelyn Mavick, the daughter of Carmen Eschelle and her second husband, has been raised in a millionaire's castle on Fifth Avenue, under the care of a radical Scottish governess. Warner is at pains to explain that Evelyn, once the object of a kidnapping attempt, has subsequently been kept entirely isolated and quarantined from all other society. She is a princess in a tower and, as in so many fairy-tale narratives, the third episode in the story breaks the spell.

Ultimately, of course, Evelyn must be presented in public or all the care and expense of her upbringing will be for nought. Philip Burnett—from whose poverty, integrity, literary ambition, and altogether unsuitable social origins we are to understand that he is the suitor who will enable Evelyn's redemption—has been longing to get a glimpse of her now that she is emerging from her seclusion. "Watch for a Wagner night," he is advised (93), and so he does. In fact, it is a *Siegfried* night, and Philip watches her in her family box as she listens. Like Curtis Henderson before him, Philip traces "the progress of the drama repeated in her face." But Evelyn is able to survive spiritually because she does not analyze the drama and its moral efficacy, as Margaret Debree did in her bluestocking way. Evelyn is all experience.

> But presently something more was evident to this sympathetic student of her face. She was not merely discovering the poet's world, she was finding out herself. As the drama unfolded, Philip was more interested in this phase than in the observation of her enjoyment and appreciation. To see her eyes sparkle and her cheeks glow with enthusiasm during the sword-song was one thing, but it was quite another when Siegfried began his idyl, that nature and bird song of

the awakening of the whole being to the passion of love. Then it was that Evelyn's face had a look of surprise, of pain, of profound disturbance; it was suffused with blushes, coming and going in passionate emotion; the eyes no longer blazed, but were softened in a melting tenderness of sympathy, and her whole person seemed to be carried into the stream of the great life passion.     (96)

Evelyn's long virginity is ended. Later, after her father's financial ruin has broken the curse and enabled the lovers to marry, Philip understands that "the soul of the woman [had been] perfectly revealed to him that night of 'Siegfried.'"

The conventional fiction of the opera box did not, of course, outlive the particular social negotiation it had so mercilessly illuminated. In one of its last avatars, *Not on the Screen* (1930), Henry Blake Fuller traces the frenetic social quest of a young woman in chapters successively situated at a prize fight, a football game, and then, somewhat archaically, "At the Opera." But the erstwhile glamour has become mere tabloid fodder, and Fuller furnishes the trope with its epitaph:

> The only persons who know how to grade and present the occupants of opera-boxes are the discriminating young women who make note of them for the daily papers. . . . To the casual observer in the parquet or the balcony, all the box-people may seem to be participating on equal terms in a brave spectacle; but when it comes to the acute dissection of the spectacle's component parts by these inquirers with note-books and pencils, it will be found that they know, they know.[56]

NOTES

A shorter version of this paper was delivered at the conference on Gender and Sexuality in Opera, SUNY at Stony Brook, September 14–17, 1995. I wish to thank the participants at that conference, and Elizabeth Harries, Daniel Horowitz, Susan Van Dyne, and Elizabeth Wood for the generosity of their many astute comments.

1. Edgar Saltus, *The Monster* (New York: Pulitzer Publishing Company, 1912), 23–24.

2. See Karen Halttunen, *Confidence Men and Painted Women: A Study of Middle-Class Culture in America, 1830–1870* (New Haven: Yale University Press, 1982), chapter 6; and William Leach, *Land of Desire: Merchants, Power, and the Rise of a New American Culture* (New York: Pantheon, 1993), chapter 3.

3. A parallel study could certainly be done—indeed, several have been done—of European novels, for the opera-box setting occurs there no less frequently. But the social meanings of opera attendance are very different in Europe, as are the relations of class and of gender that are so crucial in deciphering these scenes, and so I focus here on the work of American authors—though several of their scenes, like Saltus's, take place in Europe. European novels are briefly studied in Dominique Dubreuil, "Opéra: l'oeil de la fiction," in *Littérature et opéra* [Colloque de Cerisy, 1985], eds. Philippe Berthier et Kurt Ringger (Grenoble: Presses Universitaires de Grenoble,

1987), 177–83. English novels are the principal subject of Emily Auerbach, *Maestros, Dilettantes, and Philistines: The Musician in the Victorian Novel* (New York: Peter Lang, 1989). Approaches to the topic that are structural and critical rather than focussing on social history include Alex Aronson, *Music and the Novel: A Study in Twentieth-Century Fiction* (Totowa, N.J.: Rowman and Littlefield, 1980) and Peter Conrad, *Romantic Opera and Literary Form* (Berkeley: University of California Press, 1977).

4. "New York: Social Notes," *The American Scene* (Bloomington: Indiana University Press, 1968; orig. 1907), 164.

5. See especially Herbert Lindenberger, *Opera: The Extravagant Art* (Ithaca: Cornell University Press, 1984), 174–75.

6. "Some place in the house there was a dividing line between those who looked down on each other and those who looked at the stage, but I have not, in fifteen years of research, been able to determine just where it began" (Irving Kolodin, *The Story of the Metropolitan Opera, 1883–1950* [New York: Knopf, 1953], 58). On this "geography," see also Lois W. Banner, *American Beauty* (New York: Knopf, 1983), 67–68; and John Frederick Cone, *First Rival of the Metropolitan Opera* (New York: Columbia University Press, 1983).

7. See, for one example among many, Florence Hartley, *The Ladies' Book of Etiquette and Manual of Politeness: Complete Handbook for the Use of the Lady in Polite Society* (Boston: J. S. Locke & Company, 1873), 174–77. On opera as ritual mystification, see Bruce A. McConachie, "New York Operagoing, 1825–50: Creating an Elite Social Ritual," *American Music* 6 (1988): 181–92. For an analysis of the 1849 "Astor Place riot" as a lens into urban culture and social relations, see Peter George Buckley, *To the Opera House: Culture and Society in New York City, 1820–1860* (Ph.D. Diss., History, SUNY at Stony Brook, 1984).

8. Elizabeth Stuart Phelps, *The Silent Partner* (Boston: James R. Osgood, 1871), 16. Phelps is called "the first American novelist to treat the social problems of the Machine Age seriously and at length" by Walter Fuller Taylor in *The Economic Novel in America* (Chapel Hill: University of North Carolina Press, 1942), 58.

9. And perhaps not only in America. "The assumption that musical arousal brings out specifically feminine psychic characteristics in man and that music is— among all the arts—the most suggestive metaphor of femininity appears to a considerable number of novelists to be self-evident" (Alex Aronson, *Music and the Novel*, 113).

10. In fact, bourgeois women in the 1870s and 1880s began in large numbers to leave their drawing rooms for socially beneficial volunteer work, especially in urban centers. By and large, their orientation remained securely in keeping with Victorian gender roles, working in the spirit of "True Womanhood" to redress the excesses of male aggression and financial predation. See Mari Jo Buhle, *Women and American Socialism, 1870–1920* (Urbana: University of Illinois Press, 1981) and Carroll Smith-Rosenberg, *Disorderly Conduct: Visions of Gender in Victorian America* (New York: Alfred A. Knopf, 1985).

11. Thorstein Veblen, *The Theory of the Leisure Class: An Economic Study of Institutions* (New York: B. W. Huebsch, 1922; orig. 1899). The fact that, by tradition, nobody in the boxes actually listens to the opera—either in the novels or, apparently, in reality—makes the purchase doubly extravagant.

12. This story is well told in John Dizikes, *Opera in America: A Cultural History* (New Haven: Yale University Press, 1993), chapter 20, as well as in other histories

of opera in the United States. After a few years occupied with what New Yorkers called the "opera wars"—notoriously featuring a pitched battle between "old-fashioned" Italian opera at the Academy and "modern" German (Wagnerian) opera at the Metropolitan—the Academy succumbed. It became a venue for melodrama, and finally closed its doors in 1926. Many writers have discussed this antic (but artistically fateful) chapter in New York's social history. See, in addition to Dizikes, Henry Krehbiel, *Chapters of Opera* (New York: Henry Holt, 1908); Edward Ringwood Hewitt, *Those Were the Days: Tales of a Long Life* (New York: Duell, Sloan and Pearce, 1943); Cone, *First Rival of the Metropolitan Opera*; Louis Auchincloss, *The Vanderbilt Era: Profiles of a Gilded Age* (New York: Charles Scribner's Sons, 1989); and Joseph Horowitz, *Wagner Nights: An American History* (Berkeley: University of California Press, 1994).

13. In an effort to rectify this peculiarly motivated design years later, the Grand Tier boxes were replaced in 1940 with individual seats; some had already been removed in the renovation after an 1893 fire. See Frank Merkling et al., *The Golden Horseshoe: The Life and Times of the Metropolitan Opera House* (New York: Viking Press, 1965). The expression "diamond horseshoe" refers to the prestigious single tier of boxes into which the owners reorganized themselves after the 1893 renovation. In all this social comedy it should not be forgotten that operas were also attended by large numbers of serious music lovers, which in the case of the Met notably featured New York's extensive German-American community. The novelists, however, have not been so interested in this segment of the audience.

14. Wharton wryly describes the actual situation of New York opera production in the 1870s: "an unalterable and unquestioned law of the musical world required that the German text of French operas sung by Swedish artists should be translated into Italian for the clearer understanding of English-speaking audiences" (5). Christine Nilsson did indeed sing Marguerite at the Academy of Music several times, first in 1870; ironically, she opened the new Metropolitan Opera House in the same role on October 22, 1883; see note 12.

15. Edith Wharton, *The Custom of the Country*, ed. Stephen Orgel (Oxford: Oxford University Press, 1995), 39.

16. Neil Harris, *Cultural Excursions: Marketing Appetites and Cultural Tastes in Modern America* (Chicago: University of Chicago Press, 1990), 178.

17. *The Pit* (New York: Doubleday, Page & Co., 1903), 255.

18. Built by Adler and Sullivan, the Auditorium was completed in 1888.

19. This unproductivity, of course, is a quality that renders speculation morally questionable in the post-Victorian realm. But there is also the more concrete problem that speculators inevitably make their profits at serious cost to some innocent party: as one conscience-stricken character in *The Pit* observes, "if we send the price of wheat down too far, the farmer suffers, the fellow who raises it; if we send it up too far, the poor man in Europe suffers, the fellow who eats it" (129). Laura's female innocence about business matters is signaled by her reaction to Jadwin's announcement that the long-looked-for global short-crop in wheat has arrived; those people "over in Europe" will pay any price now, he explains, because "they've got to have the wheat—it's bread 'n' butter to them." "Oh, then why not give it to them? . . . That would be a godsend," Laura suggests. Her husband is forced to explain that "that isn't exactly how it works out" (233).

20. There is a third suitor who is not, however, taken seriously by Laura.

21. I should perhaps point out that nineteenth-century writers used the word *sex* where we would more likely use *gender*. Laura has no intimate relations with Corthell, but fears that she can never relate to him except *as* a woman.

22. Brander Matthews, *His Father's Son: A Novel of New York* (New York: Harper & Brothers, 1896).

23. Except in those cases where a greedy and corrupt woman is central to the plot, it would not be an exaggeration to claim that every single novel of financial dealings contains some version of the line, "Your mother is a very good woman—but she knows nothing at all about business. . . . She wouldn't understand anything. Women never do see things clearly—you will learn that as you grow older" (*His Father's Son*, 95). Such disclaimers, while heartfelt, inevitably signal that some virtuous and level-headed woman is trying with might and main to extricate her husband from certain financial disaster. Persis Lapham comes to mind.

24. The fact that the same money—and thus the same names—dominated both the mercantile and cultural realms created some characteristically American ironies that have been well studied by social historians. See, for example, Michael and Ariane Batterberry, *On the Town in New York: From 1776 to the Present* (New York: Charles Scribner's Sons, 1973), chapter 4; Richard Hofstadter, *Anti-Intellectualism in American Life* (New York: Vintage, 1963), chapter 9; and Sean Dennis Cashman, *America in the Gilded Age: From the Death of Lincoln to the Rise of Theodore Roosevelt* (New York: New York University Press, 1984). Cashman captures the transaction nicely by describing the impulse to art patronage as the effort "to celebrate the confidence of accumulated capital" (46).

25. "Bourgeois Opera,"in *Opera Through Other Eyes*, ed. David J. Levin (Stanford: Stanford University Press, 1994), 35.

26. Henry Blake Fuller, *With the Procession* (Chicago: University of Chicago Press, 1965), 77.

27. Sinclair Lewis, *Babbitt* (New York: New American Library, 1961), 150.

28. Sinclair Lewis, *The Job* (New York: Harcourt Brace, 1917), 196–97.

29. Daniel Horowitz, *The Morality of Spending: Attitudes Toward the Consumer Society in America, 1875–1940* (Baltimore: Johns Hopkins University Press, 1985), xviii. On the emergence of ethnic neighborhoods in New York, see Michael and Ariane Batterberry, *On the Town in New York*, chapter 4. For some musical ramifications, see Nicholas Tawa, *A Sound of Strangers: Musical Culture, Acculturation, and the Post–Civil War Ethnic American* (Metuchen, N.J.: Scarecrow Press, 1982).

30. See Russel Nye, *The Unembarrassed Muse: The Popular Arts in America* (New York: Dial Press, 1970), chapter 5.

31. See David Ward, *Poverty, Ethnicity, and the American City, 1840–1925: Changing Conceptions of the Slum and the Ghetto* (Cambridge: Cambridge University Press, 1989).

32. Lewis, *The Job*, 149.

33. James Huneker, *New Cosmopolis* (New York: Scribner's, 1915), 99, 102.

34. Saltus, *The Monster*, 74.

35. *The Buntling Ball: A Graeco-American Play*, published anonymously by Edgar Fawcett (New York: Funk & Wagnalls, 1885), 97–98: "chorus of belles."

36. Henry James, *The Portrait of a Lady* (New York: Bantam Books, 1983), 261. All quotations from the scene are taken from pages 261–62. Such terms are equally numerous in other scenes I have discussed.

37. See, for example, Stephen Koch's afterword in the Bantam edition, and several of the critical comments collected in *Portrait of a Lady: An Authoritative Text*, ed. Robert D. Bamberg (New York: W. W. Norton, 1975); James's preface to the 1909 edition is included in both of these volumes.

38. Preface to the Bantam edition, xi.

39. *Portrait of a Lady* (Boston: Houghton Mifflin, 1881), 260.

40. Hamlin Garland, *Rose of Dutcher's Coolly* (New York: Harper & Brothers, 1899), 230–31. The scene is slightly ambiguous in that it is at first referred to as "going to the opera" but turns out, in the event, to be a symphony concert. The iconography of the box, however, is intact.

41. The formation of "the 400" is contemporaneous with the passage of Jim Crow laws in the Southern states—two versions of the same impulse to distinguish the acceptable from the outcast. On the social purity movement and "the 400," see Banner, *American Beauty*, especially chapter 7.

42. Diary entry for January 21, 1848. Quoted in Vera Brodsky Lawrence, *Strong on Music: The New York Music Scene in the Days of George Templeton Strong, 1836–1875*, vol. 1, *Resonances, 1836–1850* (New York: Oxford University Press, 1988), 497.

43. See also Michel Leiris, "L'Érotisme dans l'opéra," in his *Operratiques*, ed. Jean Jamin (Paris: P.O.L., 1992),

44. Henry James, *The American* (Boston: Houghton Mifflin, 1907), 2.

45. "Frequently he took a large box and invited a group of his compatriots; this was a mode of recreation to which he was much addicted" (334).

46. A common French term for ground-floor theatrical boxes. The lowest tier of boxes in the Metropolitan Opera House—large, rather ungainly ones—were also familiarly known as *baignoires*.

47. *American Nervousness* (New York: G.P. Putnam's Sons, 1881), 67.

48. However, his penchant for argument from "scattergories" in an ineptly Borgesian manner seems to have been idiosyncratic. He describes modern civilization as distinguished by five principal characteristics—steam power, the periodical press, the telegraph, the sciences, and the mental activity of women—plus a number of subsidiary ones: "dryness of the air, extremes of heat and cold, civil and religious liberty, and the great mental activity made necessary and possible in a new and productive country under such climatic conditions" (vi–vii).

49. This topos has survived into contemporary cinema, as in *Pretty Woman* or *Moonstruck*; both the 1933 and 1993 films of *Little Women* include such a scene—in which Professor Bhaer takes Jo to the opera—even though Louisa May Alcott did not include one in her novel. (I am grateful to Susan Van Dyne for this observation.) For relevant but differently focused discussions of fictional opera as the site of passion and *jouissance*, see Herbert Lindenberger, *Opera: The Extravagant Art* and Michel Poizat, *The Angel's Cry: Beyond the Pleasure Principle in Opera*, trans. Arthur Denner (Ithaca: Cornell University Press, 1992). Both books are more oriented to the European situation than to the American.

50. Horowitz, *Wagner Nights*, 8.

51. See Horowitz's chapter 12, "Protofeminism." Although I see no reason to characterize this episode of American women's experience as merely "proto" feminism, the argument of the chapter is informative and highly important.

52. Horowitz, *Wagner Nights*, 215; M. Carey Thomas was already dean of Bryn Mawr College when she first heard *Tristan* and wrote the response recorded by

Helen Lefkowitz Horowitz in *The Power and Passion of M. Carey Thomas* (New York: Knopf, 1994), 215.

53. *The Complete Writings of Charles Dudley Warner*, ed. Thomas R. Lounsbury, vol. xi (Hartford, Conn.: American Publishing Company, 1904), 94.

54. Henry James, *The Bostonians*, ed. R. D. Gooder (Oxford: Oxford University Press, 1984), 285–86.

55. Catherine Clément, *Opera, or the Undoing of Women*, trans. Betsy Wing (Minneapolis: University of Minnesota Press, 1988). Undine Spragg is irredeemable long before we meet her.

56. Henry B. Fuller, *Not on the Screen* (New York: Knopf, 1930), 95. Opera scenes continue to occur, of course, in historical novels; but Fuller's is the latest I have found that represents contemporary practice.

## CHAPTER NINE

# "Eros Is in the Word": Music, Homoerotic Desire, and the Psychopathologies of Fascism, or The "Strangely Fruitful Intercourse" of Thomas Mann and Benjamin Britten

Daniel Fischlin

Fanaticism turns into a means of salvation, enthusiasm into epileptic ecstasy, politics become an opiate for the masses, a proletarian eschatology; and reason veils her face.—*Thomas Mann**

The entire economy of modernism is implicated in fascism in disturbing ways that have yet to be adequately assessed.—*Mark C. Taylor*[†]

I

Two of Thomas Mann's short fictions, *Death in Venice* (1912) and *Mario and the Magician* (1930), have been adapted as major operas by Benjamin Britten (1973) and Harry Somers (1992). Both literary works depict emergent nationalist and fascist sentiment. Both articulate a specific, if critically occluded, vision of the political subject characterized by narcissism, closeted homoerotic desire, and the self-annihilating transcendence experienced by their protagonists, Gustav von Aschenbach and Cavaliere Cipolla. This essay proposes a reading of *Death in Venice* by way of the issues that emerge when gender and sexuality are overwritten upon notions of national identity, political subjectivity, and state formation, especially evident in the trajectory from pre- to postfascist aesthetics—that is, from *Death in Venice*'s literary to its operatic incarnation.[1] Both the novella and opera depict a potentially disruptive, unfulfilled homoeroticism in terms closely linked, explicitly or implicitly, with nationalist ideology. Both delimit the politico-historical context of the homoerotic, oscillating between "homosexuality [seen] as the source of art and culture . . . [and] as a pernicious disease threatening the body politic" (Martin, 1992:65).

The relative absence of political analyses of the conditions of production in modern opera has remained a largely untouched subject in musicological and literary circles.[2] The aesthetics of the genre, not to mention the commercial and cultural fields to which it addresses itself as "high" art, are by definition elite, operatic conventions mirroring the social and cultural practices of its expected audience. The orthodoxies of operatic display cultivate such a mirroring at the same time as that mirroring produces the very erasures that dehistoricize and depoliticize opera as a form of mimetic idealism that apparently unifies the diverse modes of Occidental self-representation: theater, text, music, dance, visual art, and so forth.[3] An example of such an erasure occurs in the intertextual relations of Mann's and Britten's versions of *Death in Venice*. Despite the historical trajectory of the sixty-one intervening years between novella and opera (1912–1973)—a trajectory marked by two world wars, the rise of political forces aligned with national socialism and fascism, and the radical realignment of gender politics—criticism of the opera has invariably failed to address its specifically politico-erotic dimensions. Recently, to give but one example, Wayne Koestenbaum's *The Queen's Throat*, which makes playful forays into political, historical, and erotic matters associated with opera, homosexuality, and desire, does not once mention Britten or the opera, an opera characterized if not overdetermined by the way in which these topics are given explicit significance.[4] Moreover, despite the considerable body of scholarly work on the opera, almost no direct mention of its politico-erotic dimensions is to be found. The musicological criticism tends to reproduce the metaphysical transcendence that the opera putatively embodies, often with little grasp that such a metaphysics has links with political repression and aesthetic quietism. I propose a reading of the opera as marked by such ideological repression, a "closeting" that sublimates the complex psychopathologies invisibly aligned with pre- and postfascist aesthetics.[5]

Hints at the politico-erotic dimensions of the opera *do* occur. Humphrey Carpenter, for example, reports that "Robert Tear, who has himself sung Aschenbach, regards [*Death in Venice*] as a treatise about Britten's sexuality, and believes that it fails to tackle its subject adequately: 'Musically, it's a masterpiece. But there's a cop-out. It mustn't be called sexual lust. It's Beauty, or it's Greek. And that's a cop-out'" (550). Clifford Hindley expresses surprise that Britten set the Mann story given its expression of "a deeply negative and (in Mann's word) pathological approach to homosexuality as such. It may be simply . . . that Britten was influenced by an internalized sense of oppression regarding his own homosexuality. . . . It seems to me . . . that Britten saw in Mann's story not only a tale of pathological disintegration but the elements of a positive synthesis along the route from which Aschenbach turned aside—a potentiality which had eluded, or had perhaps been suppressed by, Mann" (1990:511). Hindley's attempt to recuperate the didactic value of the opera (as an example of the failure to capture the "moment of reality" in which the possibility of homoerotic fulfillment occurs and of what the price of such a failure is) ignores that the opera engages the notion of narcissism that erases the other in the imagined transcendence of self in death. In other words, Aschenbach does not fail to capture reality. He succeeds only too well. The politics of this form of negative affirmation (death as narcissistic self-consummation) cannot be ignored in postfascist aesthetic contexts.

Aschenbach's *Liebestod* is at once a revelation and a concealment of the smothering politics of Thanatos. Near the end of the opera, for example, in Scenes 12 and 16, Aschenbach wonders, "What if all were dead, and only we two left alive?" (Piper, 34). Here desire and the apocalyptic vision of the thanatological purification that unleashes Aschenbach's homoerotic desires come dangerously close to a fantasy that also entails the eradication of *every* form of repressive and liberatory otherness. Buried at the heart of this dynamic is the crucial obfuscation regarding what kills Aschenbach, a potent cocktail of homoerotic love, narcissism, and the threatening other embodied in the Asiatic cholera to which he succumbs in Venice, itself a symbol of the contagion of destructive otherness. The other mediates the demonic and death. But such a mediation is only possible through the psychopathological self-involvement that cathects on the other as symbolic of the repressed self's desire for liberatory expression. Self-loathing is converted into desire for the other, that desire expressing the very failure of the self as a marker of erotic or signifying plenitude. In such a dynamic the psychopathology of passional desire has political as well as aesthetic consequences, especially in relation to repression as a key element in the enactment of state desire vis-à-vis the political subject.

If so, the consequences of Aschenbach's unfulfilled passion for Tadzio, the young Polish boy, may be read productively in relation to Mann's own conflicted sense of the "German soul." In a public address made in October 1930 while a group of SA (*Sturm-abteilung*) disrupted the event, Mann asked, "Is there any deep stratum of the German soul where all that fanaticism, that bacchantic frenzy, that orgiastic denial of reason and human dignity is [*sic*] really at home?" (Mann; cited by Hamilton, 243). Mann describes a "German" national identity characterized by fanaticism, bacchantic frenzy, denial of reason. But Mann also implicitly represses these unwanted characteristics as not being "really at home" in that identity.[6] *Death in Venice*, written years before Mann's comments in 1930, articulates an inchoate sense of this ambiguous, national self by associating Aschenbach with a specific cultural space the novella is at pains to elaborate in its opening pages. At the beginning of the novella, for instance, Mann locates the conflicted relations between Aschenbach's ego drives and his politico-historical context: he is "Too busy with the tasks imposed upon him by his own ego and the European soul, too laden with the care and duty to create, too preoccupied to be an amateur of the gay outer world" (6). Here, as elsewhere, Myfanwy Piper's libretto diminishes or effaces such contexts, much like H. T. Lowe-Porter's English translation effaces materials that describe homoerotic relations.[7] The explicit identification of Aschenbach's nationality, for example, does not occur until Act II, Scene 8, in which the hotel barber says, "you hear less German? Ah! your compatriots are always very careful but so nice" (Piper, 23). The charged link between Aschenbach's ego and his "European soul" that the novella is at pains to articulate as crucial to the psychodrama about to occur is elided in the libretto by the banal association (however ironic) of German nationality with the epithets *careful* and *nice*.

The general historical contexts and the specific political referents in the novella itself are significant, insofar as the opera obscures those contexts and referents. For instance, the connections between the pathologies of Venice as a city, some of which have been linked by Anthony Heilbut with "homosexual prostitution" (257),[8] and Mann's disgust with the rise of nationalist sentiment in prewar Italy have been established by Giuliana Giobbi, who links Mann's notions of art, contagion, and death with his abhorrence of "Nationalism and the defenders of War; [Mann] defined the Italians as '*die Heerscharen Gabriels* [Gabriel's troops]'—'Gabriel' being D'Annunzio" (65). For Mann Venice is death and contagion. The extended treatment of Aschenbach's gondola ride to the Lido makes the allegorical significance of Venice explicit. The gondola, "black as nothing else on earth except a coffin" (21), is described as a "vision of death" (21). Furthermore, the gondolier's resemblance to Charon, ferryman to the dead, is hinted at by Aschenbach when during the ride to the Lido he imagines being hit in the head by an oar and sent "down to the kingdom of Hades" (23). By contrast, Scene 3 of the opera depicts Venice in magical even harmonious terms, thus laying the symbolic ground for the association of death with transcendence with which the opera closes. In an extended apostrophe to Venice, Aschenbach sings:

> Ah Serenissima!
> Where should I come but to you
> To soothe and revive me
> Where but to you
> To live that magical life
> Between the sea and the city?
> What lies in wait for me here,
> Ambiguous Venice,
> Where water is married to stone
> And passion confuses the senses?
> Ambiguous Venice.                                        (6)

The "magical life/Between the sea and the city" along with the image of the "marriage" of water and stone associate Venice with harmonization and the magic of life lived "between." But the "magical" life between sea and city is where the gondolier plies his trade, and such a life is therefore already verging toward "magical" death, the beckoning ambiguity that hints at a form of transcendent harmonization. Venice's ambiguity doubles Aschenbach's sexual ambiguity if not Britten's ambiguity about Mann's use of Venice as a political signifier. "[P]assion confuses the senses" in Britten's

Venice, but that confusion is tinged with the redemptive magic that transfigures a life lived "between" into the transcendent death awaiting Aschenbach after his encounter with the psychagogue Tadzio. The symbolic logic here enacts the politics of the closet, foreclosing on the degree to which the external can intrude upon the repressed interiority of Aschenbach's desires. The sensual ambiguity of Aschenbach's passion leads to a thanatological "between[ness]," a liminal space in which repressed or confused sensuality is death, but a death that is magical, matrimonial, heterosexual. Such a reading is substantiated by the gondolier's response, sung to himself, to Aschenbach's rhapsodic idealization of Venice:

> Passengers must follow
> Follow where I lead
> No choice for the living
> No choice for the dead.　　　　　　　　　　　　　　*(6)*

The imperative "must follow" and the repetition of "No choice" suggest the potent determinism of Thanatos, as if to suggest that Venice's symbolic ambiguity leads inevitably to death. When such a structure is aligned with the repression of Aschenbach's sexual ambiguity, it becomes clear that the opera reinforces, however "queerly," the closeting of desire for which Aschenbach stands. The difference between the novella and the opera in this regard, a difference exacerbated by the generic conventions particular to short fiction and libretto writing, is subtle. The novella's allegorical depiction of the trip to Venice makes explicit the thanatological significance of the gondolier. The opera, however, inverts the trope of death, substituting "magical life," marriage, and ambiguity as key Venetian tropes, thus anticipating the opera's closural purification of ambiguity in the cathartic, transcendental death that signals Aschenbach's Neoplatonic ascension. The shift in emphasis from novella to opera, however nuanced, is notable.

A similar shift occurs in the depiction of Aschenbach's family context. The opposition between his mother, "daughter of a Bohemian musical conductor" (8), and father, an upper official in the judicature" (8), which prefigures the psychic conflict Aschenbach will undergo between passion and reason, is almost completely eradicated from the libretto. Family context is especially significant for Mann, who places Aschenbach within a specific political (and patrilineal) relation to the state by way of his family, especially his father: "his forbears had all been officers, judges, departmental functionaries—*men who lived their strict, decent, sparing lives in the service of king and state*" (8; my emphasis). Note how the libretto changes the emphasis in its treatment of the same passage:

> Gustav von Aschenbach, what is this path you have taken? What would your forebears say—decent, stern men, in whose respectable name and under whose influence you, the artist, made the life of art into a service, a hero's life of struggle and abstinence?

*(He pauses, smiles to himself)*

Yes, but when heroes have flourished Eros has flourished too. It was no shame to them to be enthralled, rather it brought them praise, it brought them honour. *(Piper, 28)*

The libretto dislocates the novella's subtly politicized emphasis on the relations between the state and the kind of art Aschenbach produces, focusing instead on how art produced in the more generalized context of "heroic" respectability and decency leads to a "flourish[ing]" of Eros. Aesthetic "enthrall[ment]," the mortification of Eros, brings praise and honour in the libretto, depotentiating the novella's negative depiction of *"decent, sparing lives"* lived in *"service of king and state."* The displacement from the political to the aesthetic diminishes the explicit historical dimensions of the novella while servicing the libretto's aestheticization of Aschenbach's psychomachia. Thus in the novella the political context of homoerotic repression leads to containment and death, whereas in the opera "senses lead to passion. . . . And passion to the abyss" of transcendental death (38), the penultimate scene (Scene 16) staging Aschenbach's Neoplatonic and Phaedric motivations, but in a discursive context that has been radically dehistoricized and depoliticized.

Mann's own sense of the novella was conflicted, probably as a result of its uncomfortable insights and uncanny prolepses regarding German national identity and the complex desires associated with that identity.[9] As described by Nigel Hamilton, Mann thought that *Death in Venice* was "full of half-baked ideas and falsehood[s]" (150). And Hamilton further associates this self-criticism with Mann's professed "inability to orientate [him]self, politically and spiritually," his "growing sympathy with death" as a sign of his "inability to cope with modern times and with 'progress'" (150). The musical techniques evident in Britten's operatic transformation of Mann's fiction—especially the distinctive use of recitative[10] and the sparse orchestration—signal a compositional practice attuned to the textual origins of the opera as well as to the demands imposed on the tenor who must sing Aschenbach's role. Though one must be careful to differentiate between the musical setting of the libretto and the libretto proper as different forms of discursivity, their relations are closely imbricated, the representational context of the libretto providing a mimetic model for the musical commentary on the libretto. Such a practice is clearly text based, an aesthetic not without political contexts that can be compared productively with the textual strategies used in the novella.

## II

It will be argued, no doubt, that reading *Death in Venice* for its politics is a violation of its signifying codes, which intend suprapolitical forms of Neoplatonism, the Nietszchean agon between Dionysus and Apollo, "its personal and social response to Greek love . . . known as *Knabenliebe*"

(Martin, 1992:63), and the transcendent powers of Eros and Thanatos. Opposing such a position are Susan McClary's assertions that "music gives the illusion of operating independently of cultural mediation" (53) and that "classical music is perhaps our cultural medium most centrally concerned with denial of the body, with enacting the ritual repudiation of the erotic" (79).

The tired notion of music's nonreferentiality is too often used to deny that the illusion of nonreferentiality has its political dimensions, especially in music's ability to overcode the reception of an audience's response to visual imagery or verbal context. What is crucial is how music's *apparent* nonreferentiality erases or undermines the pertinent ideological dimensions music brings to a specific referential context. Such erasures are part of the signifying practice of music, a coding of effect that from very early on in the history of Occidental musical practice has been associated with the production of specific affects, which in turn produce specific states of subjectivity that have political valences. In book 3 of the *Republic*, Plato's prohibition of modes (399$^b$) and rhythms (400) that produce specific affects in the political subject as well as medieval controversies over melismatic as opposed to note-to-syllable compositional practices (that is, over the relative focus on music as opposed to scripture) in plain-chant are but two examples of music's political valences. Linkages clearly exist between the supposed invisibility of musical referentiality and the ideological context that makes use of such invisibility, much as Muzak's pervasive mall-presence makes it invisible in precisely the manner that makes the consumer more pliable to the ideology of material consumption.

Philippe Lacoue-Labarthe's argument that National Socialism "reveals and then obscures 'the non-political essence of the political'" and that "'no aesthetic, nor any philosophy of art either, is capable of undoing the unseverable link between art and the political'" (cited in Carroll, 720) is relevant here. That is, within Lacoue-Labarthe's referential context, fascist and totalitarian aesthetics are particularly well disposed toward media such as music in which putatively invisible effects confirm the political, a hidden dynamic exploitative of the relations between politics and aesthetics, ideology and artifice. Such a relationship is implicit in Josef Goebbels's assertion, in a letter to the conductor Wilhelm Furtwängler that, "Politics is also an art, perhaps even the highest and most extensive art that exists" (cited in Carroll, 691). Goebbels articulates the totalitarian desire to appropriate the political dimensions of art, that is, to render art totally ("extensive[ly]") political. Theories of postfascist aesthetics must address the politicization of aesthetics and the aestheticization of politics for, as Walter Benjamin notes,

[t]he logical result of Fascism is the introduction of aesthetics into political life. . . . Mankind, which in Homer's time was an object of contemplation for the Olympian gods, now is one for itself. Its self-alienation has reached such a degree that it can experience its own

destruction as an aesthetic pleasure of the first order. This is the situation of politics which Fascism is rendering aesthetic.     *(241–42)*

Fascism, specifically associated with the aesthetic pleasure of "destruction," is the logical extension of the battle over the control of the structures, production, and dissemination of the work of art. Hence it is impossible to detach art from politics without obscuring the charged ideological relations that exist between the two. When such an occultation occurs, as it does in Britten's *Death in Venice*, it produces the ideological obscurantism that postfascist criticism must make explicit to counter the sublimated effects of fascist aesthetics in a postfascist context.

This is not to cast Britten *or* Mann as villain or hero in the political dynamic I am describing. Compare, for example, Benjamin's insight with an entry from Mann's diary, Tuesday, February 14, 1939 (Princeton): "Aesthetic and political discussion. The impossibility of a satirical novel (*Dead Souls*). The phenomenon of National Socialism's being undeserving of the artist's skill. Failure or despair or renunciation of the word, the feebleness of denunciation. Have reality and art ever before been so utterly incompatible? Art not applicable to 'life.' The deadliness of nazism, the paralysis it spreads" (319). If anything, the comments reveal the extent to which Mann had failed to understand the relations between fascist ideology and aesthetics. The "paralysis" and the inapplicability of art to life to which Mann refers is symptomatic of the very paralysis that *Death in Venice*, in both its fictive and its musical incarnations, describes. The containment of desire and renunciation of action culminate in an ambiguous *Liebestod* that simultaneously signifies acquiescence to the ideology it reinforces as well as escape from the realm of "life" by way of artistic transcendence. Peter Conrad notes that Hans Werner Henze's opera *Bassarids* (1966) links the "Dionysia with a modern Teutonic epidemic which took its mythology from opera. Hitler set himself to enact in a global theater the finale of *Götterdämmerung*. Henze conceives the Dionysian cult as a political distemper; Britten treats it as a sensual plague. . . . The pestilence is erotic, killing Aschenbach by way of his love for Tadzio" (230). The significance of such a "sensual plague" suggests a somatic politics that represses the physical expression of desire.

The subtle depoliticization of the novella's context is problematic in Britten's opera, especially if the shift from the explicit political context in the novella to the narcissistic interiority of Aschenbach in the opera embodies the aesthetic shift from pre- to postfascist history. A significant example of this shift occurs in the operatic reworking of the following passage from the novella, when Aschenbach, engaged in an interior monologue, states:

> This life in the bonds of art, had not he himself, in the days of youth and in the very spirit of those bourgeois forefathers, pronounced mocking judgment upon it? And yet, at bottom, it had been so like their own! It had been a service, and he a soldier, like some of them; and art was war—a grilling, exhausting struggle that nowadays wore

one out before one could grow old. It had been a life of self-conquest, a life against odds, dour, steadfast, abstinent; he had made it symbolical of the kind of over-strained heroism the time admired, and he was entitled to call it manly, even courageous. *(56–57)*

The passage localizes an important moment of self-recognition for Aschenbach as he strives to escape the bonds that determine his response to art. Not only is art war, it is self-conquest, and, it is important to note, "symbolical of . . . [an] over-strained heroism," which reveals Aschenbach's doubts about the process of aestheticization that is art for him. The passage ironically affirms the manliness, the courageousness of such tropes, which merely echo the bourgeois sentimentality that has produced Aschenbach's inability to confront his sexual difference, the emergent homoeroticism that will subvert the values of his bourgeois origins. Not only are specific historical, political, class, and cultural contexts invoked here, but those contexts, which lead to the deadening clichés about "manly" and "war[like]" art, are explicitly critiqued. Aschenbach questions "if such a life might not be somehow specially pleasing in the eyes of the god [Tadzio] who had him in his power" (57). From Mann's perspective such a question is folly (57), the passage expressing the oppression and self-delusion of a national character overly invested in war, manliness, rituals of deification, and so forth.[11] Aschenbach symptomatizes the bourgeois self-alienation and ambiguity[12] that will lead to further repressions culminating in his death. For Mann, Aschenbach is overdetermined by the historical conditions that shape his sexual identity as well as his identity as an artist who emblematizes the conflicted masculine conventions of bourgeois culture.[13]

This historical overdetermination is made explicit in the novella, whereas the libretto sanitizes the very contexts that politicize the novella. Despite Piper's close attention to the novella (and Britten's close attention to Piper's reworking of the material), involving in some cases direct repetitions from the English translation of the novella, the libretto and the score to which it is set present a specific and transformative reading of Mann's text. In the case of the passage just cited, for example, the notion of bourgeois overstraining that "the time admired" explicitly presents a critique within a sociohistorical context. The libretto, which never once uses the word *bourgeois*, instead *poeticizes* homoerotic desire as an "inexplicable longing" (Piper, 2), a longing that Mann *explicates* in relation to specific concepts of national identity, historical circumstance, and sociopolitical and philosophical genealogy.

The psychopathological and political problem the passage from Mann expresses is directly related to Benjamin's notion that the self-alienation that produces self-annihilation becomes a pleasure intimately connected with the fascist aestheticization of politics. Self-alienation, through commitment to bourgeois order and discipline, leads to self-consumption and its illusory, transcendental after-effects in death. In pragmatic political terms, however, the subject is merely regulating and eradicating pleasure at the same time as s/he submits to the political order that determines such an eradication and regulation. Aschenbach is exemplary of this dynamic, succumbing to the self-alienation symbolically represented by his inability to speak with, much less seduce, Tadzio. His homoerotic awakening is thus played out against the apparent futility of such an awakening, his self-awareness producing a paradoxical self-alienation culminating in death. Thus, bodily pleasures are denied, as is somatic knowledge of the homoerotic, except as a function of disavowal, repression, and Thanatos.[14]

Clifford Hindley's reading of the opera proposes that "whatever the uncertainty about the reality of the Transcendent, or a fulfillment beyond death, [Aschenbach's] experience of beauty in one particular embodiment, even as he dies gazing upon it, cannot be taken away from him" (1992:429). The point, however, is that the experience *is* taken away in death, which annihilates the desire for beauty and perfection, the tropes for the aestheticization of Aschenbach's homoerotic desire, all of which is consistent with a return to bourgeois order. Aestheticization erases desire at the same time as that erasure is troped as transcendentally pleasurable. Eros is manifestly *not* in the word here as much as it is in the erasure of the word and the experiences for which it stands in death. Britten and Piper associate Tadzio's psychagogic function at Aschenbach's death with a movement toward the unattainable beauty that Tadzio represents. The final stage direction in the opera—"At a clear beckon from TADZIO, ASCHENBACH slumps in his chair. TADZIO continues his walk far out to sea"(Piper, 40)—indicates the self-contained, Hermetic[15] aesthetic for which Tadzio literally stands. Idealized as pure object, Platonic form, narcissistic other, Tadzio is the sliding signifier who gives meaning, pleasure, and direction to Aschenbach's death, even as that death eradicates Aschenbach as a conflicted register of homoerotic desire.

A disturbing alignment exists between such a closural structure and what Gottfried Benn describes, in *Weinhaus Wolf* (1937), as the need by the "great minds among the white nations . . . [to undertake] the creative camouflaging of their nihilism" (cited by Walter A. Strauss, 76). Aschenbach's death annihilates desire, substituting thanatological transcendence. The politics of transcendence after Auschwitz are heavily inflected, however, with the failure of transcendence as a signifier associated with death on such a scale. After Auschwitz, transcendent inexpressibility, formerly an expression of meaning in death, achieves a more alienated muteness, a denial that transcendence is *ever* adequate as a thanatological signifier. The historical moment of that shift is crucial for both modernist and postmodernist aesthetics, though Britten's opera engages a profoundly reactionary denial that such a historical shift has taken place in the aesthetics of death.

But this is not to suggest that the opera is void of ideology, even if there is a troubled relation between its imagination of transcendence and the historical context in which it was written. When Slavoj Žižek argues that,

"Fascist ideology is structured as a struggle against the element which holds the place of the immanent impossibility of the very Fascist project" (127), he affirms, however indirectly, the general political structure of Aschenbach's experience. Aschenbach is the site of struggles between passion and reason, chaos and order, homoeroticism and heterosexism, all of which threaten to destructure the bourgeois subject and, by extension, the bourgeois state. Homoerotic desire signifies the very "impossibility" immanent to the political system that struggles to eradicate it—and Aschenbach's psychomachia describes the (sub)liminal topography, the psychopathology of that struggle.

There is no necessary reason for Aschenbach's submission to Tadzio's unspoken command in the opera. As Žižek notes,

> the ideological power of fascism lies precisely . . . in the fact that it demands obedience and sacrifice for their own sake. For Fascist ideology, the point is not the instrumental value of the sacrifice, it is the very form of sacrifice itself, 'the spirit of sacrifice,' which is the cure against the liberal-decadent disease. It is also clear why Fascism was so terrified by psychoanalysis: psychoanalysis enables us to locate an obscene enjoyment at work in this act of formal sacrifice.    *(82)*

Twice in the novella Aschenbach resists psychoanalysis, thereby producing a structure somewhat analogous to what Žižek describes. First, Aschenbach's *The Abject* is interpreted "as a rebuke to the excess of a psychology-ridden age, embodied in the delineation of the weak and silly fool who manages to lead fate by the nose" (13).[16] Later, Aschenbach rejects "self-analysis. He had no taste for it; his self-esteem, the attitude of mind proper to his years, his maturity and single-mindedness, disinclined him to look within himself and decide whether it was constraint or puerile sensuality that had prevented him from carrying out his project [to speak with Tadzio]" (47–48). Aschenbach's inability to decide between "constraint and puerile sensuality" leads to self-sacrifice while producing the "obscene enjoyment" of denial. Denial at once prolongs the pleasure of his extended cruise and the attendant scopophilia that Aschenbach experiences even as his homoerotic desires move ineluctably toward somatic repression.

The sacrifice of Aschenbach at the altar of Beauty and Form, his containment of the desires that will proclaim him as the "liberal-decadent" threatening fascist purity, transparency, and homogeneity by virtue of his sexual difference, all structure the political dimensions of the narrative. Thus Aschenbach's death may be read as a signifier for his subjection to the Beautiful, that is, his subjection to a principle that aestheticizes the politics of subjection that lead to his death. The resonances of this reading with the Platonic dimensions of both the novella and the opera are not at all far-fetched. Socrates states, in an extended passage from the *Phaedrus*, that "Everyone chooses the object of his affections according to his character, and this he makes his god, and fashions and adorns as a sort of image which he is *to fall down and wor-*

*ship*" (71<sup>d</sup>; my emphasis). The rhetoric of submission at work in the passage has political valences that pervade the novella's discursive structures. For example, just prior to Aschenbach's death, Jaschiu, Tadzio's friend, forces him to submit physically "pressing Tadzio's face into the sand—for so long a time that it seemed that the exhausted lad might even suffocate" (74). The moment symbolizes the symmetry between Tadzio's physical subjection and Aschenbach's metaphysical subjection in death. Tadzio is very much in the world, whereas Aschenbach has already moved beyond. This seemingly inconsequential narrative gesture heightens the heroic pathos of Aschenbach's death while engaging the reader's or viewer's submission to the narrative logic of passional transcendence in the face of Beauty. But even as the novella articulates Aschenbach's submission to a passion he will be denied, Mann argues for the criminal nature of passion as a blow against the repressive forces of bourgeois order: "Passion is like crime: it does not thrive on the established order and the common round; it welcomes every blow dealt the bourgeois structure, every weakening of the social fabric, because therein it feels a sure hope of its own advantage" (53–54).

Mann precisely locates the sociopolitical field of homoerotic passion as at once liberating from the "established order" but criminal, whereas Piper and Britten sidestep the political dimensions of such an observation. Instead, the libretto focuses on confrontations between the mythic forces of Apollo and Dionysus and the Neoplatonizing drive toward transcendence as idealized signifiers for the erotic conflict of which Aschenbach is a register. The demonstrable exposition of a disruptive and "criminal" erotics in the novella is overwritten in the opera's verbal structures as a transcendental confrontation with the universalizing, ahistorical, mythic, and binarily opposed forces of reason and passion, order and chaos, that culminates in surrender to the gods.

DIONYSUS Do not refuse the mysteries.
APOLLO No! Love reason, beauty, form. . . .

ASCHENBACH O the taste of knowledge.
Let the gods do what they will with me. (Piper, 34–35)

Such an overwriting is also political, subjection ("Let the gods do what they will with me") being as potent a signifier as liberation. Crucial lines from the libretto forcefully depict how this dynamic operates:

ASCHENBACH When thought becomes feeling, feeling thought . . .
When the mind bows low before beauty . . .
When nature perceives the ecstatic moment . . .
When genius leaves contemplation for one moment of reality . . .
Then Eros is in the word.

Aschenbach's insight into the breakdown of the dissociation of sensibility for which he is striving—his submission to beauty, nature, and ecstasy—

transforms the somatic dimensions of his desire into the verbal and intellectual experience of Eros. The potent fantasy of the unifying power and aesthetics of a submission ("the mind bows low") that produces the eroticized word, transcendentalizes Aschenbach's passions. By retroping the somatic and political dimensions of passion as submission to the aesthetics of the word, the libretto unifies the split between the signifier of Eros and its signified. But inevitably, Eros is twinned with Thanatos and submission to the erotics of the word culminates in the submission to death, eroticized as the ultimate ecstatic union.

The political dimensions of such a rhetorical gesture in a postfascist context cannot be ignored. Indeed, the structure of Aschenbach's experience is comparable to a form of fascist aesthetics described by Susan Sontag: "Fascist aesthetics . . . flow from (and justify) a preoccupation with situations of control, submissive behavior, extravagant effort, and the endurance of pain; they endorse two seemingly opposite states, egomania and servitude. . . . Its choreography alternates between ceaseless motion and a congealed, static, 'virile' posing. Fascist art glorifies surrender, it exalts mindlessness, it glamorizes death" (91). Sontag's notion that "The fascist ideal is to transform sexual energy into a 'spiritual' force, for the benefit of the community . . . the most admirable response being a heroic repression of the sexual impulse" (93) is especially relevant to the politics of *Death in Venice*.[17] Aschenbach emblematizes the heroic harmonization of his disruption of the social field, the novella stating how a "respectful world" (75) takes note of his death. The opera represents death as a Phaedric, mystic ascension that quite literally harmonizes Aschenbach's relations to the community, signified by the chorus with whom he sings the last words of the opera. Insofar as Aschenbach participates in the discursive field of such a sublimated and conflicted political rhetoric, the opera and the novella stage the structures of such a rhetoric and its repression as well as the consequences of its application to homoerotic love. Even if one accepts the nonsomatic and transcendental as experientially possible and, moreover, desirable, the end results of the movement toward passion in both works are containment, repression, and death.

Recent critical appraisals of the opera, like Clifford Hindley's articulation of the nonphysical nature of Platonic love, consistently fail to address the political implications of such a rhetoric: "in its highest manifestation such love of beauty stops short of physical love-making, expressing itself rather in a communion of contemplation with the beloved and the begetting of 'spiritual children' such as wisdom and virtue" (1992:408). One must ask not only what "wisdom and virtue" Aschenbach has attained at the end of his journey, but more importantly, who determines the normative structures upon which such "wisdom and virtue" are based. Furthermore, the submission to Platonic transcendence, so frequently and arbitrarily read as a positive self-negation, is also a submission to values associated with oppression, homophobia, and the fascist predisposition to use death as an ordering principle from which emerges the purity of the political subject who has been subjected, then annihilated. Even the opera's musical structures, as Roger Hillman suggests, demonstrate how Aschenbach "is progressively being inscribed, or in-toned, by those around him" (304–305), the music thus reproducing the struggle between the individual and those who would "in-tone" or harmonize that individual.

Such a harmonization always has its extra-musical dimensions, especially in the charged political and gender contexts of *Death in Venice*'s narrative. The degree to which the musicopoetic structures of the opera participate in the harmonization of Aschenbach with Beauty and Form, and in the aestheticization of his death cannot be discounted, however disturbing the implications. On the one hand, the novella clearly frames the trajectory of Aschenbach's experiences within a social context: it begins on "a spring afternoon in that year of grace 19–, when Europe sat upon the anxious seat beneath a menace that hung over its head for months" (3) and ends with a return to the "social sphere" (Hillman, 309): "And before nightfall a shocked and respectful world received the news of his [Aschenbach's] disease" (75). On the other hand, most such contextual references are removed from the opera, an aesthetic choice that renders the interpretation of the opera more difficult.[18] The political context that Mann uses as a frame for the novella, as suggested earlier, is obscured in the opera's formal, narrative frame: the opening words of the libretto depict Aschenbach's hermetic interiority troped as a form of inexpressibility ("My mind beats on / and no words come" [1]), the final words focusing on Tadzio as a signifier of both the psychagogue and the unattainable other, whose name, repeated by both the chorus and Aschenbach, punningly bids *adieu* to Aschenbach as he dies ("Tadziù!" [40]). Within the context of pre- and postfascist history, the tendency to aestheticize the critical response to both the novella and the opera performs precisely the sort of submission to a critical orthodoxy analogous to the fascist aestheticization of politics, which inevitably demands such a submission.[19] From these interactions emerge pertinent concepts of nation, of gender and sexuality, and of idealism, at whose interstices the subject and "subjectivity" come into being.[20]

The psychopathologies of such a subject are relevant in both Mann's and Britten's work because both scrutinize the subject moving from the semblance of integration to disintegration to annihilation, a general trajectory that marks, however loosely, the narrative of fascist ideology as well, especially in regard to its victims. Such a narrative is *always already* pathological in its attempt to annihilate difference through the myth of transcendent purification. Even when applied to fascist ideology itself (as opposed to its victims) such a narrative fantasizes about the self-destruction of the evil "other" fascism has become in relation to modern politics. Hence when Lacoue-Labarthe suggests that, "it would be better to learn to stop considering fascism a 'pathological' phenomenon (from what extra-social position, asked Freud, might one make such a diagnosis?) and recognize in it not only (at least) one of the age's possible political forms—and one no more aberrant or inadequate than any other—but the political form that is perhaps best able to bring us enlightenment regarding the essence of modern politics" (107), the substitution of pathological fascism for its hypostasis as the enlightening "essence" of modern politics *must* be reconsidered. The very erasure of fascism's differences ("no more aberrant or inadequate than any other" politics) is a gesture of complicity with the pathologies of fascist narratives of purification of difference. In *Death in Venice* the historical contexts that determine the relations between the novella and the opera pose a related problem of whether it is possible in a postfascist age to escape the process of aestheticization by which fascism reproduces itself in the world. Is it possible to avoid the complicities that arise out of aestheticizing politics or politicizing aesthetics? Probably not. The attempt, however, to erase the psychopathological from the profile of fascism in a quest for the "essence" of political modernity, implicit in Lacoue-Labarthe's argument, is akin to the very denials and repressions by which fascism produces its effects in the world. Lacoue-Labarthe's totalitarian leveling of political difference in a hypostatic fascism is thus analogous to the erasure of sexual difference that occurs in *Death in Venice* by way of its containment of Aschenbach's disruptive erotics in transcendental death.

Freud's recognition of the impossibility of extra-social positioning in diagnosing the psychopathologies of fascist practice exposes the complicity of the analyst as the normative principle against which the analysand is judged, as if the myth of extra-social positioning is ever possible or even attainable in making determinations about the psychopathology of the individual or the political form under scrutiny. But this has never stopped psychoanalysts from practicing, nor should it stop cultural critics from examining the psychopathologies of fascist (or any other) political practice. Complicity, and the attraction and revulsion that accompany such complicity, are inevitable in the analysis of psychopathological states: both analyst and analysand are subject to the transferential contingencies and the normative strictures that determine their relations. Mann and Britten present versions of the dynamic between the psychopathological state of the subject and national identity, one mediated by questions of gender and sexuality in which the specific operations of individual desire are retroped at the level of national or state desire.[21] An unavoidable relational dynamic exists between the historical contexts of Mann and Britten, an ineluctable intertextuality with which Britten engaged the moment he decided to use the novella as the topic for his last opera.

## III

The psychopathological states particular to both the novella and the opera are significant in their relation to the political contexts I have described. Here the Freudian distinction between neurosis and psychosis remains useful, the former being "the result of a conflict between the ego and its id, whereas psychosis is the analogous outcome of a similar disturbance in the relations between the ego and the external world" (213). For Freud the psychopathological is part of the discursive field that emerges from the ego's structured relations with an external context. *Death in Venice* may be read (or heard) as an elaboration of such a structure, much being made of the interiority that is performatively staged in the opera's treatment of Aschenbach. Most criticism, however, while acknowledging that interiority structures the novella and the opera, fails to recognize ways in which both the novella and the opera undercut that interiority. Mann's narration of how Aschenbach deliberately baits the Venetian authorities about the extent of the contagion in Venice exemplifies the Freudian notion of psychosis as entailing a conflictual structure between the ego and the "external world": "The very next afternoon the solitary [Aschenbach] took another step in pursuit of his fixed policy of baiting the outer world" (63). The novella, despite its stream-of-consciousness techniques depicting Aschenbach's inner world,[22] also stages the political, national, and topographical "external" contexts associated with Aschenbach. Aschenbach's interiority always has a cultural context. When he dreams, for example, of the "bestial degradation of his fall" (68), a priapic, panic dream that temporarily overthrows his erotic repression, Mann carefully states that the dream overcomes "the profound resistance of his spirit . . . [leaving] *the whole cultural structure of a lifetime trampled on, ravaged, and destroyed*" (67; my emphasis).

Britten, by contrast, uses interiority to construct Aschenbach's "exteriority," not only to the other operatic players, but to the audience to whom the performance is directed. The result of both prose and stage techniques is to invert narrative interiority, thus exposing the psychopathological as a condition of Aschenbach's relations with the external world through which his internalized experience is mediated. Critical positions that essentialize Aschenbach's putative interiority without accounting for this inversion, which literally and figuratively stages the psychopathological dynamic between the external and the internal, risk effacing the degree to which the internal (individual desire) is overwritten by the external (state desire).

Individual desire never has a neutral relation to state desire. The politics of desire cannot be dissociated from the conflictual relations of the ego with the external that Freud terms psychosis. But lest fascism be reduced to a mere psychopathology of ego relations, it is useful to recall Theodor Adorno's argument that fascism is

> *not* a psychological issue and that any attempt to understand its roots and its historical role in psychological terms still remains on the level of ideologies such as the one of "irrational forces" promoted by fascism itself. . . . Psychological dispositions do not actually cause fascism; rather, fascism defines a psychological area which can be successfully exploited by the forces which promote it for entirely nonpsychological reasons of self-interest. *(135)*

The novella and the opera are about the process by which such psycho-pathological "area[s]" are marked off. The extolling of beauty as source of the creative principle, Thanatos as transcendence, the desire for the forbidden other, the homoerotic as the marker of a liminal sexuality that must be effaced, the return to a classical idealism, the Neoplatonic notions of spiritual ascendancy—all define the psychopathological conditions leading to the psychomachia that occults the political dimensions circulating around such a staged interiority.

The way in which the occultation operates in both the novella and the opera is closely tied to the operations of pre- and postfascist discourse, which both appropriate and disavow homoerotic desire as a signifier for the narcissistic desire the state has to consolidate its powers and to determine the desires of its subjects. Fascism, after all, involves potent structures of homosocial practice despite its homophobic repressions. This is in line with Freud's notion that, "The light thrown by psychology on the evolution of our civilization has shown us that it originates mainly at the cost of the sexual component instincts, and that these must be suppressed, restricted, transformed and directed to higher aims, in order that the mental constructions of civilization may be established" (111). The scopophilia—the sexual pleasure derived from the gaze or, as Mann states, "Desire projected . . . visually" (1963:5)—Aschenbach experiences in relation to Tadzio, a scopophilia consistently staged and restaged in the opera,[23] is but one example of such a "component instinct" that the novella and opera depict in relation to the repressions that work against such a pleasure. Both stage the repressive agony and guilt of the scopophiliac. Such a strategy makes explicit the operations and effects of repression thereby offering a critique of the ideological structures that produce repression. But the significant difference between the novella and the opera is that in the former a political and national context is clearly part of the narrative structure of the work, whereas in the latter that belated context is aestheticized as transcendental, Neoplatonic idealism.

Moreover, the ideological contexts of the classical sources used to explain the symbolic dimensions of both the novella and the opera also contribute to the psychopathological relations between the ego and its external world. Familiar binaries—Dionysus/Apollo, passion/reason, homoeroticism/heterosexism, transcendence (death)/body (life)—structure both works. Rarely is attention given to the ideological structures that undergird these binaries, much less to why so many critics avoid (or repress) the political and historical contexts of any of a number of equally pertinent structures. Consider, for example, the pedophilia and the extended homoerotic cruising scenes; the representational politics of the "exotic" other, Tadzio, as a transcendental signifier; the use of thanatological inexpressibility as a referent for political quietism; the notion of the closet as performative within a context of narcissistic repression; the denial of female desire and the association of femininity and effeminacy with death, especially evident in the figure of the strawberry seller who infects Aschenbach with the cholera that kills him; the connections between homoeroticism and homo-phobia[24] characteristic of fascist aesthetics; not to mention the significative import of closural tropes of denial and death. The Foucauldian notion of somatic regulation as a means of constructing desire is demonstrable in both the opera and the novella, which use Aschenbach's increasing frustration with the impossibility of somatic engagement with Tadzio as an inverted emblem of the desire he instantiates. In such a context the final death scene powerfully enacts the prohibitions that are transformed into a transcenden-tal expression in death of desire and its apotheosis. If one accepts Aschen-bach as a symbol of a German national and political, which is to say psy-chohistorical, identity, something the novella makes explicit from its start, then the paroxysms of regulatory behavior he experiences in repressing his desire for Tadzio may well signify a transcendental national longing for the otherness represented in the Polish boy. But such a longing is coincident with an overriding fear that otherness will consume and dedifferentiate the autonomy of the national desiring system. The situation is impossible: pro-hibition produces the illusion of transcendence in death, desire produces dedifferentiation, disavowal (*Verleugnung*), and self-annihilation.

An interplay exists, then, between the closeting of male–male desire in male homosocial high culture and the emergence of a politics of repression among nationalists and fascists in Western Europe through both world wars. The repression of such an interplay in the critical reception of both the novella and the opera is indicative of the symbolic potency of such a closet-ing. Nonetheless, the political and historical dimensions of both the novella and the opera cannot be ignored within a narrative context to which notions of gender, sexuality, and national ideology are crucial, especially in estab-lishing an accurate historical paradigm for understanding the relationship between Mann's and Britten's works. The psychopathologies of fascist aes-thetics, in which desire for the homoeroticized other and desire for narcissis-tic self-definition conflict with the regulatory structures of bourgeois self-discipline, ultimately produce the eradication of the other and the self in such a way as to purify the psychopathologies of such a signifying system.

Britten's work, then, performs two complex and contradictory gestures. On the one hand, it reproduces the very structures from which Aschenbach seeks to escape. Its apparent idealization of repression as a transcendental signifier for a Neoplatonic passion that is out of the body and thereby imbued with the very otherness that valorizes Neoplatonic passion is opposed to other forms of passional involvement. In addition, the opera's use of music as a signifier for the "feminine other that circumvents reason and arouses desire" (McClary, 79), symbolized in the exoticism of the gamelan orchestra-tion used in association with Tadzio[25]; its affirmation of a narrative in which, to use McClary's words, shame and death become the "price for sexual plea-sure" (79); and its dehistoricization of the very historical contexts toward which Mann directs the attention of the reader throughout the novella, all indicate the degree to which Britten's conservatism produces a radical rereading of the novella.[26] Despite the innovative musical and textual structures he created for the opera, Britten reproduces the very psychopathologies that Mann had proleptically described in the novella, but without presenting a revisionary critique of those psychopathologies within the specific postfascist historical context from which the opera emerged. On the other hand, the opera in the apparent absence of such a critique—made evident through musical gestures such as the "virtually unresolved" (Corse, 362) leading tone pedal at the end of Act II, producing a "lack of resolution [which] parallels the lack of resolution in Aschenbach's life" (ibid.), and through small but significant acts of dehistoricization apparent in the libretto—may be read as an inverted critique. The very absence of critique in a postfascist historical context *avoids* the complicity that historicization produces, *if* one decides to read absence as subversive, not complicitous.

A more radical argument could be made—especially within the ambiguous and often contradictory contexts of Britten's well-known pacifist leanings, his Christianity,[27] his homosexuality (especially his "pedophilia"), and his conservatism within the political and aesthetic cultural practices of postwar England—that the opera performs the futility of death as a signifying practice in a postfascist context.[28] It has been suggested that the "duplicity inherent in the key structures [between Aschenbach's tonality of E and Tadzio's tonality of A, at the end of the opera] re-creates the doubleness contained in the sense of irony in the narrative" (Corse, 362).[29] The pedal leading tone of G#, however, *does* resolve to A at the opera's end, just as surely as Aschenbach's transgressive sexuality *is* resolved in death. The ambiguities that have accrued around traditional interpretations of this ending are heavily invested in using death to signify Aschenbach's escape from prohibitory erotic and political structures. But an equally strong case could be made for interpreting his death as a performative closure that purifies the erotic and ideological ambiguities Aschenbach represents. The opera's movement toward tonal harmony thus represents the self-annihilating futility of that very harmony as a signifier for erotic and political quietism.

Ironically, as a measure of Mann's insight, the novella anticipates the opera's overwriting of the political dimensions of its disruptive erotic codes, especially in relation to the way in which the novella depicts the body of the state subject contained by the repressive necessities of state desire.[30] The novella's explicit politics are overwritten by the implicit ideological context of the opera, a poeto-musical intertextuality that is akin, *mutatis mutandis*, to the "Strangely fruitful intercourse . . . between one body and another mind!" (Mann, 47) that occurs as the result of Aschenbach's pursuit of Tadzio on the beach. Ultimately, the disruptive erotics apparent in Aschenbach's pedophilia, cruising scopophilia, and transgressive narcissism[31] are annihilated, whether in a questionable transcendental vision or in a performance of the death that produces erotic quietism. Thus nation and the politics of national identity (Britten/Britain) overwrite the transgressive erotics of male–male desire (Mann/man). The question then remains whether such a gesture articulates the repressive fantasy that underlies fascist aesthetics, critiques it by erasing its very presence from the context of the work, or overtly performs the symbolic effects of the subject's erotic and political quiescence.

*D. Fischlin*

228

NOTES

*Cited in Hamilton (243).

†Taylor (74).

1. The use of the term *postfascism* in this essay is deliberately problematic, both because it assumes a historical belatedness that is spurious and because it subsumes a complex ideological entity into the convenience of a trope. *Postfascism*, in the context of this essay, does not refer in any way to a condition or ideology that has receded into the event-horizon of history; instead it refers to the specific historical conditions subsequent to World War II. I also note that similar problems apply to the term *prefacist*, as if key elements of twentieth-century fascism are not to be found in earlier ideologies or sociocultural circumstances. See Hewitt's comment that the "fascist imaginary in general reformulates the possibility of a historical death" (1995:20–21), which is to say the death of history, an undertaking I argue is implicit in the operatic mutation of Mann's novella.

2. Some recent exceptions include Solie, Said, and Arblaster.

3. See Lyotard's suggestive notion that, "The peculiar importance Nazi politics placed in the mise-en-scène has often been noted. The aesthetics elaborated by postromanticism and Wagner (especially that of the 'total work of art'), in which opera and cinema are privileged as 'complete' arts, is put to the service of despotism, undermining the whole economy of the Schillerian project" (53).

4. Koestenbaum's book addresses questions relating to the use of the female voice in opera. Britten's operas idealize the role of the male voice while marginalizing the female voice so critical to Koestenbaum's project.

5. Heilbut describes Mann as the "poet of a half-open closet" (251). Despite Mann's own closetedness, Heilbut suggests that he clearly "understood homosexuality in political terms. To begin with, Paragraph 175 made it illegal in Germany, as the Eulenburg trial and the consequent ruin of many men had lately demonstrated. This knowledge contributed to the story's authenticity; Aschenbach couldn't pursue Tadzio with such equanimity outside Venice" (251).

6. See Lacoue-Labarthe's related comment that in "the modern political sphere . . . the crucial process [for Germany] was—and probably still is—that of national identification" (80).

7. See Heilbut (258).

8. Heilbut also avers that, "Nationalist rivalries flow through the story" and that, "The opening conveys a sense of imperial decline" (251). Heinrich Mann, Thomas's brother, wrote a 1913 review of the novella in which he, too, affirms that, "Aschenbach had become identified with the institution of the state" (Heilbut, 267), as evidenced in his recent knighthood. A similar, perhaps ironic, point may be made about Britten, who was institutionally aligned with the British state through, among other things, his being awarded the Order of Merit in 1965 and a peerage in 1976.

9. Aschenbach's fixation on the Polish boy, Tadzio, supposedly based on an encounter with the young Polish count, Wladyslaw Moes, has uncanny parallels to the initial events of World War II relating to the German invasion of Poland. By

contrast, Edward Timms discusses the novella as a psychohistory in the context of the World War I, arguing that it was "a story saturated with the atmosphere of a historical moment" and that it may be read "in terms of the psychohistory of Europe on the eve of World War I" (134). For more on Mann's political context, see Mayer's problematic essay.

10. See Cerf (135) and Carnegy (172).

11. See Sedgwick on the relations between German unification and the formation of homosexual emancipation groups after the proclamation of the Second Reich in 1871 (1990:132–33).

12. Mosse comments that, "The so-called fascist style demanded a strictness of form which did not allow for ambiguities or vague definitions. . . . As a movement struggling for power, fascism contained a dynamic directed against the existing order of things: it wanted to destroy bourgeois society and to preserve it at one and the same time" (153). Mosse also argues that fascism presents itself as a "community of men" (154), such a community obviously eliding the problem of sexual difference (both within and without itself) through the conversion of the homosocial into the homophobic.

13. For more on Mann's association with bourgeois culture see Lukács (25). See also Palmer's description of the "warmth of [Mann's] response to a seventieth birthday article by George Lukács which described *Death in Venice* as 'signalling the danger of a barbarous underworld existing within modern German civilization as its necessary complement'" (265).

14. This is a familiar pattern in nationalist and fascist ideology. See, for example, Hewitt's discussion of Filippo Tommaso Marinetti's *Futurismo e facismo* (1924) (1992:49).

15. Tadzio is a symbolic representation of Hermes, but also, as Hindley notes, of Apollo and Dionysus (1992:428).

16. For further discussions of abjection in relation to homoerotic desire see Edelman (276–79) and Dyer (88).

17. Nancy describes fascism as the "grotesque or abject resurgence of an obsession with communion; it [fascism] crystallized the motif of its supposed loss and the nostalgia for its images of fusion" (17). The point is that fascism aestheticizes political structures and desiring systems, articulating a double movement: on the one hand, the "obsession with communion" and "images of fusion" and, on the other, a fascination with the death and disintegration that offer, paradoxically, both communion and its dissolution.

18. This is especially so if one accepts that the opera dialogically restructures responses to the novella, as Law argues (424).

19. Sedgwick establishes significant relations among fascism, homosexuality, sentimentality, and scapegoating in *Epistemology of the Closet* (especially 154–55). In this last regard I have no desire to scapegoat either Mann or Britten, only to address issues that arise from the unarticulated political structures that are at work in both the novella's and the opera's relations to historical context. Neither Britten nor Mann can be held, anachronistically, to the standards of ethical and political "correctness" that 1990s academic discourse may have come to expect, or demand, of its subjects.

20. See Carroll's comment that "The 'nation' doesn't really even exist fully until nationalist 'aesthetic' operations manifest its unity and realize its integrity" (710).

21. Mann (in an interview given in 1925 in Milan) directly associated *Death in Venice* with Freud, not to mention a certain skepticism about the degree to which

the analyst could penetrate the "secret of his [the artist's] creative act" (see Berlin, 111, 113).

22. For more on this, see Cerf (126). I argue that the staging of narcissistic self-reflection, the public display of interiority, is in a sense analogous to the Freudian definition of psychosis as a disturbance in the relations between the ego and the external world. The operatic context reproduces the psychopathological context of that disturbance publicly.

23. See Scenes 4, 5, 6, 7, 9, 10, 16, and 17. Heilbut avers that, "When Aschenbach wordlessly contemplates Tadzio, his action is the apotheosis of the gaze, of Mann's obsession with seeing and being seen" (250). Also, see Sontag's comments on Jean Genet's notion that "Fascism is theater" (cited by Sontag, 103), especially regarding Genet's description in *Funeral Rites* of "the erotic allure fascism exercised on someone who was not a fascist" (103). Mann experienced a similar allure, Heilbut suggesting that "the Fascist love of spectacle and its cadre of gleaming warriors appealed to elements in [Mann's] personality he had grown to mistrust" (496).

24. For pertinent comments on the uses and abuses of this term, see Sedgwick (1985:219, *n.* 1).

25. Martin suggests that, "The sexual geography of *Death in Venice* will be familiar to readers of *Tonio Kröger*: the journey south and, implicitly, east, is a journey to the feminine and the repressed" (1992:63). McClary describes the use of the intervallic third as a historical signifier for femininity (see 11–12 and 77 for examples). Palmer, among others, has described the use of the third as an intervallic structure in *Death in Venice* signifying "the elements" (258). Carnegy discusses the importance of the third in relation to the "'fate' motive [which] permeates Aschenbach's soliloquies, and is later associated with the plague" (173), as well as discussing the major/minor third as the "principal musical cell which permeates the whole opera" (172). The Corses also discuss the role of the third (see especially 348, 352, 359, 362).

26. See Martin (1986) for more on this as well as Mitchell's description of Auden's influence on Britten's aesthetic (22).

27. The "operatic version of *Billy Budd* is depoliticized and de-eroticized," according to Martin, and, "In its place we have a Christianized Greek tragedy" (1983:51). Martin further avers that the operatic version of *Billy Budd* ends "in a reconciliation and an achievement of spiritual transcendence that its original clearly lacks" (55), that Britten saw erotic energy "as a threat to the creative power of social harmony" (56), and that Britten "was moving toward the dramatic monologue and dream-vision that would eventually take shape in *Death in Venice*" (55). It is no small irony that the "last piece [Mann] wrote" was a "tribute to *Billy Budd* [that] ends with ecstatic praise of the sailor's ascension to the gallows, above him a rising sun, below the crew members 'who all love their Billy'" (Heilbut, 265).

28. On Britten's supposed pedophilia, see Mitchell's comment that "*Death in Venice* embodies unequivocally the powerful sexual drive that was Britten's towards the young (and sometimes very young) male" (21). See also Carpenter (340–56, 534–37).

29. For more on the tonal ambiguities of the opera, particularly in relation to Aschenbach's tonal center of E, despite the seemingly contradictory use of serial techniques used in the opening notes he sings, see Corse (348–49).

30. Mosse affirms that fascism treats "the body as a symbolic form transcending sexuality, exemplifying nature and the nation" (153–54). In light of such an

observation, the political dimensions subsumed in Carpenter's reading of Aschenbach's death as a "return at the end to the natural world" (554) are particularly disquieting.

31. This narcissism is symbolized in the makeover by the hotel barber that Aschenbach undergoes, thus restoring to him the illusion of youth that will make him more attractive to Tadzio; see Mann (69–70) and Britten (Act 15). Also, note Mann's association, in the Phaedric interlude, of the poet with Eros and effeminacy: "yet are we [poets] all like women, for we exult in passion, and love is still our desire—our craving and our shame" (72).

WORKS CITED

Adorno, Theodor W. "Freudian Theory and the Pattern of Fascist Propaganda." *The Essential Frankfurt School Reader*, eds. Andrew Arato and Eike Gebhardt. New York: Continuum, 1993:118–37.

Arblaster, Anthony. *Viva la Libertà! Politics in Opera*. London: Verso, 1992.

Benjamin, Walter. "The Work of Art in the Age of Mechanical Reproduction." In *Illuminations*, ed. Hannah Arendt; trans. Harry Zohn. New York: Schocken, 1969:217–52.

Berlin, Jeffrey B. "Psychoanalysis, Freud, and Thomas Mann." In *Approaches to Teaching Mann's* Death in Venice *and Other Short Fiction*, ed. Jeffrey B. Berlin. New York: Modern Language Association, 1992:105–18.

Brett, Philip. "Britten's Dream." *Musicology and Difference: Gender and Sexuality in Music Scholarship*, ed. Ruth A. Solie. Berkeley: University of California Press, 1993:259–80.

Carnegy, Patrick. "The Novella Transformed: Thomas Mann as Opera." In *Benjamin Britten: Death in Venice*, ed. Donald Mitchell. Cambridge: Cambridge University Press, 1987:168–77.

Carpenter, Humphrey. *Benjamin Britten: A Biography*. New York: Charles Scribner's Sons, 1992.

Carroll, David. "Literary Fascism or the Aestheticizing of Politics: The Case of Robert Brasillach." *New Literary History* 23 (1992): 691–726.

Cerf, Steven R. "Benjamin Britten's *Death in Venice*: Operatic Stream of Consciousness." In *Bucknell Review* 31 (1988): 124–38.

Conrad, Peter. *A Song of Love and Death*. New York: Poseidon Press, 1987.

Corse, Sandra and Larry. "Britten's *Death in Venice:* Literary and Musical Structures." In *The Musical Quarterly* 73, no. 3 (1989): 344–63.

Dyer, Richard. "Coming Out as Going In: The Image of the Homosexual as a Sad Young Man." In *The Matter of Images*. New York: Routledge, 1993:73–92.

Edelman, Lee. "Tearooms and Sympathy, or, The Epistemology of the Water Closet." In *Nationalisms and Sexualities*, eds. Andrew Parker, Mary Russo, Doris Summer, and Patricia Yaeger. New York: Routledge, 1992:263–84.

Freud, Sigmund. *On Psychopathology: Inhibitions, Symptoms and Anxiety and Other Works*, ed. Angela Richards. London: Penguin, 1993.

Giobbi, Giuliana. "Gabriele D'Annunzio and Thomas Mann: Venice, Art and Death." *Journal of European Studies* 19 (March 1989): 55–68.

Hamilton, Nigel. *The Brothers Mann*. New Haven: Yale University Press, 1978.

Heilbut, Anthony. *Thomas Mann: Eros and Literature*. New York: Alfred A. Knopf, 1996.

Hewitt, Andrew. "Coitus Interruptus: Fascism and the Deaths of History." *Postmodern Apocalypse: Theory and Cultural Practice at the End*, ed. Richard Dellamora. Philadelphia: University of Pennsylvania Press, 1995:17–40.

———. "Fascist Modernism, Futurism, and 'Post-modernity.'" In *Fascism, Aesthetics, and Culture*, ed. Richard J. Golsan. Hanover, N.H.: University Press of New England, 1992:38–55.

Hillman, Roger. "Deaths in Venice." *Journal of European Studies* 22 (December 1992): 291–311.

Hindley, Christopher. "Contemplation and Reality: A Study in Britten's 'Death in Venice.'" *Music and Letters* 71 (November 1990): 511–23.

———. "Platonic Elements in Britten's 'Death in Venice.'" *Music and Letters* 73 (August 1992): 407–29.

Koestenbaum, Wayne. *The Queen's Throat: Opera, Homosexuality, and the Mystery of Desire*. New York: Poseidon Press, 1993.

Lacoue-Labarthe, Philippe. *Heidegger, Art and Politics: The Fiction of the Political*, trans. Chris Turner. Cambridge: Cambridge University Press, 1990.

Law, Joe K. "The Dialogics of Operatic Adaptation." *Yearbook of Interdisciplinary Studies in the Fine Arts* 1 (1989): 407–27.

Lukács, Georg. "In Search of Bourgeois Man." In *Critical Essays on Thomas Mann*, ed. Inta M. Ezergailis. Boston: G. K. Hall, 1988:24–47.

Lyotard, Jean-François. *The Postmodern Explained: Correspondence 1982–1985*, trans. Don Barry et al. Minneapolis: University of Minnesota Press, 1992.

Mann, Thomas. "Death in Venice." Death in Venice *and Seven Other Stories by Thomas Mann*, trans. H. T. Lowe-Porter. New York: Vintage, 1963:3–75.

———. *Diaries 1918–1939*, ed. Hermann Kesten; trans. Richard and Clara Winston. New York: Harry N. Abrams, 1982.

———. *Mythology and Humanism: The Correspondence of Thomas Mann and Karl Kerényi*, trans. Alexander Gelley. Ithaca: Cornell University Press, 1975.

Martin, Robert K. "Gender, Sexuality, and Identity in Mann's Short Fiction." In *Approaches to Teaching Mann's* Death in Venice *and Other Short Fiction*, ed. Jeffrey B. Berlin. New York: Modern Language Association, 1992:57–67.

———. "Saving Captain Vere: *Billy Budd* from Melville's Novella to Britten's Opera." *Studies in Short Fiction* 23, no. 1 (Winter 1986): 49–56.

Mayer, Hans. "On the Political Development of an Unpolitical Man." *Critical Essays on Thomas Mann*, ed. Inta M. Ezergailis. Boston: G. K. Hall, 1988:191–205.

McClary, Susan. *Feminine Endings: Music, Gender, and Sexuality*. Minneapolis: University of Minnesota Press, 1991.

Mitchell, Donald. "An Introduction in the Shape of a Memoir." In *Benjamin Britten: Death in Venice*, ed. Donald Mitchell. Cambridge: Cambridge University Press, 1987:1–25.

Morey, Carl. "Harry and the Magician." *Opera Canada* 33 (Spring 1992): 14–17, 30.

Mosse, George L. *Nationalism and Sexuality: Middle-Class Morality and Sexual Norms in Modern Europe*. Madison: University of Wisconsin Press, 1985.

Nancy, Jean-Luc. *The Inoperative Community*, ed. Peter Connor. Minneapolis: University of Minnesota Press, 1991.

Palmer, Christopher. "Towards a Genealogy of *Death in Venice*." In *The Britten Companion*, ed. Christopher Palmer. Cambridge: Cambridge University Press, 1984.

Piper, Myfanwy. *Death in Venice: An Opera in Two Acts*. London: Faber Music, 1973.

Plato. *On Homosexuality:* Lysis, Phaedrus, *and* Symposium, trans. Benjamin Jowett. Selected retranslation Eugene O'Connor. Buffalo, N.Y.: Prometheus Books, 1991.

Said, Edward W. "The Empire at Work: Verdi's *Aida*." In *Culture and Imperialism*. New York: Vintage, 1994:111–31.

Sedgwick, Eve Kosofsky. *Between Men: English Literature and Male Homosocial Desire*. New York: Columbia University Press, 1985.

——. *Epistemology of the Closet*. Berkeley: University of California Press, 1990.

Solie, Ruth A, ed. *Musicology and Difference: Gender and Sexuality in Music Scholarship*. Berkeley: University of California Press, 1993.

Sontag, Susan. "Fascinating Fascism." In *Under the Sign of Saturn*. New York: Farrar, Strauss & Giroux, 1980:73–105.

Strauss, Walter A. "Gottfried Benn: A Double Life in Uninhabitable Regions." In *Fascism, Aesthetics, and Culture*, ed. Richard J. Golsan. Hanover, N.H.: University Press of New England, 1992:67–80.

Taylor, Mark C. *Nots*. Chicago: University of Chicago Press, 1993.

Timms, Edward. "*Death in Venice* as Psychohistory." In *Approaches to Teaching Mann's* Death in Venice *and Other Short Fiction*, ed. Jeffrey B. Berlin. New York: Modern Language Association, 1992:134–39.

Žižek, Slavoj. *The Sublime Object of Ideology*. London: Verso, 1989.

## CHAPTER TEN

*Imagined Communities: Postnational Canadian Opera*

Linda Hutcheon and Michael Hutcheon

Benedict Anderson has provocatively argued that nationhood is a matter of "imagined community" and that this sense of collective identity is something that, in Europe most obviously, was conceived in the last century and born largely of the printed word and novelistic narrative.[1] But nationhood often has a darker side: the emotional but public aspect of communal identification that we call nationalism. And when it comes to documenting the art forms that historically did the most to create this affective sense of belonging and, indeed, to rally people around a national cause, not only the novel but also drama (Lindenberger, 1984:257) and especially music must be considered. The importance of music is likely related to its power to *evoke* and *provoke*—and not simply *represent*—nationalist feeling. Although many may still think of music as an apolitical art, a political scientist has recently argued that there is no other ideological force or creed that has had a more "profound and lasting impact on music in the past two centuries than nationalism" (Arblaster, 64). But, as just suggested, the same was also true in reverse.

To cut a very long story very short: in nineteenth-century Europe, music often became the locus of the search for the authentic voice of a people. The desire for a national musical idiom made music inseparable from politics in general, and patriotism and nationalism in particular.[2] Operatic narratives—perhaps because they are both oral and performative—came to play especially important roles in articulating national identity, often through their structural connections to the oral epic and communal narratives (Lindenberger, 1984:262). One theory even has it that opera houses became the covert site of political activity in countries where political expression was forbidden in the arts. So the incredible flourishing of Italian opera in the nineteenth century can be explained by its allegorical engagement with suppressed national politics.[3]

In fact, the unofficial national anthem of Italy, since the nineteenth-century drive for Italian unification, has been "Va pensiero," the oppressed Israelites' chorus from Verdi's opera *Nabucco*. Such operatic choruses are highly suggestive in their ability to represent aurally the "collective voice of a people, a nation, a community" (Arblaster, 99). The "masses" sing, and sing powerfully. However, in nationalist narratives about Canada the masses do not sing at all in the same way as when they are expressing displaced Italian patriotism. Instead they are terrifying. Equally frightening is the solo voice of the political leader as nationalistic demagogue. Here we change centuries—from the nineteenth to the twentieth; we change continents—from the Old World to the New. Nationalism and narratives of national identity are still at the core of the Canadian operas we will address—but the manner and the politics could not be more different from what we have just described as the European scene. As a bilingual, multicultural New World nation caught in the emotional and ideological double bind of being tied historically to Europe and economically to the United States, Canada is bound to figure these debates differently.

Our shift to a period after two world wars (in which nationalism played an important and devastating role) is obviously important, but so is the shift from Old to New World. The historical moment of the rise of nationalism in Europe coincided—not accidentally, of course—with the moment of European imperialism. In opera as in other art forms, Europe defined itself against its non-European other. In the eighteenth century that other was the Islamic Orient—close enough geographically to be threatening and alien enough culturally to be made exotic in terms of sexuality and violence.[4] By the nineteenth century the other could be from places as diverse but exotic as Scotland, South America, or Japan.[5]

Here is one critic's wry description of the paradigmatic plot of this kind of operatic "othering":

> Young, tolerant, brave, possibly naive, white European tenor-hero intrudes, at risk of disloyalty to his own people and colonialist ethic, into mysterious, dark-skinned, colonized territory represented by alluring dancing girls and deeply affectionate, sensitive lyric soprano, incurring wrath of brutal, intransigent tribal chieftain (bass or bass-baritone) and blindly obedient chorus of male savages. *(Locke, 263)*

Whether the opera be Verdi's *Aida* or Meyerbeer's *L'Africaine*, and be it displaced to ancient Egypt or involve fifteenth-century Portuguese imperial profiteering (Conrad, 131), the colonizing mission's orientalized[6] figuration of the other did indeed get articulated in those nineteenth-century operatic narratives of European national identity.[7] As Edward Said has argued, "[t]he power to narrate, or to block other narratives from forming and emerging, is very important to culture and imperialism, and constitutes one of the main connections between them" (1993:xiii). And musical narrative—opera, in particular—is part of the "legacy of the imperializing processes" (Said, 1991:53) of stereotyping and essentializing.

When opera crossed the Atlantic to Canada—and it did (see Willis; Kallmann; Potvin; Jones)—the link between opera (as a European art form) and the narratives of both nation and Empire was inevitably going to be configured a bit differently. Over the years there have indeed been Canadian operas on Canadian themes—often commissioned by the Canadian Broadcasting Corporation and Radio Canada. But it took the Centennial year of 1967 (and the government money made available for commissions) to see a veritable explosion of Canadian operas,[8] including the work that is the focus of the first part of our discussion—Harry Somers/Mavor Moore's *Louis Riel*.

To set the postcolonial Canadian context, we should point out that in 1967 Canada celebrated the centenary of its official founding moment of nationhood.[9] It was a moment of high English–Canadian nationalism. Given that double bind mentioned earlier, for some this was translated into relief at the diminishing weight of the British heritage, especially in cultural terms; for others Canadian nationalism meant a rejection of the increasing Americanization of Canada's economy and culture. As a result of this new self-consciousness, the years that followed were to see the first real valorization of (and serious attention given to) Canadian culture as a separate entity. Of course, some cynics would still argue that in some ways Canadians have not yet recovered from their colonial complex: they still look elsewhere for validation, but now they may look southward instead of across the Atlantic.[10]

That, very briefly, is the *postcolonial* frame. But the term used in our title is *postnational*. Here we invoke the title of Frank Davey's recent book, *Postnational Arguments*, where the word is used to describe the state of Canadian culture in the last twenty-five years since that 1967 Centenary. While acknowledging that, in Canada, narrative has been intimately tied to nationalism, Davey argues that, in the contemporary world of economic and political globalization, Canada, unlike other parts of the the world, shows little sign of any revitalized nationalist impulses. Indeed, English Canadian fictional narratives show, if anything, a decided *lack* of nationalist discourses, "unless ironically deployed" (258). He goes even further and argues that, since 1967, English–Canadian fiction has shown such a distrust of the political, the social, and the national that this thing called Canada has been linked to "treachery, betrayal, and actual or symbolic violence" (255). English Canada's narrative of identity, he implies, is not only diverse, but "deeply fractured" (5), a matter of "continued debate and irresolution" (8). But, of course, any sense of an English–Canadian communal identity (fractured or whole) would have to be considered alongside at least two other very real nationalisms today within that one nation: those of Québec[11] and of the aboriginal peoples.[12]

*L. Hutcheon*

*and*

*M. Hutcheon*

What all these nationalisms share, though, is the fact that they are social constructs, most recently rooted in the late 1960s. However, they all construct national narratives in very different ways, be it in fiction or in opera.[13] It is arguably true that, because of social and cultural change, opera does not have the same role in both representing and provoking nationalism in modern Canada that it might have had in nineteenth-century Europe. Nevertheless, it is striking that two important operas, both written by Canadian composer Harry Somers, should present such a startling critique of nationalism and its dangers and that they should do so in the particular years in which they were written: the date of the first opera, *Louis Riel*, is 1967—the year of Canada's hundredth anniversary; the date of the other opera, *Mario and the Magician*, is 1992—the year of the ill-fated National Referendum that attempted (and failed) to get a consensus on the definition of Canada as a nation as articulated in what was called the "Canada Clause" in the Constitutional Accord.

Unlike either the French or English versions of the Canadian national anthem, "O Canada," the "Canada Clause" did try to deal with "otherhood issues." In one critic's words, the clause "repopulated the country with aboriginal peoples and immigrants, it identified that Canada's 'sons' [in whom 'true patriot love' is 'commanded' in the English rendition of the national anthem] came in two sexes, whose equality was in need of attention, and it recognized both individuals and collectivities as central actors" (Jenson, 6–7). Yet not even that narrative was one a majority of Canadians could agree upon. So perhaps it was not only the *fiction* written in the 25 years between 1967 and 1992 that has denied what Davey calls any tendency to "construct the national text as unitary and thus devoid of political contestation and debate" (17). Certainly these two operas composed by Somers— and performed in 1967 and 1992—reflect a deep suspicion of unitary national narratives of identity and an even deeper distrust of the emotional power of nationalism.

Mavor Moore's libretto of the 1967 opera of *Louis Riel* was loosely derived from John Coulter's somewhat earlier play, simply called *Riel*. This is a play that has been called an important contributing factor to the growth of Canadian nationalism in the 1960s (Anthony, 62). The way this argument goes, Canadians lacked and so sought a "leader of heroic proportions" and found in the nineteenth-century Métis leader Riel, "an heroic statesman, a victimized leader, the Father of Manitoba, and the symbol of those Indian, French, and English elements that constitute Canada's heritage" (Anthony, 62). If you knew anything about Riel at all (and we realize that some readers of this essay won't . . . yet), Margaret Atwood's famous theory (in her book *Survival*) about the Canadian tendency to identify with the victims in any narrative would ring true. For just about anyone else, Riel—who was hanged as a traitor to Canada in 1885 and whose death reawoke hostilities between Ontario and Québec, Orangemen and Catholics, English and French—might seem to be a strange "leader of heroic proportions." Yet this choice was called by one critic "appropriate" for a centennial opera because its protagonist was a "potent symbol of various divisive forces which have shaped Canada" (Cherney, 129). We doubt that we are alone in finding the foregrounding of a fractious history of linguistic, regional, racial, ethnic, religious, and political difference a bizarre way—in most conventional terms—to celebrate publicly a century of national collective identity.

But it may be appropriate after all. As Canadian composer R. Murray Schafer put it, using an apt musical metaphor: Riel may personify the "dissonance at the root of the Canadian temperament."[14] The opera named after Louis Riel enacts that dissonance and those differences openly in its plot— the story of the two rebellions, the one in Red River in 1869 and the other in Saskatchewan in 1885, that ended with the defeat of Riel at Batoche. But it also enacts the nation's diversity in more structural terms. The libretto is written not only in English and French,[15] but also in Cree. There is even "a little Latin and less Greek" in the church and prayer scenes. Add to this the fact that the kinds of voice production used vary from speech through to a *parlando* or inflected "sung speech," to full singing. The music is diverse as well. The dialogue of the political scenes in Ottawa is accompanied by a kind of banal dance music, as if to underline the manipulative political dance under way. This contrasts sharply with the highly lyrical and melismatic arias of the visionary poet and leader Riel.

The opera's musical stylistic diversity is, in fact, equally marked, with four major types of music being superimposed one upon the other.[16] The core is what Somers himself (in Graham, 4) calls "abstract, atonal" orchestral music, and it is used, with its strong dissonances, for both dramatic intensity and as a kind of "platform" for the singing.[17] Against this is heard original folk music,[18] whose motives weave in and out of the entire opera. Some of these are aboriginal: for example, Riel's Métis wife sings a lullaby in Cree, "Kuyas," which is from the "Song of Skateen," a Wolfhead chief of a Nass River tribe.[19] Others are white folk songs, both French ("Est-il rien sur la terre?" and "Le Roi malheureux") and English. The chilling repetition of the song "We'll Hang Him Up the River" is from Coulter's play and was evidently a memory of the playwright's Ulster childhood.

The third type of "music" is better described as electronically produced "sounds" used to interesting effect in Riel's final trial both to jolt the listener and to give us a feeling of the kind of confusion and surreal distortion of justice and sense felt by the defendant. But Somers also uses straight, tuneful diatonic music. This is the most accessible and conventional music in the opera and—as in *Mario and the Magician* 25 years later—this is the music associated with and meant to arouse mass patriotism in the audience on the stage—if not in the theater. But if our own experience is any indication, that theater audience—rather relieved to hear melodic music—ends up being implicated by this very reaction in the politics represented on stage. Such (involuntary but noticeable) complicity is thought-provoking, for this is not Verdi's "Va pensiero" chorus "spontaneously" voicing the yearnings of a people for a liberated nation; in *Louis Riel*, it is an excited mob that has been urged to start what the libretto calls "another holy crusade / to rescue yet another land from savages" (Somers and Moore, 24). This is a mob of Ontario Protestants joining together to sing "Canada First; Canada is British. Oh Or'ngemen unite!"[20] In the musical difference between Verdi's Israelite chorus and Somers's Canadian mob lies, perhaps, the separation of Empire and colony, of the national and the postnational.

If Riel were an appropriate hero for an opera about Canada, it would be because his is a narrative in which imagined communities are formed, legally acknowledged, and then destroyed—and destroyed by the force of other national narratives; it is a story of defeat and exclusion, of enforced exile and execution for treason. The opera is not, for example, the story of his friend Gabriel Dumont—the buffalo hunter, sharpshooter, daring and shrewd fighter. Nor is it the collective story of the Métis people. Instead it is the individualized story of one Louis Riel, the self-styled religious "prophet of the New World," charismatic deliverer of his people—and, to some, dangerous traitor to the new nation called Canada.[21]

Having spent ten years, from the ages of 14 to 24, at the Collège de Montréal, Riel returned to the west educated and eloquent—in both English and French. The time: just a few years after Ontario and Québec had united with the maritime provinces to form that new nation called Canada. The place: the Red River area in what is now west central Canada and was then part of the Hudson's Bay Company's holdings that were in the process of being handed over to the new nation of Canada (to be opened up for Anglo-Protestant Ontario settlers). This was being done without consulting the set-tlers already on the land—who included the British, French, Irish, Métis (that is, those born, usually, of Indian women and French-speaking men)—not to mention, of course, the indigenous peoples. The government in Ottawa sent out survey crews to mark off the land even before the transfer was made legal; the company, now a lame-duck administration, collapsed; the enraged Red River settlers set up their own provisional government, owing allegiance to the British queen, not to Canada. This was according to the Law of Nations, an entirely legal act, in the absence of other effective government. Nevertheless the Canadian prime minister, Sir John A. Macdonald, sent out a governor—the anti-French, anti-Catholic McDougall, and that's where the opera opens, with the governor referring to the "damn half-breeds" he will teach to "be civilized" (2).

From the very first scene, Canada is the villain of the piece: the Métis repeatedly cry, "A bas le Canada d'Ottawa!" Riel, as leader of his people, wants to fight for what he calls their "British rights." Bishop Taché, the go-between, as the libretto puts it *entre les métis de l'Ouest/et les obstinés* d'Ottawa (13) ("between the Métis of the West and the obstinate ones in Ottawa"), tries to explain this position and its history to Macdonald:

> Before there was a Canada,
> the peoples of the West were free . . .
>
> their only ruler a distant queen.
> Now comes the giant Canada,
> measuring miles from sea to sea,
> taking their homes without their leave.
>
> Before you tell them anything
> you send surveyors out to grab;
> before you ask them anything
> you send a tyrant governor;
> before you give them any choice
> you order them to change their ways;
> before you grant them anything
> you take their all, and promise nothing. (9)

Riel continues to have faith in the British until their Canadian representatives prove his faith ill founded. Interestingly, in exile after the failed rebellion, Riel becomes an American citizen, before returning in 1884 to lead the Saskatchewan Métis in another uprising. His defeat and capture, his trial and execution, form the rest of the opera's narrative.

But we have omitted one important irony—one that has structured both history and the opera. In that first confrontation between the Métis and the Canadian governor, a Scottish Protestant bigot named Thomas Scott is arrested by the provisional government for attacking the leaders, both physically and verbally. To a Métis' question of "Pourquoi?" he responds, "Speak English, mongrel" (3) and then calls him a "low Popish half-breed." His physical and verbal violence—his rhetoric of miscegenation as bastard mongrelization—and his attempt to foment rebellion against the provisional government lead to his being not only arrested but put on trial by the Métis. Riel acts as both official translator and prosecutor. The trial is conducted in French, alienating Scott from the proceedings and leading to accusations of unfair legal practices—according to British law, at least, if not to Métis custom.

Riel condemns Scott to death, in full knowledge of the consequences: the outrage of Orange Ontario and the likelihood of retribution. His reason, given first in French and then repeated in English, is, "I cannot let one foolish man / stand in the way of a whole nation" (21). These are the very same words that Sir John A. Macdonald will repeat when refusing to reprieve Riel himself fifteen years later, after a trial with an equal number of legal improprieties and in equally full knowledge of the consequences: the further alienation of Québec. Between those two repetitions echo the ironies of history.

The same words may be repeated, but they have utterly different meanings: though both are equally suspect in ideological terms in the opera, Riel's Métis "nation" is not Macdonald's Canadian "nation." When the Canadian Broadcasting Corporation televised this opera in 1969, it ended the production with the words of Prime Minister Pierre Elliot Trudeau about how a country is judged by the way a majority of its people treats a minority. Trudeau added, "Louis Riel's battle is not yet won." When Elijah Harper, the aboriginal member of the Manitoba Legislative Assembly, refused to agree to a definition of Canada a few years ago (in the "Meech Lake" accord) that did not take "Louis Riel's battle" into account, that situation may have begun to change: the federal and provincial government leaders had to sit down once again and this time draft a definition that would include the Métis and First Nations peoples. But aboriginal—not to mention Québécois—distrust of Ottawa is not new, as Moore and Somers suggest in their portrayal of Canada's very different first prime minister: smug, cynical, sarcastic—though witty—Sir John A. is more than simply a political opportunist and manipulator, a prevaricator, and a procrastinator. E. D. Blodgett once ironically "Canadianized" Derridean *différence* when he noted that the "impulse to defer is at least as old as Canada's first Prime Minister, Sir John A. Macdonald, who acquired the nickname 'Old Tomorrow' because of his policies toward western indigenous people" (562).

Macdonald, however, is also the voice of Canadian nationalism, and it is *he* who articulates what, in this context, is the (now) problematic identity narrative of the nation:

Nothing can stop this country now. . . .

If we unite from sea to sea
we shall become a mighty power:
if we do not, we'll all be naught . . .
shouting unheard in French and English both. (11)

In the very next scene Riel's mother tells of hearing, as a young woman, the voice of God tell her not to become a nun, but rather to marry, because her first-born son would be "chef de sa nation" (13). Indeed, her son has visions himself in which God names him David, king of that nation. But this king is a strangely solitary leader of men, as Somers underlines by having Riel's major arias—and only his—begin without any orchestral accompaniment. The sudden silencing of the instruments effectively isolates the voice, as the narrative action isolates the man.

Riel's "mission" was not only political, however; it was also religious. By 1885 the pious, visionary Riel had rejected the Catholic Church, preferring to speak directly to God. From the start, megalomaniac madness is offered as an alternative or corollary to Christian mysticism as an explanation for his behavior. In a scene in a church, Riel casts out the priest, announcing the "fall of Rome" and giving the terrified congregation a sermon of sorts about his mission and his prophetic vision. The stage directions tell us that Riel is in a mystical trance and that the people listening to the charismatic leader are hypnotized. In other words, for all his resistance Riel turns out to be as dangerous a nationalist as Macdonald. Twenty-five years later, in *Mario and the Magician*, Somers, with Rod Anderson as librettist this time, would again bring the solo voice of nationalist pride together with associations of hypnotism, control, and violence. In fact, the chorus's response that greets Riel after this aria, with its chant of *Riel avait raison! / Riel l'avait prédit! / Riel est prophète!* ("Riel was right. Riel predicted it. Riel is a prophet."), echoes in musical style, verbal rhythm, and even thematic content the later opera's collective response to another nationalistic and demagogic orator, the hypnotist Cipolla: *Viva la cultura italiana! Viva la civiltà Romana. Viva Cipolla!* Both men are frightening; both are charismatic; both are nationalists.

In the 1992 opera the setting changes, and the concerns get displaced from those of the Métis in nineteenth-century Canada to those of visiting Germans in 1928 Italy, but the paradigm of a strong, postnational suspicion of the emotive power of nationalism continues and receives a new (but medical rather than religious) configuration. Somers and Anderson based their opera of *Mario and the Magician* on Thomas Mann's 1929 novella *Mario und der Zauberer*, adding the narrative frame of a lecture given (in spoken voice) by the narrator, here called Stefan, to an audience in Munich. His topic is what he calls "our disease" (9). With this he invokes the structuring metaphor of both novella and opera: illness—specifically, transmissible illness. "Disease?" he repeats, as he forestalls the possible objections to his seemingly exaggerated term for apparent economic prosperity in Germany. The first of many ironies, of course, is that the lecture is being given in 1929, just before the October stock market crash. Stefan claims, however, that "there is a disease infecting our world," a disease he calls a "paralysis of will" (9). To illustrate its terrifying ubiquity, he proposes to tell the audience—in the room and in the theater, of course—the story of his Italian holiday the year before. The retrospective irony of a German using Italy as the site of a cautionary tale about nationalism and fascism is one we can savor—though Mann, writing in 1929, obviously could not . . . or at least, not yet.

The novella opens with words echoed by Stefan in the opera, describing the ominous feeling of the resort: "The atmosphere of Torre di Venere remains unpleasant in the memory. From the first moment the air of the place made us uneasy" (133).[22] For those who know either the Benjamin Britten opera or the earlier Mann novella of *Death in Venice*, these references to the stifling sirocco air may recall familiar miasmic theories of disease, and in particular, of cholera. The pestilential possibilities of what Mann codes as "the South" are always risks for the "northern soul" (139) of his German travelers. Mann's narrator is both attracted to and worried about what he calls "the emotionalism of the sense-loving" south (141), a trait that starts to take on political meaning when combined with another

Italian characteristic: the pleasure in and respect for oratory. This is what makes Italians, he says, particularly vulnerable to those whose mastery of speech plays to their nationalistic pride—as does the story's titular magician, Cipolla, and, of course, the country's then leader, Mussolini.

Both this nationalism-cum-xenophobia of the Italians and their auditory sensitivity are made the focus of attention in the first major episode of conflict in the opera, as in the novella. Stefan's child coughs during a meal in the hotel dining room, and an Italian Principessa quickly has her baby taken out of the room, loudly berating people who travel with "diseased children." The Hotel Manager insists that the family move rooms—for theirs adjoin the Principessa's. Stefan assures him that German doctors have declared the child healed of her whooping cough and no longer infectious; the hotel doctor agrees. Nevertheless, the Principessa fears that her baby will be infected simply by the *sound* of coughing, through what the Manager calls "acoustic contagion"—a phrase repeated by a number of characters on stage and thereby fixed firmly in our ears and memory.

In addition to being a suggestive metaphor for the power of opera as an art form, this concept of "acoustic contagion" picks up the disease metaphor with which the entire operatic narrative is framed and sets up a further allegorical force field that structures the rest of the work. Just as Mann has his narrator return obsessively to what he calls "this stupid business of the whooping-cough" (139) to explain his unease in the Italian town, so the opera libretto returns again and again to references of aural contagion—but always connected to images of control and nationalism. For instance, in a scene on the beach, the German children are harassed because they are foreigners; they are told they shouldn't be playing with the Italian flags someone at the hotel had given them. Stefan then sings of his worries: "These flags. This stiff sense of dignity. . . . The fear of coughing. . . . Fear and pride. . . . Symptoms of an illness we might all catch" (30).

When his young child then washes the sand out of her bathing suit and is momentarily naked on the beach, there is a general outcry. Stefan is taken to the municipal offices where he is lectured about "Roman discipline" and cultural purity in relation to Il Duce's laws protecting Italian civilization from "the excesses of foreign licentiousness" (33). The librettist cleverly includes here part of one of Mussolini's own speeches, thereby setting up considerable dramatic irony when the Hotel Manager admiringly says: "*Parlate benissimo*. Il Duce himself could not turn a phrase more eloquently" (33). But this joke actually underlines the dangers of "acoustic contagion" in the form of manipulative nationalistic oratory—to which the southerners, the Italians, are deemed more susceptible than the northern Germans . . . or at least (as Mann later saw) until Hitler arrived on the northern scene.[23]

The playing out of precisely those oral nationalist dangers is the topic of the rest of the narrative. In the opera, a band of blackshirts arrives with posters announcing the visit of the Cavaliere Cipolla.[24] He is called, in

Italian, *Forzatore, Illusionista, Prestidigitatore*. The latter terms are the same as in English—"illusionist," "prestidigitator"—but *forzatore* usually means "strong-man," as in a circus, and the idea of forcing or compelling (*forzare*) is central to the identity of this manipulative and frightening performer, whose very first mention in the opera is followed by a chorus of an actual fascist anthem, "Giovinezza, giovinezza," with its call to youth to realize that in fascism lies the salvation of liberty. Just as in *Louis Riel*'s Orangemen's song about "Canada first," Somers inserts recognizably diatonic, melodic music into a basically atonal score to represent and elicit patriotic mass emotion in the stage listeners. Once again, however, the theater audience's manifest pleasure in hearing comfortably familiar tonal music for the first time implicates it in subtle and historically interesting ways: what does it mean that "Giovinezza, giovinezza"—a fascist song—is the only tune heard whistled on the way out of the theater?

Acts II and III place the theater audience in the same physical and psychic position as the characters who attend Cipolla's performance: that is, as potential victims of his compelling power. His oratory in the show is a curious and contradictory mixture of arrogant self-confidence and thin-skinned prickliness. He constantly calls attention to his own physical imperfections, his ill health, and difficult life—but always in the context of a comparison with sexually attractive young men in the audience or, rather, with young men *he* constructs as sexually attractive to women. To compensate for what he presents as his own lack of success with women, he boasts of his successes on stage, of the praise of even Il Duce's brother. The crowd then mutters respectfully, "Il Duce!" Not surprisingly, someone makes the connection—echoing the Hotel Manager's earlier one—between Mussolini and elegant speaking, complimenting Cipolla too with the words *Parla benissimo!* and *Che ispirato oratore*. Indeed Cipolla's patter constantly calls up nationalistic sentiments, flattering women for bearing glorious Roman sons or asserting that Italy "brought the flower of culture to the world."

Lest we forget the force field of that "acoustic contagion" image, Act III opens with Stefan's reminder about the miasmic, oppressive atmosphere of the town and about how that all seemed personified in the person of Cipolla that night. The original meaning of miasma—polluting, defiling—is transferred from a general theory of physical contagion to an allegory of political (and acoustically transmitted) infection, as Cipolla reveals his true identity. He is not only an effective orator but also a hypnotist.

The display of his hypnotic powers brings the nationalist allegory to the fore, for these are powers that play to the will and the instinct. Both source text and libretto illustrate the vulnerability of human reason and will in the face of the power and attraction of the Dionysian—something fascism fed into. Each of the demeaning demonstrations of his power to which Cipolla subjects the audience involves the confrontation of their will with his; in each he is victorious. The claw-handled riding whip that he cracks becomes the sadistic and insulting symbol of his domination. The librettist has said that Cipolla to him was "the symbol of the fascist leader, of the hypnotic domination of fascism over the masses, and of its expropriation of individual liberty in the name of service to a nationalistic hysteria."[25] Here there is no other nationalism to counter his—as Macdonald's effectively counters Riel's—nonetheless, as he cracks his whip, Cipolla finally goes too far.

In both opera and novella, Mario—a young, quiet waiter—is brought on stage by the hypnotist, who first praises his name as a classic one in the "heroic traditions of the Fatherland" (87). Twice Cipolla does the "Roman salute," further encoding this as a scene with political significance. But he also twice calls Mario "Ganymede"—after the beautiful youth loved by Zeus. The scene thus connects that nationalist/fascist network of associations with "acoustic contagion" with another set that, as in *Death in Venice*, organizes itself around homoerotic desire. From the start of the novella, the resort town's name has been both sexualized and ironized: it seems that Torre di Venere—tower of Venus—no longer has the phallic tower that once gave it its name. After an early confrontation with a youth in the audience whom he calls the "lady-killer of Torre di Venere" (151), Cipolla immediately calls attention to his own bodily form and does so in an openly nationalist context: "I have a little physical defect which prevented me from doing my bit in the war for the greater glory of the Fatherland," he says (151). Immediately after, he again complains about the handsome youth, the one "spoilt by the favours of the fair sex."

This youth, whom Cipolla has constructed as heterosexual, is one for whom he feels a genuine antagonism. In the narrator's words, "No one looking at the physical parts of the two men need have been at a loss for the explanation, even if the deformed man had not constantly played on the other's supposed success with the fair sex" (151). Opera, of course, has a long and now perhaps embarrassing history of associating physical malformation with moral deformation: Verdi's Rigoletto or Wagner's Alberich in *The Ring of the Nibelung* are typical examples. But Mann calls attention specifically to the *kind* of malformation he gives Cipolla. As his narrator puts it: though "the chest was too high . . . the corresponding malformation of the back did not sit between the shoulders, it took the form of a sort of hips or buttocks hump" (152). The placing of the malformation in the area of the pelvis might well be meant to suggest some sexual dimension. Indeed, the descriptions of his relations with various young men, upon whom he exercises his hypnotic powers on stage, would appear to code that sexual dimension as specifically homosexual. For example, Cipolla induces a trance by "stroking and breathing upon a certain young man who had offered himself as a subject and already proved himself a particularly susceptible one" (167).

But it is with Mario that the homoerotic suggestions take on a definitely ominous character, so strangely different from the associations that would be made in Mann's later *Death in Venice*. Cipolla teases Mario about his love for—and suffering over—a young woman named Silvestra. He characteristically follows this with a reference to his "little physical defect" (176), despite which he claims to know a lot about love. Hypnotizing Mario, he convinces him that he, Cipolla, is really Silvestra, and he does so in interesting terms: "It is time that you see me and *recognize* me, Mario, my beloved!" (177). In silence the audience watches what the narrator calls "a public exposure of timid and deluded passion and rapture" (177), as Mario kisses Cipolla. Shocked at what this form of "acoustic contagion" has made him do, Mario runs away—but then turns and shoots his mocker dead. How are we to interpret this act? Politically? Does the fascist narrative meet its own end through the violence engendered by its own irrationalist power and duplicitous self-representation? Politically and sexually? Do demagogic oratory and chauvinistic hypnotic power release repression and libidinize both authority and submission to it (Lunn, 91–92)? A recent biography of Mann that stresses the writer's (usually repressed) homosexual attractions argues that "Mann had long detected a homosexual element in the Nazis. . . . On a theoretical level, his dream of a homoerotic democracy had been killed by homoerotic fascists" (Heilbut, 504).

Both the sexualization of fascism in the story and the opera and the earlier medicalization of nationalism as something spread by "acoustic contagion" are different from those structuring force fields of religious mysticism and megalomaniac madness in *Louis Riel*, but both operas share a distrust, not to say a terror, of the power of the solo voice of the demagogic nationalistic leader. A Canadian Opera Company press release for the 1975 revival of *Louis Riel*[26] referred to the opera as a "provocative foray into Canadian political mythology" because it captured "the tragedy and high drama of an episode that almost tore the country asunder, an episode which has had important and lasting effects on the relationship between French- and English-speaking Canada" (not to mention, of course, between both and the aboriginal peoples, including the Métis). In Coulter's play, Macdonald executes Riel for "the public good," before he can "fatally" marr "everything Confederation may mean" (131). Macdonald delivers the verdict of history: he says Riel will go down in history as "one of the mortal instruments that shaped our destiny." He does this, according to the stage directions, in an ironic manner, "slightly burlesque and pompous." But the joke's on him. The people whose needs he ignored and whose rights he refused—the Métis as a New World people who racially[27] and culturally embody the hybrid nature by which some theorists (e.g., Ashcroft, Griffiths, and Tiffin) define the postcolonial condition—became the symbolic operatic representatives of the Canadian people, still caught in 1967 (and maybe 1994) between many cultures, languages, religions, local affinities, and national self-identifications.[28] *Louis Riel* may indeed be, as it was called, the "music drama from the birth pangs of the nation,"[29] but it is a very fractured and divided nation. In *A Midwinter Night's Dream*, an opera written by Somers and Tim Wynne-Jones, an Inuit Shaman says: "Stories are who we are." If so, then the Canadian "we" are not simple, single, or easy to read as narratives. And perhaps that is just as well, since, as Edward

Said has claimed, "[t]o tell a simple national story . . . is to repeat, extend, and also to engender new forms of imperialism" (1993:273).

It is amusing, therefore, to read of Said's confidence that "[d]espite its extraordinary cultural diversity, the United States is, and will surely remain, a coherent nation. The same is true of other English-speaking countries (Britain, New Zealand, Australia, Canada) . . . " (1993:xxvi). But Canada has never been either an "English-speaking" nation or a "coherent" one. If most narratives of nationhood are narratives of integration, Canada's is not: at its core is what we have been referring to as "otherhood" or what Frank Davey would recognize as the narratives of diversity, division, exclusion, of the "beautiful losers" even more than of the winners. And with all that seems to come a deep suspicion of the very narrative act of nation making. How, then, is the "imagined community" of multicultural, multiethnic, multiracial Canada ever to be invented (Itwaru, 9)? Should it be? Nationalism may well be neither reactionary nor progressive in itself,[30] but if most "nationalist politics is a politics of identity," as Said argues (1993:267), then for these two Canadian operas, both written at moments of particularly heightened national self-awareness, *nationalistic* politics seems to be a politics of identity refusal. It is not so much a lack of "narrative competence" (Prince, 61) as it is a postcolonial challenge to the narrating of the self against the internal other,[31] and a postnational deconstructing of patriotic sentiment. To make the entire context even more ironic or provisional—or perhaps simply Canadian—this message comes in an art form that itself should be suspect: the hybrid or mongrel art form of opera is, after all, a perfect vehicle of "acoustic contagion"—even if the ideology this time is antinationalist.

NOTES

We would like to thank the archivists at the Canadian Opera Company (Joan Baillie), the Canadian Broadcasting Corporation, and the Canadian Music Center, for without their help this paper would have been impossible. For their acute critical readings of this paper, our thanks go to Peter J. Rabinowitz and James Phelan.

1. See also Homi K. Bhabha, ed., *Nation and Narration.*

2. See, for example, Jane Fulcher's *The Nation's Image: French Grand Opera as Politics and Politicized Art*, on opera as the mixing of patriotic sentiment and public spectacle in the context of the larger political issues in France between 1830 and 1870.

3. On Verdi's role in the Italian Risorgimento, see Edward Said, *Culture and Imperialism*, 111–32. In their different ways Rossini and Bellini also contributed by writing operas about national oppression and struggles for liberation. See Anthony Arblaster, *Viva la Libertà: Politics in Opera*, 66–88.

4. See W. Daniel Wilson, "Turks on the Eighteenth-Century Operatic Stage and European Political, Military, and Cultural History."

5. See Elaine Brody, *Paris: The Musical Kaleidoscope, 1870–1925*, especially chapter 3, "Le Japonisme et l'Orientalisme," 60–76.

6. The term is Edward Said's, from his *Orientalism*; see the continuation of this in twentieth-century operas such as Schoenberg's *Moses und Aron*, with its "Dance around the Gold Calf, an orientalist purple patch with the lurid appeal of the

Bacchanal in *Samson et Dalila* or the Dance of the Seven Veils in *Salome*"
(Lindenberger, 1989:41).

7. Today, of course, directors are fond of foregrounding precisely this operatic
act of empire- and nation-building in their productions: in his version for the
English National Opera, Jonathan Miller took the *Mikado* out of orientalist Japan
and put it right back in the England from which it sprang.

8. For example, Murray Adaskin's *Grant, Warden of the Plains*, Kelsey
Jones/Rosabelle Jones's *Sam Slick*, Robert Turner/George Woodcock's *The
Brideship*, Raymond Pannell's *The Luck of Ginger Coffey*. This latter adds an
interestingly typical Canadian element: it was based on a novel by an Irishman
who lived for a time in Canada (Brian Moore), and its music was openly influenced by the work of Copland and Bernstein, or more generally, by what the composer has called his major musical culture, that of the United States.

9. However, it had only been a self-governing dominion since the Statute of
Westminster in 1931.

10. Canadian composer Barbara Pentland, in 1969 (to *Musicanada*), lamented
that "[w]hat comes from outside the country *must* de facto be superior. Prime example: the opening of our multi-million-dollar 'National' Arts Centre [in Ottawa]
with an imported French ballet company dancing to a score by a Greek composer
conducted by an American born in Germany." Cited in the *Encyclopedia of Music
in Canada*, eds. Helmut Kallmann and Gilles Potvin, 1033. Amusingly, Toronto's
latest theater, decorated by an American artist (Frank Stella), opened with "Miss
Saigon." *Plus ça change. . . .*

11. At a session on "Canada and the United States: Literary Studies from Cross-
cultural Perspectives" at the Modern Language Association Convention in Toronto,
December 28, 1993, Sherry Simon spoke of the two warring paradigms of "nation"
in Québec literary criticism today: that of nation-building (e.g., Jacques Pelletier's,
*Le Roman national*) and that of nation-deconstructing (e.g., Pierre Nepveu's
*L'Ecologie du réel*).

12. See Jane Jenson, "Mapping, Naming and Remembering: Globalisation at the
End of the 20th Century," typescript of plenary address to the Canadian Political
Science Association conference on "The Paradox of the Late 20th Century: Inter-
national Integration and National Fragmentation" (1993), 3–4.

13. Compare, for instance, the operatic narrative representation of the immigrant experience in Anglophone Canada in R. Murray Schafer's *Patria I* to the
Québec context of Gilbert Patenaude/Thérèse Tousignant's *Pour ces quelques
arpents de neige* (1989) to the Derek Healey/Norman Newton's *Seabird Island*
(1979) based on a legend of the Tsimshian tribe and influenced by British
Columbian aboriginal music. This latter cannot really be called an aboriginal opera,
however. What has been billed as the first of these, *Diva Ojibway* by Tina Mason
(which opened in Toronto in April 1994), is said to have been inspired by Mozart's
*Don Giovanni*.

14. Cited in Cherney (130). Canadian operas in general, it has been argued, also
"reflect the individuality of the country's composers and the diversity of their
inspiration" (Jones, 711), and so there is no recognizable Canadian national musical style or school.

15. Moore was aided here by Jacques Languirand.

16. Kenneth Winters, in the *Telegram* (September 25, 1967) called it a "pastiche
. . . big, efficient, exciting, heterogeneous."

17. Cherney's description of this core music focuses on its "nervous rhythmic figures (often entrusted to brass) and sustained single pitches or vertical aggregates with pronounced individual dynamic fluctuations" (133).

18. Marc Gagné's opera from F.-A. Savard's novel, *Menaud, Maître-draveur,* also uses folk music in its melody, rhythm, and harmonies, but to rather different effect.

19. As collected by Marius Barbeau and Sir Ernest MacMillan (Cherney, 134) and orchestrated by Somers with sleigh bells, flute, tom-tom and other drums. The melismatic music and its ornamentations become coded as "aboriginal" in the opera and have been seen as giving "authentic, realistic flavour" to the music (Cherney, 133). For us the inevitable operatic intertext of this lullaby is the Indian woman, Wowkle's song to her child in Act II of Puccini's *La Fanciulla del West,* but in contrast to Puccini's desire for a robust sound, "a little savage" and exotic (Knosp, 140; see also Carner, 406, and Ashbrook, 147), Somers did ethnographic research and sought historical material: the end of Act II features Indian dance music transcribed by Margaret Arnett MacLeod in *Songs of Old Manitoba* (Toronto: Ryerson Press, 1960). See Cherney (135). Somers also used Inuit singing (mixed with Broadway musical and pop influences) in his Inuit-theme opera *A Midwinter Night's Dream* (1988).

20. On the narrative and structural significance of reflexive songs being sung in opera, see Carolyn Abbate, *Unsung Voices: Opera and Musical Narrative in the Nineteenth Century,* especially chapter 3, "Cherubino Uncovered: Reflexivity in Operatic Narration," 61–118.

21. Compare George Woodcock's *Gabriel Dumont: The Métis Chief and His Lost World* or his *Gabriel Dumont and the North-West Rebellion* and, say, Thomas Flanagan's, *Louis 'David' Riel: Prophet of the New World.*

22. Because Anderson based his libretto on the H. T. Lowe-Porter translation of *Mario and the Magician* (in *Death in Venice and Seven Other Stories*), citations will be from this translation.

23. The opera, written in the 1990s, in full knowledge of the historical events Mann could not have known about in 1929, makes Stefan into an antifascist (as Mann himself was later to become), even before Hitler's rise to full power. It may also be for this reason that Anderson has made the rather pompous and elitist narrator of the novella into a much more sympathetic stage character.

24. Sir Onion would be a literal translation of his name, recalling the character from Boccaccio's *Il Decamerone.*

25. Rod Anderson, "*Mario* and the Medium: Necessary Liberties," printed in the libretto (2).

26. This revival was in Toronto, Ottawa, and Washington, the latter as part of Canada's contribution to the U.S. bicentennial celebrations.

27. See Earl E. Fitz, *Rediscovering the New World: Inter-American Literature in a Comparative Context,* 71; on Riel as mediating racial, linguistic and political splits in Canada, see Leslie Monkman, *A Native Heritage: Images of the Indian in English-Canadian Literature,* 119–20.

28. See Margery Fee, "Romantic Nationalism and the Image of Native People," 17, on the role of nationalism as the ideological drive behind the use of the native in contemporary Canadian literature.

29. Canadian Opera Company, press release, 1975.

30. See Andrew Parker, Mary Russo, Doris Sommer, and Patricia Yaeger, Introduction to their edition of *Nationalisms and Sexualities,* 5.

31. We cannot resist citing a 1964, utterly un-self-conscious moment in Canadian opera criticism that reads very differently for many of us today, after the consciousness-raising in 1992 around the 1492 encounter between Columbus and the Americas: "Opera and Canada—twin manifestations of the Renaissance spirit of exploration and adventure, the one intellectual in dimension, the other geographical. Both arose from the quest for something previously known but now lost, the Greek application of music to drama and the passage to a continent. Both resulted in new discoveries" (Kallmann, 10).

WORKS CITED

Abbate, Carolyn. *Unsung Voices: Opera and Musical Narrative in the Nineteenth Century*. Princeton: Princeton University Press, 1991.

Anderson, Benedict. *Imagined Communities: Reflections on the Origin and Spread of Nationalism*. London: Verso, 1983.

Anthony, Geraldine, S.C. *John Coulter*. Boston: Twayne, 1976.

Arblaster, Anthony. *Viva la Libertà: Politics in Opera*. London: Verso, 1992.

Ashbrook, William. *The Operas of Puccini*. Oxford: Oxford University Press, 1985.

Ashcroft, Bill, Gareth Griffiths, and Helen Tiffin. *The Empire Writes Back: Theory and Practice in Post-Colonial Literatures*. London: Routledge, 1989.

Atwood, Margaret. *Survival*. Toronto: House of Anansi, 1972.

Bhabha, Homi K., ed. *Nation and Narration*. London: Routledge, 1990.

Blodgett, Edward D. "Toutes Proportions Gardées: America in Canada's Text." In *Nord und Süd in Amerika*, eds. Wolfgang Reinhard and Peter Waldmann. n.p. Rombach Verlag, 1992:560–73.

Brody, Elaine. *Paris: The Musical Kaleidoscope, 1870–1924*. New York: Braziller, 1987.

Carner, Mosco. *Puccini: A Critical Biography*. 2nd ed. n.p.: Duckworth, 1974.

Cherney, Brian. *Harry Somers*. Toronto: University of Toronto Press, 1975.

Conrad, Peter. *A Song of Love and Death: The Meaning of Opera*. New York: Poseidon Press, 1987.

Coulter, John. *Riel*. Hamilton, Ont.: Cromlech Press, 1972.

Davey, Frank. *Post-national Arguments: The Politics of the Anglo-Canadian Novel Since 1967*. Toronto: University of Toronto Press, 1993.

Fee, Margery. "Romantic Nationalism and the Image of Native People." In *The Native in Literature: Canadian and Comparative Perspectives*, eds. Thomas King, Cheryl Calver, and Helen Hoy. Toronto: ECW Press, 1987.

Fitz, Earl E. *Rediscovering the New World: Inter-American Literature in a Comparative Context*. Iowa City: University of Iowa Press, 1991.

Flanagan, Thomas. *Louis "David" Riel: Prophet of the New World*. 1979; Halifax: Goodread Biographies, 1983.

Fulcher, Jane. *The Nation's Image: French Grand Opera as Politics and Politicized Art*. Cambridge: Cambridge University Press, 1987.

Graham, June. "Louis Riel." *CBC Times* 22, no. 18 (October 25–31, 1969): 3–6.

Heilbut, Anthony. *Thomas Mann: Eros and Literature*. New York: Knopf, 1996.

Itwaru, Arnold. *The Invention of Canada: Literary Text and the Immigrant Imaginary*. Toronto: TSAR, 1990.

Jenson, Jane. "Mapping, Naming and Remembering: Globalisation at the End of the 20th Century." Typescript of plenary address to the Canadian Political

Science Association conference on "The Paradox of the Late 20th Century: International Integration and National Fragmentation."

Jones, Gaynor G. "Canada." In *New Grove Dictionary of Opera*, vol. 1, ed. Stanley Sadie. London: Macmillan, 1992:710–12.

Kallmann, Helmut. "History of Opera in Canada." *Opera Canada* 5 (1964): 10–12, 78.

Kallmann, Helmut, and Gilles Potvin, eds. *Encyclopedia of Music in Canada*, 2nd ed. Toronto: University of Toronto Press, 1992.

Knosp, Gaston. *G. Puccini*. Bruxelles: Schott, 1937.

Lindenberger, Herbert. "From Opera to Postmodernity: On Genre, Style, Institutions." In *Postmodern Genres*, ed. Marjorie Perloff. Norman: University of Oklahoma Press, 1989:28–53.

———. *Opera: The Extravagant Art*. Ithaca, N.Y.: Cornell University Press, 1984.

Locke, Ralph P. "Constructing the Oriental 'Other':" Saint-Saëns's *Samson et Dalila*." *Cambridge Opera Journal* 3, no. 3 (1991): 261–302.

Lunn, Eugene. "Tales of Liberal Disquiet: Mann's *Mario and the Magician* and Interpretations of Fascism." *Literature and History* 11, no. 1 (1985): 77–100.

MacLeod, Margaret Arnett. *Songs of Old Manitoba*. Toronto: Ryerson Press, 1960.

Mann, Thomas. "Mario and the Magician." In *Death in Venice and Seven Other Stories*, trans. H. T. Lowe-Porter, 1930; reprint New York: Vintage, 1989:133–78.

Monkman, Leslie. *A Native Heritage: Images of the Indian in English-Canadian Literature*. Toronto: University of Toronto Press, 1981.

Parker, Andrew, Mary Russo, Doris Sommer, and Patricia Yaeger, eds. *Nationalisms and Sexualities*. New York: Routledge, 1992.

Potvin, Gilles. "A Short History of Opera in Canada." *Musicanada* 44 (1980): 4–6.

Prince, Gerald. *Dictionary of Narratology*. Lincoln: University of Nebraska Press, 1987.

Said, Edward W. *Culture and Imperialism*. New York: Knopf, 1993.

———. *Musical Elaborations*. New York: Columbia University Press, 1991.

———. *Orientalism*. New York: Vintage, 1979.

Somers, Harry, and Mavor Moore, with Jacques Languirand. *Louis Riel*. Toronto: Canadian Opera Company, 1967.

Somers, Harry, and Rod Anderson. *Mario and the Magician*. Toronto: Canadian Opera Company, 1992.

Willis, Stephen. "Opera Composition." In *Encyclopedia of Music in Canada*, 2nd ed.; eds. Helmut Kallmann and Gilles Potvin. Toronto: University of Toronto Press, 1992:968–69.

Wilson, W. Daniel. "Turks on the Eighteenth-Century Operatic Stage and European Political, Military, and Cultural History," *Eighteenth-Century Life* 9, no. 2 (1985): 79–92.

Woodcock, George. *Gabriel Dumont: The Métis Chief and His Lost World*. Edmonton: Hurtig, 1975.

———. *Gabriel Dumont and the North-West Rebellion*. Toronto: Playwrights Co-op, 1976.

## Part III

Genre, Performance, and the Cultural Politics of AIDS

Diamanda Galas performs the *Plague Mass* at Alice Tully Hall, New York City, 1989. (Courtesy of Paula Court.)

## CHAPTER ELEVEN

*Mozart and the Politics of Intimacy:* The Marriage of Figaro *in Toronto, Paris, and New York*

Richard Dellamora

I

In the fourth act of *The Marriage of Figaro* an unexpected reversal occurs. Figaro, who has hitherto mastered the complexities of the court of Count Almaviva, suddenly finds the tables turned when the countess and his new wife, Susanna, trick him into thinking that she plans go to bed with the count. Turning to the audience, Figaro directs to male listeners an outspoken attack on the perfidy of women. A string of expletives follows: women are witches, sirens, screech-owls, she-bears, and so on.[1] This outburst can be taken in one of three ways: (1) As the conventional lyric and musical structure suggest, the aria can be regarded as a parody, whose violence and exaggeration tell against the usually imperturbable Figaro. For once, the joke is on him. (2) The aria can be viewed as cynically inverting the celebration of true love issuing in marriage, with which the opera ends. (3) The aria can be staged in such a way as to draw into question assumptions about human individuality that most productions of the opera depend upon. But in the New York City Opera production, directed by John Copley, which aired live on PBS on September 25, 1991, Figaro's bewilderment opens a bottomless abyss of distrust that demands an altogether different conception of desire and relationship from that offered in the opera's closing moments. Conventional productions of the opera and critical readings of the play of the same name by Pierre de Beaumarchais, upon which Mozart and the librettist, Lorenzo Da Ponte, based their work, are usually of this sort.

In *Viva la Libertà* Anthony Arblaster has written that opera always has a political dimension.[2] The work of restoring this meaning, however, can be done in a way that confines it to a particular time and place in the past while simultaneously privileging the present in our ability to understand the past better than those who lived in it could. This position is similar to that of the audience of *The Marriage of Figaro*, who enjoy a cognitive advantage over the scheming, mistaken, often deluded characters. In the terms of an abbreviated class analysis, Susanna and Figaro represent middle-class energy, wit, and intelligence in successfully resisting the count's clandestine attempt to reassert feudal privilege.

The menacing shaking of pikes by countrymen at the end of Act III in John Eliot Gardiner's production of the opera at the Théâtre du Châtelet in Paris depends on this conventional view. After the count follows the newlyweds from the hall at the end of the marriage ceremonies, the countrymen kick over his chair and begin to disassemble the walls of the room. At the beginning of the next act the audience sees that the count and countess's palace has been converted into the angled ruins that serve as props for the final action. These details, which remind the observer that Mozart's opera premiered in Vienna only three years before the outbreak of the French Revolution, signify the import of the *The Marriage of Figaro* as a pre-revolutionary text—and act.

This version of historicity aligns the public implications of the opera with the domesticity of many of its scenes, focusing as they do on the reunification of parents with children, conjugal reconciliation, and embarkation on marriage at the point of narrative closure (Arblaster, 4). Arblaster argues that this emphasis guarantees the contemporaneity of *The Marriage of Figaro*, because Mozart's concerns remain "common property" (3) with audiences today. At this point, Arblaster's account itself becomes political in a way that he does not quite recognize. Insofar as the opera is taken to be "about" the triumph of marriage-bound love over the corrupt designs of others, it becomes a form of domestic ideology. In that sense *The Marriage of Figaro* continues to do bourgeois political work even if and when this work is carried forward in terms either of a Marxian analysis, as by Arblaster, or of a formal analysis, such as that by Charles Rosen.[3]

In recent years the advent of feminist critique has altered our understanding of the nature of this "common property." Christie McDonald, for example, argues that Beaumarchais's attempt to improve the condition of women by siting the discussion of marital relations in a context of individual human rights rather than of the priority of fathers comes to grief in the third play of the trilogy, of which *The Marriage of Figaro* (1784) is the second installment. In the third play, *La Mère coupable* (1792), Beaumarchais shows that the legalization of divorce in France not only failed to emancipate women but provided their husbands with a new weapon to use against their wives. At the same time the tendency of revolutionary ideology to idolize women in their capacity as mothers reinforced their subordination to men.[4] McDonald points out that Beaumarchais himself undercuts the Enlightenment discourse of rights constituted through civil contract.[5] Moreover, he repeatedly shows how the attachment of individual figures to roles within the terms of heterosexual normativity results in the loss of agency, the capacity for mutual commitment, and reciprocal desire. Hence Figaro's words before he begins his screed against women: "I'm already beginning/ To play the wretched part/ Of the jealous husband . . ." (*MO*, 270). Exactly!

In *The Marriage of Figaro* the principal spokesperson of a feminist viewpoint is the wronged mother, Marcellina. The fourth act aria in which she criticizes men's injustice toward women is usually cut in production.[6] Even with this loss, however, she retains the crucial lines:

*Ogni donna è portata alla difesa*
*Del suo povero sesso,*
*Da questi homini ingrati a torto oppresso.*[7]

In the play, Marcellina's outburst is longer and more argued.[8] Concluding, she says, "Even in the highest ranks, women get from you only derisory consideration: lured by apparent respect, but in a real servitude; treated as minors for our own property."[9] In his preface to the play Beaumarchais reports that the actors at the Comédie-Française refused to deliver the lines *craignant qu'un morceau si sévère n'obscurcit la gaieté de l'action.*[10] The speech remained unperformed until Jean Vilar succeeded in restoring it in a production at the Théâtre National Populaire in 1956.[11]

A revisionary viewpoint can result in the portrayal of the count as a sexual sleazeball. This approach, though, is inconsistent with the way in which Beaumarchais and Mozart customarily observed the sexual oppression of women. Although Beaumarchais's stage directions include moments of unwanted sexual contact extorted by the count, he also cautions that, "Count Almaviva must be played with great nobility, but also with lightness and freedom. The corruption of his heart must not remove the *good form* of his manners. In keeping with the customs *of those days* the great considered the conquest of women a trifle" (98). The petulant bully of John Eliot Gardiner's production is not noble, light, or free. Given Beaumarchais's suggestion, a more traditional approach, as in the New York Opera production, may better hit upon a crucial aspect of Beaumarchais's moral and political vision, namely, his emphasis on the discrepancy between the appearance of social decorum and the actual abuse of power relations. This awareness makes the text critical and, in that respect, prerevolutionary. What impresses me most about the opera is the tension between the continual comic improvisations of Susanna, Figaro, and the countess, on the one hand, and the continual threat of the unthinking abuse of superior means by the count. Even after he confesses and is forgiven at the end, who is to say that the comedy will not begin all over again on the morrow?

Against this probability, Beaumarchais directs the critique of asymmetrical power relations toward particular elites. He does so, for example, in Basilio's aria in Act IV. For that reason it is unfortunate that this aria too is usually cut. In the New York City Opera production, refurbished on the occasion of the Mozart bicentenary, Copley chooses to emphasize comic action and the principals at the expense of what I refer to as prerevolutionary aspects of play and opera. He even omits the following important lines, which Gardiner retains. When Figaro complains about Susanna's planned infidelity, Basilio remarks:

> . . . In this world, my friend,
> It has always been dangerous
> To clash with the powerful few:
> They give you ninety percent, and they've
> still won over you. *(268)*

I say "important" because these lines as well as those of Figaro's extended speech in the Beaumarchais text indicate that the blaming of women in the aria transcodes a number of specific grievances. Beaumarchais's Figaro complains about the unmerited privileges enjoyed by the nobility; he complains about censors cutting plays. In Vienna, where Mozart's opera was launched, Da Ponte could mention neither of these items; he could, however, retain the attack on women.[12] The censored limits of political expression have the effect of intensifying the assault on women by condensing other grievances within them.

At the same time, the binary structure that opposes faithful wife to "deceitful creature" (Beaumarchais, 237) is another example of the ideological structure of stereotype, which Da Ponte demonstrates in the structure of the aria. Because the existence of one term implies the existence of the other, the definition of sex/gender relations within the terms of bourgeois marriage will always carry with it the unwanted terms (and conditions) of abuse. Hence the need for other ways of thinking desire between men and women (not to mention between men and between women). Stereotypes project vicious truths upon representative Others, but these terms, which are always predetermined, need to be continually reinscribed as new discoveries. In that way they attribute subjectivities to Others, who thereby merit the abuse they receive, and the opposition serves to constitute the subjectivity of the speaker.[13] The stereotype permits, indeed requires, Figaro, directing his speech to men, to assert that "everyone already knows" (*MO*, 271) that women are incapable of love when, at the same moment, he is discovering this truth for himself. A reader can, of course, work out the pattern of analysis; but in production such insights need to be communicated in another way. In this respect one might again well pay heed to Beaumarchais's direction to observe an apparent normalcy whose disturbing obverse is registered in our peripheral vision.

In contrast, a director who chooses to move sexual predation to stage center is well advised to set the action in another time, as Peter Sellars does in his 1990 production of *The Marriage of Figaro*—from the Trump Tower in New York City.[14] Occurring in the present (i.e., when the economic boom of President Reagan's second term soured), Sellars's *Figaro* places the insecurities of the countess and others in the context of a new economic elite who have abandoned any sense of responsibility to others, on either individual or collective grounds. By emphasizing aspects of the sexual politics of the opera and play that have traditionally been downplayed, Sellars succeeds at the same time in lending the play a *national* significance. Performed in the United States, the count's abuse of his wife and employees further signifies the crisis implicit in decisions to defund the welfare state taken in Washington since 1980. In other words, by restoring a neglected feminist context of the play, Sellars also causes the play to resonate with contemporary concerns.

Adrianne Lobel, the set designer, captures the self-enclosure of the New Rich that produces in turn a sense of isolation and ennui in the windowless servants' quarters of Act I and the glass-enclosed penthouse of Act III. Lobel underscores the point in the final act, when the scene is reversed with the window wall now set downstage, thereby permitting the "garden" scenes to be played in front of lit Christmas trees on the condominium balcony. Figaro's solipsism as he sings the aria is figured in the transparent glass barrier that separates him from Susanna, who stands looking at him from the living room where the wedding ceremonies have just taken place.

Sellars departs from usual practice in casting Cherubino as a cross-dressed dyke in her mid-thirties who appears at first to be permanently excluded from romantic possibility. In Act I s/he enters, returning fully equipped from a predawn hockey match. When Susanna and the countess dress her in a flesh-toned blouse in Act II, s/he seems to acquire a new skin, inhabiting a feminized body for the first time. At the end of the opera, s/he is left briefly and surprisingly alone for a moment on the stage.[15]

Retaining the two Act IV arias that are usually cut, Sellars presents a *Marriage* in which the final acts of contrition and forgiveness continue to carry conviction but in which their arbitrariness is more exposed than ever. When Marcellina, who emerges as an important figure in this production, sings her aria of feminine protest, the audience is forcibly reminded that the happy ending to come leaves unaltered the systematic structure of inequality that has permitted the count to twist his wife's arm in Act II and to grope Susanna at the beginning of Act III. At the end of the aria, Bartolo has to restrain Marcellina from jumping off the balcony.

The other restored aria reminds us that there is a second queer in the opera: namely, Basilio. Frank Kelley plays him as sexually "neuter" in the way in which D. A. Miller suggests that Roland Barthes uses the term in *S/Z* as one that "can never exactly be ungendered or unsexed. It does not register a *general* deprivation of gender but the specifically *male* experience of such deprivation; still more important, neither does it restrict this deprivation to a loss of 'masculinity,' that is, to the dread castration by which the general imagination of the neuter is usually monopolized, but makes no less definitive of itself a man's barred access to 'femininity.'"[16] As sung by Kelley, Basilio's aria provides an account of how this desexing, degendering has occurred. In the aria Basilio explains that he has learned how to avoid "insults, danger, shame, and death" by wearing a smelly ass's hide. He says that a *Donna flemma*—translated in the video of the Sellars production as "fairy godmother"—taught him this trick. What "shame," however, has Basilio escaped? Who is or was this "fairy godmother"? Who is the "savage beast" that subsequently threatened him? And what is the "foul smell"? Could it be that the woman (or man) who led Basilio as a child to a "little hut" and taught him the double lessons of shame and concealment sexually abused him? Or that someone else did? The aria is staged so as to convey the suggestion. "Smell" signifies Basilio's outcast position—impotent pimp and voyeur, neither man nor woman, inadequate on either score.[17]

Phantasmatically, this coded narrative is likewise hinted in the chair scene of Act I. Carolyn Abbate notes that the trio of the count, Susanna, and Basilio is interrupted by an inset piece of recitative, in which the count explains how yesterday, visiting Barbarina in search (as we learn later) of a secret tryst, he finds her locked in her room with (her lover) Cherubino. At the moment when the count explains how he found the page hiding under the tablecloth, he removes the dress from Susanna's chair—and to his surprise discloses Cherubino hiding underneath. This "story" is a narrative about the disclosure of sexual misconduct—adolescent, lesbian, or what have you—discovered by a powerful male adult whose interest in the situation is explicitly sexual. Since Basilio is one of the singers of the disrupted trio and since Abbate notes that, in the recitative, the count repeats the notes sung by Basilio earlier in the scene to refer to Cherubino's illicit intentions, it is reasonable to infer that the narrative of a primal scene unveiled by an authoritative adult refers forward to Basilio's confessional aria.[18]

In the New York City Opera production, the plangent mistrust expressed by Figaro unsettles the fixed character of the subject that is one leading, if somewhat unintended, effect of Da Ponte and Mozart's work. As I have suggested, this operatic effect resulted from the threat of censorship that necessitated important revisions in adapting the play to the opera stage.[19] As Arblaster argues at length, Da Ponte, Mozart, and Beaumarchais all faced exacerbated economic and social uncertainties as artists at a time when the stability previously afforded such composers as Haydn by aristocratic patronage was ending (24). Hence all three knew that economic realities made the prospect of a stable domestic existence for men like themselves highly unlikely.

In contrast to the way in which the opera at times reinforces conventional sex/gender roles, the unpredictability of human desire and relationship is suggested in the cross-dressed role of Cherubino.[20] Dressing Cherubino *en travesti*, Mozart follows Beaumarchais, who, in his stage directions, says, "The part can only be played, as it was in fact, by a young and very pretty woman."[21] Copley exploits the opportunities thereby presented for a range of subtle erotic responses between Cherubino and the countess in Act II, where the countess and Susanna dress him/her in the countess' clothes and s/he sings an aria of youthful sexual awakening. In the stage directions for Act II Beaumarchais three times refers to the countess as "dreaming." This dream, which we learn in the third play of the trilogy will have resulted in her bearing a child by Cherubino, signifies a larger delirium. Although the aria has been sent as a letter to the countess, the addressees are multiple and the possible responses varied:

> *Voi che sapete*
> *Che cosa è amor.*
> *Donne, vedete*
> *S'io l'ho nel cor.*[22]

The projection of a characteristically masculine sexual errancy in a female voice and androgynous figure underscores Beaumarchais's vision of a world in which desire is ever in unpredictable flight.[23]

Mozart and Da Ponte endow Susanna and Figaro with a resourcefulness and axiomatic naturalness that contrasts with the aristocratic decadence of the count and the passivity of his wife. The count's romantic abandonment of the countess threatens to deprive her of agency altogether. As I have mentioned, however, Beaumarchais already had in mind a sequel in which the countess would be revealed to be Cherubino's co(r)respondent.[24] Moreover, in Beaumarchais, Figaro's ceaseless search for place renders him a character virtually without interiority.[25]

Figaro is an eighteenth-century picaro, placeholder in an episodic narrative, rather than a person in his own right. At the end of a long catalogue of failed efforts, in Act V of Beaumarchais's play, he concludes:

> What an odd series of events? How did it happen to me? Why these things and not others: Who fixed them in my head? Forced to go through the road of life, not knowing where it leads and bound to leave it against my will, I have strewn it with as many flowers as my cheerfulness has permitted. Still I say my cheerfulness without knowing if it's mine any more than those other things: nor do I know who this *I* may be with which I am concerned: it's a shapeless collection of unknown parts, then a puny imbecile being, a playful little animal, a young man thirsting for pleasure, having a real zest for enjoying, plying any trade to live: master here, valet there, according to the whim of fortune, ambitious from vanity, industrious by necessity, but lazy . . . with delight! an orator in danger, a poet for relaxation, a musician when the occasion arises, a lover in mad fits: I've seen everything, done everything, used up everything. My illusion is shattered, my eyes are open only too well!                    (*240–41*)

This unfixedness is, of course, yet another sort of fixity. But the compulsive repetitiveness of Figaro's continual self-invention places him at a pole removed from that of the bourgeois paterfamilias.

When Figaro looks directly into the camera in the video of the Gardiner production to address male viewers, he intermits the onrush of innocent sexual play, romantic feeling, and proper marriage in such a way as to emphasize that they too are a set of artifices. In the 1994 restaging of the Metropolitan Opera production, a comparable effect is achieved by raising the house lights so that Figaro can make his complaints directly to the men of the audience.[26] Putting in doubt the narrative of true love, Mozart and Da Ponte call in question the axiom of naturalness that late eighteenth-century moral and social reformers assumed in their assault on aristocratic privilege. If love and trust are phantasms of male desire that necessarily produce feminine deceit, the "natural state" and bourgeois moral superiority are equally illusory.

## II

A comparable moment of disillusion articulates Dwayne Williams's AIDS short story "Behind Glass," in *Queeries*, a collection of Anglophone Canadian short stories edited by Dennis Denisoff. Williams's story differs from Mozart's in that the moment of apparent betrayal is not staged. Williams does, however, stage the representation of heterosexual romance as a way in which gay men can hope to protect themselves from the risk of HIV-infection. "Behind Glass" is about a young man named Ian James who is dying with AIDS. The story turns on the word *safety*, a term whose salience is driven home to him by a poster he sees mounted in a bus shelter: "a pretty male face sharpened against a plane of grey that separated his female counterpart. The caption advised, 'Better a Safe than a Sorry.' Ian despised the affected yearning of their faces captured behind glass that reflected his own sullen face."[27]

Ian resents being compelled to recognize his desire through the distorting medium of heterosexual representation. But he also resists the poster's not very subliminal double message: on the one hand, that heterosexual desire is estranged, both models needing to "affect" it; on the other, that the source of safety is not a condom (signified dissonantly in the image as a "plane of grey") but the proper choice of sex object. Ian is obsessed with the moment of infection since he "allowed inside him" (138) only one other man, his companion Sammy, who has already died. "Why did he never speak of safety?" (139), Ian thinks. More to the point, why didn't Ian? Ian's imminent death is a silent witness to an unrepresented moment of intimacy during which "love" and "trust" have proven to be ineffective prophylaxes.

In watching Figaro's breach of the transparent barrier between players and audience, I am prompted to recognize ways in which AIDS and, more generally, HIV infection have compelled gay men to acknowledge that neither love nor trust suffices to articulate the relation between responsibility and erotics. Although this new demand has further complicated the relation of gay men to the "plane of grey" in which they are forced to mirror their desires in relation to representations of attraction and repulsion within the heterosexual economy, the situation also requires young men to rethink the ethics of sexual dissidence. For many of the writers who have contributed to Denisoff's anthology, this necessity has resulted in disidentification from the terms *gay* and *gay man* in preference for *queer*, a word that insists on the difference between dissident sexualities and heterosexual representation. Nicholas Muni queers Verdi's *La Traviata* in another New York City Opera production in which "Violetta's consumption" has been "re-coded into AIDS-related disease."[28] But even with regard to conventional productions, effects can operate in the opposite direction through the permeable glass of sexual difference, so that the losses to AIDS among gay men and members of other groups in New York inflect, palpably if without name, the presentation of a classic opera in a time of plague. Hegemonic representation itself becomes queered.

This possibility is pertinent in considering the production of *The Marriage of Figaro*, presented by the Canadian Opera Company at the Elgin Theatre in November 1993. The new production was directed by Robin Phillips, former director of the Stratford Festival and at the time director general of the Citadel Theatre in Edmonton, Alberta. An expatriate Englishman and "out" homosexual, Phillips would appear to be extremely well suited to tracing the difference between bourgeois moral assumptions and the ethical dimensions of sexual attraction and intimacy during an epidemic of a fatal, sexually transmissible disease. Instead, although it is the work of a gay director, the Canadian Opera Company (COC) *Marriage of Figaro* is oddly quarantined from contemporary realities in Toronto. The celebration of sexual play, emblematized in the large circular bed that features prominently in this production, functions to exaggerate rather than to call into question the normative heterosexuality of the Susanna–Figaro plot. In Act IV Phillips emphasizes the parody (or, at best, cynicism) of infinite male bile in Figaro's aria. There is no moment of recognition, shared through the looking glass, that, however delusive Figaro's state of mind may be, his disabuse is neither unique nor merely comic.

Phillips chooses to emphasize not Figaro's aria but another, "Deh, vieni" ("Ah, come, my joy, do not delay"), which Susanna sings a few minutes later while Figaro hides to await the count's arrival. The lyrics, referring to babbling brook and laughing flowers, are just as clichéd as Figaro's. But the melody, the loveliest in the opera, operates beyond the words to show a Susanna, displaying not pert affection but, for the first time, romantic ardor.[29] She does so, properly, only *after* the wedding ceremony has taken place. Just as significantly, however, the song can be addressed to two very different objects: Figaro *or* the count. Susanna (and Mozart) depend upon the ambiguity. Gardiner, for his part, floating evening mist across the stage, chooses to link the aria with the temper of the closing lines of Cherubino's aria in Act I—lines not in Beaumarchais's text but added by Da Ponte and Mozart:

*Parlo d'amor vegliando,*
*Parlo d'amor sognando. . . .*
*E, se non ho chi m'oda,*
*Parlo d'amor con me.*

Bliss does not require marriage or even a partner: "I talk about love when I'm awake, / I talk about love in my dreams. . . . / And if there's no one to hear me, / I talk about love to myself" (*MO*, 183). Gardiner also moves the aria so that, instead of following Figaro's and in that sense "answering" it, it occurs between Figaro's recitative and aria. The displacement underwrites the solipsism of Figaro's outburst by emphasizing the autoerotic reverie of Susanna's absorption in romance.

Phillips opts for the sentimental gesture. The ambiguity that permits Susanna's utterance in Copley's presentation is erased by the sincere assurance that Susanna (and the audience) knows that this song is sung to Figaro alone. The moment is one of ideological suture as the audience is called upon to confirm her confidence that love will triumph.[30] Phillips's decision to direct Act IV as he has offers an example of a paradoxical inability of a particular minority culture in Canada to inflect Anglophone high culture. I say "paradoxical" not only because Phillips is gay but because AIDS is very much on the cultural agenda—witness the special issue on AIDS that appeared in the Arts and Book section of the Toronto *Globe and Mail* while *The Marriage of Figaro* was playing. Moreover, the same opera company that hired Phillips also commissioned a disturbing and innovative production of Béla Bartók's *Bluebeard's Castle* and Arnold Schoenberg's *Erwartung* directed by Robert Lepage.[31] In this double bill and in other productions—such as *Elsinore*, the single-actor adaptation of Shakespeare's *Hamlet*, in which Lepage plays the roles of Gertrude and Ophelia along with others—Lepage calls into question the conventional structure of gender and sexuality. For this vanguard Québécois producer, undercutting "normal" ideas of characterization is standard practice. This is not so on Anglophone Canada's main stages, where Aristotelian mimesis reigns.

### III

With *The Ghosts of Versailles* (1992), John Corigliano and William M. Hoffman demonstrate that the institutional contexts in which new operas are generated need not preclude the articulation within them of the voices and needs of members of subordinated groups. Corigliano and Hoffman began writing *The Ghosts of Versailles* after James Levine in 1979 suggested that Corigliano undertake an opera to celebrate the centenary of the Metropolitan Opera in 1992. One can scarcely imagine a more official context in which to undertake such a project. At the time, Corigliano was already thinking of adapting Beaumarchais's melodrama *La Mère coupable* (1792) to the genre of opera buffa. Levine prompted him to think of staging it within a larger context more capable of filling the stage of the Met. Hence the emergence of *Ghosts* as a work of double genre, in which a Mozartean opera is staged for an audience composed of the ghosts of King Louis XVI, Marie Antoinette, and their aristocratic courtiers. In this way *Ghosts* constitutes a new genre of "grand opera buffa."[32] As I have mentioned, Corigliano imagined this work *before* the onset of the AIDS epidemic in New York in the early 1980s. He and Hoffman then wrote it during the decade in which AIDS became the most salient aspect of gay existence.

Marie Antoinette and her circle signify the institutional contexts of production of new texts: Louis XVI initially forbade the production of *The Marriage of Figaro*. It was only after Beaumarchais led a long campaign at court that the king was eventually forced to permit the play to be performed for the first time—for an audience comprised of his courtiers, a number of whom reappear as "ghosts" in Hoffman's text.[33] Within the libretto, Marie Antoinette also carries the weight of the Terror that, in Act II, transforms the work into a grand opera whose overarching sign is the guillotine, to which her double is drawn and subsequently executed. The "work" of the opera is to release Marie from the condition in which she is frozen at the opening of Act I. Similarly, "first wave" gay literary responses to AIDS are often structured in terms of a narrative typology in which the experience of blockage within a narrative leads the author and/or narrator to turn to an earlier historical moment in order to devise a second narrative that might enable the protagonist either to surmount the impasse or at least to understand why it can be neither evaded nor overcome.[34] Is it surprising to find that the same composer who wrote the *AIDS Mass* provides a similar narrative structure for *Ghosts*? Moreover, as often in opera, the implications of sexual dissidence are not confined to male dissidence, because, as Terry Castle has recently reminded us, Marie Antoinette has long been a focus of interest within the terms of a lesbian cultural imaginary.[35]

Sexual politics can inflect not only a new work like *The Ghosts of Versailles* but also the presentation of standard works within the operatic repertoire. In this way producers and directors address the challenge of how to present opera in a way that is political without also being historicist. Consider, for example, the production of Richard Strauss's *Ariadne auf Naxos* that premiered with Jessye Norman in the starring role at the Metropolitan Opera in March, 1993. At the end of the opera, Bacchus invites the abandoned Ariadne aboard a ship "that sails to night and gloom."[36] Ariadne recognizes the implication of mortality even though Bacchus's words contradict his funereal attire. He assures her that "sooner will perish the stars in their places / Than death e'er in my arms o'ertake thee."[37] On this double edge of *Liebestod* the opera ends, celebrating both the transformation of human existence that occurs at death and a romantic absorption that regards no cost. The ambivalence of the ending emphasizes both loss and an imperative yearning to become other in sensation and/or romantic love. The mixture calls vividly to mind the bitter range of experience that faces all too many people in the age of AIDS.[38] In a 1955 lecture entitled "Bourgeois Opera," Theodor Adorno argues that opera becomes the leading musical genre in works such as *The Magic Flute* and *Fidelio* at a time when it expresses a double realization on the part of Mozart and Beethoven: "namely, the interlocking of imprisonment in a blind and unselfconscious system and the idea of freedom, which arises in its midst."[39] In New York City in 1993, the devastation wrought by AIDS occasioned a comparable awareness that could be heard in the swelling notes of Jessye Norman and the apocalyptic staging of the opera's second act.

*Ariadne auf Naxos* is a two-part opera. First the audience sees a below-stairs, backstage Prelude, replete with the pratfalls of the actual relations between patronage, production, and performance. After the intermission, *Ariadne auf Naxos*, the opera proper, takes place. Paul Griffiths, reviewing the production for *The New Yorker*, provides a detailed account of how the Met's new production draws the most extravagant contrast possible between these two parts.[40] The *opera seria*, however, is punctuated by the antics of a company of commedia dell'arte characters, who feel the main piece could use some enlivening. Moreover, the nobleman in whose home the entertainment is being staged has decided that *Ariadne* should be played simultaneously with an opera buffa.

There could scarcely be a better test case for the ability of classic opera to register complaint than *Ariadne* because no other opera more clearly demonstrates the problematic relationship between the theatrical culture of opera, the norms of production and stage technology, on the one hand, and opera's emergence from a world in which magic, ritual, and myth still held the belief both of elites and ordinary folk, on the other. When delivered with all the incongruity, awkwardness, and panache of operatic tradition, what capability of meaning does myth retain? Adorno answers by observing that opera is a secular genre. The decline of profane and sacred faiths is necessary before its staging of myth can occur. This fact registers the significance of opera as an aspect of enlightenment. It also enables music to console. For, in Adorno's argument, in *The Magic Flute* "music intervenes in and transforms fate's blind, inescapable ties to nature (as they are represented in Western myths)—and the audience is called upon as a witness, if not indeed as an appellate court" (35). Listening to *Ariadne*, the audience (or at least *some* audiences) experiences the human ability to face complete loss.

Early in the twentieth century, when medical model definitions of sexual deviance were becoming widely circulated and when lesbian and male homosexual artists used aesthetic and decadent means to turn sexological typology to their own purposes, Strauss revived the female *travesti* role in a number of operas.[41] "*Der Rosenkavalier* (1911) opens with an erotic bedroom scene (enacted with increasing explicitness in recent years) between the Marschallin and the cross-dressed Octavian." In *Ariadne* (1916), Strauss "takes the even more subversive step of assigning the role of the Composer to a cross-dressed mezzo-soprano."[42] As we know from operas such as Jacques Offenbach's *The Tales of Hoffmann* (1881), in the nineteenth century, *female* figures were supposed to inspire *male* composers to write great music; they were not supposed to dress up like men and do the work themselves. When Strauss, who had Mlle. Artôt in mind for the part, announced his plan to the librettist, Hugo von Hofmannsthal, his collaborator balked: "Your opportunism in theatrical matters has in this case thoroughly led you up the garden path. . . . To prettify this particular character, which is to have an aura of 'spirituality' and 'greatness' about it . . . strikes me as, forgive my plain speaking, odious. . . . Oh Lord, if only I were able to bring home to you completely the essence, the spiritual meaning of these characters."[43] Prettiness, however, won out. Or, rather, what Abbate refers to as "Strauss's homage to this re-sexing of our archetypal Opera Composer," besides implicitly acknowledging the centrality of male homosexual and lesbian practitioners in early modernist performance, makes the polemical point that operatic composition, from the very start, has operated in critical relation to the hegemonic values that it appears to exalt. This aspect of operatic practice places in a new context Adorno's view that situates the essence of opera in the bourgeois demand that existence (what Lacan would refer to as "the real") be experienced as transfigured and transfigurable (34, 38). And it virtually guarantees that the experience of AIDS will make itself felt in the opera house.

It is unsurprising, then, that in New York City the losses to AIDS, even when not specifically mentioned, can inflect a new production of an opera like *Ariadne*. In contrast, in Phillips's production, dissident effects are bracketed. Toronto critic Urjo Kareda observed that the tall, handsome Swedish mezzo-soprano Charlotte Hellekant's "Cherubino, gracefully sung, wonderfully free in physicality and transparent in feeling, dominated the performance."[44] What Kareda found transparent, however, others found oblique. Hellekant's Cherubino didn't look like a (heterosexual) woman, and she didn't look like a man either.[45] To my fancy, she is a dream figure: a dominant femme who goes both ways. Despite the pleasurable female–female eroticism of Act II, however, disturbing aspects of the opera were elided in favor of the light-filled normalcy of the final curtain. As in the photograph of Douglas Chamberlain, cross-dressed and wearing a powdered wig topped with a model sailing ship, that the Stratford Festival used to advertise its 1995 production of Gilbert and Sullivan's *The Gondoliers*, (male) *travesti* roles have become the signature of "safe" fun for the aging audience of Canada's national theater.[46] Hence a missed opportunity in the fourth act of *The Marriage of Figaro* is symptomatic of *a tone not heard* in the dominant culture of English-speaking, central Canada. Anglophone high culture, despite its gay practitioners, continues to exclude the queering of contemporary consciousness that would otherwise appear to be an unavoidable, if contested, effect of contemporary cultural politics.

I use the phrase "national theater" advisedly because the overdetermined relationship of Robin Phillips's career to the formation of a national theater in Canada inhibits him from taking part in the work of constituting Canadian existence beyond the limits of the bi- or tri-national model that dominates mainstream political discourse.[47] Phillips was first invited to

Canada in the early 1970s to head the Stratford Shakespeare Festival. The festival was founded twenty years earlier in response to the report of the Massey-Lévesque Commission, which in 1951 recommended federal funding of higher education and the foundation of the Canada Council. As had occurred earlier in England with the forming of the Arts Council in 1945 and the BBC Third Programme in 1946, the intervention of an expansive central government in the cultural sphere focused on making traditional high culture more available to a wider audience.[48] As a result, "in the first three years of the 1950s, we had the founding of the National Ballet, Les Ballets Canadiens, [and] the Stratford Festival."[49] Although Stratford was dedicated to *England's* foremost writer and in that sense is part of Canada's colonial heritage, it is important to remember that this homage was made in the terms of a universalizing rhetoric: Shakespeare was elevated as an index of humanity. Hence theatrical tradition was simultaneously constituted as English *and* Canadian *and* universal. This trinity has continued to characterize "English Canadian" concepts of national identity.

By the time that Phillips arrived, Stratford had become a commercial and critical success. It was also behind the curve of revisionary production that had transformed the presentation of Shakespeare in England since the early 1960s. Phillips, a rising star on the London scene, was brought over to renew the connection between Canadian Shakespeare and the cultural significance of Shakespeare in contemporary London.[50] Although this move was immediately construed by "English Canadian" nationalists as craven, it could also be read, more accurately, as an attempt to open a dialogue that would keep Shakespeare-in-Ontario from devolving into a pleasant, summertime experience insulated from ongoing contests elsewhere over the meaning of Shakespeare. Six Canadian directors issued a public challenge to the board of directors of the festival. Read in retrospect, it underscores the narrowly ethnic concept of national and international culture prevalent at the time: "During the past twenty-five years," they wrote,

> theatre in Canada has advanced to [sic] a direction that Stratford does not reflect. Canadian theatre is now working consistently to present world theatre in Canadian terms, to reveal a truly Canadian sensibility, and to advance, under the best circumstances at its command, Canadian plays, and the work of theatre artists in every field. The time has come when we have a right to expect leadership from your theatre, which is the national theatre of our country whether it accepts that title and the accompanying burdens or whether it does not. Your theatre receives the largest public subsidy of any theatre in Canada, and we think the time has come for some public statement as to its function, and its plans for fulfilling that function.[51]

Accordingly, Phillips was hired not only to direct a "world theatre," to quote another phrase from the letter but also, if he was to attempt the task at all, to consolidate Stratford as English Canada's national theatre.

For Phillips as for many other contributors at Stratford and similar institutions in Anglophone Canada, the universal values that theater represents have provided a shelter and an opportunity to take part in cultural work that might otherwise have been denied sexual dissidents as monstrous others. Since the passage of a federal law in 1969 that partially decriminalizes sex between men, many in the theater have gradually been able to come out as gay men. But, with exceptions, the general rule still holds, at Stratford and elsewhere, that there is no place for the particularities (sexual and otherwise) of existence beyond the general terms available as "Canadian" and "human."

## IV

These reflections on the continuing bracketing of Anglophone Canadian high culture were prompted by another experience of "no place" that I encountered when I read a new collection of queer fiction edited by Dennis Denisoff. Denisoff and a number of contributors attempt to "queer" desire between men by crossing it with a range of ethnic differences (Jewish, Chinese, etc.). However, these crossings are for the most part marked by the curious absence of a specific nationality. Public transport, by contrast, does signify, for example, the bus shelter that gives "Behind Glass" its title. The young protagonists of these stories spend a lot of time waiting for buses or en route. As a sign of transit, the bus provides the most available image of Canadian existence in the book. Economical and egalitarian without being noble or very efficient, public transit is an equally apt sign of queer existence for the young men who use it to travel the Trans-Canada highway.

In "Home," Peter Dickinson writes:

Consider this. It is that buying time between darkness and unreality, between remembering and forgetting, that unmapped hour of consciousness just after the clubs have closed and just before your mind does the same. You are sitting on a bus, alone at the back, on your way home. Somewhere someone is listening to something. And you think: I've been to the end of the world and back on this road. Winding. Snaking. Of this you are sure. All else: forests of memory, whizzing by peripherally, anonymously. Trapped as you are in the hereness and nowness of Hyundais and high beams, you yearn for the thereness and thenness of another time and place. And you know: like the Trans-Canada, the ribbon of asphalt you're travelling, the highway of the mind runs west to east.                                    (49)

Dickinson's narrator explicitly rejects being called Canadian: "I prefer to think of myself as a citizen of the world, especially in these dark times." More prosaically, he is another Anglophone Canadian whose identity comes from somewhere else, in this case, England, the colonial mother. His parents named him Christopher Robbins. His occupation, street hustler, synchronizes with the mapped grid of Anglophone Canada. Yet at the end of the story, Christopher, who fled from Toronto to Vancouver after his lover's death, is taking the bus back "home." Dickinson attempts to reconcile this term with queer nationality, which, as I have suggested, connotes motion. Appropriately in a cultural context in which heterosexuality remains the norm while gay identification repels sexual dissidents, Christopher falls for Mike. Mike is a highly suitable protagonist for a story set in Toronto, Anglophone Canada's media-saturated metropolis. "Mike, I was to discover, spent his whole life looking the part" (50). "A part-time actor" (52), his relationship to sex is as oblique as his relationship to cultural praxis. He and Chris live together for seven years in a celibate relationship: "As for Mike's sex life, I think his celibacy was a carefully negotiated mediation between his long-suppressed homosexual desires and his very real heterosexual marriage. Poor Mike, I think he only had sex twice in his life. The first time someone got pregnant. The second time someone died" (51).

Dickinson explores the consequences of queer identification with reference to relations existing in time. Mike invites Chris to move in with him; his wife, Helen; and their seven-year-old son, Kevin. The arrangement survives until Mike's death as a result of complications arising from AIDS. After calling Helen from the hospital to inform her of her husband's death, Chris leaves for Vancouver. There he hustles to keep body and soul together. Six weeks later, after a john finds a photograph of Mike, Helen, and Kevin in one of Chris's pockets, Chris decides to return to Toronto. As the story ends, he is on the way back: "The highway of the mind ends here," Dickinson writes: "home."

There's a show-stopping moment at the beginning of the second act of *The Marriage of Figaro*, when a new character, the countess, enters. It's the sort of moment divas kill for. But it is tricky. The countess has only a brief cavatina with which to bring into the opera a tone absent from Act I:

> *Porgi amor, qualche ristoro*
> *Al mio duolo, a miei sospir.*
> *O mi rendi il mio tesoro,*
> *O mi lascia almen morir.*[52]

The song indicates how devastating romance can be. When the countess later sings the aria, "Dove sono," she likewise reveals how elusive home can be. The count's palace is her home but because she has lost her husband's love, home exists somewhere else in moments of remembered bliss and devotion. The countess's song resonates with the acute sense of bereavement in face of AIDS; at the same time, it sounds a note of warning in face of the injunctions, heard frequently since the onset of AIDS, specifically directed to gay men to form monogamous relationships. The example of the countess indicates that the most intense experience of loss can exist within marriage.

In the midst of an epidemic the institution of the couple seems to offer a home. In the troubled 1980s it offered Ian and Sammy the promise of safety: "Their love for one another had become a refuge, protecting them from their desires for other men. In that love and in the apartment that had become their home, they salvaged a reason to stay together—safety" (138).

But Sammy infects Ian with HIV, and the work of memory takes over the story as Ian reaches back into a past that discloses no secure place but only secrecy and ambivalence. Ian remembers the moment in his childhood when his uncle, believing the two to be home alone, asked to join him in bed. Ian is silent, "trembling with desire and fear" (142). Ian's uncle touches him. When he opens his eyes, he sees his mother silently observing the two of them in bed. Shortly afterward, Ian comes home to find an ambulance in front of the house. His uncle's body is being removed. Only on his own deathbed does Ian realize that his uncle committed suicide "*to protect me and to protect. . . .* " To protect what? The fiction of domestic security. But such protection is purchased at a high price. The counterpart of the countess's lost past in "Behind Glass" is "the only photograph" Ian has of "his mother smiling. . . . Years later, when she disapproved of his *lifestyle* (as she called it), it was the only image that survived her distance. Eventually he could not control its appearance in his mind. It came back to him again and again until he was there, behind the camera, cajoling her with forgiveness to give him a smile" (137).

Mozart's opera ends, as opera buffa is supposed to, with the count, embarrassed by public exposure, receiving his wife's forgiveness. The curtain falls, so we don't have to face worry about what another day may bring. In "Behind Glass," Ian's mother does not forgive. At the end of the story, which is also the moment of death, Ian sees a vision of an altogether desirable young boy:

> The boy walks towards him, his tanned skin glistening.
> "You called for me?"
> "Yes. Will you lie down beside me?"
> His feet are wet. On his lips, he tastes the faintest trace of salt. His body surges, reducing the room to two.
> Then one.
> Then none. *(144)*

Ian, at the end, awaits himself in a dream of fusion. His vision provides an example of a self-unity that he never experienced while alive.

The ambivalent transcendence of this ending recalls not so much the here-and-now forgiveness with which Mozart ends *The Marriage of Figaro* as the moment at the end of Strauss's *Ariadne auf Naxos*, when Ariadne, united with Bacchus, ascends to the skies. For those who do not enjoy such sublations, going home means acknowledging the continuing reality of absence and loss. However incomplete this situation may be, it is a better "no place" to inhabit than the "no place" of sexual dissidents within "English Canadian" high culture.

NOTES

1. Special thanks to Elizabeth Baisley, Assistant Producer, *Live from Lincoln Center*, for making available to me a screening copy of *Live from Lincoln Center: New York City Opera—Marriage of Figaro*, which aired live on September 25, 1991.

Lisa Vala of the COC provided materials related to the COC's 1993 production of *The Marriage of Figaro*.

1. "Aprite un po'": "Open your eyes!" *Le Nozze di Figaro*, *The Metropolitan Opera Book of Mozart Operas*, 270; hereafter cited in text and notes as *MO*.

2. Arblaster, *Viva la Libertà*, 6; hereafter cited in text as Arblaster.

3. Charles Rosen combines both kinds in "Inventor of Modern Opera," *New York Review of Books*, October 27, 1988, 8–14.

4. McDonald, "Anxiety of Change," 45–78.

5. Ibid., 76.

6. Both Copley and Gardiner omit the aria.

7. "Every woman's inclined / To come to the defense of her own poor sex, / So wrongly oppressed by these ungrateful men" (*MO*, 265).

8. "Marceline" in Beaumarchais's text. In general, I adopt the names used in the opera for the characters of both texts.

9. Beaumarchais, "*The Barber of Seville*" and "*The Marriage of Figaro*," 203; hereafter cited in text and notes as Beaumarchais.

10. "Fearful lest so severe a speech dim the high spirits of the action" (Rat, ed., *Théâtre de Beaumarchais*, 163).

11. McDonald, "Anxiety of Change," 68.

12. In case it is not already obvious, let me state that I do not see the Beaumarchais text as an original that determines the meaning of the Da Ponte–Mozart adaptation. I am describing discursive effects within institutional contexts. McDonald traces effects of censorship on Beaumarchais's text.

13. For a classic analysis of the stereotype, see Bhabha, "The Other Question: Stereotype, Discrimination and the Discourse of Colonialism," in *The Location of Culture*, 66–84.

14. For an unsympathetic but detailed account of Peter Sellars's presentation of Mozart operas, see Littlejohn, *The Ultimate Art*, 130–55.

15. I am relying on the video presentation here.

16. Miller, *Bringing Out Roland Barthes*, 14–15.

17. *MO*, 268–269 (translation slightly modified). Except where I cite the Sellars version, citations from Italian and English refer to this text.

18. Abbate, *Unsung Voices*, 64.

19. *MO*, 163.

20. Margaret Reynolds, "Distractions," 133. In an excellent study Reynolds traces the shift from the prominent place of castrati, in both male and female roles, in Handel's operas to the thoroughly heterosexualized operatic worlds of Verdi and Puccini by way of the transition through *travesti* or trouser roles in operas by Handel, Mozart, Rossini, and others.

21. Cited in Reynolds, "Distractions," 140.

22. Oh, you who know
   What love's all about,
   Tell me, my ladies,
   What's in my heart.                                        *(MO, 203)*

23. Cf. Reynolds, "Distractions," 140, 141, 148–49. Beaumarchais writes: "Excessively timid before the Countess, he is elsewhere a charming scamp; a vague restless desire is at the bottom of his character" (100).

24. Brown, *Preromanticism*, 256.

25. Cf. ibid.

26. Allan Kozinn, "Figaro's Back with His Bag of Tricks," *New York Times*, January 26, 1994, B3.

27. Williams, "Behind Glass," 138. Subsequent page references to stories in *Queeries* are included in the text.

28. Hutcheon, "'Life-and-Death Passions': 'Operatic' AIDS and the Stage," 126.

29. Compare the comments of Hughes, *Famous Mozart Operas*, 74.

30. Gagnier, *Subjectivities*, 113.

31. The production won a $50,000 prize at the Edinburgh Festival earlier in 1993.

32. Information is from Michael C. Nott, *Composing the "Grand Opera Buffa*," printed text included with the video transcription of the Met telecast of John Corigliano and William M. Hoffman, *The Ghosts of Versailles* (New York: The Metropolitan Opera, 1993), 3.

33. Grendel, *Beaumarchais*, 211, 214–216.

34. Dellamora, *Apocalyptic Overtures*, 1.

35. Castle, *The Apparitional Lesbian*, 107–49. In the book Castle takes the figure of the ghost to be an apt metaphor of the liminal visibility of subjects of female–female desire in Western culture (1–19).

36. Von Hofmannsthal, *Ariadne auf Naxos*, 59. The set of Act II is dominated by a dark ship.

37. Ibid., 58.

38. The cover of the program for the premiere performance of this production is an image of the crossed red ribbon that signifies a common effort to address issues attending AIDS.

39. Adorno, "Bourgeois Opera," 34; hereafter cited in text as Adorno.

40. Griffiths, "Jovial Pursuits," *The New Yorker*, March 29, 1993, 97. Nonetheless, he was willing to exclude everything except "a disarming pursuit of pleasure and enjoyment" from his awareness. Contrast Bernard Holland's review of the restaging of the same production a year later ("'Ariadne' Brings Its Mix of Tragedy and Pratfalls," *New York Times*, April 18, 1994, B3).

41. For lesbian cross-gendering, see Vicinus, "The Adolescent Boy," 90–114.

42. Blackmer and Smith, Introduction, *En Travesti*, 14.

43. Cited in Reynolds, "Ruggiero's Deceptions," 145.

44. Urjo Kareda, "Toronto," *Opera News*, March 5, 1994, 44.

45. In March, 1996, Hellekant debuted at the Metropolitan Opera in New York in another trouser part, the role of the Page in Richard Strauss's *Salome* (Anthony Tommasini, "A Cool, Willful Salome in a Fascistic Setting," *New York Times*, March 9, 1996, 14 [national edition]).

46. Stratford would spell the phrase *national theatre*.

47. I challenge this model in contrast to the development of what I term "posthegemonic" culture in Canada in "John Greyson's *Zero Patience*."

48. Alan Sinfield is the most perspicacious commentator on postwar British cultural politics. See *Literature, Politics, and Culture*.

49. Mavor Moore, quoted in an untitled article by Simona Chiose, *The Globe and Mail*, August 19, 1995, C1.

50. For the scene in London, see Alan Sinfield, "Royal Shakespeare: Theatre and the Making of Ideology."

51. Cited in John Pettigrew and Jamie Portman, *Stratford*, 2:47.

52. Oh love, grant some relief
   To my sorrow and my sighs.
   And if you won't give me back my loved one,
   At least, I beg you, let me die.          *(MO, 197)*

*R. Dellamora*

274

BIBLIOGRAPHY

Abbate, Carolyn. *Unsung Voices: Opera and Musical Narrative in the Nineteenth Century*. Princeton: Princeton University Press, 1991.

Adorno, Theodor W. "Bourgeois Opera." In *Opera Through Other Eyes*, ed. David J. Levin. Stanford: Stanford University Press, 1994:25–43.

Arblaster, Anthony. *Viva la Libertà: Politics in Opera*. New York: Verso, 1992.

Beaumarchais, Pierre A. Caron de. *"The Barber of Seville" and "The Marriage of Figaro,"* trans. Vincent Luciani. Great Neck, N.Y.: Barron's Educational Series Inc., 1964.

Bhabha, Homi K. *The Location of Culture*. New York: Routledge, 1994.

Brown, Marshall. *Preromanticism*. Stanford: Stanford University Press, 1991.

Castle, Terry. *The Apparitional Lesbian: Female Homosexuality and Modern Culture*. New York: Columbia University Press, 1993.

Dellamora, Richard. *Apocalyptic Overtures: Sexual Politics and the Sense of an Ending*. New Brunswick, N.J.: Rutgers University Press, 1994.

———. "John Greyson's *Zero Patience* in the Canadian Firmament: Cultural Practice/Cultural Studies." Special issue, "Cultural Studies in Canada," *University of Toronto Quarterly* 64 (Fall 1995): 526–35.

Dickinson, Peter. "Home." In *Queeries: An Anthology of Gay Male Prose*, ed. Dennis Denisoff. Vancouver, B.C.: Arsenal Pulp Press, 1993:49–58.

Findley, Timothy. "My Final Hour: An Address to the Philosophy Society, Trent University." *Journal of Canadian Studies* 22 (1987): 5–16.

Gagnier, Regenia. *Subjectivities: A History of Self-representation in Britain, 1832–1920*. Oxford: Oxford University Press, 1991.

Grendel, Frédéric. *Beaumarchais: The Man Who Was Figaro*, trans. Roger Greaves. London: Macdonald and Jane's, 1977.

Hofmannsthal, Hugo von. *Ariadne auf Naxos*, trans. Alfred Kalisch. New York: Boosey and Hawkes, n.d.

Hughes, Spike. *Famous Mozart Operas: An Analytical Guide for the Opera-Goer and Armchair Listener*. New York: Dover, 1972.

Hutcheon, Linda. "'Life-and-Death Passions': 'Operatic' AIDS and the Stage." *Essays in Theatre/Études théâtrales* 13, no. 2 (May 1995): 112–31.

Littlejohn, David. *The Ultimate Art: Essays Around and About Opera*. Berkeley: University of California Press, 1992.

McDonald, Christie. "The Anxiety of Change: Reconfiguring Family Relations in Beaumarchais's Trilogy." *MLQ*, 55 (March 1994): 45–78.

*The Metropolitan Opera Book of Mozart Operas*, ed. Paul Gruber; trans. Judyth Schaubhut Smith, David Stivender, and Susan Webb. New York: HarperCollins, 1991.

Miller, D. A. *Bringing Out Roland Barthes*. Berkeley: University of California Press, 1992.

Pettigrew, John, and Jamie Portman. *Stratford: The First Thirty Years*. Foreword by Robertson Davies. Two volumes. Toronto: Macmillan, 1985.

Rat, Maurice, ed. *Théâtre de Beaumarchais*. Paris: Éditions Garnier Frères, 1956.

Reynolds, Margaret. "Ruggiero's Deceptions, Cherubino's Distractions." In *En Travesti: Women, Gender Subversion, Opera*, eds. Corinne E. Blackmer and Patricia Juliana Smith. New York: Columbia University Press, 1995:132–151.

Rosen, Charles. "Inventor of Modern Opera," *New York Review of Books*, October 27, 1988, 8–14.

Sinfield, Alan. *Literature, Politics, and Culture in Postwar Britain*. Berkeley: University of California Press, 1989.

——. "Royal Shakespeare: Theatre and the Making of Ideology." In *Political Shakespeare: New Essays in Cultural Materialism*, eds. Jonathan Dollimore and Alan Sinfield. Ithaca, N.Y.: Cornell University Press, 1991:158–181.

Vicinus, Martha. "The Adolescent Boy: Fin de Siècle Femme Fatale?" *Journal of the History of Sexuality*, 5, no. 1 (1994): 90–114.

Williams, Dwayne. "Behind Glass." In *Queeries: An Anthology of Gay Male Prose*, ed Dennis Denisoff. Vancouver, B.C.: Arsenal Pulp Press, 1993:135–44.

## CHAPTER TWELVE

## Strange Meeting: *Wilfred Owen, Benjamin Britten, Derek Jarman, and the* War Requiem

Jim Ellis

According to Michael Tippet, Benjamin Britten once remarked that "I would be a court composer, but for my pacifism and homosexuality."[1] Donald Mitchell reacts to this statement by arguing that,

> Britten—if he said it—did not mean *courtier* composer—a royal servant—but someone willing and, above all, able to provide music of character and quality for public occasions—even to find them a source of inspiration! That *would* have appealed to him. How any of Britten's operas—not excluding *Gloriana*—could be interpreted as the work of a *courtier*, God only knows. Even his arrangement of the National Anthem was conspicuously anti-jingoistic, anti-pomp and circumstance.[2]

Mitchell's defensiveness here is spurred on by Tippet's opinion that Britten was in fact a court composer. Mitchell is, I think, correct to point out that he was not. The most obvious reading of Britten's statement is that a jingoistic and homophobic nation would not accept Britten as its court composer, which is certainly not an inaccurate reading, given the place of homophobia in the cold war discourse operative through much of Britten's productive life. Interestingly, however, Mitchell's argument implies the possibility of the reverse reading: that Britten would not consent to be a composer for such a nation.

In his recent study of the place of homosexuality in British colonialism, Christopher Lane has suggested that there are times when homosexuality can act as an "unassimilable element" that has the power of shattering national allegory, specifically by "fostering a contrary interest, or counter-allegiance, with the colonized." Lane is attempting to trouble the usual picture of the role of homosexuality in Britain's colonial project which uses "a model of 'integrated' homosexuality (the integration was generally a fantasy), in which proponents of the empire such as Rhodes and Kitchener bolstered the most egregious imperialist strategies by rejecting or sublimating their physical desire for other men."[3] As Lane shows, there is no single way in which homosexual desire necessarily relates to the nation, a point that is also demonstrated in Richard Dellamora's discussion of competing models of homosexuality in nineteenth-century Britain, which hinged upon differing relations to the nation.[4] Interestingly, Lane's positing of homosexuality as a force that can shatter national allegories echoes to a certain degree Leo Bersani's claim that homosexual sex can act to shatter the "masculine ideal of . . . proud subjectivity"[5]; this connection between sexualities and politics, "between how we organize our pleasures with one other person and the larger forms of social organization,"[6] has long been insisted upon by both gay and feminist thought. This connection can also be seen in the work of Benjamin Britten (and is more prominent still in the work of Derek Jarman) and is signaled in the comment of his with which I opened: his sexuality and his political beliefs are logically consistent with each other. Why the nation cannot accommodate either of them is something that Britten's operas often gesture toward but that the *War Requiem* makes clear: that the nation depends upon the sacrifice of young men, and this is a sacrifice that neither his homosexuality nor his pacifism is willing to concede.

Is this sacrifice foundational? Are homosexuality and pacifism necessarily unassimilable elements? Is, as Britten's comments seem to imply, another version of the nation possible? Just as Britten's *War Requiem* makes the critique of the sacrificial basis of the nation more explicit than the operas, Derek Jarman's film of the *War Requiem* makes this critique more explicit still, adding a narrative and characters that move the work back in the direction of opera. Jarman's film works to consolidate a tradition of protest in twentieth-century British culture. The film links together the work of three artists, Wilfred Owen, Britten, and Jarman—patriots, antiwar activists, and homosexuals all—who protested against three successive British wars and, more specifically, against the sacrifice of youth in the name of the nation. Their work does not foreclose on the idea of nation, only on those nationalist ideologies predicated on the sacrifice of youth. This critical relation is characterized by a similar aesthetic move in all three artists: the interruption of "classical" forms—whether romantic poetry, the mass, or 35-mm narrative film—by other, more "personal" forms—realism, song, and video, respectively. The dominant is not thereby wholly rejected, but rather interrupted and interrogated through the addition of foreign elements. This is not to suggest that the artists are interested in a liberal accommodation in the nation; rather, they want to commandeer the present version of the nation in order to redraw its boundaries. Their work draws upon the idea of the nation for its emotional power and challenges the present ownership of it. Jarman's *War Requiem* constructs a countertradition through the referencing of a series of countermoves, a history of interruption that is peculiarly appropriate for the construction of a gay history. In an interview regarding his relation to homosexual figures in history, Jarman first notes that, "They may have had the same sexual preferences but 'gay' is a late twentieth century concept." He goes on to say, however, that, "an orgasm joins you to the past. Its timelessness becomes the brotherhood; the brethren are lovers; they extend the 'family.' It was then, is now and will be in the future. I like the idea that we are linked in orgasm with Alcuin, St. Anselm or St. Aeldred, all of whom loved men physically."[7] Homosexuality has long been noted (and feared) for its tendency to disregard class, racial, and national lines in pursuit of its desire. This is not to say, of course, that homosexuals have not been racist or nationalist, but rather to observe that their relative disenfranchisement may produce a corresponding disinvestment in ideologies predicated on the maintenance of difference. Jarman uses this privileging of similarity over difference to characterize a homosexual mode of cultural and historical transmission envisioned as a brotherhood of lovers rather than a lethal struggle between fathers and sons. In the case of the *War Requiem* this homosexual tradition is constructed on both ethical and sexual lines, a discontinuous tradition of symmetrical oppositional moments.

It is one of the perversities of Benjamin Britten's career that the operas for which he was once regarded with homophobic suspicion are once again becoming a source of criticism, now for their political and sexual conservatism.[8] Robert K. Martin argues of *Billy Budd* that Britten "depoliticized and de-eroticized" the Melville story on which it is based.[9] Philip Brett criticizes *Death in Venice* for "the stereotypical warnings it appears to give against being gay or pederastic."[10] Daniel Fischlin claims in this volume that *Death in Venice* is characterized by fascist aesthetic principles. Jarman himself writes that, "Auden's criticism of Ben as a 'queen's man' hell-bent on papering over his insecurities in the bosom of the Establishment and its Church, seems justified."[11] Part of this reaction to Britten is no doubt the result of Britten's place in the official culture of his day and his relation to the establishment, although this relation was at best precarious, as his interrogation by Scotland Yard during the height of the homosexual witch-hunt of the 1950s seems to indicate.[12] Much has also been made of his relation to the royal family, as witnessed by his knighthood and the condolence telegram sent to Peter Pears on Britten's death, although neither of these seem particularly remarkable given Britten's prominence in the international music world and his role in promoting English music.[13] Although I would not claim that Britten's works were politically radical on the subject of homosexuality in any easily discernible way—indeed, if they were, they would probably never have been staged, much less discussed—it cannot be ignored that for the length of Britten's career he staged operas that, covertly or not, dealt with erotic and political relations between men, during times when it was impolitic, to say the least, to do so.[14] It is worth remembering that homosexual acts in private between consenting adult males over the age of twenty-one were decriminalized in Britain only in 1967, nine years before Britten's death.

Catherine Clément argues that traditional opera depends upon the sacrifice of the woman to sustain the patriarchy.[15] This would put Benjamin Britten's operas, which often depend upon the sacrifice of youth, in an oppositional, or at least tangential, relation to the dominant ideology of opera. It has long been noted that in Britten's operas, "the theme of innocence destroyed or betrayed, or evil triumphing over good, of purity besmirched, or grace and virtue defiled or derided, frequently occurs."[16] For perhaps as long, this interest in the career of innocence has been linked to Britten's sexuality and to his strong emotional investment in children and youths, especially male. That is to say, the operas are often read as a record of repression or torment, either of pedophilia or of homosexuality, or some nasty combination of both. (There is, in fact, no evidence that Britten was a pedophile.[17]) Britten's friends and colleagues occasionally confronted him over his affection for youths, expressing anxiety about his choice of subject matter for the operas, or the number of roles he wrote for young singers, or his relations with these singers. Given the general hysteria in this century around the sexuality of children, this discomfort in Britten's circle is hardly surprising. When this is linked with the continued virulence of homophobia, it is also cause for little surprise that Britten's relations with youths were (and continue to be) read suspiciously and that darker motives are assumed regardless of the lack of evidence and Britten's own completely public conduct of these friendships. My point here is not that Britten was not strongly attracted to youths (obviously he was) but that it is impossible to know the precise nature of that attraction (except to call it love) and that it is irresponsible to simply label it "pedophilia," given the overwhelmingly negative connotations that word currently carries. At the same time, it should be remembered that there is a wealth of evidence that Britten had a sexual relationship with the adult Peter Pears, with whom he shared a house and a creative partnership for much of his adult life.

What if the repression hypothesis were to be rejected and the operas were read as productive of something? What if, indeed, they were read as Britten read them, as protests against the destruction of innocence? To read them in this way would not necessarily be to reject the idea that Britten's homosexuality fueled, or was at least related to, this protest, but to complicate the relation between them. This would entail abandoning the critical investment in Britten's "pedophilia," which may have directed attention away from a more politicized reading of the operas, or indeed, an ethical project in the operas.

In this regard it might be helpful to reflect on Michel Foucault's comment that "what most bothers those who are not gay about gayness is the gay life-style, not sex acts themselves . . . the common fear that gays will develop relationships which are intense and satisfying even though they do not con-form to the idea of relationship held by others. It is the prospect that gays will create as yet unforeseen kinds of relationships that many people cannot tolerate."[18] Leo Bersani warns that Foucault's comments could be seen as a desexualizing of homosexuality, but he also recognizes that the power of Foucault's suggestion is in seeing the potential in homosexuality for creating new modes of relationalities, or a different ethics of relations. Bersani argues that male heterosexuality is marked by a "traumatic privileging of difference," one that reads difference as a threat to the sanctity of the self-hood.[19] Jarman has a remarkably similar reading of male heterosexuality, noting that, "It must be very odd to be a straight man because your sexual-ity is hopelessly defensive—like an ideal of racial purity."[20] Homosexuality, on the other hand, partakes of an economy of sameness that is founded in a recognition of the nonidentical status of identity: "Homosexual desire is less liable to be immobilized than heterosexual desire in that, structurally, it occupies several positions. Its privileging of sameness has, as its condition of possibility, an indeterminate identity. Homosexual desire is desire for the same from the perspective of a self already identified as different from itself." This leads Bersani to postulate that, "Homo-ness is an anti-identitar-ian identity."[21] One of the political consequences of this structure of iden-tity is that homosexuality will tend toward a sociality based on sameness. Hegemonic heterosexual masculinity, on the other hand, is dependent on a policing of the borders of the self, to ward off what it sees as a potentially annihilating difference: its response is to fear those who seem to embody that difference. It is specifically in this regard that I want to consider Britten's relations to youth, both in his life and in his work. To make this shift in think-ing, however, will require a more adequate notion of what constitutes inno-cence in his work and what precisely it is that threatens it.

Jeremy Tambling's reading of Britten's explicitly pacifist opera *Owen Wingrave* (1971) supplies some answers as to what is at stake in the forces besetting the innocent. Based on a short story by Henry James, the opera tells the story of a young man who refuses to join in the family tradition of soldiering. Owen mounts a spirited defense against his father and his fam-ily, but he is sacrificed in the end by the ghosts of his ancestors. According to Tambling, "Owen confronts maleness in its fantasied forms, and cen-trally in the woman, aligned with the power of the Father. The opera seems to suggest that the struggle cannot be resolved positively. From an opening that looked simply like a credo for pacifism, the work has become a study in the sexual basis of violence." The credo for pacifism and the study of the sexual basis of violence are of course related, and it is arguable that Britten explored the relations between them in a number of his works. As Tambling argues,

281

Strange
Meeting: Wilfred
Owen, Benjamin
Britten, Derek
Jarman, and the
*War Requiem*

It seems clear that Britten locates the war-spirit as linked to the oppression of the Father: "But the old man would not so, but slew his son / And half the seed of Europe one by one" is the end of the "Parable of the old men and the young" in the Offertory section of the *War Requiem*: the same happens in *Owen Wingrave*, as it does too with Peter Quint and Miles in *The Turn of the Screw*.[22]

A similar thing seems to occur in the antifascist work *Our Hunting Fathers*, a "symphonic cycle for soprano solo and orchestra" written in 1936 with W. H. Auden. Donald Mitchell notes the "urgent political, historical dimension" of the work, with its "startling juxtaposition of 'German, Jew' in the coda of the 'Dance of Death,'"[23] a juxtaposition that links our hunting fathers with the forces of fascism. Standing in opposition to our hunting fathers is the pacifist son, who is in fact the father's game. The son is both a political and a sexual dissident. In his study of Britten's use of Balinese musical themes, Brett notes that,

> In *Owen Wingrave* the gamelin makes a special appearance for Owen's biggest aria, the lyrical statement of belief about peace. In view of his earlier work the use is suggestive, so that when we hear the character exclaim, at the climax of the aria, before the emergence of the ghosts who are to seal his doom, that "peace is love," we may be pardoned for wondering what kind of love is involved.[24]

If not explicitly, then (explicitness in this regard was not an option for Britten), the opera argues for an ethics that encompasses homosexuality and pacifism.

Brett and Tambling thus directly or indirectly make the connection in Britten's work between pacifism and homosexuality, a connection that we have already noted in Britten's life. In *Owen Wingrave* the patriarchal family can accommodate neither, and Owen is sacrificed. Brett and Tambling both also suggest that the concerns of the pacifist *Owen Wingrave* are on a continuum with the concerns of Britten's other operas. Owen may stand in a similar relation to his family as Miles does to Peter Quint, or Billy Budd to Captain Vere. Lining up the relations in this way should complicate those readings of the operas as apolitical, if indeed operas about male desire could possibly be apolitical in the twentieth century. The older figure is most often associated with patriarchal authority and hegemonic masculinity, erotically invested in youth but fully prepared to sacrifice it to further its own interests. For Britten the transition from the state of youth into adult heterosexual masculinity seems to be just such a sacrifice, or at least this is what *Owen Wingrave* implies. Read in this light, the perennial theme in Britten's operas of the sacrifice of innocence becomes more pointed and political than is generally granted. *Owen Wingrave* suggests that the problem of war is the same as the problem of hegemonic masculinity, which is not the same as saying that testosterone causes wars. Rather, hegemonic masculinity produces and is produced by those institutions in whose interests wars are fought; this observation is central to Virginia Woolf's examination of the sexual politics of war in *Three Guineas*.[25] The operas, it might be argued, are thus more often about heterosexual masculinity and its lethal desires than they ever are about homosexuality or pedophilia.

283

Strange
Meeting: Wilfred
Owen, Benjamin
Britten, Derek
Jarman, and the
*War Requiem*

Like *Owen Wingrave*, the dedication of the *War Requiem* suggests that there are for Britten different sacrifices and different wars but that their origin is in a common source. The piece is dedicated to four young men, all of whom served in World War II and three of whom died there. The fourth, Piers Dunkerley, was one of Britten's young friends, with whom Britten remained in sporadic contact until the end of Dunkerley's life. Carpenter suggests that Dunkerley could not accommodate himself to postwar British society, and he committed suicide on the eve of his wedding in the summer of 1959. World War II is perhaps, then, not the war of the title of the piece, but only the most obvious symbol of a more general war, continually waged.

In the letter in which he asked the German baritone Dietrich Fischer-Dieskau to sing in the premiere of the *War Requiem*, Britten describes it as "a full-scale Requiem Mass for chorus and orchestra (in memory of those of all nations who died in the last war), and I am interspersing the Latin text with many poems of a great English poet, Wilfred Owen, who was killed in the First World War. These magnificent poems, full of the hate of destruction, are a kind of commentary on the Mass."[26]

Michael Kennedy argues that the Latin text and the poems remain distinct, constituting "two plains of emotion, the ritualistic Latin and the deeply personal English words."[27] Britten seems to have been more interested in the settings for the Owen poems than in the mass, which Kennedy notes bears similarities to masses by Verdi and Mahler: "It is not surprising that the Owen settings are the finest and most characteristic music, for Britten is at his best in dealing with the dark and secret places of the heart, with the private rather than the public."[28] Kennedy's opposition of public and private, although suggestive, is not entirely accurate. Despite Owen's intimate and subjective portrayal of the sufferings of war, the causes of these sufferings are continually signaled in the poetry and are, in fact, made in the name of the public. "The Next War," for example, in the "Dies Irae" section of the requiem, comments on the perversity of a war that kills men in the name of national ideologies. Although Owen's focus is frequently on the sufferings of individuals, he continually shows why these men suffer and die, and not incidentally, the role organized religion plays in their suffering. Owen's poetry may then function within the requiem mass as an unassimilable element (to recall Christopher Lane's formulation) that works specifically to prevent an easy recuperation of the losses the requiem memorializes, preventing us from seeing them as necessary and worthwhile sacrifices in the interests of the nation.

It is not hard to see why Britten would be attracted to the poetry of Wilfred Owen or how this poetry would fit into a work that exploits structural oppositions to create productive dissonances. As a recent editor of Owen comments,

> Owen's major poems, drawing upon his searing experiences of the Great War, comprise a sustained subversion of poetic tradition. In his use of old and new techniques of parody, his ironic subversion of romantic forms and expression, and his innovating half-rhyme, he mocks the whole tradition of poetry. And in his content—the anti-romance, the anti-civilization of war in all its detail—he exposes the "order" from which war emanated.[29]

These elements of Owen's work have long been noted. What has been less commented on is the place of the male body in his poetry, an element that surely would have been of interest to Britten. Douglas Kerr writes of Owen that following his meeting with the French modernist poet Laurent Tailhade, "The male body becomes established as the central theme of his work, a focus for his curiosity, desire and pity. And for him the question of writing modern poetry was henceforth never quite to be separated from the question of sexuality."[30] For Owen as for Britten, the body of the youth was threatened by the Father, as is seen most immediately in Owen's rewriting of the Abraham and Isaac story. There Abraham chooses to sacrifice Isaac and "half the seed of Europe" (16) rather than the "Ram of Pride" (14). In its condemnation of the Father this poem corroborates Bersani's reading of hegemonic masculinity and its insistence on "the sacrosanct value of self-hood, a value that accounts for human beings' extraordinary willingness to kill in order to protect the seriousness of our statements."[31] Another Owen poem, "A Terre," not included in the *War Requiem* (but which Jarman quotes in the published script), shows a critique of hegemonic masculinity similar to that found in Britten's works, most obviously in *Our Hunting Fathers*:

> Little I'd ever teach a son, but hitting,
> Shooting, war, hunting, all the arts of hurting.
> Well, that's what I learnt, that—and making money.          *(7–9)*

To oppose the male body to the nationalist ideologies sacrificing it is not to retreat from politics but to enter them at a more profound level. To privilege the body in this way is to begin to move toward a new form of sociality, one not based on a traumatic relation to difference.

In the published script and production diary for his adaptation of the *War Requiem*, Derek Jarman records that,

> At lunch today the conversation circled around Clause 28 and the homophobia that Benjamin Britten and Peter Pears were subjected to in the 1950s. Aldeburgh was sometimes referred to then—shame-fully—as the 'two queers' festival.' Perhaps, as my friend Duncan Campbell thought, the old consensus would seek its revenge. Donald

[Mitchell] told me not to underestimate the genuine anger that had fuelled the writing of this work. Benjamin Britten was a pacifist.[32]

In Jarman's brief account of the lunch conversation, a familiar conjunction recurs—the homophobic nation, homosexuality, and pacifism. Jarman draws a connection between his era and Britten's: a cold war Britain that linked homosexuality and communism, and that pursued a terror campaign against suspected homosexuals (in which Britten was caught up), and 1980s Britain, when Thatcherite forces fought for both family values and the Falklands/Malvinas Islands. The notorious Clause 28 of the Local Government Bill, which forbids the promotion of homosexuality as a pretended family relationship by local councils, was passed on March 9, 1988, as production was beginning on *War Requiem*. Jarman was not alone in seeing a connection between the two time periods: "The Arts critic of *The Times*, on Feb 4 [1988] argued that the resounding majority of the Clause proved that 'we have clearly returned to a pre-Wolfenden era of gay bashing. . . . if not to Victorian values then at least to the long lamented witchhunts and blackmail charters of the 1950s."[33] This return was reflected in the courts as well: "in England and Wales in 1989, the police recorded 2,022 offenses of 'indecency between males,' a figure which almost equals those recorded at the height of the witch-hunt of the mid-1950s."[34] Just as he was caught up in the first witch-hunt of the 1950s, Britten in death came under official suspicion in the second: as a result of the new Section 28, schools in Kent and Sussex canceled the performances of a traveling production of Britten's *Death in Venice*.[35]

Like Britten, Jarman was profoundly attached to the idea of the British nation. When asked by a journalist why the establishment is so upset by him, he replied, "It's so simple. I am the Establishment." This would no doubt come as a shock to many, given the famous attack on Jarman in the *Sunday Times* by Norman Stone, a prominent adviser to the Thatcher government ("Sick Scenes from English Life"),[36] the denunciation of his films in the House of Commons, and the general furor raised in the press when Channel 4 proposed to show some of his films on television. Jarman goes on to partially explain this paradoxical statement by protesting against "a land in bondage to the estate agent, PR, and runtish Tory MPs whose faces are deep in the trough, selling off the Welfare State our fathers and grandfathers died to create, to line their pockets. What patriots these?"[37] Jarman, like Britten, is committed to a possible version of the British nation, but not to the present one, as his radical activism (in support of OutRage) and a film such as the apocalyptic *The Last of England* (1987) would show.

Anna Marie Smith documents the continuities between Enoch Powell's racist rhetoric of the 1960s and Thatcherite homophobia, especially with regard to the right's demonization of two communities—blacks and queers—in order to consolidate a particular version of the nation. She argues that "Thatcherite homophobia . . . borrows its structure from

Powellian/Thatcherite racism in the sense that it reconstitutes the Powellian image of the nation under siege through the substitution of the dangerous queer for the black immigrant."[38] The dangerous queer had of course figured on the British political landscape before Powell, in the cold war spy scandals, and Stephen Jeffery-Poulter notes that AIDS fostered a resurgence of this image: "At the very time when the thawing of the cold war was making the old model of the homosexual as an automatic traitor outmoded, his role as a sexual fifth columnist was given a nasty new contemporary twist."[39] Leading the way in the promotion of this image of the treacherous queer were the British tabloids, who used the promotion of AIDS hysteria as a handy gambit in an ongoing circulation war.[40]

Also making a killing on the new political conservatism was the heritage industry, which flourished alongside Thatcher's call for a return to Victorian values and the dangerous nationalist nostalgia of the nation. The British film industry in the 1980s was dominated by what Andrew Higson has called the heritage film, a genre invested in "the reproduction of literary texts, artefacts, and landscapes which already have a privileged status within the accepted definition of the national heritage." Higson argues that, "This version of the national past, this version of history, in which a critical perspective is displaced by decoration and display, 'an accumulation of comfortably archival detail,' is not in any way confined to the cinema: it is the very substance of the heritage industry and its commodification, idealization, and marketing of the past."[41] The decade started with the hugely successful *Chariots of Fire* (1981), saw *Brideshead Revisited* (1984), the various E. M. Forster adaptations, and a slew of films about the Raj. Of the last of these, Salman Rushdie writes that "the rise of Raj revisionism, exemplified by the huge success of these fictions, is the artistic counterpart to the rise of conservative ideologies."[42] The end of the decade witnessed the emergence of Kenneth Branagh's Renaissance Films, the first production of which, an adaptation of *Henry V*, premiered on St. Crispin's Day, 1989 (the day on which the historical Henry won the battle that is the climax of the film).

Branagh's *Henry V*, when seen as a representative of this trend in British cinema, can stand as a useful point of comparison with which to assess Jarman's adaptation of the *War Requiem*, which was released in the same year. Both directors claimed that their films carried an antiwar message, and both attempted to establish this critique through the juxtaposition of traditional religious music forms with scenes of battlefield realism. Both also came with complex cultural filiations: Branagh's film was closely related to a more or less explicitly anti-Falklands production of the play in 1984 by Adrian Noble (it features many of the same actors but little of the political commentary) but is more obviously related to Laurence Olivier's patriotic 1944 film version of the Shakespeare play. Coincidentally, *War Requiem* and *Henry V* both invoke Olivier as the specter of a past war, and a past version of the British nation. It is worth noting, however, the differing ways in which Olivier is presented or invoked by each of these films: in *Henry V* it is the youthful, vigorous Olivier of memory, reincarnated by Branagh as he delivers his St. Crispin's day oration from the same cart on which Olivier's Henry spoke. In *War Requiem* Olivier appears as a very frail veteran, hands shaking too much to pin his medals on his chest. As he is wheeled out of a hospital by a nurse (Tilda Swinton), Olivier in a voice-over reads Wilfred Owen's "Strange Meeting."

287

Strange
Meeting: Wilfred
Owen, Benjamin
Britten, Derek
Jarman, and the
*War Requiem*

Although Branagh states that he intended the film to have an antiwar message, this has to be balanced with his stated desire to popularize Shakespeare and to present Henry as an action hero.[43] He attempts to convey the antiwar message through a conventionally realistic portrayal of battlefield carnage and to secure the effect with religious music. Branagh describes the climactic scene in his autobiography: "To the accompaniment of a single voice starting the *Non Nobis* hymn, the exhausted monarch and his men would march the entire length of the battlefield to clear the place of the dead. As they marched, the music (provided on playback by Pat Doyle) swelled to produce a tremendous climax. There would be no question about the statement this movie was making about war."[44] Indeed, even for sympathetic viewers there is little question: "Embodied in this massive musical interlude in the film is the quintessence of four centuries of popular British patriotism. Its incredible build-up in volume and intensity is like nothing so much as the old Promenade Concerts at Royal Albert Hall, where a thousand voices finally joined as one in singing 'Rule, Britannia.' It creates a dream that is difficult to want to awaken from."[45] The clash between the visual and the aural is unfortunate in its effect. Although Branagh's battlefield scenes are not meant to trivialize the sufferings of war, the music encourages a particular attitude toward the spectacle. The many-voiced choir singing a traditional hymn of victory removes the spectator from any implication in the scene, or rather encourages a pious attitude of acceptance and gratitude: this was a necessary loss, a worthwhile struggle.

Suzanne Collier remarks upon the "curious presentation of [*Henry V*], by publicists and critics alike, as the human triumph of Kenneth Branagh, subjectified as both King Henry and as Olivier's usurper/heir apparent."[46] Graham Holderness elaborates on the possible reasons for this: "Branagh's film version of *Henry V* is very clearly a product of this new age of individualism. . . . Denied a home in nationalist politics, the emotional resources of patriotism gravitate inexorably towards their true heartland in the individualism of the new entrepreneur whose conquest of new economic and artistic modes continually endorses the cultural and ideological power of the old."[47] Collier and Holderness thus identify in the film's cultural filiation a peculiarly Oedipal dynamic. The son, Branagh, kills off the father, Olivier, to accede to his place. The whole drama is played out in the context of a play that is centrally concerned with usurping and becoming the father.

But if the critics were quick to read the *Henry V* as the story of the Kenneth Branagh, the very incarnation of Thatcherite individualism and economic initiative, the film itself does not invite any other comparisons between the story and the present day. This is, in fact, consistent with the genre of the heritage film, which prides itself above all else on visual authenticity: "Period authenticity and heritage conservationism represent precisely the desire for perfection, for the past as unimpaired paradigm, for a packaging of the past that is designed to please, not disturb."[48] Branagh's version of *Henry V* differs markedly from Olivier's in this respect. Whereas Olivier plays the whole first act in an Elizabethan playhouse, and the rest of the film on nonrealistic sets, Branagh insists on period values. The result is precisely a film designed to please rather than disturb.

Jarman's war film is in some regards closer to Olivier's than to Branagh's *Henry V*. The film clearly references the present, most pointedly, of course, by starting in the present and staging the rest of the film as a kind of memory (although it is impossible to know who is doing the remembering). Although period costumes and some props are used for the central Great War narrative, the possibility of creating the sustained illusion of the period film is impossible given the use of suggestive rather than realistic sets, and the disruption of the 35-mm sequences by super-8 and video. Chris Lippard and Guy Johnson argue that the set itself constitutes a concrete political statement: "That the AIDS virus has created war conditions in Britain is materially expressed by Jarman's filming *War Requiem* in the newly abandoned hospital at Darenth Park in Kent. . . . Its setting, resonant of a decline in public health facilities, continues the demand for attention to physical suffering that pervades the earlier films."[49] The set is used to forge a direct link between the past and the present, between "the Welfare State our fathers and grandfathers died to create"[50] and the actual struggles of these men. Like the set, the war footage acts as a bridge in the film from the time of the central narrative to the present day. The footage is initially almost all from the Great War, but over the course of the film the wars come inexorably closer to our own time. Although largely set in the past, Jarman's film demands to be read in relation to contemporary British society.

With the exception of a brief opening sequence, the soundtrack to Jarman's film consists of the 1963 recording of the *War Requiem* conducted by Benjamin Britten, with the soloists for whom it was written: Galina Vishnevskaya, Peter Pears, and Dietrich Fischer-Dieskau. Jarman's script for the film starts with an old soldier wheeled out of a hospital by a nurse. In a voice-over, Olivier reads Owen's poem "Strange Meeting," which is sung in the final section of the requiem. The film follows Wilfred Owen (Nathaniel Parker) as he trains, goes to the front, and is eventually killed. Intertwined with Owen's story is that of an English nurse (Tilda Swinton again), an Unknown Soldier (Owen Teale) who is in Owen's regiment, and an Enemy Soldier (Sean Bean). The careers of the three soldiers come together in No Man's Land, where the Unknown Soldier is playing a piano. The German Soldier stumbles upon him, and rather than shooting him, throws a snowball. The Unknown Soldier lobs one back, but when Owen comes upon the scene, he mistakes what is up and shoots the German Soldier in the hand. The German Soldier thinks it is a trap and kills the Unknown Soldier and is subsequently bayonetted by Owen. Later, when Owen is killed, the Unknown Soldier (now dead) bears him off the field to the afterlife. In the final section of the requiem, Owen meets the German Soldier in a subterranean space (in the script Jarman calls it Hell) as "Strange Meeting" is sung by the English and German soloists (Pears and Fischer-Dieskau).

The story of the strange meeting in no man's land forms the central narrative thread of the film; indeed, the idea of the strange meeting is central to the film's meaning. The history of the *War Requiem* is of course full of strange meetings, from the nationalities of the soloists (German, Russian, and English—especially strange when it is remembered that the cold war was still very much alive at the time of its composition) to the final conjunction of Owen, Britten, and Jarman. The film is composed of 35-mm, super-8, and video; the video contains footage of many of the major wars fought this century, without bothering to differentiate one from another.

It is crucial that this meeting takes place in no man's land, which accounts in large part for its strangeness. Jarman's inspiration for the snowball fight was "the legendary Christmas Day when the English and German soldiers exchanged greetings and played football in no man's land. Tilda's grandfather led the British team."[51] The strangeness, then, has to do with the privileging of human interests over national ones; it is a meeting of similarity rather than, or in spite of, difference. The film continually juxtaposes the realm of the human with the mechanized and dehumanized world of war, which is also the world of the nation and the Father. The former is often associated with memories of the domestic and is often shot in super-8, a medium that, significantly, Jarman says is closer to the body.[52] The three soldiers are all given memories of home, of childhood games, of family and familiar landscapes. These memories of the domestic and the bodily are often linked to sensual moments in the trenches when the men smoke, shave, wash, or comfort each other: Owen removes a thorn from the Unknown Soldier's foot in their first scene together; an older soldier comforts a younger one suffering from shell-shock; a soldier washes the feet of the Unknown Soldier. The emphasis on men physically caring for other men is indicative of a larger tendency of the film: the male body becomes, quite unusually, the recipient of tenderness rather than violence at the hands of other men. This emphasis on caring for the male body is more potentially radical than might be thought, at the very least in its portrayal of what we might call the pacification (rather than the feminization) of the male subject. Through this willing acceptance of passivity the male subject renounces, at least temporarily, any claim to the wholeness or self-sufficiency that is a key feature of hegemonic masculinity. What the film demonstrates is a Foucauldian *ascesis*, an art of the self that can lead to a different ethics of relations. Toward the end of the film we are offered further demonstrations of this strange mode of relationality in the war video footage, where we see repeated images of wounded and dying men. One particularly poignant series of images shows Afghan soldiers

binding the face of a dead or dying comrade, and then later lovingly comb-
ing his hair. These moments evoke the portrayal, at once sorrowful and loving, of the suffering or dead male body in Wilfred Owen's poetry.

Juxtaposed with the world of the bodily or the human or the domestic in
the film is the world of the nation, represented by politicians and businessmen. We see these figures first in a burlesque show where four soldiers in
clumsy drag surround a grotesque Britannia draped in the Union Jack,
"while behind them four fat businessmen, in top hats and tails, carry
scythes."[53] The same spirit of sinister grotesquerie recurs during the
"Parable of the Old Man and the Young," which the film stages as a scene
in Owen's imagination. Abraham is dressed as a Victorian bishop, Owen is
the biblical Isaac, and businessmen again observe in the background. The
businessmen are dressed in the style of the capitalists of 1930s leftist agit-
prop theater (fat, cigar-smoking, with clownish makeup), and they vigor-
ously applaud the sacrifice of Isaac by Abraham. The film immediately cuts
to video footage of "George V and his General Staff, the victory parade,
and a sea of white crosses in Normandy."[54] As is perhaps metonymically signaled by the businessmen's appearances, the sequences strongly echo
Brechtian theatrical practice, most importantly in the use of the fable to convey unequivocally a political point and to establish an immediate relation
between the fable and the world outside the theater. (Brecht frequently
effected this "by big screens recalling other simultaneous events elsewhere,
by projecting documents which confirmed or contradicted what the characters said."[55]) The use of Brechtian staging in these episodes is consistent
with Jarman's practice in the film as a whole to avoid what Brecht identifies
as the sentimentalizing effects of traditional opera, which prevent a more
politicized approach to the opera's subject.[56]

By adding the Wilfred Owen narrative to Britten's work, and by apparently tying some of the actions or identities of the on-screen characters to
the solo parts of the *War Requiem*, in Jarman's film the work takes on the
character of opera. This is most marked during a sequence in which the
nurse sits beside Owen's tomb and weeps; the scene consists of one extraordinary seven-minute take of Tilda Swinton braiding her hair (which continues the images of bodily care) and weeping in an obviously theatrical yet
oddly affecting way. The scene is operatic in the extravagance of the emotions portrayed, and in this scene Swinton is very much the diva, a role for
which she is especially suited, given her reputation in the rarefied world of
art house cinema. The obvious and crucial difference between her and
Maria Callas is, of course, that this diva is not singing. There is a soprano
solo at this point, and Swinton does occasionally make gestures in time with
the music, although at other points she covers her ears with her hands.
Another aspect of the scene that prevents us from seeing her as a diva is that
we are not sure what her relation to the dead Owen might be—sister?
friend? patient? lover?—and so her grief remains at least partially opaque.
We are not invited, as with the great operatic aria, to revel in the exquisite

grief of the diva, or as Brecht would put it, "to submit to an experience uncritically (and without practical consequences) by means of simple empathy with the characters."[57]

What is the point of this withholding? Certainly Jarman could have easily specified the relation between Owen and the nurse. We can take this question further and ask, "Having suggested some relation between the characters he creates and the solo parts Britten wrote, why did Jarman not simply cement the relation, either through having the characters lip-sync (which admittedly would have been dreadful) or through some other means?" There are at least two moments in the film when Jarman does join soundtrack and image, when at two different points we have a video image of a choir singing with battle footage matted in behind them. A final, tantalizing moment when the image almost matches the sound occurs in the "Strange Meeting" sequence, when the German soldier mouths the word *hopelessness* soon after it is sung. Fusing the soundtrack and the narrative was obviously a possibility, then, and one that would have resulted in something very much like a filmed opera.

It is crucial to recognize that the film both holds out this possibility and pointedly refuses to carry through on it. What this refusal entails is at least in part a refusal to provide an interiority for the characters. The nurse's grief, for example, is not localized or psychologized but remains simply the grief of a nurse for a dead soldier. Our attention is not allowed to be distracted from the cost of the soldier's death by a sentimental investment in character. A similar strategy is at work in providing the soldiers with near identical memories, each remembering himself as a boy at home with his mother. This refusal of differentiation on the basis of nationality, which repeats the pattern of the strange meeting, prepares us for the actual war footage, in which the participants are similarly unknowable. This is perhaps the point: it is unnecessary to know anything about them; we merely need to know that they are suffering. The maintenance of nationalist difference would distract us from a more profound similarity. Jarman writes of one sequence: "In the footage of Afghanistan there is a moment when the cameraman films two young soldiers who have been left to die. The look they give him is of utter despair. It must be dreadful not being able to help, but just observe. There is a terrible impotence in this film that makes one feel helpless. . . . In that moment there are no nations or ideologies, just suffering. Nations and ideologies must die so that we may live."[58] It would be easy to dismiss this as naive or apolitical, but to do this would be to miss the profound political point the film makes. By not giving us a story that might in some way explain, ameliorate, contextualize, or give meaning to the loss of the individual lives, we are faced with the brute fact of their loss. The refusal of identity is a refusal of the categories of difference that the nation imposes, and which are overridden in the film's no man's land.

The war footage continually reminds us of what is at stake in this particular nationalist mode of relationality: wars are, after all, about fixing certain lines, and establishing terrains and subjects as Other. The power of the *War Requiem* is to remind us that along with nations go subjectivities and that subjectivities respond to national allegories, a point that Britten also makes in *Owen Wingrave*. By rejecting the borders of the nation through privileging the space of no man's land, Jarman points toward a community based on what Foucault calls new ways of being together: "The problem is not to discover in oneself the truth of sex but rather to use sexuality henceforth to arrive at a multiplicity of relationships."[59] An important element of this new mode of relationality, as I have been suggesting, is a different relation to the male body. This different relation is one that through the acceptance of passivity denies the "sacrosanct value of selfhood."[60] Both the pacifist and the homosexual do not or cannot share in this masculine ideal of selfhood, on which full participation in the nation depends.

Jarman's filming of the requiem can be said to act out certain of these other ways of being. In his introduction to the script, the film's producer, Don Boyd, remarks upon the unusual degree to which Jarman collaborated with others.[61] This communal approach to directing was not limited to this film; Jarman began making films by and of his community.[62] This approach to directing is related to Jarman's sexual politics. He once said that it was his ambition to direct a film made entirely by his collaborators,[63] an interesting evacuation of ego from an egoistic profession, which recalls Bersani's discussion of the radical potential of gay sex to lead to the annihilation of ego. We might contrast this filmmaking practice to that of Kenneth Branagh, who turns Shakespeare's equivocal examination of Henry V into an unequivocal celebration of the individual greatness of Kenneth Branagh.

To fully appreciate Jarman's approach to filmmaking as a community practice that encourages further community, it must be seen in the context of 1980s Thatcherite politics. The community that Jarman calls upon in making this film and the community of care that the film portrays are under assault by the same forces. The history that Jarman writes through the film works to challenge the dominant construction of the past that the heritage film promoted. If, as Eric Hobsbawm observes, "What makes a nation *is* the past . . . and historians are the people who produce it,"[64] then it can be seen that Jarman is actively contesting both the outlines and the ownership of the British nation by contesting the writing of its history. The Thatcherite construction of nation depended upon demonizing relations between men, relations that are terrifying not because of sexual practices, but because of their potential to reconfigure the basis of the social: hence, of course, the fear of the promotion of the "pretended family relation" that is inscribed into Section 28. The fear is not that gays will have families, but that the meaning of the family and hence the social may be radically reconfigured. This fear is amply inscribed in any number of the heritage films, regardless of the original politics of their source texts, in their nostalgia for an era of stable social relations that in fact never existed.

The force of Jarman's film of the *War Requiem* is to reconfigure the lines of the nation by portraying modes of relationality and sociality at odds with the ones currently structuring the nation, modes that are the consequence of his homosexuality and his pacifism. It was precisely this conjunction that was at the heart of the ethical project of Benjamin Britten's operas: a project that protested the sacrifice of youth in the name of a heterosexual nation. Jarman's film constructs a tradition of opposition that embraces the work of both Britten and Owen, a tradition based on a brotherhood of lovers rather than a murderous pact between father and son. The *War Requiem* challenges the current outlines of the nation through a contestation both of the history of Britain in the twentieth century and the ways in which that history was being filmed during the Thatcherite regime.

293

Strange
Meeting: Wilfred
Owen, Benjamin
Britten, Derek
Jarman, and the
*War Requiem*

NOTES

This paper began as a collaboration with Daniel O'Quinn, but unfortunately time constraints militated against our working together. The argument has, nonetheless, benefitted greatly from his comments and suggestions throughout the writing process, for which I thank him. Thanks also to Jennifer Henderson and Richard Dellamora for their perspicacious and productive comments.

1. Humphrey Carpenter, *Benjamin Britten: A Biography* (London: Faber and Faber, 1992), 194.

2. Ibid.

3. Christopher Lane, *The Ruling Passion: British Colonial Allegory and the Paradox of Homosexual Desire* (Durham, N.C.: Duke University Press, 1995), 2, 4, 4.

4. See especially his chapter on "Dorianism" in *Apocalyptic Overtures: Sexual Politics and the Sense of an Ending* (New Brunswick, N.J.: Rutgers University Press, 1994), 43–64.

5. Leo Bersani, "Is the Rectum a Grave?" in *AIDS: Cultural Analysis/Cultural Criticism*, ed. Douglas Crimp (Cambridge: MIT Press, 1989), 222.

6. Leo Bersani, *Homos* (Cambridge: Harvard University Press, 1995), 81.

7. Derek Jarman, *At Your Own Risk: A Saint's Testament* (London: Hutchinson, 1992), 27.

8. Philip Brett observes of criticism written during Britten's lifetime that, "On the one hand Britten's music was characterized as 'mere cleverness,' 'devilish smart.' On the other it was accused of sentimentality. Behind both attitudes, of course, lay the unspoken fascination with Britten's homosexuality, both labels being the reverse sides of the opposition craft/cleverness, sincerity/sentimentality. . . . critics also embraced a strategy of choosing an approach to the themes of Britten's operas that would mask, parry, or render ridiculous their homosexual content" ("Musicality, Essentialism, and the Closet" in *Queering the Pitch: The New Gay and Lesbian Musicology*, eds. Philip Brett, Elizabeth Wood, and Gary C. Thomas [New York: Routledge, 1994], 19).

9. Robert K. Martin, "Saving Captain Vere: *Billy Budd* from Melville's Novella to Britten's Opera," *Studies in Short Fiction* 23, no. 1 (1986): 51.

10. Brett, "Musicality," 21.

11. Derek Jarman, *War Requiem: The Film* (London: Faber and Faber, 1989), 6.

12. For the few surviving details, see Carpenter (334–35). For discussions of the witch-hunts of the 1950s see Stephen Jeffery-Poulter, *Peers, Queers and Commons:*

*The Struggle for Gay Law Reform from 1950 to the Present* (New York: Routledge, 1991), or Alan Sinfield, *Literature, Politics and Culture in Postwar Britain* (Oxford: Basil Blackwell, 1989), 60–85. Like the present argument, Richard Dellamora's chapter on Alan Hollinghurst's *The Swimming-pool Library* discusses the relations between the 1950s and the 1980s in Britain as they are invoked in a contemporary work. See his *Apocalyptic Overtures*, 173–91.

13. John Gill writes of this: "When Britten died in 1976, the Queen sent a telegram of condolence to Pears. 'It's a recognition of the way we lived,' he told a friend, implying that the missive represented a kind of blessing from the establishment. In fact, the telegram was a private note (she sends hundreds of them, as this former telegraphist's fingers will attest) from a member of a royal family with more than its fair share of queers among its acquaintances. The establishment was by no means willing to recognize the way Britten and Pears lived" (*Queer Noises: Male and Female Homosexuality in Twentieth-Century Music* [Minneapolis: University of Minnesota Press, 1995], 19–20). Noel Annan's *Our Age: Portrait of a Generation* (London: Weidenfeld and Nicolson, 1990), although not addressing Britten and Pears specifically, confirms this reading of the establishment's relation to homosexuality. He writes that among his generation (which came of age between the wars), homosexuality "had become normal, but not in the world of good form. If a homosexual were compromised he was dead to official life" (119).

14. Britten's operas *Peter Grimes* (1945), *Albert Herring* (1947), *Billy Budd* (1951), *The Turn of the Screw* (1954), *Owen Wingrave* (1971), and *Death in Venice* (1973) have all been discussed by critics such as Philip Brett, Jeremy Tambling, and Humphrey Carpenter for their treatment of nonconformist male desires. On the potential repercussions of Britten being completely candid about his sexuality, Brett writes of Britten and Pear's influence on British culture that, "This great achievement above and beyond Britten's music would scarcely have been possible, in a country where homosexuality is tolerated as an eccentricity but not accepted as a way of life, if Britten had been as overt as, say, Angus Wilson or David Hockney." Brett, "Britten and Grimes," in *Benjamin Britten: Peter Grimes*, ed. Philip Brett (Cambridge: Cambridge University Press, 1983), 189.

15. Catherine Clément, *Opera, Or, The Undoing of Women*, trans. Betsy Wing (Minneapolis: University of Minnesota Press, 1988).

16. Michael Kennedy, *Britten*, rev. ed. (London: J. M. Dent, 1993), 118.

17. Carpenter discusses the accusations (341–58).

18. Michel Foucault, *Politics, Philosophy, Culture: Interviews and Other Writings, 1977–1984*, ed. Lawrence D. Kritzman; trans. Alan Sheridan (New York: Routledge, 1988), 301.

19. Bersani, *Homos*, 39.

20. Jarman, *At Your Own Risk*, 28. Jarman's connection here between sexuality and race is very much to the point, as I will argue.

21. Bersani, *Homos*, 58–59, 101.

22. Jeremy Tambling, *Opera, Ideology and Film* (Manchester: Manchester University Press, 1987), 119, 122.

23. Benjamin Britten, *Letters from a Life: The Selected Letters and Diaries of Benjamin Britten*, vol. 1, ed. Donald Mitchell (London: Faber and Faber, 1991), 449.

24. Philip Brett, "Eros and Orientalism in Britten's Operas," in *Queering the Pitch*, 251.

25. Virginia Woolf, *Three Guineas* (Harmondsworth: Penguin, 1977). Woolf's brilliant analysis of the relation of women to the nation is in many ways parallel to what I am arguing about the relation of the homosexual to the nation. Particularly relevant are her comment to her male interlocutor that she "has no wish to be 'English' on the same terms that you yourself are 'English'" (116), and her statement that "as a woman, I have no country. As a woman I want no country. As a woman my country is the whole world" (125). Also relevant to the present argument are Woolf's brief comments on Wilfred Owen (10–11), whom she counts as an ally.

26. Quoted in Carpenter, *Benjamin Britten*, 404–405.

27. Kennedy, *Britten*, 209.

28. Ibid., 213–14.

29. Jennifer Breen, ed., *Wilfred Owen: Selected Poetry and Prose* (New York: Routledge, 1988), 171.

30. Douglas Kerr, *Wildred Owen's Voices: Language and Community* (Oxford: Clarendon Press, 1993), 271.

31. Bersani, "Is the Rectum a Grave?" 222.

32. Jarman, *War Requiem*, xii.

33. Jeffery-Poulter, *Peers, Queers, and Commons*, 228.

34. Ibid., 257.

35. Brett, "Musicality," 21.

36. *Sunday Times*, January 10, 1988, C1–C2. For a brief account of the attack and Jarman's response the following week, see Chris Lippard and Guy Johnson, "Private Practice, Public Health: The Politics of Sickness and the Films of Derek Jarman," in *Fires Were Started: British Cinema and Thatcherism*, ed. Lester Friedman (Minneapolis: University of Minnesota Press, 1993), 281.

37. Jarman, *War Requiem*, 29.

38. Anna Marie Smith, *New Right Discourse on Race and Sexuality: Britain, 1968–1990* (Cambridge: Cambridge University Press, 1994), 26.

39. Jeffery-Poulter, *Peers, Queers, and Commons*, 265.

40. Simon Watney has written extensively on the British media's representation of AIDS. See, for example, *Policing Desire: Pornography, AIDS and the Media* (London: Methuen, 1987). In *At Your Own Risk* Jarman discusses the tabloids' treatment of AIDS (91–97), as well as their irresponsible coverage of his own illness (125–28). See also *Modern Nature: The Journals of Derek Jarman* (London: Vintage Books, 1992), passim.

41. Andrew Higson, *Waving the Flag: Constructing a National Cinema in Britain* (Oxford: Clarendon Press, 1995), 27, 47.

42. Salman Rushdie, "Inside the Whale," *Granta* 11 (1984): 130.

43. See Suzanne Collier's fine essay on the relation between the stage and screen version of *Henry V*, as well as the relations among Branagh, Olivier, and Henry, "Post-Falklands, Post-Colonial: Contextualizing Branagh as Henry V on Stage and on Film," *Essays in Theatre/Études Théâtrales* 10, no. 2 (1990): 143–54.

44. Kenneth Branagh, *Beginnings* (London: Chatto & Windus, 1989), 236.

45. Michael Manheim, "The Function of Battle Imagery in Kurosawa's Histories and the *Henry V* Films," *Literature/Film Quarterly* 22, no. 2 (1994): 133.

46. Collier, "Post-Falklands, Post-Colonial," 149.

47. Graham Holderness, "'What ish my nation?': Shakespeare and National Identities" *Textual Practice* 5, no. 1 (1991): 87.

295

Strange
Meeting: Wilfred
Owen, Benjamin
Britten, Derek
Jarman, and the
*War Requiem*

48. Higson, *Waving the Flag*, 122.

49. Lippard and Johnson, "Private Practice, Public Health," 288.

50. Jarman, *War Requiem*, 29.

51. Ibid., 24.

52. Lippard and Johnson, "Private Practice, Public Health," 285.

53. Jarman, *War Requiem*, 16.

54. Ibid., 31.

55. Bertolt Brecht, *Brecht on Theatre*, ed. and trans. John Willett (New York: Hill and Wang, 1964), 71.

56. See especially the essay "On Opera," in *Brecht on Theatre*, 33–42.

57. Brecht, *Brecht on Theatre*, 71.

58. Jarman, *War Requiem*, 14.

59. Michel Foucault, *Foucault Live: Interviews, 1966–1984*, ed. Sylvère Lotringer; trans. John Johnston (New York: Semiotext(e), 1989), 204.

60. Bersani, "Is the Rectum a Grave?" 222.

61. "Preface" to Jarman, *War Requiem*, vii.

62. Jarman trained as a painter, and initially worked as a set designer for ballet, opera, and film. In the late 1960s he began making films in the gay subculture of London. See the chapter "Home Movies" in *Dancing Ledge*, ed. Shaun Allen (London: Quartet Books, 1991), 114–38.

63. Colin MacCabe, "Throne of Blood," *Sight and Sound* (Oct. 1991): 14.

64. Eric Hobsbawm, "The Opiate Ethnicity," *Alphabet City* 2 (1992): 8.

## CHAPTER THIRTEEN

*Metropolitan Opera / Suburban Identity*

Kevin Kopelson

There are two kinds of queer theorists. Some, like Eve Kosofsky Sedgwick (*Epistemology of the Closet*), want to know how we make sense—or nonsense—of different desires. Others, like Kaja Silverman (*Male Subjectivity at the Margins*), want to know why we desire differently.[1] The former tend to be Foucauldian and analyze discursive constructions of sexuality. The latter tend to be Lacanian and offer psychoanalytic explanations—if only because these explanations are easy to find and hard to disprove. Wayne Koestenbaum (*The Queen's Throat: Opera, Homosexuality, and the Mystery of Desire*) wants to know why we desire differently.[2] He wants to know why some men love men—and opera, and why some women love women—and opera. But he's too smart to look to psychoanalysis for answers. Like Roland Barthes, from whom he's learned a thing or two, Koestenbaum disturbs our faith in psychoanalysis—an institution, or discourse, that like any religion has too much faith in itself. Koestenbaum does identify "the curiosity of the 'homosexual' who wants to know the origin of his preference" with the curiosity of Oedipus, "who wanted to know the secret of his birth," but he can't believe Oedipus ever learned it (54). Nor can he believe, as Silverman does, that something as simple (and demeaning) as a "negative" Oedipus complex will ever satisfy his own curiosity. Desire is "mysterious," Koestenbaum asserts, and therefore inexplicable. "When I as [a] gay person," he writes, "*go backward* to find or write the story of my sexuality, I am making it up, because sexuality has no absolute origin or motivation" (54).

What, then, does *The Queen's Throat* do? If Koestenbaum doesn't presume to explain desire—a rhetorical stance like-minded theorists might wish to replicate—why bother reading him? Because he enables us to explain it ourselves. Koestenbaum tells stories about his homoerotic and operatic inclinations, orientations, fantasies, impressions, and experiences. But he withholds morals. He turns readers into moralists, or theorists. He has us reproduce his Barthesian text, re-create his purple prose. He assumes, however, that most of us need help and so suggests inferences (his suggestions are always generous—multiple and indeterminate) we might make. Here, for example, are Koestenbaum's reflections on one voice manual: "If I imitate Guilbert and make my face Serene, Gray, or Neutrally Amiable, will I have introduced new desires, or will I have restaged old ones? Maybe old desires, when mimicked, become new: maybe there are no new desires, and all we can do is imaginatively and wittily reinhabit old ones" (170). Are we to conclude that desire is imitative or that it is nonimitative? (In other words, what is our take on René Girard [*Deceit, Desire, and the Novel*]?[3]) That desire is performative or nonperformative? (What is our take on Judith Butler [*Gender Trouble*]?[4]) That it is fantasmatic or nonfantasmatic? (On Freud, Lacan, and Silverman?) I say: all of the above. No, make that some. No, none. I guess I'll have to think about it—and Koestenbaum makes me want to think about it.

For the most part, however, Koestenbaum is far more suggestive—and poetic—than this example would indicate. His typical move, characteristic of his first book (*Double Talk: The Erotics of Male Literary Collaboration*) as well, is to indicate metaphoric connections between otherwise unrelated phenomena, to hint that profound relation is always only metaphoric, and to let us make what we will of his intriguing juxtapositions.[5] In *Double Talk* Koestenbaum juxtaposed collaboration and copulation, and implied that homosocial partners always understand themselves as heterosexual partners—a notion nonheterocentric readers may choose to resist, but Koestenbaum chooses to repeat. "When men collaborate," he writes of composers and librettists, "they often imagine that they are doing the miraculous work of gestation together, homoerotically. . . . Every opera is a coupling: not an affair of actual flesh, but an abstract romance of words and music" (187). (This would even seem to apply to composer-librettists. See Jean-Jacques Nattiez's *Wagner Androgyne*.[6]) Most of Koestenbaum's latest juxtapositions, however, are far more startling, his implications far less obvious. Now bilingual libretti suggest bisexuality. Spindle holes are reminders of "the emptiness at the center of a listener's life and the ambiguities in any sexual body, including a homosexual body, concerning the proper and improper function of orifices" (56). Monophonic recordings seem homosexual, and stereophonic recordings heterosexual. Homosexuality and bel canto, although "not the same thing, [are both] wrapped in languages of control and cure" (159). Opera and homosexuality are equally unreal, "and so gays may seek out art that does not respect the genuine" (145). More important, they're equally vocal. "Training a voice" and "voicing a sexuality" are parallel processes, because "sexuality (as we know it) is always vocal, is ineluctably vocal, is structurally vocal" (174–75).

Some readers—ones who require "rigor"—won't want to make anything of these and other similar juxtapositions. So what if homosexuality and opera are both vocal? What's that supposed to mean? Michael Shae, for example, who reviewed *The Queen's Throat* in a gay studies newsletter, complains that Koestenbaum never "resolves his hunger for opera into a coherent narrative or conceptual apparatus," and finds that his "elaborately spun web of analogies between singing and sexuality, between vocal production and the production of a sexual self . . . dissolve[s] in its figurations."[7] Other readers will want to make much. Most reviewers, in fact, provide their own explanations of opera queens—explanations Koestenbaum incites, but in ways his reviewers can't quite articulate. Charles Rosen, for example, picks up on Koestenbaum's suggestion that Mae West, although "not an opera singer . . . thought like one" (91). Rosen writes:

> The diva, like Mae West, presents an erotic charge with no sexual threat. . . . The coarseness of Mae West's verbal comedy, combined with the way her appearance both represents and distances an erotic invitation at the same time, allows the homosexual to approach female sexuality without fear of aggression. The cult of the diva offers him similar and even greater freedom . . . . The diva helps him escape the shame with which society has characterized his inadequate response to the female anatomy. At last he can find genuine passion for a woman, not merely as a mother or as a nanny, but as an erotic object, for the sexuality embodied—or disembodied—in her voice.[8]

I doubt that Koestenbaum, who shows no such sense of threat or fear of aggression, would endorse this reductive and somewhat misogynist explanation. He would, however, appreciate the way Rosen uses *The Queen's Throat*. Koestenbaum would have any queer reader "read resistantly for inscriptions of his condition [and search] for signs of himself."[9] In fact, his final chapter ("A Pocket Guide to Queer Moments in Opera"), a series of impressions that begins with Butterfly's entrance and ends with Isolde's "Liebestod," shows how Koestenbaum himself does this. (It was gay Walter Pater, of course, who queered impressionism from the get go.) But by writing an open text that asks them to do so, Koestenbaum risks being written off by opera queens who don't recognize themselves in *The Queen's Throat*. Alex Ross, for example, concludes his review by rejecting Koestenbaum's reading of the "Liebestod":

> Koestenbaum . . . writes, "A complete harmonious society (an audience, an orchestra) surrounds Isolde, and affirms her as power's mouthpiece, even while she performs the diminuendos of a scapegoat." It's an echo

of Theodor Adorno's incomparable "In Search of Wagner," which [finds] solace in the tumultuous third act of "Tristan": "By voicing the fears of helpless people, it could signal help for the helpless, however feebly and distortedly. In doing so it would renew the promise contained in the age-old protest of music: the promise of a life without fear." Amid piles of records in my lonely homosexual apartment, I am listening in vain for this solace, this harmoniousness. "It could . . . it would"—what of that? It didn't.[10]

Readers like Ross tend to see Koestenbaum as narcissistic—to think: He's interested in himself, but not interested in *me*. Ross calls *The Queen's Throat* "sumptuously self-contained." Brooks Peters calls it "self-indulgent."[11] What Ross and Peters fail to realize is that they are narcissistic, not Koestenbaum. It is they who assume that they typify "the" opera queen, "the" gay man. Koestenbaum knows there's more than one kind of opera queen. He even sees himself as atypical: "I have always felt that my opera queendom is paltry and postmodern because I don't pursue it literally enough" (22). But atypical tastes are extremely interesting. They're interesting in and of themselves, and they're interesting insofar as they help explain typical tastes. Conceptions of homosexuality, for example, circumscribe both homosexual and, insofar as it sees itself as nonhomosexual, heterosexual experience—which is why queer theorists, including ones who happen not to be queer (and so can't be accused of narcissism), study them.

Koestenbaum maintains this dual focus. He scrutinizes his unconventional fanaticism in order to appreciate himself and to understand "the" conventional queen—"Mendy in [Terrence McNally's] *Lisbon Traviata*," the opera expert "who knows everything, who puts your humble tastes to shame," who uses his "intense, phobic knowledge [as] a bludgeon" (34–35). (Edward Rothstein fails to see this and chastises Koestenbaum for ignoring Mendy, whose fanaticism Rothstein calls "a sad escape from human interaction."[12]) Unfortunately, conventional connoisseurs may resent Koestenbaum because his understanding is itself rather phobic:

> The opera queen who only likes Monteverdi, the opera queen who doesn't go to the Met anymore, the opera queen who can't stand Sutherland, the opera queen who gave me his 1953 Callas Cetra *Traviata* because he said her voice was fingernails against a chalkboard, the opera queen who disagrees with the maestro's tempi, the opera queen who hates Wagner or loves only Wagner, the opera queen who doesn't recognize himself in this description, the opera queen who thinks homosexuality has nothing to do with opera, the opera queen who never has body odor but then, suddenly, unexpectedly stinks. *(34–35)*

They should realize, however, that Koestenbaum isn't trying to demonize them. He's trying to problematize his urge to demonize them. He's *staging* his phobic understanding.

Attentive readers, especially ones opera experts "humble," will notice the subtlety of that staging. Just as heterosexuals make homosexuals feel like failures (i.e., see us as badly gendered versions of themselves), connoisseurs make Koestenbaums feel inadequate (i.e., see us as insufficiently acculturated versions of themselves). They also make us feel angry, insecure, and envious. But just as most homosexuals wouldn't rather be heterosexual, most Koestenbaums wouldn't rather be connoisseurs. We're happy with our own fabulousness—our culture, our humor, our pleasure. Our strange tendency to shun performances. (We like recordings.) Our unjustifiable fondness for Anna Moffo (whom Rosen derides as "second-rate"[13]). Our inexplicable unwillingness to knock on dressing-room doors. Koestenbaum writes, "The opera queen who is a part-time nudist and runs a bed-and-breakfast and won't go to the local Falstaff because Moffo isn't singing Nannetta: that is the opera queen I could be, a hack, an amateur, who will never go to La Scala, who has never met a diva, but *who has his own province of affection that no one can usurp*" (35, emphasis added). It's a passage that both transcribes and transcends Roland Barthes. Like Koestenbaum, Barthes—who was more of a Lieder queen than an opera queen—prefers amateurs to connoisseurs and virtuosos; he "freely exalts some little-known, secondary, forgotten artist, and . . . turns away from some consecrated star."[14] Barthes prefers Panzéra to Fischer-Dieskau; Koestenbaum prefers Moffo to Callas. But Barthes, unlike Koestenbaum, never transvalues amateurism. Barthes always pretends to be a better musician, as well as a better homosexual, than he really was.[15] Koestenbaum never does. He embraces, or *tries* to embrace, musical and sexual "inadequacy." It is tempting to trace this embrace to the fact that whereas Barthes played the piano, and so approximated the musical expertise he couldn't attain, Koestenbaum can't sing ("If I could sing I would not be writing this" [154]), and so can't quite identify with divas he desires. (I'm alluding to somatic identification. Psychic identification, Koestenbaum suggests, is relatively easy to establish: "I spent much of childhood trying to distinguish identification from desire, asking myself, 'Am I in love with Julie Andrews, or do I think I *am* Julie Andrews?' " [18].) In fact, he can barely talk: "I speak from my throat, not my diaphragm [and am] perennially hoarse. . . . I speak huskily, like Harvey Fierstein" (13). But I'd trace Koestenbaum's embrace to something else.

Barthes feels constrained by stereotypes, sexual stereotypes in particular, and tries to eradicate them. Sexuality, for Barthes, will be liberated when it fails to signify. Male homosexuality, for example, mustn't denote "the invert" or "the mama's boy." (Barthes, to his discredit, is less troubled by noneffeminate stereotypes that adhere to gay men—"the trick," "the cruiser."[16]) Koestenbaum doesn't share this view of gay liberation. He inhabits, and transvalues, the negative stereotypes—including the stereotypes "opera queen" and "*amateur* opera queen"—that Barthes finds inhospitable:

> I'm a neat, fussy homosexual: you know the type. I don't look for the
> source of my conduct (why am I neat? why am I fussy?), but I simply acknowledge the discourses looming like gargoyles at the helm
> of my life, the discourse of hygiene intersecting with the discourse
> of homosexuality, and I, trapped, shut into these languages, shaped
> by them—though I also find them obliquely inspiring, and a source
> of wonder. (58)

Readers must decide for themselves whether Koestenbaum's position is
more or less advanced than that of Barthes. I myself am undecided. I feel
empowered as well as disempowered by "reverse" discourse (the term is
Foucault's),[17] and mesmerized as well as repulsed by Barthes's ludic project.
I do know this, however. At a time when queer theorists tend to celebrate
successful (i.e., ironized or campy) sexual performances, Koestenbaum
(unlike Butler, unlike Barthes) has the brilliance and temerity to celebrate
unsuccessful ones, and in so doing tries to deconstruct the notion of sexual
"failure" altogether. "The tendency of a diva's voice to break down," he
writes, "makes queer people feel at home. Collapsing, the diva says, 'I am
discontinuous. I am vulnerable. I cannot bear the martyrdom of performance and exposure'" (126). Callas is a case in point. Koestenbaum worships Callas "because she made mistakes. . . . she was a mess *and* she was a
goddess" (136). No other gay critic takes this tack. Richard Dyer, for example, when considering gay male interest in early Judy Garland (a nonoperatic diva), emphasizes her success:

> Not being glamorous is to fail at femininity, to fail at one's sex role.
> [Garland] might be valued for her peppy singing, but pretty much as
> one of the boys. Lack of glamour—and the painful sense of this registered in the torchy numbers which are often occasioned by a sense of
> inferiority—might correspond with several different ways in which
> gay men think about themselves in relation to their sexuality and sexual attractiveness, as gender misfits . . . , as physically deformed (if
> not bodily, at least biologically), and so on. But of course Judy does
> get Mickey [Rooney], does get to sing for Clark Gable at his birthday
> party, does get to be the star of a Ziegfield show. The pleasure of
> identification with this misfit could also be that she does get her
> heart's desire, as in wish fulfilment alongside her we may too.[18]

Whereas both Dyer and Koestenbaum realize we identify not only with stars
who remind us of the failed selves we know ourselves to be, but also with
stars who remind us of the successful selves we'd like to be, Koestenbaum
alone refuses to characterize sexual failure as "unglamorous." This refusal
should inspire new and interesting work in queer theory, but it will also puzzle some readers—especially those who, like Rosen, don't see themselves as
failures. According to Rosen, "Koestenbaum writes well about [Callas's]
faults [but] does not sufficiently acknowledge her purely musical intelli-

gence, or remark about what two conductors have told me—that she had an uncanny ability to take account of the orchestra and alter the timbre of her notes according to the accompanying harmony."[19] Personally, I'd rather read about her faults, because I've had it up to here with intimidating queens who prattle about her musical intelligence. And as long as I'm ranting, how could Rosen expect Koestenbaum to comment on something he himself had to be told by two conductors?

I'm not surprised by Rosen's puzzlement. He's a first-rate pianist—and writer—who deserves to be self-satisfied, who can afford to imagine Callas as fault-free. He's also a New Yorker. A *true* New Yorker. Unlike Koestenbaum, who was born in San Jose and now lives in New Haven, Rosen is a Manhattanite, is a Parisian, and speaks several foreign languages (the languages of opera), which makes him both metropolitan and cosmopolitan. Koestenbaum has no such facility. Neither have I. Although opera queens are supposed to be—and usually suppose themselves—men of the world, few are. Most of us are parochial and monolingual. We don't live in Paris, Vienna, Milan, or any other city with an opera house. We don't speak French, German, Italian, or any other language that would enable us to know the libretto as well as we know the score, to fully appreciate opera as drama. We're *pseudo*-metropolitan and *pseudo*-cosmopolitan. Deep down, of course, we know it. We know we'll never go to La Scala. We know we need bilingual (if not bisexual) libretti. And, even with them, we know our understanding of opera—understanding presumed to situate us as both urban (if not urbane) and international—to be, at best, approximate. In other words, if I really know the meaning of Aida's "O patria mia," I needn't tell myself, when all is sung and done, that I'm merely one of those *American* opera queens whose primary province of affection happens to have been, well, Queens.

Koestenbaum, however, is a first-rate writer as well, a fact I find troublesome. Lurking behind—or beyond—his transvaluation of musical failure is his sense of himself as a literary success. Koestenbaum knows, and wants us to know, that, as Rosen puts it, he "writes well." (He pretends not to, however: "When a nondiva writes diva prose, she writes to admire or to impersonate" [85].) He'd have us agree with Thomas Disch, who characterizes *The Queen's Throat* as a star turn: "Like the art of the diva that he celebrates, anatomizes and obsesses over, Wayne Koestenbaum's *The Queen's Throat* is . . . a cornucopia of extravagant gestures and precise observations, bon mots, home truths, and preposterous propositions that, like the soprano voice in its full oracular glory, will either raise your hackles or leave you breathless."[20] Koestenbaum presents himself as a *sexual* success as well. Unlike the conventional queen, and unlike Barthes, he's neither closeted nor lonely. Koestenbaum is an attractive, gregarious, sexually active, "married" gay man who doesn't feel he's failed at either heterosexuality or homosexuality. Does this mean that the only critics who ever really transvalue failure aren't really failures themselves? Does it mean that transvaluations of failure are really revaluations of success? Perhaps. But I hope not. My love of deconstructive inversion goes only so far.

My love of camp, however, knows no bounds, which explains why, misappropriating a campy caption Koestenbaum uses to cathect Callas, I titled the earlier version of this review-essay "Tawdrily, I Adore Him." One of the pleasures of his text is, in fact, that it's very campy. This is as it should be, because queer readings of opera often reflect camp "sensibilities." (Note the plural.) But not only does Koestenbaum utilize camp, he theorizes it as well—a critical enterprise with which many queer theorists concern themselves. Sometimes he theorizes camp indirectly, defining it without actually naming it. "I adore Callas," Koestenbaum writes, "because she so frequently expresses fury—a wrath that is its own reward and its own argument, that seeks no external justification, that makes no claim beyond the pleasure of drive, of emotion, of expressing *why I have been wronged*" (147). "Divaspeak," he explains, "is the language of put-on (faked aristocracy, faked humility) but it utterly believes in the effectiveness of its gestures— or pretends to" (132). Sometimes, however, he theorizes camp directly. Koestenbaum sees it as reliant upon Wildean paradox:

> Superficially, Maria Callas took away opera's campiness by making it believable and vivid. And yet by importing truth into opera, an art of the false, she gave the gay fan a dissonance to match his own. Bestowing verisimilitude on Lucia or Norma or Elvira, Callas perforated the operagoer's complacency; her voice and her presence, arsenals of *depth*, when brought to bear on music that had become *superficial*, upset the audience's sense of perspective. Though it seems sacrilegious to call Callas's musically compelling creations camp, she performed the same kind of reversal that camp induces. . . . Callas "camped" *Lucia* not by mocking it (*Lucia* is too easy to mock) but by taking it seriously. (*145*)

He also sees camp as reliant upon Barthesian production. Campy readers, according to Koestenbaum, (re)produce texts that noncampy readers consume:

> Susan Sontag defined "camp" as the anarchic jolt we experience in the face of artistic artifacts that try to be serious and fail. But it is not the object's or artist's failure that makes the artifact campy: the camp sensation is produced by our own joy in having discovered the object, in having been *chosen*, solicited, by it. Experiencing the camp glow is a way of reversing one's abjection, and, by witnessing the depletion of cultural monuments, experiencing one's own power to fill degraded artifacts to the brim with meanings. (*117*)

Koestenbaum's notes on camp are worth considering. The indirect theorizations, for example, shed new light on such drag acts as Glenn Milstead's "Divine" and Barry Humphries's "Dame Edna Everage." But they're hard to characterize. The indirect theorizations reflect a modern camp sensibility. "Fury," "faked aristocracy," and "faked humility" are touchstones of a bygone era, aspects of curious artifacts like *Little Me*, by Patrick Dennis.[21] The direct theorizations, however, reflect a postmodern sensibility. Whereas modern camp (Oscar Wilde, John Waters, Charles Ludlam) values surface over depth, playfulness over seriousness, artificiality over authenticity, and ineptitude over aptitude, postmodern camp inverts these inversions, and values profundity, sobriety, sincerity, and talent—qualities Koestenbaum associates with Callas. The drag queens in *Paris Is Burning* (1992), for example, seem—and try to seem—"real." Sandra Bernhard, in *Without You I'm Nothing* (1990), constantly gestures toward the skillfulness of her unskillful impersonations, as well as toward the genuine (i.e., African-American) femininity she fails to approximate. On balance, though, Koestenbaum's camp sensibility, like (and along with) his opera queendom, is quite postmodern—which explains three things. It explains his distance from his pre-postmodern subject. ("The opera queen is a dated species: very 1950s" [31].) It explains the directness of his postmodern and the indirectness of his modern theorizations. (He wants camp to be postmodern but can't help it if it's not.) And it explains his somewhat Barthesian inability to fully transvalue failure. (Unless, of course, the *failure* to transvalue failure is a covert transvaluation of failure—but I doubt it.) Koestenbaum, unlike Ludlam (the author of *Galas* [1983], a play based on Callas), is simply too postmodern, as well as too successful, to appreciate fully the extent to which Callas *was* a mess.

What does it mean to love someone, or something, "tawdrily"? I wish I knew. And I'm glad I don't. Camp, like poetry, inscribes indeterminacy. Just as poets cultivate "negative capability" (Keats's term for sustaining "uncertainties, Mysteries, doubts, without any irritable reaching after fact & reason"),[22] campy writers cultivate literal irresolution. One way they do so involves italics. Campy writers use italics to be suggestive and to indicate citation—to no source in particular. Ronald Firbank, the marginalized modernist who invented ecclesiastic camp, is terrific at this, as when in *The Flower Beneath the Foot* the Countess of Tolga gives the Queen of Pisuerga "a glance that was known in Court circles as her *tortured-animal* look."[23] Who knows what it means to look like a tortured animal, and who knows which courtier said it first? But we (sort of) get the point. (Glenn Gould, by the way, calls Barbra Streisand—another nonoperatic diva—"one of the great italicizers, no phrase is left solely to its own devices, and the range and diversity of her expressive gift is such that one is simply unable to chart an *a priori* stylistic course on her behalf."[24]) Another way campy writers cultivate irresolution involves offbeat adverbs. Campy adverbs never denote. They only, and always, connote. When Firbank writes: "Mademoiselle Blumenghast clasped her hands *brilliantly* across the nape of her neck," I (almost) feel I know the girl—even though I can't imagine her improbable gesture.[25] Koestenbaum—a poetic critic who camps it up, a campy critic who thinks like a poet—flirts with both techniques. Not that reading Koesten-baum is like reading Firbank. Koestenbaum adores Callas "tawdrily," but he uses campy adverbs far less frequently and rarely italicizes words the way Firbank does. But the two share a "sensibility," a campy and poetic tendency toward enigmatic figures and mystical phenomena, that may be modern as well as postmodern.

In "The Answer Is in the Garden," an elegy about a friend who died of AIDS, Koestenbaum offers two explanations of this modern/postmodern sensibility. One of them opens the poem:

> . . . campfire fables—
> Bermuda Triangles, Kennedy death plots—
> Touched me as only the watery, unrigorous
> Mind can be shaken: of my epiphanies
> I demand little more than an impression of speed,
> Illusion that I am moving toward an end
> Unseen by all but the wisest spectators, who ask
> Not for real prophecy, but the skeleton
> Of enchantment, private auguries, a ringing phone.
>
> (*lines 41–49*)

The other ends it:

> . . . Metro's last
> Fevered sentence was, "The answer is in the garden."
> I meet Metro in his still-tended garden
> And am wearing his clothes, given to me because
> We are one size. I want to read Metro's lips
> For he is facing the invisible, and speaking
> Eloquently of efforts taken too late,
> The many souls wandering in the air, not pinioned
> As children are. I am too corporeal
> To hold the attention of one so weightless, to say,
> In a tone of sad confusion, that the good
> Suit he wore in life fits me well, too well, like a charm.[26]
>
> (*lines 150–61*)

The wonderfully unrigorous mind, with its healthy suspicion of facile eti-ology; the epiphanies of which he demands little more than an impression of speed; the illusory movement toward ends he can't quite envision—Koestenbaum tells us how he reads, and how to read him. He tries to deci-pher things he doesn't fully understand, things he's too honest—and too humble—to claim to understand. Koestenbaum the poet would read the lips of a dead friend who's told him, yet hasn't told him, the answer he needs to know. Koestenbaum the critic, listening to a hundred-year-old recording, feels "as if Adelina Patti were whispering something I could not understand, or as if the medium of reproduction itself were whispering instructions, codes, opacities" (83). They are, of course, one and the same person.

I'm reminded, once again, of Barthes. Unlike André Gide, who loved Chopin and who played him in a plodding manner that reflected a cautious sensibility,[27] Barthes loved Schumann and played him in a rapid manner that reflected an incautious sensibility. Barthes especially loved Schumann's use of the word *rasch*. *Rasch*, Barthes realizes, "signifies only: *quick, fast (presto)*." But mightn't it also, he asks, signify "the truth of the signifier: as if I had a limb swept away, *torn off* by the wind, whipped toward a site of dispersion which is precise but unknown?"[28] And mightn't it also signify Schumann's extemporaneousness, which Barthes extols as "closed to any general meaning . . . in short a pure *wandering*, a becoming without finality"?[29] (Note the similarity to Gould's description of Streisand's italics: "one is simply unable to chart an *a priori* stylistic course on her behalf.") Like Barthes, like Gould, Koestenbaum is rather hasty (another meaning of *rasch*), and rather improvisatory. He's a speed-reader who enjoys illegible texts (musical scores, sexual scripts) that, to cite Disch's description of *The Queen's Throat*, "leave you breathless." He's an epistemological vagabond who doesn't know—and who doesn't really need to know—his origin, his location, or his destination, but who'd like to get there, or at least to get going, as soon as possible.

Campy queens who, like Koestenbaum, happen to be "hasty" will love *The Queen's Throat*. Cautious ones won't. But one needn't be campy—in fact one probably shouldn't be—to appreciate Koestenbaum's sentimentality. Yes, there's something sentimental about camp. As Sontag notes, "the relation of Camp to the past is extremely sentimental."[30] But neither Koestenbaum's sentimental relation to opera, which he calls "an outdated art form" (145), nor his (related) sentimental relation to modern homosexuality, which he calls equally passé, can be seen as campy. For one thing he's far too serious about them. (Campy sentimentality doesn't take itself very seriously.) He has to be, because "sentimentality," with its Romantic and Victorian, not to mention its effeminate and emotional connotations, is a dirty word in academic circles, including the circles described by "queer theory" and "lesbian and gay studies." Barthes realized this, which explains the defensive posture of *A Lover's Discourse: Fragments* (1977), his sentimental interrogation of sentimentality, as well as the fact that the book hasn't instigated many cultural studies of love. As Barthes puts it, even scholars who approve of (sexual) transgression see the introduction of even "*a touch of sentimentality* [as] the *ultimate* transgression . . . the transgression of transgression itself."[31] *The Queen's Throat* is one such introduction. Like *A Lover's Discourse*, it's a sentimental interrogation of sentimental cathexes (Koestenbaum's, for the most part) that violates the transgressive norms of a discipline not yet queer enough to take lovers— let alone *opera* lovers—as seriously as they take themselves. Which helps explain why it's proven to be more popular among sentimental folk who couldn't care less about queer theory than among antisentimental academics who see themselves as queer theorists.

Koestenbaum's own sentimentality, however—the sentimentality of his interrogation of sentimentality—isn't exactly Barthesian. Barthes's text is a fragmentary "affirmation" of erotic experiences that are still alive and well, but fundamentally depressing.[32] Barthes sees love—and seems to have experienced it—as Wertheresque. Koestenbaum's text is a fragmentary "elegy" concerning experiences we no longer have, but found euphoric. Like "The Answer Is in the Garden," *The Queen's Throat* is a doleful interrogation, a woeful celebration of opera ("I am performing an autopsy, an elegy; peering into opera's corpse, I am mournful and coldly curious, with my gloves, tools, and formulae" [192]), of opera queens ("This book is an elegy for the opera queen. I am an opera queen, but I am also mourning him" [41]), and of the recordings queens used to listen to ("This is an elegy for opera records and for those who loved them" [48]). A sentimental "air of melancholy" pervades the text, not because opera never really fulfilled our "least sanctioned desires"[33] (a critique I'll explore momentarily), but because it's not supposed to do so anymore.

Another reason that Koestenbaum's sentimentality isn't very campy is that it's somewhat cathartic. As Sontag notes, "Camp refuses . . . the risks of fully identifying with extreme states of feeling." "Camp and tragedy," for example, "are antitheses."[34] Koestenbaum agrees but can't say the same of tragedy and sentimentality. Tragedy and sentimentality, he suggests, are both related and unrelated. (Poststructural theorists often attend to nonoppositional, nonhierarchical difference.) In "The Answer Is in the Garden," Koestenbaum writes:

> . . . Metro died at thirty-five,
> A waste huge enough that I can address my parents
> Within the magic circle of his passing:
> Let the fact of my body be the *Piramide*
> Memorial to your once marriage, and don't
> Cry about things only seventy-five-percent sad—
> Save tears for the fully tragic.
>
> *(lines 144–50)*

In *The Queen's Throat*, he considers the extent to which opera enabled him to recognize, and respond to, Metro's "fully tragic" death:

> Even before AIDS, I listened to death scenes so that I might identify with the dying woman and the bereft man, and so that I might produce "sentimentality" in my body: sighs, tears, extravagances I can never explain. Call by its proper name the pity and terror we feel when an opera mauls us, suffocates us with sentiment, makes no reasoned dramatic claim. Not camp, not bathos, not sentimentality: dignify queer emotion by saying *catharsis*, even if opera induces the wish, condemned as effeminate, never to reassemble the socialized self, but, instead, to remain in tears forever, to stay where Puccini's *La Bohème* (1896) places us. *(235)*

I find this passage doubly—no, make that triply—transgressive. Koestenbaum violates the norms of a transgressive discipline (queer theory) by being sentimental, then proceeds to violate the norms of sentimentality by exposing, verifying, and validating the tragic aspects of gay experience. Other queer theorists deconstruct discourses surrounding AIDS, of course, and other theorists analyze non-AIDS-related conflations of homosexuality and tragic early death (from Orpheus to Dorian Gray). None, however, share Koestenbaum's daring. None, that is, are willing to weep—and to weep long and hard—at a time when rage (and I don't mean campy rage) is seen as the only politically viable reaction to senseless loss.

Some readers will doubt that Koestenbaum, who privileges queer impressions (and so couldn't possibly know what's *really* going on), sees *La Bohème* as "fully" tragic. But Koestenbaum, contrary to what Rothstein would have us think, isn't the kind of queen for whom queer "moments and scenes become *substitutes* for a nonexistent [nonqueer] whole."[35] He's the kind of queen who does double takes—who, notwithstanding the fact that he can't speak Italian, recites "the entire plot [of *La Traviata*] with mind-numbing thoroughness, including what Violetta feels in the final moments of the opera when she disbelieves her own imminent death ('rinasce!')" (40) *and* who finds that the opera fulfills his least sanctioned desires. In other words, he's the kind of queen who experiences *La Traviata* as both tragic and euphoric. Many of his critics aren't quite so adept. Ross, "sitting amid piles of records in [his] lonely homosexual apartment," listens in vain for the sexual solace Wagner offers both Koestenbaum and Adorno. Rothstein feels that operas, seen whole, "defeat" our least sanctioned desires. "Only in fragments and with irony," he writes, "is opera ever completely unfettered and liberating."[36] But Koestenbaum never claims queers find texts like *La Bohème*, *La Traviata*, and *Tristan und Isolde* "completely" liberating. He thinks we read—and *should* read—along as well as against the grain. He recommends that we *consume* heterocentric texts (heterocentrically, tragically) as well as *(re)produce* them (homoerotically, euphorically). Which is yet another transcendent transcription of Barthes, who writes off textual consumption and fails to realize the extent to which it can be profitable as well as pleasurable.

*Profit, pleasure*—these, of course, are terms Marxists never valorize. Then again, Koestenbaum is no Marxist. "Yes," he writes, "I fetishize records; and yes, I fetishize men's bodies" (59). Unlike Michael Bronski,[37] he doesn't underscore the fact that opera queens amass cultural capital. He doesn't call them snobs and doesn't castigate them for supporting social systems in which people who can't afford to appreciate opera count as odd men out. Koestenbaum, in other words, wouldn't bother to read Rosen's "nanny" symptomatically. ("At last he can find genuine passion for a woman, not merely as a mother or as a nanny, but as an erotic object.") But why should he? The line deconstructs itself. Which is one reason I, for one, wouldn't care to consume a Marxist analysis of opera queendom: it probably wouldn't tell me anything I don't already suspect. Another and more important reason is that I don't enjoy seeing queer pleasure repudiated for "political" purposes, be they right-wing and puritanical or left-wing and ascetic. We still need queer critics to articulate, and celebrate, pleasures (both sexual and nonsexual) that are central to queer identities—even though well-meaning friends on the left, most of whom wear very nice clothes, want us to clean out *our* closets and donate the contents to Goodwill.

As you may have gleaned by now, *The Queen's Throat* is performative. It's performative insofar as it stages Koestenbaum's phobic understanding of connoisseurs. It's performative insofar as it's celebratory. It's performative insofar as it's sentimental. It's also performative (nonconstative) insofar as it makes readers do things. I've already indicated that Koestenbaum has us come up with explanations. I haven't mentioned, though, that he has us come out of closets:

> Opera queen, whether or not you choose to call yourself "opera queen": opera queen, whether or not you choose to identify yourself as "gay" (the label is reductive, but do we have another?): impresario, conductor, singer, costume designer, makeup artist, lighting designer, prompter, usher, ticket-booth agent: fan, solitary, standing-room-only habitué, record collector, weeper-at-telecasts, hoarder-of-programs: come out. *(41)*

Some of us do so slyly. Walter Clemons, for example, drops a few hairpins: "Anna Moffo is an original choice. My own, Claudia Muzio, is more conventional."[38] (His by-line reads: "Clemons, a freelance critic who owns almost as many opera recordings as books, is completing a biography of Gore Vidal.") Some of us do so spectacularly. Ross's comment about sitting "amid piles of records in [his] lonely homosexual apartment" is particularly stunning. I find it remarkable, but not surprising, that we do what we're told. Most successful performative critiques—and I don't know of many—are Barthesian. Barthes (a lover who "affirms" the lover), like Koestenbaum (an opera queen who "mourns" the opera queen), is especially compelling when he doesn't distance himself—or us—from problematic subject positions. Barthes adores Garbo (but not Audrey Hepburn), and so can't quite demystify her. ("The face of Garbo is an Idea, that of Hepburn, an Event."[39]) Koestenbaum adores Callas (but not Hepburn), and so can't quite demystify her. ("While Hepburn seemed born to be beautiful, Callas had an effortful, wounded relationship to her glamour" [139].) Both, however, make us understand—and (mis)recognize ourselves as equally prone to—these cathexes in ways that nonperformative, noninterpellative texts don't. In other words, they make us realize why queers (including postmodern, poststructural queers) can't help but seek pleasures nonqueers find perverse.

Some of Koestenbaum's readers, however, don't do as they're told. I can think of two reasons why. First, they may be *afraid* to come out. Far be it from me—whose parents, siblings, friends, and colleagues haven't been especially homophobic—to call these readers cowards. But I'm troubled by the fact that they prevent *The Queen's Throat* from realizing its political potential. (Should Koestenbaum have found a way to make fearful readers reveal themselves? Could he have?) A second reason is that they may not want essentially private pleasure publicized. Publicity, they feel, will take the fun out of being a (closet) fan. David Deitcher, for example, resents the inclusion of Koestenbaum's text in a book display at the Whitney Biennial. "I was dismayed to come upon the pale-green and pink slip case of [*The Queen's Throat*], which I happened to be enjoying at home. Its presence on the Whitney's hit list felt unmistakably grotesque."[40] (Don't take the phrase "which I happened to be enjoying at home" to mean that Deitcher is a self-confessed opera queen; he refers to queens in the third person.)

I'm thankful Koestenbaum has no such scruples. His public performance of private pleasure has enabled me to enjoy, and to understand, my own—pleasure as well as performance—all the more. What I don't understand, though, is why Koestenbaum accedes to the notion that opera queens are dying off, a notion he himself calls both "illogical" and "homophobic." ("We consider the opera queen to be a pre-Stonewall throwback because we homophobically devalue opera love as addictive behavior and as displaced eroticism. . . . After sexual liberation, who needs opera?" [31]) Why write an "elegy," why act as though all opera queens are somewhat closeted, when he knows (1) that queer sexuality, like any sexuality, will always articulate itself through "displacement" (I'd use a non-Freudian term, but can't think of one); (2) that "liberated" queers will always consume, and (re)produce, nonqueer texts (including heterocentric operas); and (3) that they'll probably do so sentimentally as well as campily. After all, even post-Stonewall queers know heartbreak.

Koestenbaum begins *The Queen's Throat* with a primal scene:

> The first opera I ever saw: *Aida*. San Francisco War Memorial Opera House, 1969. I was eleven. By the last act I was exhausted, bored. All I remember now is the color of the sky above the Nile—beyond midnight blue, a shade redolent of witchcraft and spice.
>
> In childhood, I stored all my programs in a crate. Recently I found that first opera program: the Radames was Jon Vickers. Only now do I appreciate the name's weight and valor. A house's foundation, even if invisible, exists—has once, long ago, without witnesses, been poured. And so as I try to compose this fragmented history, I must begin with my first *Aida*, unremembered except for the high blue sky. *(9)*

I'm haunted by the expression "high blue sky." For some ineffable reason, I see it as a transcendental (and synecdochic) signifier of the book it sets in motion. Perhaps Koestenbaum knows why. Perhaps not—he'd have to know himself better than he (says he) does. He'd also have to know me better than I do. Needless to say, I can't really help him with the first requirement. (This essay is the best I can do, I'm afraid.) But I can help him with the second (do you read me, Wayne?) by describing a primal scene I've never understood—and hope he can.

The first opera *I* ever saw: *Le nozze di Figaro*. The New York State Theater, 1967. I was seven and wore a tuxedo—rented, of course, not for the occasion, but for my sister's wedding, which had taken place the day before. All I remember now is a single line of recitative, sung (in English) by the countess. Or to be precise, all I remember is that I used to remember the line—and that I've never found it in the libretto. Koestenbaum writes: "Listen to the Countess, and learn to sublimate your own abjection" (213). Yes, of course. But why do I feel I learned something else—something I can't quite put my finger on—as well?

NOTES

An earlier version of this review-essay appeared in *19th-Century Music*.

1. Eve Kosofsky Sedgwick, *Epistemology of the Closet* (Berkeley: University of California Press, 1990). Kaja Silverman, *Male Subjectivity at the Margins* (New York: Routledge, 1992).

2. Wayne Koestenbaum, *The Queen's Throat: Opera, Homosexuality, and the Mystery of Desire* (New York: Poseidon Press, 1993).

3. René Girard, *Deceit, Desire, and the Novel: Self and Other in Literary Structure*, trans. Yvonne Freccero (Baltimore: Johns Hopkins University Press, 1988).

4. Judith Butler, *Gender Trouble: Feminism and the Subversion of Identity* (New York: Routledge, 1990).

5. Wayne Koestenbaum, *Double Talk: The Erotics of Male Literary Collaboration* (New York: Routledge, 1989).

6. Jean-Jacques Nattiez, *Wagner Androgyne: A Study in Interpretation*, trans. Stewart Spencer (Princeton: Princeton University Press, 1993).

7. Michael Shae, "Outing Opera," rev. of *The Queen's Throat*, *Lesbian and Gay Studies Newsletter* (July 1993): 34.

8. Charles Rosen, "The Ridiculous & Sublime," rev. of *The New Grove Dictionary of Opera* and *The Queen's Throat*, *New York Review of Books*, April 22, 1993, 14.

9. Koestenbaum, "Wilde's Hard Labor and the Birth of Gay Reading." In *Engendering Men: The Question of Male Feminist Criticism*, eds. Joseph A. Boone and Michael Cadden (New York: Routledge, 1990), 176–77.

10. Alex Ross, "Grand Seductions," rev. of *The Queen's Throat*, *New Yorker*, April 12, 1993, 120.

11. Ross, "Grand Seductions," 117; Brooks Peters, "A Queen for Days," rev. of *The Queen's Throat*, *Out* (March 1993): 27.

12. Edward Rothstein, "Classical View; Doting on Divas: Private Jokes, Open Secrets," rev. of *The Queen's Throat*, *New York Times*, March 28, 1993, II, 25, 28.

13. Rosen, "Ridiculous & Sublime," 14.

14. Roland Barthes, "The Grain of the Voice." In *The Responsibility of Forms: Critical Essays on Music, Art, and Representation*, trans. Richard Howard (New York: Hill & Wang, 1985), 276.

15. Compare, for example, Barthes's celebratory preface to Renaud Camus's *Tricks* with "Soirées de Paris," in *Incidents*. Barthes, "Preface to Renaud Camus's Tricks," in *The Rustle of Language*, trans. Richard Howard (New York: Hill & Wang, 1986), 291–95; *Incidents* (Paris: Seuil, 1987), 71–116.

16. See my *Love's Litany: The Writing of Modern Homoerotics* (Stanford: Stanford University Press, 1994), in which I analyze this differential treatment.

17. Michel Foucault, *The History of Sexuality*, vol. 1, *An Introduction*, trans. Robert Hurley (New York: Vintage, 1980), 101.

18. Richard Dyer, *Heavenly Bodies: Film Stars and Society* (London: Macmillan, 1986), 167.

19. Rosen, "Ridiculous & Sublime," 14.

20. Thomas M. Disch, "Opera and the Diva's Disciple," rev. of *The Queen's Throat*, *Washington Post*, March 21, 1993 ("Book World"), 3.

21. Patrick Dennis, *Little Me: The Intimate Memoirs of That Great Star of Stage, Screen and Television Belle Poitrine* (New York: Dutton, 1961).

22. Keats, from a letter to George and Thomas Keats (December 1817), quoted in *The Critical Tradition: Classic Texts and Contemporary Trends*, ed. David H. Richter (Boston: Bedford, 1989), 320.

23. Ronald Firbank, *The Flower Beneath the Foot*. In *Five Novels* (New York: New Directions, 1961), 3.

24. Glenn Gould, "Streisand as Schwarzkopf," rev. of "Classical Barbra" (Columbia M33452), *Hi Fidelity* (May 1976): 74.

25. Firbank, *Flower Beneath*, 17 (emphasis added).

26. Koestenbaum, *Ode to Anna Moffo and Other Poems* (New York: Persea, 1990), 75–79.

27. See André Gide, *Notes on Chopin*, trans. Bernard Frechtman (New York: Philosophical Library, 1949), 21–22. Chopin's *Impromptus* should be played "in such a way that they seem to be improvised, that is with a certain, I dare not say slowness, but uncertainty; in any case, without that unbearable assurance which a headlong movement carries with it."

28. Barthes, "Rasch," in *The Responsibility of Forms*, 311.

29. Barthes, "The Romantic Song," in *The Responsibility of Forms*, 291.

30. Susan Sontag, "Notes on Camp," in *Against Interpretation and Other Essays* (New York: Farrar, Straus & Giroux, 1961), 280.

31. Barthes, *Roland Barthes by Roland Barthes*, trans. Richard Howard (New York: Hill & Wang, 1977), 65–66.

32. It is Barthes who calls it an "affirmation." Barthes, *A Lover's Discourse: Fragments*, trans. Richard Howard (New York: Hill & Wang, 1978), 1.

33. Rothstein, "Classical View," 28.

34. Sontag, "Notes on Camp," 287.

35. Rothstein, "Classical View," 28 (emphasis added).

36. Ibid.

37. Michael Bronski, *Culture Clash: The Making of Gay Sensibility* (Boston: South End, 1984).

38. Walter Clemons, "Divas to Die For," rev. of *The Queen's Throat*, *New York Times*, February 28, 1993, VII, 14.

39. Barthes, "The Face of Garbo." In *Mythologies*, trans. Annette Lavers (New York: Noonday, 1991), 57.

40. David Deitcher, "Queens in the Reading Room," rev. of *The Queen's Throat*, *Artforum* (May 1993): 13.

## CHAPTER FOURTEEN

*Divas and Disease, Mourning and Militancy: Diamanda Galas's Operatic*
Plague Mass

Rebecca A. Pope and Susan J. Leonardi

In *The Great Singers* (1966) Henry Pleasants laments the "police escort" that, in the contemporary opera world, supervises "the singers' every utterance" (348).[1] He bemoans the "philosophy of the sanctity of composition and the immutability of the written note" that informs the training of contemporary opera singers and informs as well the expectations of many contemporary listeners. The Western operatic voice is now restricted, controlled, policed in ways unthinkable in earlier centuries. Pleasants further argues that the difficulty of contemporary serious music—difficult to sing, difficult to listen to—and the incompatibility of popular music with classical voice training contribute to the stagnation of the standard repertoire, a repertoire itself adhering to the conventions of the sanctity of the composition and the immutability of the written note. Confined and stagnant, young singers, Pleasants suggests, should continue the efforts of Callas and Sutherland to revive an older tradition in which the musical line "must be shaped, varied, embellished" (352).

Since the publication of *The Great Singers*, opera singers have, of course, done just that. Along with the increased popularity of early music, singers like Julianne Baird have helped restore an earlier tradition that many major opera houses now work to represent in their schedules. What singers gain from this trend and from the proliferation of small ensembles that specialize in such performance is not only a more expansive repertoire but the archeological satisfaction of digging in and re-creating the past, the artistic satisfaction of embellishing what they find, and the creative satisfaction of improvising. Though the early music movement has, as does any musical tradition, its own set of policing procedures, there is for singers an excitement, freedom, and even danger about such performance rare in twentieth-century opera culture. "Improvising and embellishing," Julianne Baird remarks, is like going out on a limb: You can go out a certain distance safely and still get back. But you don't know how far that is until you test it" (Crutchfield, 38). Baird and other singers of early opera specialize in and experiment with the not-written and not-taught as, in part perhaps, a way of evading the opera police and courting danger while remaining within an operatic tradition.

More obviously and more frequently, young people who want to sing and perform choose another idiom altogether in which to express themselves freely, stake out their territory, and court danger, an idiom that, Pleasants says, very few "serious" singers can master (349). Popular music—folk, gospel, country, jazz, and of course pop/rock—is not only a less policed but a more democratic idiom. It does not require the extensive (and expensive) training of the opera singer, nor does it require the same vocal equipment. The popular singing voice, especially in its pop/rock incarnation, is often cyborgian—enhanced, that is, by an array of electronics unimaginable to composers of early opera. This is not to suggest that many popular singers are not highly trained musicians with powerful and aesthetically interesting voices. Many are, and are as well their own composers and lyricists/librettists. Few opera singers, perhaps with the exception of Francesca Caccini (c. 1587–1640), have had such control over so many aspects of their art. Victorian diva Pauline Viardot wrote music and planned to write an opera with George Sand, but most of the music Viardot sang came from the established repertoire, composed, of course, by men. Many divas have had music written *for* them, and they have been instrumental in creating operatic roles. But most of the roles opera singers perform and almost all the music they sing are created and written by others, again almost always men.

Pop/rock artists and performance artists like Laurie Anderson often write and arrange their own music and lyrics, create or direct their own stage performances and videos, accompany themselves on instruments, manipulate their own electronic equipment, distribute on their own recording labels. This control (though itself limited and policed by access to equipment and airwaves, by the decisions of producers and bookers, by the taste of those who buy tickets and CDs, and by the fluctuations of the wider marketplace) over the production of their sometimes quite elaborate performances exceeds the control of even the most demanding and demanded prima donna of the opera world. Until recently, such control was largely limited to male performers, who dominated—with notable exceptions—the rock, jazz, blues, and country scenes. But the last ten years have seen a remarkable proliferation of female performers who do more than sing, many of whom exhibit more similarities to than differences from their sisters in opera. Some of these singers, like Madonna and Annie Lennox, have themselves explicitly flirted with or fled from the title "diva." American singer, composer, and performer Diamanda Galas, dubbed variously by the press as the "Scream Diva" and the "Diva of Disease," has a classically trained voice and records on a rock label, Mute Records, an exemplary contradiction that illustrates the way her music is a hybrid of "serious" music and the extreme fringes of rock. Unlike early opera singers and pop singers, Galas moves both ways: she retrieves what she can from earlier classical forms like opera and sacred music and takes vocal freedoms with and within them similar to those pop singers take. These are, of course, political moves, made in the service of explicitly political ends. Galas uses her classically trained voice to, in her words, "explore the nature of the time we are living in," in other words, to make music an explicitly political discourse: "I don't think that I could survive if the work I was doing was detached from the time in which I was living, and that time includes AIDS. That's why I'm not going on stage and singing *Tosca* or *Norma*, with all due respect to those works and as much as I love them. . ." (Avena, 194–95).[2] Although she doesn't publicly perform Verdi heroines, Galas does, as Verdi himself did, compose works that are fairly explicit in their political positions and claims. Her trilogy of works on AIDS, *The Masque of the Red Death* (and another shorter version performed and recorded as *Plague Mass*), is Galas's best-known work and the work that most explicitly argues that AIDS defines the time in which we live.

Galas's work before the *Plague Mass* was also explicitly political and often focused on the politics of gender. For example, long before Lorena Bobbitt's knife incited a national debate over the boundary between anger and insanity, rage and pathology, so neatly tied together in notions of female "madness," Galas wrote and performed *Wild Women with Steak Knives*, a "Homicidal Love Song for Solo Scream."[3] The word *solo* is somewhat misleading; as in most of the work Galas writes and performs, her voice in *Wild Women* takes on a multitude of parts/roles—here the voices of the fragmented "selves" of a schizophrenic woman. Anger and insanity combine there; female insanity is figured as a symptom of anger. The roles/voices are distinguished through varied timbres, textures, registers, and vocal styles that exploit to the full Galas's extraordinary three-and-one-half octave range. Screams, wails, whispers, glossolalia, and cries of "listen" bespeak rage, terror, isolation. The effect is amplified, in all senses of the word, by Galas's use of multiple microphones and other technological aids that multiply and fracture one voice into multitudes.[4] The voices are the frenzied Maenads' (also known as Bacchae, whom George Eliot's eponymous diva Armgart claims as sisters when she declares that she carries her revenge in her throat). The politics are Medusa's: she who is the object of the gaze gazes back. Galas's performances often work to disrupt the objectifying gaze of masculinist power and lay bare the politics of spectatorship. Although traditional representations of the diva conventionally cast her as an object of masculine desire and fear in perpetual and excessive competition with other women, a feminist counterdiscourse from George Eliot to contemporary women writers and singers represents the diva's voice as a point of identification for other women, as a vehicle for their anger and desire and a site for female community.[5] Galas's narrative of her own vocal history participates in this revisionary countertradition, although, as ever with Galas, in the extreme: "Some of my earliest performances were in mental institutions. . . . The response I got was very positive; it was very much a shared kind of community expression. A lot of women were interested in the way I was using my voice—extroversion of the soul, so to speak" (Avena, 180).

Predictably, reviews in the mainstream press of Galas's performances often employ rhetorical strategies that, Perseus-like, try to cut her down to size—to domesticate and reinscribe her in traditional women's roles. In his *New York Times* review of *Insekta*, Edward Rothstein calls up the conventional figure of the demented diva—her voice "always on the edge, touching on the forbidden, breaking the boundaries of earthly melody"—and enrolls Galas among their numbers. By the close of this very mixed review, however, he decides that Galas is somehow beyond divahood: "Ms. Galas has redefined the diva: She is already over the edge, already beyond madness. She is neither noble nor heroic nor tragic. She is merely a victim" (13)—as though victimhood doesn't always haunt the diva, since she plays victims and sings to avoid becoming a victim herself. Galas's threat to the system of binary oppositions on which cultural constructions of gender and sexuality depend leads another critic to engage in a massively defensive but finally incoherent remarshaling of other oppositions: "That operatically trained instrument is a force of nature, climbing from an ashen whisper to Callas-like brilliance, and beyond that to a harsh mechanical purity, like a tea-kettle whistle" (Brown, "Galas's Screams," D3). Brown's use of the nature/culture opposition fails to stabilize the system and inadvertently deconstructs it. (How can a trained voice be a force of "nature"?). But he can still close with a triumphant image of "nature" domesticated. The female voice that aspires to climb, to rise, is punished through ironic reversal. To be beyond Callas—who, despite her rages and other nontraditional gender behaviors, still tried to perform traditional femininity (as her dramatic weight loss suggests)—is to be beyond divahood and beyond womanhood. Galas as Callas is transformed into Olympia, the singing mechanical doll in Offenbach's *The Tales of Hoffmann*.

*Wild Women*, an early composition, which, in its use of a variety of vocal techniques and electronics is typical of much of Galas's work, privileges themes common to traditional, masculinist, representations of the opera diva—excess, transgression, and female "madness" in its multiple senses. Galas is a diva who not only sings mad scenes but writes them, and a revisionary political impulse is at work here on the stereotypes of both the female malady as opera represents it and the demented diva. Rothstein's attempt to read Galas as an over-the-top Lucia notwithstanding, Galas's mad protagonists are not Lucias or Elviras. As Susan McClary points out: "like other performance artists, she enacts her pieces upon her own body. This is politically very different from the tradition of male composers projecting their own fantasies of transgression as well as their own fears on to women characters. Galas is not interested in the narrative of raising the specter of the monstrous, flirting with madness, and then reimposing control. . . . she enacts the rage of the madwoman for purposes of protesting genuine atrocities" (110).

The works Galas has composed and performed take up a number of tragedies and horrors—imprisonment, political torture and murder, mental illness, and now AIDS. *The Masque of the Red Death*, which Galas has described as a "one-woman opera," is one of the first serious musical responses to the epidemic (Hilferty).[6] As we noted, sections of *The Masque* reappear with new material in the *Plague Mass*. Galas's work is protean; it refuses the limits and boundaries of traditional forms, and one work often seems to generate another. For example, a portion of the *Plague Mass* served as the germ of the more recent *Vena Cava*, one long "mad scene" that seeks to articulate the fractured voices of someone suffering from AIDS dementia.[7] Heteroglossia, both *Wild Women* and *Vena Cava* suggest, is the essence, as it were, of subjectivity. Screams, pleas, and obscenities mix in *Vena Cava* with spirituals, snatches of Purcell, and a powerfully sung rendition of "Porgi Amor" from *The Marriage of Figaro*. In its new context the countess's plaintive and painful "Grant, O love, some sweet elixir to heal my pain, to soothe my sighs! To my arms restore my loved one or vouchsafe that I may die" becomes a militant, political anthem. By quoting one of the most beautiful (despite its retrograde politics) musical expressions of desire that Western culture has to offer, *Vena Cava* recoups desire and beauty for the HIV+ body, the very body that the dominant culture has argued should renounce its desire and has figured as having been, through illness, punished for its desire. The coupling of mourning and militancy achieved in *Vena Cava*'s quotation of Mozart is the defining strategy of the *Plague Mass*.

As commentators have pointed out, Galas's most important operatic model is Maria Callas; "the vocal and visual resemblances are remarkable" notes Thomas Avena (177). Galas herself lists Callas among her idols, and photographs of Galas wearing large dark glasses or heavy eye makeup—"no diva performs without her *full* eye makeup," Galas insists—pose her as more Callas than Callas herself (Juno and Vale, 9). But Callas is not the only Greek singer with whom Galas identifies; she also places herself and her work in the tradition of women singers of *moirologia*, dirges and lamentations for the dead that sometimes call for vengeance. Since antiquity death has been an occasion for female vocal performance in Greece. Women not only prepare the corpse for burial but also sing dirges, their formulas passed down through an oral tradition. Often the women pull their hair, beat their breasts, and rent their clothing as they sing, cry, and wail.[8] Thus the disruption of death becomes, as well, the occasion for the disruption of women's traditional silence and eruption of women's voices; the women sing and lament with, according to Galas, "the violence of somebody who's been in a hole for a really long time" (Gehr, 118).

R. A. Pope and
S. J. Leonardi

A number of features of the *moirologia* tradition are important for understanding Galas and her *Plague Mass*.[9] Some of the more accomplished *moirologia* singers became, in effect, some of the first professional female singers in Greece. Tradition required that kinswomen be the primary dirge singers, but particularly skillful singers were sometimes asked to join them and were compensated in some way for their participation (Alexiou, 10, 40–41). Not surprisingly, civil and religious authorities during both the classical and Christian periods tried to control, at times silence, these women's voices: in the *Laws* Plato forbids "hired songs," and Church Father John Chrysostum condemns dirges as "blasphemies" (Alexiou, 10, 28). Historians have offered a number of possible reasons—some of them unrelated to gender—for official attempts to limit and control funeral rites and practices, but the terms with which the early Church tried to condemn and curtail these popular and pagan practices so as to appropriate them in the service of its own patriarchal power are highly gendered.[10] Chrysostum, for example, lists dirge singing and breast beating as symptoms of "this disease of females" (Alexiou, 28) and argues against female performance by calling for female modesty. His argument is similar to other church arguments about women "displaying" themselves on stage, arguments that long kept women off the opera stage in Rome and the Papal States. Women who perform are ever pathological and/or corrupt: "What are you doing, woman? Tell me, would you shamelessly strip yourself naked in the middle of the market-place . . . ? And would you tear your hair, rend your garments and wail loudly, dancing and preserving the image of Bacchic women, without regard for your offence to God?" (Alexiou, 29).

Again the Maenads are called up, here to link female voice and performance to madness, transgressive sexuality, disorder, and disease in order to foreclose the possibility of linking them to politics, art, and anger.[11] As Margaret Alexiou shows, patriarchal complaints about female dirge singers inaccurately and unfairly figured their performances as artless, as spontaneous and disordered exercises in excess and self-indulgence (28,34). Galas's work has been characterized similarly, as "primal screaming," a charge she rejects: "Although my work is very emotional and concerned with things that are larger than life, it is also very disciplined. I prefer to call it 'intravenal electroacoustic voice work' " (Holden, C3). Other listeners have tried to place the *Plague Mass*, and thus by extension Galas herself, on the side of the "good" feminine, the sentimental. She rejects this reading as well:

> In 1986 my brother was diagnosed with AIDS. It is bizarre that I was working on this two years before Philip was diagnosed, but that is how things are. Unfortunately, people tend to want to sentimentalize

the work, to see it as a reaction to my brother's illness. . . . "Oh, she's mourning the death of her brother from AIDS!" This is seen as sufficient explanation. It is also used by idiots and misogynists as a deprecation of the work, as if it is some pathetic sentimentality. . . .

(Avena, 187–88)

Galas herself connects the emotional intensity of her work with her heritage: "The intensity of my work has a lot to do with my being of Greek descent. . . . Greeks pretty much scream about everything—it's part of the family. What I do is commandeer and control these emotional forces and propel them in different directions in order to take the audience on an emotional voyage" (Holden, C3). The military rhetoric—*commandeer, propel*—is important. In a number of interviews Galas traces both her ancestry and her dirge singing to the Spartan Maniots, whose lamentation tradition was well developed and stressed not just grief, but militancy (see, for example, Juno and Vale, 11). The voice of militancy in Maniot culture is a woman's voice; when men died in wars or blood feuds, Maniot women called for revenge. According to Alexiou, "Although the act itself rested with the men . . . the women maintained the consciousness for the need to take revenge by constant lamentation and invocation at the tomb. . . . The dirge is always the strongest where the law of vendetta flourishes, as in Sicily or Mani today" (22). In other words, Maniot women transformed lamentation into political discourse and grief into political action. "Patronizing sympathy is revolting," Galas contends, "it has nothing to do with Greek tragedy or Middle Eastern . . . mourning, which not only expresses the mourning of the family, but—more importantly—the *anger* of the dead" (Juno and Vale, 12). As call to action and cultural critique, Galas's work exemplifies what Douglas Crimp has argued is the most necessary kind of art about AIDS: "a critical, theoretical, activist alternative to the personal elegiac expressions that [have] appeared to dominate the art-world response to AIDS" (15).

From this vantage point we see why critics have likened the *Plague Mass* to Haydn's *Mass in Time of War* and Britten's *War Requiem* and why Galas herself is careful to separate her work from traditional requiem masses. "It's a plague mass, as opposed to more traditionally a requiem mass, in the sense that it's very active mourning," Galas observed. "It's a political discussion. It's for the dead, but its for people living with AIDS, for the AIDS community, for the families. It deals with a geography of the plague mentality, a slow death in a hostile environment. It discusses how to stay alive in this kind of place" (Brown, "With Songs"). For Galas, requiems induce political quiescence; as a "plague mass," her work emphasizes that epidemic diseases have long been the occasion for the division and policing of people and groups: " 'Plague' refers specifically to a quarantine mentality as represented in Leviticus, by the way in which the disease is received within the community, the way people with it are isolated as 'unclean,' much as lepers used to be," she argues. "A requiem mass helps to pacify the living so they can feel the dead are resting in peace. . . . the dead from this disease, I don't think of them as resting in peace" (Polkow, 3). Mourning is transformed into a call for action. The final section of *The Masque*, "You Must Be Certain of the Devil," is an angry and aggressive call to act up and fight back, against the Roman Catholic Church and evangelical preachers who are quick to condemn and slow to show compassion, against skinhead gay-bashers, and against everyone who ignores or merely watches the spectacle of suffering and disease. Further, like so many American composers of "serious" music, Galas breaks open traditional classical forms by using folk and popular motifs, melodies, and genres. Using gospel idioms and reworking such well-known spirituals as "Swing Low, Sweet Chariot" and "Let My People Go" (a setting that closes the *Plague Mass* recording), Galas taps for the *Masque* and *Mass* an American folk tradition that, she claims, is about survival and resistance, and appropriates it for a new fight against the forces of marginalization and bigotry.

Galas borrows the title of her longer work, *The Masque of the Red Death*, from American writer Edgar Allen Poe, of course, and in addition to the reworkings of gospel music, the trilogy includes settings of passages from Lamentations, Leviticus, and the Psalms; settings of poems by Corbière, Nerval, and Baudelaire; and settings of her own lyrics. As the work's musical styles, genres, and idioms are varied, so too are the sources of her lyrics. To understand how AIDS has been constructed in America, the strategy suggests, we must return to the sources of traditional discourses about disease, desire, punishment, and homosexuality in Western culture as a whole. To address these constructions and the political oppression they motivate and sanction, the use of spiritual and gospel music implies, political struggle is necessary. As Richard Gehr notes, in "confronting the historically determined residue of 2,000 years of Judeo-Christian ethics [and some of its critics], Galas sorts through the preexisting structures of feeling and thought that the culture has provided as tools, sometimes inappropriate or actually destructive ones, with which to face the disease" (117). Not just to "face" the disease, we would argue, but to know/represent it, as Gehr's sense of *The Masque* as a Foucauldian "genealogy of the idea" of plague, and its capacity to generate social division and oppression, implies (117). *The Masque*'s strategy of quoting many and varied discourses reminds listeners that the new is always read through epistemological frames provided by earlier discourses, discourses that always have ideological investments. There was, in other words, a set of representations of disease and (homo)sexuality that was already, as it were, waiting for AIDS to appear, representations (that disease is punishment for sin, that homosexuality is a disease, for example) through which AIDS was read and that were used to construct the "meaning" of AIDS.

"The most dangerous thing about the AIDS epidemic is the way we are conditioned to think about it, which encourages the sense of isolation that people end up with," Galas has argued (Avena, 182). The opening movement of "The Divine Punishment" section of *The Masque*, a piece that reappears in the *Plague Mass*, is a setting of Leviticus 15, titled "The Law of the Plague." That law, Galas sings in a tone that both mocks and mimics such patriarchal pronouncements, is "To teach when it is clean/And when it is unclean." Epidemics present ideological opportunities by which power regulates persons and increasingly transforms private realms into public ones. Fear of disease becomes a vehicle of social control, for the reassertion of traditional binary identity categories (clean/unclean, monogamous/promiscuous, heterosexual/homosexual) and for the construction of new ones ("innocent victim," "general population," "risk group"). In this way the repression, marginalization, and punishment of people confined to penal categories like "risk group" can masquerade as the destiny arising "naturally" from a particular identity. Galas unmasks this masquerade by claiming repeatedly that AIDS is "homicide."

"When any man hath an issue out of his flesh, / Because of that issue he is unclean. / Every bed whereon he lieth is unclean," Galas sings. These lines from Leviticus 15 about "unclean" issues from men's flesh call to mind another famous, but here unspoken, verse from Leviticus, the command, in 18:22, that a man not lie with another man as with a woman. The omission resonates for any listener familiar with the religious right's polemics against homosexuality. The *Plague Mass* reminds listeners that Leviticus is a founding text both for the ideological use of disease as an occasion for social division and discipline and for the West's discourse against homosexuality, a discourse that has allied it with sin, disease, and contagion. "The Divine Punishment" was first performed in 1986, a time when AIDS was consistently figured as a gay disease by the popular American media and as a punishment for "sinful" sexual practices by the American political and religious right. By citing the Levitical equation of illness with punishment, Galas emphasizes that conservative and phobic discourses about AIDS in the early and mid-1980s used the syndrome and the fear it generated to reinvigorate older discourses about the sinfulness and pathology of homosexuality and to argue for the punitive identification and quarantine of gay men as a public health measure.

As the *Plague Mass* looks back to earlier discourses, so, we have suggested, it reworks earlier forms. Traditional *moirologia* is often structured antiphonally, and the parts are often in antithetical relation. In some *moirologia* this structure is used to construct an imagined dialogue between the living and the dead.[12] (The personification of the voices of the dead is a convention of Greek dirges.) The *Plague Mass* mobilizes these conventions for its own ends. For example, in "This Is the Law of the Plague," the judging, excluding patriarchal voice of Leviticus is interrupted by responses from the suffering and dead, settings of Psalms 22 and 59, and a text written by Galas herself, which plead for deliverance and compassion and imply that the judging, Levitical voice is the voice of evil. This section is followed by a section of spoken dialogue, recitative, called "I Wake Up and See the Face of the Devil," which dramatizes an escalating exchange ("How do you feel today? . . . Are you sure you are facing things? . . . There's something unnatural about this thing.") between a patient and another person or persons—physician, caretaker, visitor—that drives the patient to hysterical responses. A narrative is implied; roles are sung. Galas's *Mass*, in other words, is rooted not only in her *Masque*, but in the genre of the masque, those early dramatic spectacles dependent on machinery. Formally structured musical compositions (solo and technologically produced "choruses") alternate with passages of spoken dialogue. A liturgical form is transformed into a dramatic form that takes up traditional operatic themes—death, desire, madness, political resistance. Mass becomes opera. In the tradition of Act-Up's 1989 demo and die-in at St. Patrick's Cathedral in which Galas participated, Mass becomes political action.

Epidemics, we noted, have long served as the pretexts for increased social regulation, division, and surveillance—the means and ends of what Galas has called the "quarantine mentality." What Foucault calls in *Discipline and Punish* "spectacles of enforcement" (public executions, for example) also function to regulate behavior and to divide people from each other.[13] In the *Plague Mass*, Galas's revisionary introit—called "Were You a Witness?"—draws an explicit parallel between the crucifixion of Christ and the deaths of people with AIDS. The linkage is heavy with irony in a culture in which AIDS is often figured as the wages of sin, where homosexual practices are still in some places illegal, where some suspect that the government's slow reaction to the epidemic was/is ideological, and where the person living with AIDS (PWA) is so often represented, like the criminal, as the person with whom identification is forbidden. (Recall the many media images during the middle and late 1980s of solitary and cadaverous PWAs hooked up to medical machinery. These images served as monitory emblems, spectacles of enforcement, arguing that a lonely and painful death was always the fate of gay people and IV drug users.) Exploiting the multiple senses of "witness" in legal and religious discourse, she sings to "you cowards and voyeurs" that, "There are no more tickets to the funeral / The funeral is crowded / Were you a witness / Were you a witness." The chantlike repetitions of "Were you a witness?" demand a response, albeit a silent one, from listeners. The strategy reworks the antiphonal structure of the traditional introit and reminds listeners that they will have to answer for their own behavior, for their own passivity. (The trilogy's reference to Poe's work, which argues that no one can escape an epidemic, has a similar resonance.) The singer some critics have called the "Diva of Disease" works to force her audience to give up its complacent ease about AIDS.[14] While the *Plague Mass*, she argues, is *for* people who are living with AIDS, people who have died of AIDS-related illnesses, and those who care about them and suffer with them, the work is *aimed* at, in all senses of the word, the bigoted and the complacent. In the tradition of the requiem mass's *Dies irae*, the *Plague Mass* reminds that there will be a reckoning, a judgment. Rejecting conservative claims that AIDS is a judgment on how the dead have lived their lives, Galas argues that there will come a time of reckoning for those who have stood by and done nothing. Those who have died of AIDS-related disorders do not, she claims, rest peacefully, so Galas refuses to allow listeners to rest peacefully. Galas not only highlights here the difference between passivity and action about AIDS and contends that silence equals complicity with murder, but, by figuring her audience as voyeurs, draws a parallel between the masculinist gaze that seeks to frame women in order to control them and the framing of PWAs, the tendency to represent the HIV+ body as other and the PWA as silent and monitory emblem of transgression punished.

Galas's genealogy of the plague mentality makes clear that representations of gays and PWAs are interested constructions. The work has another agenda as well, which it shares with *Wild Women*, *Vena Cava*, and her other compositions: to explore/express what it's like to be subject in/to a system of discursive oppositions that confine as they define. (The speaker in *Vena Cava* repeatedly quotes the pedagogue's "boy, girl, boy, girl.") To this end Galas employs what might be called a strategic essentialism. In interviews Galas claims repeatedly that the *Plague Mass* is the wound of the epidemic itself: "Most pop music is descriptive; it's *about* the thing, not the thing *itself*. Whereas my work is the thing itself, it *is* the sound of the plague . . ." (Juno and Vale, 14). This claim recalls her description of how she uses her voice, "extroversion of the soul, so to speak" (the qualification is significant). In other words, her work aspires to reproduce rather than represent, to express while circumventing cultural codes, to give a voice to those who are traditionally silenced and objectified in cultural discourse—women, gays, the mentally ill, PWAs. Of course Galas runs into the same difficulty as feminists before her: how can those who are constructed by the system as silent and objectified become speaking subjects within that system? Thus Galas's frequent use of glossolalia and the discourse of the mentally ill; their unintelligibility reminds listeners of the epistemological and representational limits of the discursive system (Galas figures glossolalia as a "space of freedom" ["Diamanda Galas," 18]). Though critics might find this a utopian and nostalgic project, we think her insistence that there are real people who are suffering and dying and who therefore shouldn't be deconstructed away is necessary: "I'm talking about blood and muscle hanging from the cross and stinking up the room. Death by crucifixion is prolonged torture—the back breaks one vertebra at a time" (Gracie and Zarkov, 78).

Not surprisingly, Galas's ironic use of Biblical texts and liturgical forms ("You Must Be Certain of the Devil" closes not with a benediction but a "malediction") to represent people living with and dying of AIDS as Christ-like martyrs to social bigotries has led some to accuse of her of blasphemy. The Christian right in the United States has denounced her work as satanic, and during one her European tours, Italian officials, in the tradition of Chrysostum's denunciation of earlier female dirge-singers, accused Galas of blasphemy. Cast as demonic iconoclast, she appeals to tradition: "I was simply performing the mourning rituals of the old women of the south of Italy and Greece. . . . I don't think these old women would have been shocked at all" (Avena, 193). In an interview she quotes an Italian editorial with pride, " 'After the fake scandal and fake blasphemy of Madonna, now we have a real blasphemer' " (Polkow). Although Galas and Madonna both take female stereotypes (the hysteric, the vagina dentata, the phallic woman) to the limit in order to reclaim them for women's own interests,[15] Galas is always careful to distance herself from Madonna: "And people like Madonna are only too willing to propagate the idea that, 'If you want to feel better about a terrible situation, you can dance' " (Juno and Vale, 14). Indeed, Galas tries to distance her work from pop music itself, which, she argues, "generally dilutes the subject [like AIDS] so that people live with it without confronting anything unpleasant" [Gracie and Zarkov, 76]). Like traditional requiem masses, pop music, she argues, induces political quiescence.

The spectacle of enforcement that was Christ's crucifixion was also, Christianity tells us, his sacrifice, and in her performances of the *Plague Mass* Galas presents herself as a sacrificial spectacle. Covered in stage blood and naked to the waist, her exposed and bloody breasts remind the audience that it occupies the discomfiting position of the voyeurs in "Were You a Witness?" who either keep a passive and disengaged distance from the suffering they see or find the suffering of others titillating. Here again the strategy of the critique is to display the extreme, to make the unspoken assumption and conventional mode of thought spectacularly obvious: "The People of the Catholic Church see suffering as something old—like the martyrs—by which they are voyeuristically thrilled and titillated. I'm talking about blood and muscle hanging from the cross and stinking up the room. . . . I'm not talking about pain as eroticism" (Gracie and Zarkov, 78). The blood is Christ's sacrificial blood (in performance she pours blood on herself during the Consecration) and the infected blood of the PWA, but it also recalls the lamenting women of the *moirologia* tradition who draw their own blood and figure their dead as sacrificial victims. Galas likens her performances to sacrificial rites, and she finds her primary model for sacrifice not, as we might expect, in the mass or the tradition of the Levitical scapegoat, but in the *moirologia* tradition of vengeance: "Traditionally, they would sacrifice everything to avenge that person's death. So sacrificing one's public image, or sacrificing the intelligibility of the performance, when confounded by this intense emotional experience, is a small price to pay in comparison" (Avena, 193–94).[16]

But what finally gets offered up, and put at risk, is her voice. To hear Galas perform is to be constantly worried that what she is doing with and to her voice will ruin it, to hope that her extensive training, skill, and discipline will protect her instrument. In this Galas seems to participate in a long tradition that includes Callas. As Koestenbaum makes clear, anxiety that the diva's voice might break is always a part of diva worship (we might call this a kind of "vocal voyeurism"). He argues further that some operas exploit this anxiety/expectation: "The audience is excited by the danger that hysterical or extreme parts pose to the voice: opera requires the preservation of a singing instrument, and yet opera also explodes the boundaried, obedient self, moving listeners and performers away from respectability and toward rage, even if the throat is silenced by the travail of speaking out" (127). Here again Galas calls up and reworks the conventional diva narrative. Unlike earlier divas, Galas writes for her own voice; she knows where the outer reaches of safety for her instrument are and can respect them. She exploits, in order finally to refuse, the romantic scenario of triumphant/tragic voice/lessness that opera, or at least Koestenbaum, finds thrilling. She makes us aware that she knows we expect everything to end in the silence of vocal rupture even as she refuses to be silent.

Galas links voice and rupture in another way. If every diva needs eye make-up to perform, so she needs a narrative of origins for her voice. Galas constructs a postmodern diva narrative that marks out rupture or discontinuity as the origin, rather than the potential climax, of voice.[17] Asked by an interviewer if there was "a break, when suddenly you were free to excavate the voice," Galas shies away from the depth metaphor of "excavate" (and the model of an essential and unified selfhood the metaphor implies) and locates origin instead in disruption: "*My* break happened shortly after living and working in a situation that had very little to do with art. It had to do with distrusting everything, distrusting every means of expression I had learned, so that all the means of my previous expression became too facile, like gestures. . . . I felt I was in search of a new vocabulary of expression. By no means was I alone in doing that" (Avena, 180–81). But as she closes this decentering myth of origins, she decenters it in turn by providing another: "I often sang while working on the street; as a matter of fact, I discovered my voice. There I was with these queen sisters—in particular Miss Gina— saying, 'Do you know that you have a lovely voice, Miss Thing?' "Oh, why thank you' " (Avena, 182). Two elements of this tale are striking. In this narrative, the singer is a "whore," as the patriarchal voice has warned and as masculinist diva narratives repeatedly insist. Further, her first fans, and those who help her to recognize her voice, are transvestites (and thus themselves figures of disruption, as Garber's *Vested Interests* makes clear). In this version, then, Galas "discovers" her voice in a world where boundaries are already blurred and identity categories already unsettled. As her early setting of Baudelaire's *Litanies of Satan* (1982) suggests, Galas is drawn to the figure of the unrepentant outlaw and constructs her own self-representations along the same line, but she also illustrates here an important strategy of both her work and her politics: to own proudly the very traits/identities the wider culture assigns and then uses to condemn, confine, isolate.

As Madonna has been called a "pop diva," so we might call Galas a "pomo diva." Critics have called her an "avant garde diva," and she has worked with avant garde and New Music composers and performers, although here too, perhaps disingenuously, she distances herself: "I don't think of my work as avant-garde or bizarre, I think of it as natural expression. When you come from a place like San Diego you don't know about the avant-garde" (Gaer, 431). In the bourgeois tradition of diva narrative, the diva's voice is often figured (with some qualifications) as a manifestation of—or the expressive vehicle for—a unique, unified, autonomous selfhood. Thea Kronberg's voice in Willa Cather's *The Song of the Lark*, for example, gives her a "sense of wholeness." Galas, on the other hand, as techno-pomo diva deliberately alienates her voice from her-/it-self; she distorts and multiplies her voice electronically, a fitting strategy for works that, like *Wild Women*, *Plague Mass*, and *Vena Cava*, assume a divided, fragmented, multiple human subject. We suggested earlier, for example, that *Vena Cava* figures psychic life as a tissue of quotations from the discourses that constitute us; we hear there the voices of parents and pedagogues as well as quotations from Mozart and "Amazing Grace," obscenities, multiplication tables, bingo-calling.

These multiple voices speak to a politics of multiple identification that figures identity categories as fluid and constructed, and understands gender and sexuality as performative. Speaking of the time she spent as a sex worker in Oakland, Galas credits her transvestite co-workers with not only encouraging her voice but educating her on womanhood: "I learned a lot about *being a woman* from those black drag queens—the power behind the role, how you can use it" (Juno and Vale, 21). This may sound retrograde to some ears, but at least part of the power is a kind of freedom for multiple identification, an embrace of all identities that subverts the notion of identity as fixed and essential and rejects the divisive identity politics that this model produces and sustains. This politics of multiple identification encourages both multiple gender identifications and national/ethnic identifications. Significantly, Galas allies this politics with her female voice and her Greek heritage: "From the Greeks onward, [the female] voice has always been a political instrument as well as a vehicle for transmission of occult knowledge or power. It's always been tied to witches and the shamanistic experience—the witch as transvestite/transsexual having the power of both male and female." Indeed, her identifications are positively promiscuous: "People ask me, 'How do you feel as a woman onstage?' and I say, 'A *what*? Woman, man—I am a fucking nigger, a white person, lesbian, homosexual, witch, snake, vampire—whatever!' I don't think in any one of those terms—that's so limited!" (Juno and Vale, 10–11). We have suggested elsewhere that literary and historical divas of the revisionist tradition break down binary gender and sexuality categories through their "masculine" behavior and stance toward the world. Galas, as always, pushes further. By explicitly embracing all social positions and identity categories simultaneously, she seems to be trying to avoid—and perhaps this is an impossible, utopic, nostalgic project—reinscribing on another level both those categories and the binary structure that produces and depends on them.

This stress on the performative, and her sense of the political power of performance, should not, however, lead to the conclusion that Galas's politics are merely an exercise in striking a pose. Tattooed on her hand is the claim, "We are all HIV+." "People always ask me why I am singing to a special interest group," Galas has complained, "I tell them I am the special interest group, *we all are*" (Gaer, 432). Gay male opera culture often figures the diva as a model of anguish and anger and a model for the rejection of conventional gender behaviors; the archetype/object is Callas. Galas, an avowedly feminist diva, does what Callas never really could—she publicly, and against the advice of many in the music business, identifies with gay men. She embraces their concerns even as she understands that AIDS is not merely, simply, only a gay issue. Long before the opera scene in Jonathan Demme's *Philadelphia* (1993) linked divas (Callas), disease (AIDS), and gay men, Galas linked them. Long before the now alarming rise in the infection rates of women, Galas's work and public statements suggested that she understood that AIDS is an issue for feminists. As Constance Penley points out, like women, "gay men too inhabit bodies that are still a legal, moral, and religious battleground" (157). As the religious right's increased activism against gay rights legislation makes clear, the same forces that would legislate what women can and cannot do with their bodies seek to do the same for gay bodies. "That's what the whole trilogy is about," Galas argues, "the witch hunt . . ." ("Diamanda Galas," 25).

In her operatic, confrontative, frightening, and active mourning, Galas loudly rejects opera's tight control of singers' voices and rejects as well any concern for the longevity of her own voice. She defies every operatic rule and every prescription for the healthy voice in order to scream out her own American-pastiche version of the vendetta of her ancestors—in the context of a specifically American response to AIDS. She thus urges her audience to action while refusing them the cathartic ending of the classical tragedy, the dramatic conclusion of Western opera in which women lie slain and silenced like the AIDS dead. This may be why, though she refers to *Masque* as an opera, Galas hates to be called an opera singer. She explains, "My approach to the voice is like Mike Tyson when he goes into the ring. It's live or die" (Carr, 188).

NOTES

1. Much of the material in this essay appears in somewhat different form in our *The Diva's Mouth: Body, Voice, Prima Donna Politics*.

2. New Music soprano Dora Ohrenstein makes a similar argument in the liner notes to *Urban Diva* (CRI Emergency Music, 1993), her "one-woman, multi-character, music-theater piece": "Divas, it seems, were intended to love and lament. When confronted with anything more complex and threatening, a soprano's only option was to go mad. Despite my admiration of Verdi and Puccini, I found these 19th century notions cramping my style. What I wanted was the freedom . . . to express the emotions of *my* time, no matter how crude and impolite."

3. Indeed, Galas prefigured Lorena Bobbitt's solution: "ten years ago I came up with the concept of 'Black Leather Beavers,' a group of feminist diesel dykes who went around committing revenge on rapists. We had a veterinarian to perform the

castrations, a tatoo artist to engrave 'BLB' on the rapists' foreheads, an arsonist to burn their houses down. . . . A girlfriend has formed a West Coast chapter in San Francisco, and I would encourage more women to do the same . . ." (Juno and Vale, 7). The vigilante frontier justice that figures so prominently in the mythology of the American West is here recast in a feminist key, but Galas's interest in and identification with women's role in the ideology of the vendetta in certain Mediterranean cultures is also at work here. This fusing of the vendetta and vigilante reappears, as we will see, in the *Plague Mass*.

4. Or, as Galas herself described the work in "Intravenal Song": "Theatrically, this diffraction of the mind is made infinite through a ceaseless navigation of the following variables: physical body effort & shape; changing light series which are choreographed; vocal timbre chains, incremental change of room reverberation; manipulation of sonic spatial coordinates and trajectories through the use of four microphones sent to a triphonic sound system. With the exception of the changing light series, the performer has control over all of the above during performance" (61).

5. For details of these two opposed representational traditions, see Leonardi and Pope.

6. *The Masque of the Red Death* was first released by Mute Records in three separate recordings: *The Divine Punishment* and *The Saint of the Pit* in 1986 and *You Must Be Certain of the Devil* in 1988. The *Plague Mass* (1991) contains new work as well as selections from the three parts of *The Masque* and is structured like a mass, with settings of scripture, a confessional, and a consecration. (Like the masses of Verdi and Berlioz, Galas's is a concert work.) Galas sees her mass as an ongoing project that won't be finished until the epidemic is over. In this her work recalls the Names Project's Quilt but also illustrates her general rebellion against boundaries and against conventional aesthetic norms, values, and forms.

That she conceives of *The Masque* as an opera is important. Although she is often called a "performance artist," Galas rejects the term: "I use the word *auteur*. . . . I compose the music and I perform the music and I compose the libretto and I design the lights until I turn it over to a professional lighting designer. But Wagner did that, too! People who call this performance art do it out of sexism—any woman who organizes *Gesamtkunstwerk* is condemned to this territory" (Gracie and Zarkov, 79).

7. Galas's analysis of the PWA's position in relation to medical authority and its strategies to keep the PWA from having a voice in his/her own treatment parallels the cultural links between women, madness, and medicine: "Often people with AIDS dementia are seen as victims of atrophy of the brain, and 'incapable of making decisions.' So when a person with AIDS starts to act in a way that people don't understand, he may be classified as having AIDS dementia, which means that he is no longer listened to, no longer taken seriously. His treatment preferences are not taken into consideration. The person is demoralized by doctors and people around him. Induced madness" (Gracie and Zarkov, 78).

8. Constructing a rhetoric to talk about these practices is difficult for us, who live in a culture where mourning practices are more sedate. "Wail," for example, seems pejorative. And is there a difference, we wonder, between grieving and performing grief? Both of us, Italian Americans, can recall family funerals during which aunts or grandmothers cried and screamed at the grave of a husband whom—we had always thought—they hadn't liked very much. Behavior we saw then as extravagant, embarrassing (aspiring WASPS that we were), unauthentic, we began to see

as conventional; we learned eventually that relationships are more complicated than they seem, that emotion is always mediated and expressed through convention, that *artful* does not equal *duplicitous*.

9. Galas is not the only writer to bring together AIDS and the *moirologia* tradition; for an analysis of this linkage in Edmund White's short story "An Oracle," see Dellamora, especially pp. 162–72.

10. For a survey of early civil and religious attempts to control funeral rites and, by extension, women's voices and a summary of possible reasons, see Alexiou, especially pp. 4–35.

11. This tradition of patriarchal discouragement of female singing continues. Like Chrysostum, Galas's father, a musician himself, tried to keep her from shifting from piano to voice by arguing that women singers were tone deaf and were "a bunch of whores. . . . as a Greek Orthodox, singing wasn't one of the things I was encouraged to do" (Gaer, 431).

12. For an analysis of the conventions and themes of *moirologia*, see Danforth.

13. Foucault associates spectacles of enforcement with earlier forms of power since superseded by forms of power that work by more subtle disciplinary means; the occasion for this shift, he argues, was the plague of the late seventeenth century. The parallel Galas establishes between AIDS and crucifixion and her figuring of social and governmental indifference to AIDS as a kind of "homicide" (a genocidal cleansing of social "others" by conservative and homophobic forces, images of which are brought to us on the nightly news) call into question the marked shift from spectacular enforcement to disciplinary power in Foucault's reading of the history of power. For another important reading of how AIDS has unsettled Foucault's version of history, see Judith Butler's "Sexual Inversions" in Stanton's *Discourses of Sexuality*.

14. The heavily amplified vocal assault Galas unleashes on listeners during a performance is matched by her sometimes vehement and deliberately insulting off-stage comments about the effect she hopes her work will have on those who see AIDS as an issue of/for "others." In a talk for the 1988 New Music Seminar she claimed, "I've just completed a trilogy that is dedicated to my brothers and sisters, persons with AIDS who are now living and dying in Cadillacs, in hotel rooms, crucified in hospitals, and everywhere you don't think they are. And let me tell you something else . . . while you're sitting here having a good time, think about somebody who's lying in vomit bags, lying in perspiration and in dirty old sheets . . . and when you aren't too busy eating pussy and getting autographs, you might go to an ACT-UP meeting tomorrow night" (Flanagan, 170–71).

15. McClary comments on the risks and rewards of this strategy: "What Galas does is undeniably risky, given the tendency for women in Western culture always to be understood as excessive, sexually threatening, mad. She can be read as simply reaffirming the worst stereotypes available. But she can also be read as extremely courageous as she confronts these stereotypes head-on, appropriates them, and rechannels their violent energies in other directions. Her images enter into public circulation, challenging the premises of the prestigious male-constructed madwoman preserved within the musical canon and giving voice to what has always been represented as radically 'Other' " (111).

16. She also sacrifices conventional success and financial reward. In a number of interviews she recounts how often she has been advised that to be associated with AIDS is bad for her career.

17. We say "diva narrative" not only because she is, like most divas, conscious of herself as "diva," but also because the many interviews she has given to a variety of publications are beginning, when taken together, to constitute an autobiography in different versions. Despite significant changes in emphasis and tone, many of the same themes and events are repeated from interview to interview: her Greek heritage and *moirologia*, her early success as a classical pianist, her interest in the free jazz movement, her days on the street, her shift from piano to voice (figured as a rebellion against the patriarch), her rigorous and disciplined vocal training, the reading and research she does for her compositions, the work on *The Masque of the Red Death* and *Plague Mass*.

WORKS CITED

Alexiou, Margaret. *The Ritual Lament in Greek Tradition*. Cambridge: Cambridge University Press, 1974.

Avena, Thomas, ed. *Life Sentences: Writers, Artists, and AIDS*. San Francisco: Mercury House, 1994.

Brown, Joe. "Galas's Screams of Suffering." *Washington Post*, April 13, 1991, D3.

——. "With Songs of Rage." *Washington Post*, April 7, 1991, G1+.

Butler, Judith. "Sexual Inversions." In *Discourses of Sexuality*, ed. Domna C. Stanton. Ann Arbor: University of Michigan Press, 1992:344–61.

Carr, C. *On Edge: Performance at the End of the Twentieth Century*. Hanover, N.H.: University Press of New England, 1993.

Crimp, Douglas. "AIDS: Cultural Analysis/Cultural Activism." In *AIDS: Cultural Analysis/Cultural Activism*, ed. Douglas Crimp. Cambridge: MIT Press, 1988:3–16.

Crutchfield, Will. "A Soprano Fascinated with the Past." *New York Times*, September 29, 1985, H23, H38.

Danforth, Loring M. *The Death Rituals of Ancient Greece*. Princeton: Princeton University Press, 1982.

Dellamora, Richard. *Apocalyptic Overtures; Sexual Politics and the Sense of an Ending*. New Brunswick: Rutgers University Press, 1994.

"Diamanda Galas: Tura Satana Without Cleavage." *Forced Exposure* 15, no. 5 (1989): 11–33.

Flanagan, Michael. "Invoking Diamanda." In *Life Sentences: Writers, Artists, and AIDS*, ed. Thomas Avena. San Francisco: Mercury House, 1994:161–75.

Foucault, Michel. *Discipline and Punish*, trans. Alan Sheridan. New York: Vintage/Random House, 1979.

Gaer, Jillian G. *She's a Rebel: The History of Women in Rock and Roll*. Seattle: Seal Press, 1992.

Galas, Diamanda. "Intravenal Song." *Perspectives of New Music* 20 (1981–1982): 59–62.

Garber, Marjorie. *Vested Interests: Cross-Dressing and Cultural Anxiety*. New York: Routledge, 1992.

Gehr, Richard. "Mourning in America: Diamanda Galas." *Artforum* (May 1989): 116–18.

Gracie & Zarkov. "Killing Floor: The Harrowing Spirituals of Diamanda Galas. *Mondo 2000* 8 (1992): 75–79.

Hilferty, Robert. "The Avenging Spirit of Diamanda Galas." *High Performance* (Spring 1990): 22–25.

Holden, Stephen. "Diamanda Galas, Avant Garde Diva." *New York Times*, July 19, 1985, late ed., C3.

Juno, Andrea and V. Vale. *Angry Women*. San Francisco: Re/Search Publications, 1991.

Leonardi, Susan J. and Rebecca A. Pope. *The Diva's Mouth: Body, Voice, Prima Donna Politics*. New Brunswick: Rutgers University Press, 1997.

Koestenbaum, Wayne. *The Queen's Throat: Opera, Homosexuality and the Mystery of Desire*. New York: Poseidon Press, 1993.

McClary, Susan. *Feminine Endings; Music, Gender, and Sexuality*. Minneapolis: University of Minnesota Press, 1991.

Penley, Constance. "Brownian Motion: Women, Tactics, and Technology." In *Technoculture*, eds. Constance Penley and Andrew Ross. Minneapolis: University of Minnesota, 1991:135–61.

Pleasants, Henry. *The Great Singers: From the Dawn of Opera to Our Own Time*. New York: Simon and Schuster, 1966.

Polkow, Dennis. "Beating the Devil, Galas Tries to Face Reality of AIDS in her 'Plague Mass.'" *Chicago Tribune*, April 3, 1991, final ed., "Tempo," 3.

Rothstein, Edward. "A Diva Makes a Cage Her Vehicle." *New York Times*, July 10, 1993, 13.

Co-editor: *Richard Dellamora* recently completed a term as a Visiting Fellow at the Centre for the Study of Criticism and Theory at the University of Western Ontario and a year as Visiting Fellow in the department of English at Princeton University. Dellamora is acting director of the Graduate Program in Methodologies at Trent University. He is the editor of *Postmodern Apocalypse: Theory and Cultural Practice at the End*, New Cultural Studies Series, University of Pennsylvania Press (1995) and author of *Apocalyptic Overtures: Sexual Politics and the Sense of an Ending* (Rutgers University Press, 1994) and *Masculine Desire: The Sexual Politics of Victorian Aestheticism* (University of North Carolina Press, 1990). He lives in Toronto.

Co-editor: *Daniel Fischlin* teaches in the department of English at the University of Guelph. He has edited *Negation, Critical Theory, and Postmodern Textuality* (Kluwer, 1994) and co-edited, with Mark Fortier, *James I: The True Law of Free Monarchies and Basilikon Doron*, the first publication in the Tudor and Stuart Texts series of the Centre for Reformation and Renaissance Studies at the University of Toronto (1996). In addition to being the author of *In Small Proportions: A Poetics of the English Ayre, 1596–1622* (Wayne State University Press, 1997), he is currently working on a study of early modern kingship and Foucauldian theories of representation entitled *The Sovereignty of Words: Early Modern Absolutism and the Politics of Uncertainty.*

*Victor Anand Coelho* is professor of musicology at the University of Calgary. He has also held visiting professorships at Cornell University, the Ecole Normale Supérieure, and the University of Melbourne, and is a Fellow of Villa I Tatti in Florence. His publications include *Music and Science in the Age of Galileo* (Kluwer), *The Manuscript Sources of Seventeenth-Century Italian Lute Music* (Garland), and *Lute, Guitar, and Vihuela: Historical Practice and Modern Interpretation* (Cambridge), as well as numerous articles on seventeenth-century Italian music and culture.

*Jim Ellis* teaches in the department of English at the University of Calgary. Another essay on the films of Derek Jarman, "Queer Period: Derek Jarman's Renaissance," is forthcoming in a volume of essays on queer film theory, *Out Takes*, edited by Ellis Hanson.

*Todd S. Gilman* holds a Ph.D. in English from the University of Toronto and teaches literature in Boston. He is also a professional viola da gamba player. He has been a Visiting Fellow of the Houghton Library, Harvard University, the Huntington Library, and McMaster University Library. He has published articles on early opera and musical drama, Shakespeare, and cinema in *Theatre Survey*, *The Musical Quarterly*, *The University of Toronto Quarterly*, *Restoration*, *Literature/Film Quarterly*, *Hamlet Studies*, and *Children's Literature Association Quarterly*. He is currently completing two books entitled *Appropriative Acts: Handel and English Theatre* and *Our English Amphion: The Theatre Career of Thomas Augustine Arne, 1732–1778*.

*Linda Hutcheon* is University Professor of English and comparative literature at the University of Toronto. A devoted opera buff, she discusses Wagner's *Ring* cycle at length in her book *Irony's Edge: The Power of the Unsaid* (Routledge, 1994). Most recently, she is co-author with *Michael Hutcheon* (professor in the School of Medicine, University of Toronto) of *Opera: Desire, Disease, Death* (University of Nebraska Press, 1996).

*Kevin Kopelson* is an associate professor of English at the University of Iowa and is the author of *The Queer Afterlife of Vaslav Nijinsky* (Stanford University Press, 1997), *Beethoven's Kiss: Pianism, Perversion, and the Mastery of Desire* (Stanford University Press, 1996), and *Love's Litany: The Writing of Modern Homoerotics* (Stanford University Press, 1994).

*Lawrence Kramer* is a musicologist, composer, and critic who is a professor of English, music, and comparative literature at Fordham University in New York City. He is the author of *Music as Cultural Practice: 1800–1900* (1990), *Classical Music and Postmodern Knowledge* (1995), and *After the Lovedeath: Sexual Violence and the Making of Culture* (1997). He co-edits *19th-Century Music*.

*Ralph P. Locke* is professor of musicology at the University of Rochester's Eastman School of Music. He is a co-editor of the *Journal of Musicological Research* and senior editor of *Eastman Studies in Music*. His publications include *Music, Musicians, and the Saint-Simonians* (University of Chicago Press, 1986), as well as articles on the musical life of early-nineteenth-century Paris. His current research interests include operas set in the non-European world and women music patrons in America; on the latter topic he has several chapters in a forthcoming collection that he co-edited with Cyrilla Barr, *Cultivating Music in America: Women Patrons and Activists Since 1860* (University of California Press).

*Susan McClary* (professor of musicology at UCLA) has published critical essays on music ranging from Monteverdi to Madonna. Her books include *Feminine Endings: Music, Gender, and Sexuality* (University of Minnesota Press, 1991) and *Georges Bizet:* Carmen (Cambridge University Press, 1992). While living in Minneapolis, she wrote and produced a music-theater piece, *Susanna Does the Elders* (1987). She delivered the Ernest Bloch Lectures at the University of California at Berkeley in 1993. McClary was awarded a John D. and Catherine T. MacArthur Foundation Fellowship in 1995.

*Felicia Miller* is the author of *The Mechanical Song: Women, Voice and the Artificial in Modern French Narrative* (Stanford University Press, 1995; published under the name Felicia Miller Frank). The book includes a discussion of modernity and artifice focused on the shift from emphasis on the voice of castrati to the voices of sopranos in Romantic opera in France. She is also the author of "*L'Inhumaine, La Fin du Monde*: Modernist Utopias and Filmmaking Angels" in *MLN*, 111.5 (December, 1996).

*Rebecca A. Pope* (Georgetown University) and *Susan J. Leonardi* (University of Maryland, College Park) are the authors of *The Diva's Mouth: Body, Voice, Prima Donna Politics* (Rutgers University Press, 1997). Leonardi is also the author of *Dangerous by Degrees: Women at Oxford and the Somerville College Novelists* (Rutgers).

*Patricia Juliana Smith* is a visiting professor in the department of English at the University of California at Los Angeles. She is co-editor with Corinne E. Blackmer of *En Travesti: Women, Gender Subversion, Opera* (Columbia University Press, 1995) and author of *Nothing Happened: Lesbian Panic and the Disruption of Narrative* (Columbia University Press, 1997). She is presently editing a collection entitled *Queering the Sixties*.

*Ruth A. Solie* is professor of music and a regular participant in the Women's Studies Program at Smith College. Her published work is in the social history of music in the nineteenth century. Most recently, she is editor of *Musicology and Difference: Gender and Sexuality in Music Scholarship* (University of California Press, 1993) and is an associate editor of the journal *19th-Century Music*.

Castellini, Teresa, 64, 76

Castle, Terry, 14, 109n. 1, 265

castrati, 3–4, 13–14, 19, 33, 80, 89, 272n. 20; in eighteenth-century London, 13, 49–66, 76; as symbol of luxury and corruption, 59–60; in the film *Farinelli*, 73, 75, 76–8, 79; and gender, 13, 49, 50–8, 61, 62; sexual prowess/aspects of, 50–8, 76, 77; and sodomy, 50–8

Catalani, Ottavio, 38

Cather, Willa, 110n. 8; *The Song of the Lark*, 328

Cavalieri, Emilio de, 38

Cavalli, Francesco, 12, 61

Cesti, Antonio, 12

Chambers, Ross, 82, 83

Chanan, Michael, 3

Charles, emperor of Austria, 79

Cherney, Brian, 250n. 17

Chrysostum, John, 320, 325

Church of St. Ignatius (Rome), 30, 39

class: in Bizet's *Carmen*, 118, 124; and homosexuality, 279; in *The Marriage of Figaro*, 19, 256, 262; in Mérimée's *Carmen*, 116; and opera, 11, 18, 86, 185, 186–8, 197–8, 203n. 3

Clément, Catherine, 2, 21, 100, 103, 105, 126, 180n. 35, 202, 280

Clemons, Walter, 310

Coelho, Victor Anand, 12–13

Collier, Suzanne, 287

colonialism: in the *Apotheosis ... of Francis Xavier*, 13, 31–3; in *Norma*, 100; in operas about the New World, 38. *See also* imperialism

Conrad, Peter, 179n. 26, 216

Consolino (castrato), 62

contralto voice, 14, 73, 80, 81, 82–3, 86

Copland, Aaron, 249n. 8

Copley, John, 255, 258, 261, 264, 272n. 6

Corbiau, Gérard, 79

Corbière, Édouard-Joachim, 322

Corigliano, John, 264–5

Coulter, John, 238, 239, 247

Crimp, Douglas, 321

Crispi, Francesco, 111n. 12

cross-dressing: in *The Marriage of Figaro*, 259–61, 267; in opera, 5, 13, 19, 62, 69n. 46, 80, 89, 272n. 20; in

Renaissance theatre, 62; in Strauss's operas, 266–7; in the theatre, 86, 267

Curll, Edmund, 52

*The Custom of the Country. See under* Wharton, Edith

Dahlhaus, Carl, 125

Da Ponte, Lorenzo, 256, 258, 260, 261, 262, 263, 272n. 12

Davey, Frank, 237, 238, 248

David, Félicien, 164

David, Marc, 79

*David musicus* (Catalani), 38

Dean, Winton, 123, 124, 126

death/Thanatos: in *Death in Venice*, 211, 212–13, 215, 218, 219–20, 221–2, 223, 225–6, 227, 231n. 30; in Galas's work, 319–21; response to, and opera, 308–9

*Death in Venice* (novella), 17, 209–31, 243, 246

*Death in Venice* (opera), 10, 209–31, 243, 279, 285, 294n. 14

Debat-Ponsan, Edouard-Bernard, 167

Defoe, Daniel, 51

Deitcher, David, 311

Delacroix, Eugène, 165

Delibes, Léo, 164

Dellamora, Richard, 19–20, 278

Denisoff, Dennis, 262, 269

Dennis, John, 51, 59–60

Dent, Edward J., 96, 109n. 3

Dickinson, Peter: "Home" (short story), 269–70

*Dido and Aeneas* (Purcell), 9

*Didone* (Cavalli), 61

difference. *See* other/outsider

Dionisi, Stéphano: in the film *Farinelli*, 77

dirges, Greek. See *moirologia* tradition

Disch, Thomas, 303, 307

disease: in Galas's work, 322–3; in *Mario and the Magician*, 243, 244, 245. *See also* AIDS

*Diva Ojibway* (Mason), 249n. 13

*The Divine Punishment*, 330n. 6

Dizikes, John, 8

Domingo, Plácido, 7, 128

Donati, Alessandro, 38

*Don Carlos*, 102